Threshold of a New World

Threshold of a New World

INTELLECTUALS AND THE EXILE
EXPERIENCE IN PARIS, 1830–1848

Lloyd S. Kramer

Cornell University Press   Ithaca and London

First published 1988 by Cornell University Press.

International Standard Book Number 0–8014–1939–5
Library of Congress Catalog Card Number 87–19899
Printed in the United States of America
*Librarians: Library of Congress cataloging information
appears on the last page of the book.*

*The paper in this book is acid-free and meets the guidelines for
permanence and durability of the Committee on Production Guidelines
for Book Longevity of the Council on Library Resources.*

To my parents,
Ruth and Frank Kramer

CONTENTS

ILLUSTRATIONS

ACKNOWLEDGMENTS

This book bears the trace of many influences, supporters, critics, and friends over a period of several years. I especially acknowledge the early help and criticism of Dominick LaCapra, Steven L. Kaplan, and R. Laurence Moore at Cornell University. The critical insights of Dominick LaCapra and his knowledge of European intellectual history played a significant role in shaping my concern with the problems I address in this book and in directing me toward a wide range of issues in contemporary historiography. I thank him for his support and for his openness to a historical method that differs from his own, though it also carries the influence of his theoretical priorities from beginning to end.

The comments of others who have read various parts of the manuscript—notably Gordon Craig, Peter Paret, Robert Finlay, and the participants in Keith Baker's workshop on culture and political practice at the University of Chicago—helped me to clarify my themes. I especially thank Robert Finlay for his thorough and perceptive critique. None of these readers will agree with all that I have written (and of course they have no responsibility for any errors that may appear in the book), and yet they have helped me to explain what I am trying to do and why I am trying to do it.

Among others who have contributed at different times and in different ways, I am grateful for the help of Clark Anderson, Deborah Anderson, Paul Bailey, Sally Barbour, Roger Chartier, Jane Dickinson, Dena Goodman, Peter Hayes, Stanley Idzerda, Cynthia Koepp, Robert Love, Sarah Maza, and Linda J. Pike. Colleagues in the history departments at Stanford and Northwestern universities and the University of North Carolina offered congenial environments in which to expand my interests and perspectives as I revised the manuscript. These various friends have provided encouragement and assistance of all kinds as well as the personal conversations so important for intellectual progress and social survival.

Research fellowships from the history department and the Western Societies Program at Cornell University, a Bourse Chateaubriand from the French government, and an academic leave from Northwestern University enabled me to pursue research in France and to complete the writing in the United States. I gratefully acknowledge these sources of aid, without which this project would not have been possible. I also acknowledge the permission of *Historical Reflections/Réflexions Historiques* to incorporate parts of my article "Exile and European Thought: Heine, Marx, and Mickiewicz in July Monarchy Paris" (vol. 11, 1984, pages 45–70); Penguin Books Ltd. and Random House, Inc., to quote material from Karl Marx, *Early Writings*, edited by Quintin Hoare, translated by Gregor Benton and Rodney Livingstone, introduced by Lucio Colletti, translation copyright © 1974 by Rodney Livingstone and Gregor Benton, reproduced by permission of Penguin Books Ltd.

Special appreciation goes to Gwynne Pomeroy; the support and valuable perspective she contributed during the final revisions of the manuscript helped me to see more clearly what is important and what is not important in the processes of intellectual development and of living.

Finally, I have benefited for a long time from the perspectives of my parents, Ruth and Frank Kramer, whose insights have affected me in more ways than they can know and whose enduring encouragement I acknowledge with deep appreciation by dedicating this book to them.

Chapel Hill, North Carolina   L. S. K.

Threshold of a New World

We are going to France, the threshold of a new world. May it live up to our dreams! At the end of our journey we will find the vast valley of Paris, the cradle of the new Europe.

Arnold Ruge, *Zwei Jahre in Paris*

To be a stranger is naturally a very positive relation; it is a specific form of interaction.... The stranger, like the poor and like sundry "inner enemies," is an element of the group itself. His position as a full-fledged member involves both being outside it and confronting it.... He is not radically committed to the unique ingredients and peculiar tendencies of the group, and therefore approaches them with the specific attitude of "objectivity." But objectivity does not simply involve passivity and detachment; it is a particular structure composed of distance and nearness, indifference and involvement.

George Simmel, "The Stranger"

Introduction

Exiles in Paris and Intellectual History

When I read a book, what gratifies me is not so much what the book itself is as the infinite possibilities there must have been in every passage, the complicated history, rooted in the author's personality, studies, etc., which every phrase must have had and still must have for the author.

Soren Kierkegaard, Journal, 1838

This book explores the historical connection between social experience and ideas. Although most people believe that such a connection exists, historians disagree about the processes through which it evolves across time. Some stress the primacy of social experience in shaping ideas; some emphasize the decisive role of ideas in shaping social experience; and some argue that experience and ideas are always mutually dependent. I do not propose to resolve this perennial debate. On the contrary, I accept this open-ended discussion as an opportunity to investigate the experiences and ideas of foreigners in nineteenth-century France without the obligation to prove the exact proportions of social and intellectual influence in their lives or thought—though I do argue that the French influence was highly significant. If it were possible to determine the precise balance between social and intellectual influences in the historical development of societies, individuals, or texts, this book might have taken the form of graphs and mathematical calculations. As a matter of fact, however, there is ambiguity in the interaction between social realities and interpretation which defies quantitative methods, though it is intrinsic to what we know as history. Ambiguity and complexity do not impede the expansion of historical knowledge and perspective; they make it necessary. It is therefore the ambiguous intersection of lived experiences and

1

written texts which creates the subject of this book and shapes my interest in interpretive processes that give meaning to all forms of history.

I approach these broad issues of experience and interpretation through two specific themes: the formative influence of exile as a social-intellectual experience for people who are forced (or choose) to live outside their native social and cultural milieu, and the importance of Paris as a social-intellectual center for creative Europeans in the period between 1830 and 1848. These themes overlap throughout this book and lead to distinctive, individual examples of the dialectical relationship between social contexts and thought. This relationship is complicated because those who interpret social reality inevitably understand that reality in terms of a particular interpretive framework. All people "read" and interpret their social context through the conventions of their culture, though this is not always apparent to the interpreters themselves. In the case of exiles, however, the reading of the context may take a more self-conscious form because outsiders often become more aware of the assumptions by which they and others interpret social experience.

I argue in the following chapters that July Monarchy Paris offered a modern, urban context that foreigners interpreted from the perspectives of their own traditions, and a social-intellectual community that facilitated for exiles the development of new theories about their native national cultures, about France, and about themselves. Parisian realities helped to transform the ideas of outsiders who went there, but their ideas also helped to transform the historical meaning and realities of Paris. Exile provokes new forms of interpretation by defamiliarizing the familiar and familiarizing the unfamiliar. That experience becomes especially provocative in a place such as July Monarchy Paris, where foreigners encountered well-developed French social, political, and intellectual traditions and where they also came upon some of the most stimulating and disturbing tendencies in modern European society. The social and intellectual reality of exile in nineteenth-century France thus constitutes the experience that I analyze in connection with the ideas of three influential European writers: Heinrich Heine, Karl Marx, and Adam Mickiewicz.

The Tradition of Exile and the Significance of France

The creative possibilities of exile appear in a remarkable variety of important historical figures; in fact, the creativity of exiles has occurred often enough to suggest a pattern rather than an accident. A list of intellectuals who have lived at different times outside their native societies would include many of the most influential writers in Western history—from Herodotus and Ovid, Dante and Erasmus through Dostoevsky and Joyce to Thomas Mann and Nabokov— and people from every nation and cultural tradition. Indeed, the number of exiles in the world has increased steadily through the wars, revolutions, military repressions, and economic disruptions of the modern era. Emigré writers and political dissidents have lived by the thousands in foreign cities (especially during the last two centuries), organizing opposition movements, seeking support for their causes, analyzing developments at home, and struggling to survive amid alien and difficult circumstances. Despite their frequent isolation and their vast differences in culture, political values, reasons for expatriation, and personal experiences, all of these displaced persons have been able to draw upon an extraordinary exile tradition to give meaning or consolation to their situation.

The concept of exile in Western culture goes back to Greek and Hebrew texts—the *Odyssey*, the Old Testament accounts of the Jews in Egypt and Babylon—and it shows up often in early Christianity. In ancient texts, exile can mean separation from a geographical home or, more broadly, separation from God. Saint Augustine, for example, believed that exile or separation in this religious sense was the universal Christian (and human) condition.[1] Throughout most of Western history, however, the wandering Jew served as the archetypal exile figure: separated from the place of his ancestors, isolated from much of the society in which he lived, and relegated to the status of permanent social and cultural scapegoat. Exile seemed always to suggest both a specific physical position (what the seventh-century writer Isidore of Seville called "outside his own ground") and a spiritual condition of suffering and pain, a dual definition that was expanded during the Renaissance to encompass also the political persecution in Italian city-states. During the Middle Ages and the Renaissance, exile became more institutionalized (the refuge of monastaries, for example) and codified (as in the laws pertaining to exile status or rights in Italian cities). Even more important, perhaps, medieval and Renaissance exiles built on ancient Greek, Roman, and biblical precedents to produce a new exile literature. The texts of Dante—his poetry and his life—contributed to definitions of exile through all subsequent periods in European history.[2]

By the beginning of the modern period, exile therefore carried a rich history of religious, political, geographical, and literary meanings that expatriated and alienated persons might use for purposes of personal identity and self-justification, even after exile became associated with somewhat different historical patterns and problems. Although the classical texts continued to influence the interpretation of exile during the eighteenth and nineteenth centuries, the experience in this period of evolving nation-states became more explicitly linked to nationalism. Modern people increasingly defined themselves through their national identity. Apart from gender or race, few characteristics contributed more to formation of the modern idea of self, especially as social and economic developments gradually weakened other sources of identity (religion, family, native city, artisan work, inherited privilege) and greatly increased the contacts between people from different parts of the world. The new national cultures, shaped in the nineteenth century by education, language, and the needs of an emerging industrial economy, began to provide some of the clearest identifications that individuals could establish for themselves: "I am French," "I am German," and the like.[3]

The consolidation of powerful nations and national identities nevertheless aroused opposition from persons who challenged specific policies or ascendant ideologies and eventually found themselves either being forced or choosing to leave their native society. This modern form of exile extended the earlier traditions by placing greater emphasis on separation from national culture and the national state—which were now becoming synonymous. (Significantly, Renaissance Italians who were forced to leave their native cities usually continued to live in Italian linguistic and cultural territory.)

Like many tendencies in the modern world, the stronger nationalist meaning of exile evolved out of the French Revolution. The people who left their home countries for political or cultural reasons in the early nineteenth century were thus among the first to become national exiles of the modern type. Their experiences helped to give the exile tradition its national, revolutionary dimensions, and their political motivations (as compared, for example, with religious motivations among earlier exiles) made France the most popular place for them to live. Emigrés who might use the ancient tradition or texts of exile to explain why they left home could also use the recent political tradition or texts of France to explain why they chose Paris as their destination.

Paris emerges as an important place in any discussion of the

Foreigners entering Paris. Frontispiece by Henry Emy for the book edited by Louis Desnoyers, *Les étrangers à Paris* (1844). Bibliothèque Nationale, Paris.

exile experience because it has perhaps attracted more foreigners (especially intellectuals) than any other city in the world. To be sure, other exile havens have served as centers of creative exile life: Amsterdam (seventeenth and eighteenth centuries), Geneva and Zurich (from the Reformation to the twentieth century), Brussels (nineteenth century), London (nineteenth and twentieth centuries), and New York (twentieth century). Yet Paris appears to have been the most common destination for intellectual exiles and expatriates since the eighteenth century, drawing Germans and Russians before and after their wars and revolutions; Poles after their recurring attempts to win national independence; English novelists and romantics at all times; Americans after World War I; Italians and Spaniards during the era of fascism; Asians, Africans, Arabs, and Third World political figures during and after the era of colonialism; and dissidents from almost everywhere in every recent decade. It sometimes seems that every modern revolution, every modern literary or artistic movement, every modern protest, and every modern reaction has had advocates and critics who planned, plotted, or lamented their programs in Parisian cafés, journals, and meetings. It is impossible to study the political or cultural history of any modern nation without coming upon persons who established themselves for a time in Paris.

Among the various golden eras in Parisian expatriate life, the decades of the 1830s and 1840s stand out as a period of exceptional importance because so many creative people went there to pursue political activity and writing that were forbidden in other parts of Europe.[4] Louis-Philippe's Paris provided a cosmopolitan and relatively free environment for expatriates and a network for disseminating the new creeds and theories that appeared in such profusion among reform-minded intellectuals during those decades. France's reputation for revolution and radical politics established its appealing symbolic status for all Europeans who opposed the conservatism and repression of their own governments. "Exile in France" could therefore convey a specific political and intellectual meaning, especially for central and eastern Europeans: it suggested sympathy with the French Revolution, democratic government, Enlightenment tolerance, nationalist or internationalist movements, and modern or romantic literature and art. Of course, the exiles and expatriates from various cultures used different aspects of these French traditions, and few persons supported or identified with everything that France could represent. But the revolutionary and Napoleonic upheavals in France fascinated almost all nineteenth-century Europeans as the most significant events in modern history and gave the French capital a quasi-mythic quality for persons who felt overwhelmed by the constraints, contradictions, and inequalities in their native societies.

The trip to Paris thus became a flight from familiar conflicts and hardships to the alien conflicts and hardships of a foreign (and idealized) city. From their outsider position in France, though, many émigrés were able to develop a new understanding of social, political, and cultural traditions or texts on both sides of the frontier. These shifting perspectives among foreigners in July Monarchy Paris exemplify patterns that have appeared also among displaced intellectuals at other times and places. Indeed, as I argue throughout this book, new interpretive insights often seem to evolve through specific social and intellectual characteristics of the exile experience, an experience of marginality that places self-conscious individuals both inside and outside two cultures at the same time.

The Social and Intellectual Experience of Exile

The study of exile as a social and intellectual experience raises questions about the relationship between social and intellectual history. By stressing the reciprocal influence between experience and texts, I want to avoid those historiographical hierarchies that make either social forces or ideas the ultimate causal agents in history. All social experiences (including poverty, political repression, work, love, friendship, and exile) take place within interpretive systems that derive from inherited ideas or texts. Without ideas, experience does not make sense. All ideas and texts (including the most abstract theories, the greatest fiction, and works by exiles) appear within social systems that derive from inherited economic or political structures. Without society, ideas do not make sense. Sharp divisions between social and intellectual history therefore distort what actually happens in the historical process. True, the intricate, overlapping nature of social and intellectual reality often necessitates analytical separations into different kinds of history, but the example of exile suggests that those separations can misrepresent the way in which social experience and ideas depend upon one another. I want to emphasize to social historians that exile social experiences, like all other experiences, are mediated through textual traditions and meanings; I want to emphasize to intellectual historians that creative exile texts, like all other texts, are embedded in social experience and relationships. In short, the problem of exile offers special opportunities to show the enduring connection between social and intellectual history.[5]

I use the term exile to refer to persons who leave their native culture because they feel that they are physically unsafe or threatened with imprisonment; or unable to express their ideas, act upon their political and personal beliefs, or continue the work they want to do. They may choose to emigrate without direct government pressure (I apply the words exile and émigré to the same people), yet they usually find it difficult or impossible to return to their home country as long as political and cultural power remains in the hands of their opponents. The exile differs from other expatriates in feeling less free to return home without danger. Exiles may sometimes exaggerate their peril, but if the fear is great enough to keep them away from home, their position differs from that of persons who live in a foreign country with little fear of repression in their native society. The line between these positions is by no means clear or absolute; many of the persons whom I discuss in Chapter 1, for example, developed new perceptions of themselves and of France even though they were only temporary expatriates. But expatriates by choice can always go home, whereas exiles feel that the home country is somehow closed to them—as did Heine, Marx, and Mickiewicz. Some exiles want desperately to go back; others become reconciled to permanent residence in another country. Few exiles, however, lose interest in their native culture, and their long-distance perspective on that culture provides an example of how the exile position, for all its hardships, can facilitate the development of new insights.

The creative possibilities in this position result largely from the fact that the experience of exile establishes a new interaction between social context and intellectual analysis in individuals who, as outsiders, can become unusually conscious of their social and cultural biases. The exile experience is, in the first place, an encounter with a new social environment that almost always stimulates some new awareness and analysis of social realities.[6] Nobody can live in a foreign culture without experiencing the social environment in ways that it is never experienced at home. Almost all aspects of the alien society—streets, buildings, money, laws, fashion, language, food, race, gestures, religion—intrude upon the outsider and attract his or her attention. The social context is just as influential in the home country, yet few people feel it as acutely at home as they do abroad. The outsider position provides a distinctive view of the social system that defines reality for insiders and thereby prevents them from deciphering some of its most basic characteristics. Furthermore, the social and economic problems of exile life (housing, work, precarious legal status) reveal to most émigrés the biases of the social system and expose the nature of power in ways that many natives never experience firsthand. It is this new sense of social realities that often makes foreign accounts of any society such valuable, informative documents.

Yet exile texts do not simply reveal the social reality of an alien culture. Foreigners always bring from home certain expectations and assumptions that inform their response to the new place and inevitably transform or even create the social context as they describe it to themselves and others.[7] Anyone who uses exile texts as simple mirrors overlooks the complex interaction of competing interpretations and intellectual traditions which occurs within these texts and within the people who write them. Exile writings often become notable as works in which contrasting intellectual and cultural orientations meet, interact, and evolve through a kind of multinational dialogue. The problems and presuppositions of different traditions may appear more clearly to exiles than to others as they compare or contest, say, French materialism and German Hegelianism or Polish Catholicism. These dialogic tendencies in exile texts generate questions about tradition and convention which cross cultural boundaries and open the view of the ideological center to creative assaults from the periphery. It should also be stressed that exiles come upon new books and new theories that contribute to a critical analysis of both their own intellectual tradition and the one in which they live as outsiders. The interaction between contrasting theoretical tendencies frequently challenges inherited intellectual identities and encourages a search for conceptual syntheses.

Exile challenges more than social and intellectual identities, however, for it often brings about major psychological adjustments as well. The experience of living among alien people, languages, and institutions can alter the individual's sense of self about as significantly as any of the traumas known to psychologists. The referents by which people understand themselves change dramatically when they are separated from networks of family, friends, work, and nationality. Although this separation affects each individual somewhat differently, the resulting disorientation commonly provokes important changes in self-perception and consciousness. Intellectual exiles frequently respond to their deracination by describing home (idealistically) or rejecting home (angrily) or creating a new definition of home (defiantly); in any case they almost always explore problems of national and personal identity in new ways and write about their conflicts in texts that can become unusually rich revelations of both conscious and unconscious needs, motivations, and anxieties.[8]

Along with this new perspective on the self, exiles often gain insights into the collective consciousness of their society and historical epoch. Extended contact with a foreign *mentalité* helps them to recognize the unconscious social or ideological hierarchies that create order and meaning in their native culture but pass unnoticed by the people who never leave home. The "normal" (or normative) values of the home country become more relative: simply *one* way of explaining reality or social experience rather than *the* way. Exiles learn from their own difficult experience about the relationship between language and mentality: the words by which they name ideas or things at home lose meaning abroad, and the whole linguistic system that organizes experience must change if the outsider is to cope with a different culture. Alien social environments reveal unconscious mental structures because these structures often do not work well in the new place. Indeed, the unnoticed assumptions that enable people to function in their own context frequently become impediments to life in another culture. The shock of recognition that accompanies this experience allows exiles to describe their native-country attitudes with unusual critical distance and to analyze aspects of collective consciousness in their new culture from perspectives unavailable to people raised and educated within that culture. Located on the margin of two cultures, the exile can become one of the most astute interpreters of collective consciousness, prejudice, and ideology and an extraordinary informant for people who want to understand the unexamined values of their own society (as well as for historians who want to reconstruct collective mentalities from the past).

Exile creativity surely evolves also from factors that go beyond the social, intellectual, psychological, and ideological aspects of the experience outlined here, but these and other characteristics of exile all relate in some way to the problem of identity—that definition of self which contributes so much to intellectual work. Thus, the starting point for this emphasis on exile is the recognition that personal and cultural identities never exist in any pure or complete form, that they always depend upon interactions with other referents on the outside or margin; all identities evolve in relation to some difference.[9] This creation of identity through the exploration of difference, which became increasingly important in European thought with the development of nationalism and the expanding contact between people from various cultures, appears conspicuously in the history of expatriated intellectuals. While all modern people have in some respects confronted the issue of difference, exiles face the problem most explicitly and often most creatively because it enters their lives every day.

Heine, Marx, and Mickiewicz in July Monarchy Paris

The general patterns of exile and the particular significance of post-Revolutionary France both appear in the lives of many foreigners who went to Paris in the 1830s and 1840s. I have chosen to focus on Heine, Marx, and Mickiewicz in July Monarchy Paris because these writers became especially influential examples of exile creativity and because these decades form an important transitional period in the evolution of modern French society. In choosing to analyze well-known intellectuals, I am following a historical method that emphasizes the achievements and texts of original thinkers more than the behavior and attitudes of the anonymous majority. This emphasis does not mean that the experience of famous writers is more important than the experience of others, but it does assume that the literary and analytical abilities of creative persons help them to interpret their experiences more clearly or profoundly than most people in similar situations. The tendency to write about their experiences separated intellectuals from most other exiles, even though they encountered the same streets, crowds, markets, laws, and problems of material and psychological survival which confronted all foreigners in Paris. Like others who went to France, intellectual exiles arrived with hopes and met with disappointments, but for them the hopes and disappointments often carried more explicit literary or theoretical meanings. The textual interpretation of Parisian society thus enabled Heine, Marx, and Mickiewicz to become self-conscious, imaginative analysts of experiences that were shared in various ways by thousands of expatriated people in nineteenth-century France. As intellectuals, they were both typical and untypical of all exiles in Paris.

In order to place these three writers in the Parisian context and to suggest how their work connected with the experience of other people, I begin with a discussion of how foreigners commonly responded to the French capital during the era of the July Monarchy. Almost all of the issues that concerned famous intellectuals (and appear in subsequent chapters of this study) also attracted the attention of lesser-known visitors, journalists, and writers who came to Paris from abroad: the crowds, the social classes, the political disputes, the nationalism, the revolutionary heritage, the theater, the language, the newspapers, the academic institutions, the commerce, the shops, the restaurants, the congestion, and the noise. The city that was expanding rapidly under the bourgeois guidance of Louis-Philippe's government seemed to fascinate and to frighten those foreigners whose travel books described the capital's great attractions and strange risks. The social and political evolution of July Monarchy France continued a long transformation from the old regime to modernity which began before the French Revolution and that accelerated after the Revolution of 1830 finally displaced the kings and advisers of the Bourbon Restoration.[10] These changes affected the culture as well as the social structure in Paris and contributed to the contradictions that visitors regularly discovered: the city was crowded and lonely, beautiful and ugly, fashionable and filthy, well policed and dangerous, open to ambition and inaccessible, polite and rude, wealthy and poor, jovial and anxious, free and repressive.

The leaders of July Monarchy Paris were willing to support (or tolerate) the development of modern social and cultural institutions that assured the city's status as the cultural capital of Europe. Newspapers, journals, publishing houses, academies, and universities took on the characteristics of a modern culture industry that attracted and helped to sustain a large community of French and foreign intellectuals. Paris became a place where people from different nations met one another, where they could publish their work, and where they could draw the attention of Europe to problems and movements in their native countries. The intellectuals who went there in the 1830s and 1840s (especially those who traveled from eastern or southern Europe) therefore encountered the emerging economic, political, and literary organization of modern Europe. July Monarchy Paris became the threshold of a new world because those who crossed into it could find themselves crossing boundaries between periods of history as well as between nations and cultures and phases of their personal lives. It was this experience of crossing all kinds of familiar boundaries which made the journey across the Parisian threshold both exhilarating and threatening for almost everyone who made the trip. Like all creative experience, work, and thought, the transition encouraged the extension or transgression of familiar limits. Once they had settled in the city, however, foreigners began to discover social and intellectual possibilities that could evolve in different directions for every new arrival.

The similarities and differences of the Parisian exile journey show up specifically in Heine, Marx, and Mickiewicz, all of whom went to Paris with attitudes about France and with expectations about what emigration might mean and then gradually transformed their views and expectations in the course of their French experience. They responded to many of the same tendencies and contradictions in French culture, but they expressed these responses in relation to significantly different literary, theoretical, and nationalist priorities. Heine became an exemplar of the new international literary culture that was based in Paris; the network of Parisian publications and friendships enabled him to establish his literary identity as a cultural mediator and to dramatize his personal experiences through books that made him famous in Germany and France alike. His French career attests to the literary opportunities that exile in France could provide for someone who was capable of transforming that position into witty, cross-cultural texts.

The case of Marx suggests how a more theoretically oriented exile could interpret French intellectual traditions and social conditions to develop a new conception of history and society. Although his French experience was much shorter than Heine's and his use of Paris somewhat more abstract, Marx exemplifies the new social theory that emerged in these decades through the synthesis of French socialism and republican political theory with German Hegelian philosophy. Heine exploited French social conventions and connections to pursue his literary objectives; Marx exploited French revolutionary traditions and economic ideas to extend his search for a critical social theory. Taking from France those features that best served their own interests, both men demonstrated the creative possibilities that arose when Germans began comparing French history and society with the traditions and society at home.

The Poles, too, compared French traditions with their own as part of a creative search for national identity which nobody pursued with more resolve than Adam Mickiewicz. Through a remarkable series of Parisian texts and lectures, he developed influential religious definitions of Polish nationalism both by explaining what Poland shared with France and by stressing how Poland was different. He serves as the outstanding example of the connection between an evolving eastern European nationalism and French nationalist traditions in the early nineteenth century. France provided the all-important model of a nation that had achieved both cultural autonomy and political independence. Mickiewicz's analysis of French and Polish history therefore showed how these nations followed their similar national destinies in the separate directions of east and west. While Heine and Marx were using France to pose critical alternatives to German politics and culture, Mickiewicz was using Poland to pose critical alternatives to French rationalism and social organization. This notion of otherness in Mickiewicz contributed to that strong cultural identity which has often transformed exiles into influential leaders of modern national independence movements.

Heine, Marx, and Mickiewicz thus become distinctive examples of exile responses to the French social-intellectual milieu and suggest how the exile experience in Paris entered into the general development of nineteenth-century European literature, social theory, and nationalism. To be sure, there were important differences in their interests, their contacts, their access to Parisian institutions, and their length of residence in France; and many significant themes in their lives and thought bore little or no direct relation to their French experience. I nevertheless emphasize what they shared more than how they differed. I claim no comprehensive explanations of three figures who have been subjected to continual analysis by an army of scholars for more than a century. Instead, I propose simply to investigate how these persons used exile and the French context to work out new theories, new texts, and new identities in ways that I take to be characteristic of the creative thought that often accompanies expatriation. The chapters of this book may therefore be read as connected essays that speculate on the complex interaction between experience and texts and that emphasize the importance of exile and the significance of Paris in the evolution of nineteenth-century European thought.

Chapter 1

The Capital of Europe

It is admitted by candid persons of all nations, that, after a long residence in Paris, the society of all other capitals produces the impression of provinciality.

Catherine Gore, *Paris in 1841*

Paris became a legend in the nineteenth century. Although it also happened to be the largest city on the European continent, its legendary attributes surpassed almost all of its real-life characteristics. Several centuries of *ancien régime* manners and culture, an unprecedented political-social revolution, a decade of Napoleonic conquests and architecture, an expanding commerce and population, another revolution in 1830, and a never-ending supply of popular books, irreverent wits, and scandalous stories made Paris the most famous place in Europe during the first half of the nineteenth century. Its history had transformed the French capital into a symbol of extremism in politics, mores, culture, and theory; its vivid social contradictions (high style and low life, wealth and misery) had produced the most striking combination of grandeur and squalor. Paris therefore became a symbol that also gave its interpreters the excitement and excesses of a permanent sensory spectacle.

The city offered something for everybody: elegance and privilege for aristocrats, a market for merchants, intrigue for diplomats, contacts and ideologies for revolutionaries, an audience for writers and artists, jobs for laborers—and wine, sensuality, and amusement for all. Opportunities for work and leisure, combined with the city's historical reputation, attracted a continual stream of French provincials and foreign visitors. Many stayed for months or years—or a lifetime, contributing new customs and causes to Parisian life and providing the cosmopolitanism that Catherine Gore found so conspicuous in 1841.[1]

Gore's comment about the comparative provinciality of other capitals was not unusual. Living in Paris during the middle years of the July Monarchy, she saw for herself the mix of social classes, nationalities, immigrants, and tourists that made the city a legend and attracted the interest of people throughout Europe. It was during the reign of Louis-Philippe that Paris functioned as the principal meeting place for expatriates from Germany, Poland, Russia, and Italy and as *the* stop on the continent for American and English travelers, writers, diplomats, and merchants. This convergence promoted intellectual exchange and political enthusiasms, and it created the lively center that Walter Benjamin called "the capital of the nineteenth century."[2] That is a bold claim for the influence of Paris, and yet it is a claim that Parisians made and foreigners accepted throughout the 1830s and 1840s.

Travelers and foreign residents generally assumed that Paris had a special role in world history. The assumption appeared often in the introductions to memoirs and travel books of the period as authors explained why they had written about Paris. Polish émigré Charles Forster offered a typical account when he asserted that Paris was the "new capital of the world" and a "magic word" that resounded among civilized people everywhere. The city stimulated anyone who went there or who knew about recent history, and its "grandeur" was certain to impress all thinking persons who saw it.[3] Another Pole, Karol Frankowski, undertook a "physiological study" of the French capital in which he compared Paris to a flashing meteor. As a place that changed daily, Frankowski explained, it demanded total immersion on the part of anyone who (like himself) wished to describe it. London, by contrast, scarcely changed at all.[4]

Parisian prestige may have turned more heads in Russia, however, than anywhere else. The Russian critic P. V. Annenkov emphasized the vital importance of Paris for his generation when he wrote about the "extraordinary decade" (the 1840s) in Russian letters: "The impression Paris produced on the travelers from the North was something like what ensues upon a sudden windfall: they flung themselves on the city with the passion and enthusiasm of a wayfarer who comes out of a desert wasteland and finds the long expected fountainhead."[5] Some visitors decided that the oasis was really a mirage, but that part of the story did not appear until the late 1840s. Alexander Herzen, who did his share of debunking, remembered that Russian tourists in the post-1830 period "glided over the veneered surface of French life, knowing nothing of its rough side, and were in raptures over everything."[6] Their reports encouraged very high opinions of French society, opinions that did not always survive when their compatriots had a look for themselves. The images nevertheless lasted a long time and brought many legend-chasing Russians to France.

Visitors of all nationalities agreed that Paris was the unrivaled cultural capital of Europe. Guidebooks of the day ascribed this dominance to the open-minded habits of Parisians, who welcomed foreigners because they believed them to be spiritual brothers. "London is a more opulent city," noted one guide, "but it is egotistical and arrogant; it is only the capital of industry, while Paris is the home of philosophes, the heart of Europe, in a word, the capital of civilization."[7]

This French explanation for the permanent flow of foreign visitors was confirmed by the exclamations of countless foreign observers. Eduard Gans, a German, reported that he found everything in Paris "important and meaningful."[8] Americans were no less enthusiastic. After a winter of lectures, plays, and conversation, Margaret Fuller called Paris an extraordinary school: a place where "ignorance ceases to be a pain, because there we find such means daily to lessen it"; it was also the only "school" she had ever known in which the teachers could bear examinations by the students.[9] Her praise was typical of the image-enhancing reports that made the French capital an obligatory stop for any New Worlder in search of Old World culture and experience. In fact, James Fenimore Cooper, who lived in Paris for several years before and after the Revolution of 1830, thought the city provided the best introduction to the whole of Europe:

> Paris is effectually the centre of Europe, and a residence in it is the best training an American can have, previously to visiting the other parts of that quarter of the world. Its civilization, usages, and facilities, take the edge off our provincial admiration, remove prejudices, and prepare the mind to receive new impressions, with more discrimination and tact. I would advise all our travellers to make this their first stage, and then to visit the North of Europe, before crossing the Alps, or the Pyrenees.[10]

All roads led from Paris.

Americans usually went to France for culture and Old World charm rather than for politics. They were mostly convinced that Americans could not learn much from European political life—even in France, home of the era's most advanced political theories.[11] For many other visitors, however, the French reputation for revolution and radical politics was a major attraction. Paris was the center and the symbol of progressive thought in the 1830s and 1840s. This political role gave "Paris" a highly charged significance throughout much of central and eastern Europe. It became the refuge for displaced radicals and hence the "enemy" for conservative regimes everywhere.[12]

Despite the conservatism of Louis-Philippe's government, foreigners—revolutionaries and reactionaries alike—continually attributed radical inspiration in their own countries to French influence. Germans and Russians could therefore reveal their political and religious attitudes simply by expressing their hostility or sympathy for France. Arnold Ruge stated the common radical perspective when he outlined his plans for the *Deutsch-Französische Jahrbücher* in 1844. Anyone who opposed France opposed liberty, Ruge argued, because "France represents alone in Europe the pure and unalterable principle of human liberty.... This nation fulfills a mission of cosmopolitanism." The French had proclaimed human rights, thereby altering the history of all European nations. "One can judge the intelligence and independence of a man in Germany by his appreciation for France.... Any German who understands France becomes an enlightened man, a free man."[13]

Ruge's enthusiasm clearly reflected a German, Hegelian desire for radical precedents and alternatives. When Poles and Russians searched for alternatives to what they knew at home, they too settled on France. Annenkov remembered that Russian intellectuals often debated the merits and problems of France during the 1840s. In Russia, as elsewhere, "it was the hidden France, and not the France in plain view, which was the object of interest." This hidden France was of course the country of revolution, "the earlier, still quite recent, universally well-known, typical France, the France that had categorical solutions for all questions of a social, political, or moral character, the one that, when those solutions were slow in coming, had taken measures to produce them by force. It was this latter, older France which for many people in Europe was then still the immemorial, the eternal France." Thus, many Russians idealized an "imaginary, fanciful" France that did not exist and knew practically nothing about the real France of Louis-Philippe.[14]

Yet conservative governments in Germany and Russia likewise assumed that France in 1840 was still very close to the France of 1793. The Russian government declared the country "off limits" for Russian travelers, and German authorities looked for French influence whenever political groups or publications seemed to question German traditions and values.[15] Annenkov, for one, believed that the Revolution of 1830 frightened the leaders of every conservative regime in Europe. Like the radicals, they perceived that revolution as the reappearance and expansion of something that would not go away. "The wound which, in 1830, France had inflicted on the customary order of things and trend of ideas in Europe was far from fatal," Annenkov explained, "but the wound, nevertheless, ached and provoked grim thoughts about the eventual outcome of the malady. Hence—the hue and cry, the summoning of endless numbers of doctors, and the search for possible means of an immediate cure."[16] Although the French injury to the old European order was less dangerous than radicals hoped and conservatives feared, they all believed that something important had happened there, and they went to Paris to take heart or despair, to live their dreams or confront their nightmares.

The Paris that many foreigners dreamed about, however, was by no means the city of culture and politics but rather the city of decadence and pleasure; that reputation may have drawn as many visitors in a year as the lectures and concerts attracted in a decade. Charles Forster described the image of Paris that grew as one traveled east in Europe: "In Germany, and especially in Russia, they are convinced that Paris is a new Babylon; that the air one breathes there is so saturated with vice that one need only enter the city to witness every imaginable depravity. Parisian women in particular have such an equivocal reputation that it is thought to be nearly impossible to meet a single honest women among them."[17] Forster rejected the stereotype, claiming that French women were as virtuous as others and that London was more depraved than Paris.[18] The city's alleged immorality, however, formed only one aspect of its more general reputation for criminality. Historians have collected a great deal of demographic and statistical evidence to show why crime became a pervasive theme in Parisian society during the nineteenth century, and there can be little doubt that the lurking figure of the Parisian criminal contributed significantly to perceptions of the city among foreigners, French provincials, and the residents themselves.[19] Paris seemed dangerous, but danger has its own allure, and it never stopped the influx of travelers who came to see the world.

Nor did it destroy the city's reputation for gaiety. German and English visitors were especially impressed by the apparent high spirits of the Parisians. Novelist William Thackeray reported from France that nothing there seemed serious; he described French society as "rant, tinsel, and stage-play" and warned the English to distrust a solemn French face because it was never genuine. Thackeray nevertheless considered the "innocent gaiety" of French people more pleasing than the "coarse and vulgar hilarity" of the English.[20] Another observer from Britain, journalist James Grant, called the Parisians "a remarkably light-hearted and lively-looking people" for whom a melancholy face was abnormal.[21]

The English writer Frances Trollope found the same *esprit* during an extended visit in 1835. She had never seen so many happy people; indeed, as she went about the city, she wondered "where all the sorrow and suffering which we know to be the lot of man continues to hide itself in Paris." The cheerful Parisians were unlike any people she had met before. "Everywhere else you see people looking anxious and busy at least, if not quite wo-begone and utterly miserable: but here the glance of every eye is a gay one." She suspected that this happy bearing might be worn and removed as others wear a hat; perhaps it was. Like others who were drawn to Parisian gaiety (including Germans such as Heine), Trollope could doubt the sincerity of all the smiles, and yet she admitted that "the effect is delightfully cheering to the spirits of a wandering stranger."[22] Paris of course had its share of "sorrow and suffering," but it was the stories of Gay Paree that made the city famous.

In short, the Parisian legend drew thousands of visitors and new residents to the city in every year of the July Monarchy. At the same time, there were many who went because they had no choice. The repressive policies of Metternich and his allies in Germany and Italy forced opponents to choose silence or exile. In Germany, for example, Metternich's laws prohibited almost every kind of political activity: associations and meetings, publication of pamphlets, liberty trees, hissing the flag, and liberal journals. Strict censorship hampered would-be writers and political activists in all of German-speaking Europe and encouraged many dissenting Germans to move to France.[23]

Meanwhile, several thousand Polish nationalists fled into exile in the 1830s to escape tsarist repression after an unsuccessful revolt against Russian control of Poland.[24] The largest number went to France, where they found other exiles from Italy, Portugal, Spain, and Russia. People moved to Paris from all of these countries because Louis-Philippe's bourgeois regime allowed more freedom for publishing and political activity than any other government in southern or central Europe. It was a place to hide, to study French politics, to write, and to follow the news from home. The Russian critic Annenkov left one of the best descriptions of this exile life when he explained what eastern Europeans found in the French capital during the 1840s:

> Among the distinguishing features of the Paris of those days belonged its additional important quality of providing the people in search of solitude for whatever reason the quietest spot in all of continental Europe. One could conceal oneself in it, keep hidden and out of sight of people, without ceasing to live the general life of a big, cosmopolitan city.
>
> In Paris one did not need to employ special efforts to find a neutralized corner, so to speak, from which one could easily and freely observe just the day by day creative activity of the city and of the French national spirit in general, an occupation, moreover, of a kind sufficient to fill whole days and months.[25]

Not surprisingly, some people went to Paris because they felt they had no choice but chose to stay when they might later have gone somewhere else.

Yet the political and literary refugees actually formed only a small part of the foreign community in Louis-Philippe's France. They were far outnumbered by laborers and artisans from Germany, Spain, Belgium, and Italy. Most émigré laborers worked near the border between their native country and France.[26] The Germans, however, came in large numbers to Paris, thereby constituting the largest foreign colony in the capital. This immigration evolved as a consequence of a long-term German economic crisis that began after the Napoleonic wars and continued until midcentury. The root of the crisis was an overcrowded agricultural labor market and an underdeveloped industrial base. Put simply, the absence of large-scale German industry in these years forced a growing population to stay in the countryside, where there was never enough work. The problem became increasingly severe because German agricultural products were losing their market in western Europe, especially after passage of such protectionist legislation as the revised English Corn Laws of 1815. As German agriculture stagnated, many unemployed farm workers emigrated or took up other trades. Many went to America, crossing France in long caravans to take ship at Le Havre or Brest. Others entered France as apprentices and journeymen in order to return home eventually as master artisans.[27] Many of the craftsmen in Paris

Table 1. Population of Paris, 1830–1848

Year	Population	Year	Population
1830	780,726	1840	928,071
1831	785,862	1841	935,261
1832	808,552	1842	958,986
1833	831,242	1843	982,715
1834	853,932	1844	1,006,442
1835	876,623	1845	1,030,169
1836	899,313	1846	1,053,897
1837	906,501	1847	1,053,770
1838	913,691	1848	1,053,643
1839	920,881		

Source: Louis Chevalier, *Laboring Classes and Dangerous Classes*, trans. Frank Jellinek (New York, 1973), p. 325, by permission of Howard Fertig, Inc.

were therefore Germans who had come to work for several years. Some tailors, bootmakers, and cabinetmakers settled permanently and dominated much of the Parisian market. For most French citizens in this era, the "German immigrant" was not a writer publishing political tracts but a tailor or a shoemaker.[28]

It was economic circumstances, then, rather than politics or culture, that brought most foreign residents to Paris. Their economic preoccupation gave workers a material purpose somewhat different from that of most intellectual exiles. They nevertheless played a major part in the expatriate community and in the wider society of Paris; together with those who wanted to be there and those who had to be there, they created an active cultural and political life. But how many foreigners lived in Paris, and what did they find when they moved from the legend to the city?

Population and Economy

Paris was by far the largest city in France during the July Monarchy, and it was growing all the time. Its population rose from 785,862 in 1831 to 1,053,897 in 1846 (see Table 1 for yearly figures), an increase of 34 percent. This growth rate was nearly four times greater than the rate for France as a whole during these years. Although the city still accounted for barely 3 percent of the total French population in 1846, it had more inhabitants than the ten next largest cities combined.[29] The capital's growth occurred during two periods of rapid expansion, separated by five years of comparative stagnation (when the economy was also weak). The early years of Louis-Philippe's reign (1831–36) coincided with a Parisian population boom during which the city grew by 14.5 percent. Thereafter (1836–41), the growth rate fell to 4.1 percent before resuming a rapid increase of 12.5 percent toward the end of the regime (1841–46). Another economic crisis in the year before the Revolution of 1848 finally halted the expansion.

Most of this growth was due to immigration; in fact, one study of the demographic patterns attributes at least 88 percent of the city's new population in the July Monarchy period directly to immigration.[30] The right bank was generally growing more rapidly than the left, though the old central *quartiers* on both sides of the Seine grew very slowly. The Latin Quarter and the right-bank market areas around Les Halles actually had more emigrants than newcomers between 1841 and 1846—their population growth came entirely from a surplus of births over deaths—but even these *quartiers* housed a great many nonnative Parisians and were always the most densely populated areas in the city. The twenty-three *quartiers* inside the grand boulevards on the right bank made up 42.7 percent of the population in 1831 and 38.9 percent in 1846.[31] Since these were also the smallest *quartiers*, this population lived in an extraordinarily congested environment. The Arcis *quartier* in the seventh *arrondissement* had a density of 243,000 per square kilometer in 1846. That was exceptional, but seven other *quartiers* on the right bank exceeded 100,000 people per square kilometer, and the density rate in the entire city approached 31,000.[32]

Although there was much more space on the periphery, the theme of the statistics is clear: Paris was already a densely populated city in the 1830s and 1840s, perhaps more crowded in these years than at any other point in its history. Major annexations in 1860 and the rebuilding of Paris during the Second Empire widened the city's space and encouraged growth in new areas. Louis-Philippe's Paris, by contrast, contained a rapidly growing nineteenth-century population in the space of an eighteenth-century city.[33]

People were moving to Paris from all areas of France, but especially from departments in the North and East. No one could live in the capital without noticing the constant influx of newcomers. A. Cuchot, who evaluated the population statistics for the *Revue des Deux Mondes* in 1845, decided that it was wrong to claim that Paris governed France; on the contrary, he suggested, the people of France had taken control of Paris.[34] A majority of residents in practically every part of the city had been born elsewhere. Population figures for 1833 show that 527,000 (or 63 percent) of the city's people were of non-Parisian origin.[35]

The immigration to Paris altered the characteristics of the population as well as its numbers. The majority of newcomers were young, unmarried men who worked as laborers or artisans, and most were not well off. Cuchot estimated that only one Parisian in ten had the luxury of knowing where the next meal might come from. In order to explain how people actually earned their bread, Cuchot divided the population according to professions.[36] Using data from the 1831 census, he counted the totals as follows: liberal professions, 16 percent; business, 9 percent; laborers, 43 percent; salaried employees, 22 percent; military, 10 percent. His categories were vague, and they suggest that more than one out of every ten Parisians had some economic security. Still, the main points of his analysis have been confirmed by modern research. One study calculates that no more than 20 percent of the capital's population belonged to the bourgeois or leisured classes in the period of the July Monarchy.[37] For the rest, the material problems of daily life were never far away.

The stream of new, often disconnected young men fostered social tendencies typical of modern urban life. The crime rate went up, and more persons were arrested for derangement and madness. There were also more suicides, a fact that reflected in part the large male population: men accounted for two-thirds of the suicides in Paris.[38] The number of unmarried persons considerably outnumbered the married population in the city, and a third of all children born in Paris during the July Monarchy were born out of wedlock.[39] Figures for indigence and prostitution provide further evidence of the anomic modernity in nineteenth-century Paris. There were more than 68,000 persons on relief in the capital in 1832, or one of every eleven people; by 1847, the number of those receiving relief had grown to nearly 74,000, with the largest number living in the working-class *quartiers* on the eastern side of the city.[40] And to serve the crowd of lonely immigrants, wandering workers, and would-be adventurers, there were well over 3,000 prostitutes: the police registered 3,479 in October 1831, but there may in fact have been more, and the number probably increased as the population grew over the next fifteen years.[41]

They surely drew part of their clientele from among the foreigners in the city. Approximately 850,000 foreigners were in France by the end of 1847, most of them living in border areas or in the

Table 2. Foreign population in the Department of the Seine, 1830–1847

Year	Resident foreigners on January 1	Transient foreigners	Total population of Department
1830	47,000	19,928	
1831	39,000	19,983	
1832	37,000	25,733	
1833	47,000	38,746	
1834	57,000	44,434	
1835	66,000	48,035	
1836	75,000	54,585	
1837	83,000	53,713	
1838	91,000	56,182	
1839	97,000	57,525	
1840	104,000	53,844	
1841	110,000	51,954	1,194,603
1842	118,000	53,559	
1843	127,000	56,835	
1844	136,000	58,557	
1845	147,000	57,315	
1846	159,000	61,379	1,364,467
1847	174,000	38,601	

Sources: Jacques Grandjonc, "Eléments statistiques pour une étude de l'immigration étrangère en France de 1830 à 1851," *Archiv für Sozialgeschichte* 15 (1975): 229, by permission of Institut für Sozialgeschichte; Louis Chevalier, *La formation de la population parisienne au XIXe siècle* (Paris, 1961), p. 284.

department of the Seine.[42] The count of foreign residents in Paris was never very accurate because officials normally listed only those living in hotels and roominghouses; since many also lived in private homes or in their workplaces, the official figures were almost certainly too low.[43] In spite of these statistical problems, modern research suggests that the number of foreigners living in the department of the Seine rose from about 47,000 in 1830 to 174,000 in 1847 (see Table 2). Growing at an average annual rate of over 9,000 between 1832 and 1847, the foreign community increased from roughly 5 percent to 13 percent of the total population in the department.[44] In addition to the long-term residents, there was a constant flow of foreign visitors—on average, about one visitor for every two permanent foreign residents. For example, approximately 104,000 foreigners were living in the department of the Seine in 1840, and there were almost 54,000 foreign visitors; thus, some 158,000 foreigners lived in or passed through the Paris region that year. The same calculation gives a total of 194,000 for 1844. (Table 2 provides figures for each year of the July Monarchy.)

Most foreigners in Paris were German, English, Belgian, or

Table 3. Distribution of foreigners by nationality and percentage of foreign colony (Department of the Seine)

Nationality	1831		1832	
	Total	% on 1 Jan.	Total	% on 15 June
English	6,435	16.5	5,280	15.4
German	6,708	17.2	5,510	16.1
Belgian and Dutch	7,410	19	6,200	18.1
Swiss	4,680	12	3,970	11.6
Italian and Savoyard	6,825	17.5	5,820	17
Spanish	1,755	4.5	1,570	4.5
Portuguese	1,287	3.3	1,160	3.3
Polish	156	.4	1,870	5.4

	1836		1839	
	Total	% on 1 Jan.	Total	% on 15 Nov.
English	12,525	16.7	16,740	18.1
German	15,450	20.6	23,200	25.1
Belgian and Dutch	12,900	17.2	14,950	16.2
Swiss	8,250	11	9,560	10.3
Italian and Savoyard	12,225	16.3	14,300	15.5
Spanish	3,000	4	3,280	3.5
Portuguese	750	1	750	.8
Polish	2,250	3	2,800	3

	1841		1846	
	Total	% on 1 Jan.	Total	% on 31 Dec.
English	20,570	18.7	35,192	20.8
German	30,030	27.3	59,334	34.1
Belgian and Dutch	17,270	15.7	24,882	14.3
Swiss	11,000	10	15,760	9
Italian and Savoyard	16,610	15.1	24,360	14
Spanish	3,410	3.1	4,550	2.5
Portuguese	550	.5	500	.3
Polish	3,300	3	4,000	2.4

Sources: The figures for 1832 and 1839 are drawn from statistics in police bulletins; the others are estimates, based on trends in available statistics and on nonquantitative sources, from Grandjonc, "Eléments statistiques," p. 234, by permission of Institut für Sozialgeschichte.

Italian (the Italian figures include Savoyards). Germans formed the largest foreign group in all the years of Louis-Philippe's reign. Their number increased from roughly 6,000 in 1830 to 60,000 by the end of 1847, and their percentage of the foreign community grew from 17 percent to 34 percent over the same period (see Table 3).[45] The English colony also grew rapidly, reaching 35,000 (20 percent of foreigners) by 1846. The percentages of Belgians and Italians in the foreign community fell somewhat, even though they continued to arrive in large numbers throughout the period. The Poles showed the greatest increase, however: their population in the department of the Seine grew from about 150 in early 1831 to 4,000 by 1846.

Foreigners and French provincials immigrating to Paris during these years were similar in social class, gender, and age. The majority of the diverse foreign community—both resident and transient—always consisted of workers. Among the 110,000 foreign residents of the Seine department in 1841, for example, 66,000 may be classified as workers (artisans, migrant laborers, and the like). The others lived in the capital as students, writers, businessmen, diplomats, or long-term visitors. In that same year, 31,200 of the 52,000 foreign transients were workers. Immigrants from abroad, like their French counterparts, were mostly male and mostly young. It was common for young men to go to Paris for a *compagnonnage* apprenticeship when they were between sixteen and eighteen years old. Many stayed ten and even twenty years before settling permanently or returning to their native counties.[46] For the most part, they lived in the crowded central *arrondissements* that extended to the north and east of the Palais-Royal.

The economy of Paris depended to a great extent on the labor of French provincials and foreigners. In 1844, Louis Desnoyers explained that non-Parisians essentially controlled a number of the capital's trades and professions. Nearly all the carpenters, masons, and locksmiths came from the provinces; building painters were mostly Italian; tailors, cabinetmakers, and bootmakers were usually German; and mechanics were often English. There were also tailors, barbers, and doormen from Poland.[47] A Chamber of Commerce investigation of Parisian industry in 1847 found the same nationalities in the professions Desnoyers discussed, and in other trades as well; for example, the report estimated that some 34,500 Germans were working as tailors, shoemakers, or cabinetmakers in the capital.[48] Although this was less than the total German dominance that Desnoyers described (it accounts for about a third of the workers in these trades), the study showed that Desnoyers's impressionistic comments about the capital's economy were based on real-life situations.

Workers in all trades had long hours. *Galignani's New Paris Guide* (1837) reported that the workday averaged ten to twelve hours except for cotton spinners, who frequently worked as much as fifteen hours. Most artisans and laborers did not work on Sunday afternoon or Monday morning. The spinners received only one or two francs per day for their long hours, but the daily wage for most tradesmen varied from three to five francs. A rag collector made less than two francs per day, and shopgirls—who received room and board as well—averaged between ten and thirty sous (twenty sous equaled one franc).[49] The ordinary journeyman needed twenty to thirty sous a day for food and about six francs a month for lodging. Dinner could be had in a cheap restaurant for twenty-five or thirty sous, or sometimes less: *Galignani's Guide* mentioned a dinner of soup, main dish, dessert, bread, and wine for twenty-two sous. Dinner and wine in a better restaurant was about two francs.[50]

The English authors of *Galignani's Guide* thought these Parisian prices were cheap, perhaps because the British pound was then worth about twenty-five francs. Frances Trollope, however, found the necessities of life about as expensive in Paris as in London. It was the luxuries that made Paris a bargain: "Wine, ornamental furniture, the keep of horses, the price of carriages, the entrance to theaters, wax-lights, fruit, books, the rent of handsome apartments, the wages of men-servants, are all greatly cheaper, and direct taxes less."[51] Aristocrats had a good life at a good price in the French capital.

Most Parisians, though, were looking for necessities rather than luxuries, and those were not easy to find. Housing was inadequate throughout the years of the July Monarchy. With population growth far outpacing new building, many people lived in Paris without any kind of permanent residence. The 1846 census estimated the city's "floating" population at 88,000, and there may always have been at least 50,000 homeless people.[52] Wealthy visitors could find good hotels, where prices ranged from two to five francs per night.[53] Most new arrivals, however, lived in overcrowded roominghouses or cheap hotels. An 1847 almanac reported that Paris had 650 hotels and 2,200 restaurants and cafés. This Paris of hotels and restaurants was the Paris that many immigrants knew best. It was where their stay in the city began and where they often lived for a long time thereafter. A police report on the roominghouse population in December 1838, for example, listed 9,530 foreigners among the 62,075 lodgers identified.[54]

The housing problem was most severe in the densely populated center of the city (around Les Halles), where unsanitary conditions took a very high toll in disease and death.[55] Many contemporaries believed that Paris caused rapid physical deterioration. *Galignani's Guide* noted that men in particular soon lost their health and that

Parisian families often became extinct within a couple of generations.[56] Congestion in the crowded old buildings and ancient streets
helped to spread any epidemic or infection that reached the capital;
nevertheless, those buildings and streets were so full of activity,
so full of people and distractions of every sort, that newcomers
could rarely resist their fascination. By all accounts, Paris street
life was a sight to see—and something to hear.

The Streets of the City

   The streets of Louis-Philippe's Paris still wound through the city
in medieval narrowness and disorder. Most were built for people
instead of vehicles; the French capital had the smallest streets of
any major European city. At least this was the opinion of William
and John Anthony Galignani, and they did not expect the situation
to change: "The interior of Paris," they wrote, "must for ever retain
the appearance of a town of the middle ages."[57] This meant, among
other things, that the city would probably always be dirty and that
English visitors would always have something to complain about.
Indeed, the English preoccupation with Parisian mud and filth
provides an interesting view of the Paris that revolutionary change
and imperial architecture had scarcely touched.
   The city still lacked running water and therefore depended on a
small army of water carriers to keep its kitchens and bedrooms in
livable condition. Water buckets hardly provided the refinement
that English visitors expected; even worse was the scarcity of
drains and sewers.[58] It was difficult to get water into a house, but
it was nearly impossible to get water out of a street. A hard rain
invariably left the streets covered with puddles and mud, which
produced very strong odors. Frances Trollope thought the bad
drainage and bad smells inevitably coarsened the thoughts and
language of many French people and also encouraged them to
commit "the indelicacy which so often offends us in France":
namely, to urinate in the streets.[59] English people never grew accustomed to this "indelicacy," though they apparently encountered
it wherever they went in Paris.
   The journalist James Grant offered some typical English impressions of the sanitation in Paris in the early 1840s. Among the significant differences between the English and French capitals, he
was especially appalled by the poor drainage system in Paris,

but, bad as the evil referred to is [bad drains], there are nuisances of a still more offensive kind which are hourly, indeed almost momentarily witnessed; and (which is more unfortunate still) which you cannot fail to witness as you pass along the principal streets of Paris. In England, warnings are given, by perpetual inscriptions, against committing the indecencies to which I allude; and delicacy is, in consequence, but seldom shocked in this way. In Paris, so far are the civic or other authorities from putting down these offenses against all sense of decency, that they actually, by small exposed constructions, invite the passers by to their commission. And this, too, in what Frenchmen tell us is the finest, the fairest, and most fashionable city in the world![60]

For Grant and many of his compatriots, the mud and the public "indecencies" were among the French government's most serious failures and perhaps the most disagreeable feature of Parisian life.

Grant made additional comparisons that suggested a better quality of life in London. True, there seemed to be fewer ragged people and fewer drunks in Paris. But there were also fewer horses and carriages and omnibuses, and the Parisian streets were not as well lighted.[61] Weather comparisons were in France's favor, however. William Thackeray, among other English visitors, considered the "bright, clear French air" far superior to the unhealthy coal smoke and yellow fog of London; he called the French air intoxicating. Catherine Gore also praised the "clearness" of French skies, which she attributed to the habit of burning wood instead of coal. She thought the clear air, dry soil, and bright sunshine made Paris a healthy place to live.[62] This enthusiasm of the English for Parisian weather may have said more about their own country than about the French climate. One contemporary report noted that Paris enjoyed 174 days of good weather per year.[63] Still, those good days could be separated by a lot of rain; when Margaret Fuller left Paris in early 1847, she could remember only one fine day during a visit of more than three months. "Let no one abuse our climate," she wrote. "Even in winter it is delightful, compared to the Parisian winter of mud and mist."[64]

Rainy weather, dirty streets, and mud puddles did not keep Parisians at home, however. They went out on the boulevards to look for amusement and to look at each other. Indeed, the best way to see the city was to take long walks in the streets and parks. Parisian streets were a permanent parade in which every visitor and every resident participated at one time or another. A stroll on the city's boulevards, noted the Polish writer Karol Frankowski, was an "intellectual promenade" without rival in Europe.[65] Frankowski lived in Paris during the middle years of the July Monarchy and published his imaginative "physiological study" of its characteristics in 1840. His goal was to describe the city as a biologist might describe an organism by explaining where its vital parts were located and how it lived. Significantly enough, he devoted much of his study to boulevards and back streets, where he found the capital's beauty and ugliness on full display. As Frankowski explained repeatedly, all the tensions in the Parisian social body showed up there. He called the streets a "vast field for observation," a place where incident constantly followed upon incident and where one could see best what Paris carried in its head and heart: "Paris lives there, Paris plays there, Paris thinks there, speculates [and] loafs there. It lives in this river of people which foams in two opposing currents; it plays with the senses in the gilded parlors of its cafés and with the spirit in the halls of its thirteen theaters." The boulevards were an extraordinary marketplace. "When you look, you are astonished; when you reflect, you applaud."[66]

Frankowski's account of Parisian streets emphasized one dominant impression: the crowd of people. The crowd, which appeared most forcefully in revolutionary moments, was part of every Parisian's daily life, and it impressed foreigners such as Heine or Marx as much as it impressed the peasants and artisans who arrived every year from the French provinces.[67] Frankowski wrote about Parisian crowds with metaphors of nature and economics that conveyed both his fascination with the modern city and his fear of its unfamiliar, threatening, and even criminal qualities. The crowds were a "river" that flowed in the streets, and those streets were a huge "boutique" where everything was for sale and almost everyone was selling.[68] He described the city as a huge commodity warehouse in which thousands of antlike human beings collided with one another every day while they searched madly for their share of the goods, forever committing crimes as they gathered their loot and keeping the whole city in perpetual motion.

[Paris] is rapid,—it is ardent,—it is seething. . . . In the streets, in the passages, in the gardens, on the squares, on the quais, on the bridges, and under the bridges, men, animals, carts, and boats walk, run, roll, and slide. The air vibrates. It is torn by brusque notes and long notes, and it is worn out by blasts of bizarre sound that suddenly erupt and suddenly vanish. The street is always babbling, and the paving stones groan or complain, grind or hiss. Nobody takes offense. . . .

There is the clamor of travelling merchants, of daily news bulletins, and of cracking whips on prancing post-horses, the horn of stagecoach drivers, the neighing of heavy wagon stallions, the "watch out, watch out" of the dandy in a carriage, the false sounds of the blindman's bird organ, the grating harmony of the Savoyard's hand organ, the rumbling of thousands and thousands of wheels on all kinds of vehicles ...and all that without cease. In short, it is a human anthill with swarms of antlike businessmen, as tireless as bees, rushing to search for the conventional myrrh and honey called *money* or returning, nimble and cheerful, loaded with precious booty they have pilfered as only they know how and as only they they can do it.[69]

Frankowski's Paris thus combined the chaos of an inferno with the purposeful activity of an anthill, and it was a very noisy place.

The city's sounds fascinated him as much as the rushing people. As in nature, the sounds at night were different from the sounds of day, but Frankowski heard enough to decide that the city never slept:

The clamor of individuals and groups in Paris seems even more shrill at night than in the day. Its vast composition includes: the sharp, hoarse notes of horns, the tinkling bell of the coco merchant, the heavy clanging bells of the late wagon driver, the ringing bell of the omnibus conductor, and stanzas from the *Marseillaise* shouted by jovial workers and unlucky conscripts or students in search of adventures, all walking in groups through the streets and screaming as if they were deaf when they are not singing like fools.[70]

It all added up, he said, to a "modern Nineveh" of fervent labor and fervent pleasure. It might even be called a "carnival of hell," especially in the busy center.[71]

The greatest congestion was in the rues Saint-Martin, Saint-Denis, Montorgueil, and Montmartre, where the crowds were so dense that even the sidewalks seemed to sweat under the load. Preoccupied, expressionless people hastened through the congestion, pushing their way past other pedestrians and swearing at obstacles. These were the work areas of Paris. On Sundays and holidays, however, the crowd moved to the boulevards and to the better neighborhoods along the rues de la Paix, de Rivoli, de Castiglione, and Royale. Frankowski thought the crowds in the leisure streets were more cosmopolitan than those in the work streets, where people seemed very French.[72] The boulevards were well lighted, and they attracted a more relaxed crowd of strolling couples and cigar-smoking men. It was the most pleasant part of Paris. "A promenade on the boulevards . . . gives you sensations and pleasures that are always new, always fresh."[73] The principal drawback was the public "indecency" that so distressed the English. Frankowski warned women that a walk in even the nicest areas of the city was often disrupted by acts of "bestial filth" and concluded that American spitting was far less offensive than the Parisians' habit of urinating wherever they happened to be.[74]

Still, there was no denying that these people had style. The Englishman James Grant expressed a common perception when he called the French "exceedingly fastidious" in their appearance. He reported that it was rare to see dirty or poorly dressed persons in Paris. The men wore elegant hats and more stylish beards and mustaches than he had ever seen. As for the women, Grant thought they excelled in makeup and walking, but were less beautiful than English women.[75] The American Margaret Fuller said nothing about comparative national beauty but did note that "groups of passably pretty ladies, with excessively pretty bonnets" on the Champs-Elysées marked the colorful approach of spring. Parisian children were charming, and even the horses were handsome— which was more than she could say for the cigar-smoking, sauntering French men with their self-assured "half-military, half-dandy" attitudes.[76] It was a question of taste. Grant liked the men's hats; Fuller preferred the women's bonnets.

But there was a hat—and much, much more—for every taste in Paris. Frankowski referred to the city as an enormous "store divided into galleries" where everyone was buying and selling at the same time.[77] As he explained it, Louis-Philippe's Paris had in fact become a city of shopkeepers. There were "merchants of old clothes, old laces, old boots, rabbit skins [and] broken bottles"; in the crowded streets one was likely to see "menders of broken pots, orange sellers, fruit sellers, then women who fry potatoes on portable grease pans, water carriers, postmen with letters, [and] traveling salesmen with their wheelbarrows full of . . . manufactured knick-knacks of all different shapes, styles, and quality, but priced on average ten, fifteen, twenty, or twenty-three [sous] less than in the shops!"[78] So at least they claimed. Bargain hunters, though, could easily check for themselves because there was always another vendor and always another shop.

The most popular shops lined the galleries of the Palais-Royal. No serious shopper—indeed, no visitor to the city, however serious or fun-loving—could pass up the Palais-Royal. Everyone agreed

View of the gardens at the Palais-Royal in the 1840s. Lithograph by Jean-Baptiste Arnout and Louis-Jules Arnout. Musées de la Ville de Paris © by SPADEM, 1987.

that it offered the best shopping, gayest amusement, and finest restaurants in the capital. It was a center for social life day and night, particularly for foreigners. "There are many persons who pass not only days, but years, in carelessly sauntering through it," noted *Galignani's Guide,* "and who are to be found in it at all hours of the day and at all seasons of the year."[79] Gas lights illuminated both the arcades and the gardens, making the Palais-Royal one of the brightest places in Paris by night as well as day. "The first impulse of a foreigner, on entering the sunshiny place," wrote Catherine Gore, "is to exclaim—'How Gay!' "[80] It had gained a bad reputation among some Parisians and visitors during the Restoration because it was the meeting place for gamblers. The government closed the gambling houses after the July Revolution, however, and also posted guards to keep away prostitutes. The atmosphere had thus become wholesome enough for Gore to recommend a visit for anyone "not too fastidious or refined."[81]

Although the Palais-Royal attracted the lower classes more regularly than the rich, its shops were among the most elegant in the city. Frankowski counted eighty-five watchmakers, goldsmiths, and money-changers selling gold in one form or another. There were also jewelers (specializing in diamonds or silver), opticians, fashionable clothing stores, bookshops, and foodshops where one could buy exotic edibles from many parts of the world.[82] The variety of food was one feature that brought together what Gore called the "people of all nations and languages." Thirty restaurants fed this crowd, and three theaters entertained them.[83] Idlers could lounge in the courtyard to watch the stream of shoppers and tourists flow through the arcades. The Café de la Rotonde placed chairs and tables in the gardens and became one of the most famous meeting places in the city. According to one observer, even persons from hostile nations would meet at the Café de la Rotonde, a "central point where all the roads of the universe came to an end."[84] Other famous cafés and restaurants lined the arcades: the Café de Foy, Café de Chartres, Café Montansier, the Valois, the Véfour, and many others.[85] There were inexpensive restaurants too; a hungry person with little money could not find a better place to go than the Palais-Royal.

Finally, when visitors tired of shopping, eating, or watching the people, they might find a place to read: there were four pavilions in the gardens where anyone could borrow a journal for one sou. Or they could listen to the politicians and crusaders who gathered under the trees to debate the issues of the day.[86] The newspaper readers and the debaters added a political dimension to the Palais-Royal's many social and economic activities. One could see Parisian crowds and fashion in many parts of the city—on the boulevards, for example, or in the Tuileries—but the Palais-Royal brought together more of Paris and its visitors than any other place during the 1830s and 1840s. It was a social institution of considerable importance, a place where Parisians were most likely to see foreigners and where foreigners were likely to begin watching Parisians and each other. It was also a place where new arrivals started learning firsthand about the French political and cultural institutions that had attracted many of them in the first place and that the writers among them never tired of describing for the people at home.

Politics and Cultural Institutions

Most educated Europeans in the nineteenth century knew more about the politics and political history of France than about any other country except their own. The French Revolution, the exploits of Napoleon, and the July Revolution were famous wherever people discussed politics, and the history of these events continually drew curious foreigners to Paris. The French newspapers, political pamphlets, utopian tracts, and novels that were read throughout Europe further confirmed the common notion that the French were a highly politicized people. Though some visitors found a less active political life than they expected, and though the strength of French conservatism usually changed their stereotypical images of radical France, most foreigners decided that French political culture was unusually pervasive: "The very air they breathe," said Frances Trollope, "is impregnated with politics."[87] The Russian critic Annenkov recalled that the city's political activity was nearly irresistible to foreigners, combining as it did shrewd articles in the press, frequent debates by professors and nonprofessors alike, propaganda in the theaters, lectures on social theory, and the meetings of reformist or radical organizations. Since most of this activity criticized Louis-Philippe's government, the foreigners who participated in it were usually hostile to the French Monarchy, and the citizen-king became known as *"le tyran."*[88]

At the same time, however, many foreigners concluded that this constitutional monarchy managed to avoid both radicalism and reaction and that its policies were never as bad as its critics portrayed them. Conservatives found the regime reassuringly stable; liberals found it surprisingly open. The tradition-minded Mrs. Trollope, for example, praised Louis-Philippe's firm rule and sensible leadership. She assured the English that the French king was in no way revolutionary: "It is not to him that the radicals of any land must look for patronage, encouragement, or support: they will not find it."[89] Most radicals would have agreed with this assessment, and a few of them (such as Marx) were expelled from France. Even so, some expatriates (including Heine) became discreet admirers of France's constitutional regime, though it was not fashionable to express this admiration in radical circles.

The liberal Annenkov was willing to call Louis-Philippe a "distinguished bourgeois king" and to praise François Guizot for leading the most liberal European regime of the period. To be sure, Guizot had his flaws, yet Annenkov thought France was a much freer place in the 1840s than before or after:

> Out of fear of being reputed an egotistical "bourgeois" bereft of the faculty for understanding popular aspirations and the hidden miseries of the working classes, few people could bring themselves to give full voice to all they felt about the Paris of the 1840s. It is an undeniable fact, however, that travelers to Paris at the time came in contact with a city of irreproachable manners and customs, distinguished, as a natural outcome of the constitutional order, by an ease of social intercourse, by the possibility for any foreigner of finding appreciation and sympathetic response for any serious opinion or initiative, and finally, an integrity, relatively speaking, in all transactions between private parties. All this, as we know, immediately vanished with the advent of the Second Empire. To verify this brief sketch, it is sufficient to draw a comparison between it and what the city of Paris became after the loss of the July Constitution.[90]

Annenkov's account has the tone of nostalgia. He forgot or ignored the problems of opposition groups and newspapers and foreigners. His memory of Louis-Philippe's Paris nevertheless shows how attractive the July Monarchy could be for eastern Europeans.

Most liberal visitors from England or America, by contrast, did not feel the political openness that Annenkov remembered. James Grant, for one, described France as a "civil and military despotism." He reported that visitors would encounter uniformed men in every part of Paris—in the streets, the libraries, the theaters, and at all public places; the city resembled an enormous garrison.

"Crowned by the Academy of Soft Pears." Caricature of Louis-Philippe and Guizot after the Revolution of 1848. Lithograph by Becquet brothers. Musées de la Ville de Paris © by SPADEM, 1987.

Counting the regular army (30,000 to 35,000), the National Guard (60,000 to 65,000) and the police (1,500), Grant figured that at least a tenth of the capital's population was in uniform.[91] Even worse, Paris was a den of spies. Police informers attended every public meeting and most private ones, and the slightest criticism of king or government went immediately into the files at the Prefecture of Police. People could be arrested for casual remarks at a private party if one of the guests happened to be an agent.[92]

The military presence affected foreigners almost as much as the French. A foreign visitor, Grant explained, must constantly produce his passport: "The French authorities deal with all foreigners as if they were a set of rogues." Grant conceded that other nationalities might find such treatment normal enough, but for an Englishman it was "unspeakably galling." The harassment insulted English travelers, most of whom (according to Grant) became thankful for their English birth. "The sum of the matter is this; that France, though nominally a free country, is not so in reality. In all that constitutes true freedom, England is incomparably before it."[93] There was ethnocentric smugness in Grant's assertions, but he described what many people may have felt in their daily contacts with civil and military authorities: guilty until proven innocent.

Police surveillance stifled some of the accumulating resentment toward Louis-Philippe's government but did not make it go away. Almost all foreigners agreed on this. Annenkov remembered that the strength of opposition social movements was one of the first things a visitor noticed in Paris; Mrs. Trollope worried about the "noisy portion of the mob," and Grant stated categorically that "a Republican feeling everywhere prevails in France."[94] Foreigners who came looking for the opposition in France could usually find what they wanted. Margaret Fuller reported during the cold winter of 1846–47 that hunger was fostering criticism of the regime and that an explosion could not be far off. "While Louis-Philippe lives," she wrote, "the gases, compressed by his strong grasp, may not burst up to light; but the need of some radical measures of reform is not less strongly felt in France than elsewhere, and the time will come before long when such will be imperatively demanded."[95]

Meanwhile, it was difficult for the opposition to produce much light. Convening public political meetings was illegal, and no meeting of more than twenty people could take place without police permission. As Grant explained in 1843, this constraint on political groups and public meetings partly accounted for the influential role of French newspapers. The press offered the principal outlet for public opinion, and it was an institution that foreigners often observed closely. Paris newspapers were almost always connected with political groups in the capital. Guizot's supporters, for example, edited and usually read *Le Journal des Débats* (with a circulation of 9,305 in 1846). Republicans edited *Le National* (4,280 in 1846), and the socialist newspaper was *La Réforme* (1,860).[96] These journals covered the news with highly partisan perspectives and provided meeting places for otherwise illegal political gatherings.

Yet none of them had as many readers as the newer mass circulation newspapers that began to appear in Paris during the 1830s. *La Presse* (22,170) usually supported Guizot; *Le Constitutional* was close to Adolphe Thiers; while *Le Siècle*, which had the largest circulation (32,885), often agreed with left-leaning critics of the government (Odilon Barrot, for example), though it remained vaguely monarchist.[97] These were the most important among the twenty-three dailies that were published in Paris during the mid-1840s. The police kept a close eye on their activity (newspapers needed government clearance and a security deposit to publish) and regularly reported on the work of leading journalists.[98] Newspapers argued with one another, filled their columns with political tracts, and ran lengthy pieces by prominent novelists.

The French press aroused James Grant's journalistic interest and envy. He decided that Parisian editors had enormous influence over public opinion and that cabinet ministers could not afford to ignore them, as often happened in England. The English had no idea— "and can have none"—of the great power wielded by the press in France. The daily circulation of Paris newspapers was nearly twice that of the London press, though Grant believed that this might be explained in part by the fact that French journals were cheaper.[99] The power and prestige of French newspapers was most evident, however, in the public attitude toward the people who wrote for them. "No class of professional men occupy so high a place in French society as public journalists," Grant reported enviously. "They are the associates of nobles, ministers, and statesmen of the highest order." In fact, almost every government official had at one time been a newspaper writer. It was no disgrace to be connected with the daily journals in France; distinguished Englishmen and authors thought it dishonorable to write for newspapers, but the French seemed eager to publish in the press. And they were rewarded for it. "The appointment of newspaper editors to the highest, most honourable and most lucrative situations in the state, is a matter of constant occurrence," Grant explained. "How different, in this respect, the state of things in France and England!"[100]

Other observers were less sanguine about the role of French newspapers. After hearing French journalists argue for a free press, Frances Trollope concluded that the government had every right to protect itself and the common people from the "malign influence" that such persons exercised through their newspapers. Her stay in Paris gave her no faith in the social functions of journalism. "The influence of the press is unquestionably the most awful engine that Providence has permitted the hand of man to wield."[101] Charles Forster, the Polish writer, was equally dismayed by the partisanism and irresponsibility of French newspapers. He complained that the press, "this terrible weapon of intelligence," was too dependent on special interests and powerful persons who deceived the nation. Like Grant, Forster believed that French journalists were very close to power, but he regretted that they used their newspapers to encourage rivalries and deception. Most dangerous of all, however, were those who wanted to bring the working class into the nation's political life. Politicized workers thought about things that did not concern them. Once distracted in this way, they wandered from their proper task, which was to work. "Thus, to instill the working class with the taste of politics is to render it the worst possible service." Forster singled out the weekly *L'Atelier* as the worst offender. Here was a paper (published by workers) that frankly encouraged political discussion rather than hard work, a crime for which Forster vehemently condemned its very existence.[102] Working-class newspapers were still new in Europe, and Forster, among others, was not happy to see them.

But foreign residents and visitors could always relax after dinner with something besides a newspaper; they could go to a theater or a soirée. The Parisian stage and Parisian actors had a very high reputation during the July Monarchy. There were more than twenty-five theaters in the city where one could see everything from French classics and Italian opera to the most outrageous vaudeville. They drew big crowds from all social classes—perhaps 18,000 people each night.[103] In addition to the large theaters (such as the Odéon and the Comédie Française) that offered the famous pieces of classical French drama, many small neighborhood playhouses specialized in farces and horror shows for the working classes.[104]

Most visitors to the city felt obliged to comment on the quality of French theater or the performances of French actors and (like Heine) frequently used the theater to explain the codes of French culture. Margaret Fuller, for example, included a lengthy portrait of the famous actress Mademoiselle Rachel in the reports she sent from France. She called Rachel a genius and informed American readers that her acting revealed the pure power and symmetry of French tragedy; Rachel's language was a "divine dialect, the pure music of the heart and soul." She had no rival as an actress, but there was plenty of good entertainment in the city's small theaters, where the comic shows provided "excellent acting, and a sparkle of wit unknown to the world out of France."[105] Parisian plays and their appreciative audiences contributed more than a little to the French reputation for gaiety, frivolity, and superficiality.

French salon life added to that reputation. By tradition, the conversation at a Parisian soirée had to sparkle. The French themselves insisted on this and acknowledged that a brilliant salon never happened by accident. One famous hostess, Madame de Girardin, compared a good salon to an English garden in which the apparent disorder actually hides a very careful organization. If the right people were put together, the conversation would take interesting turns, and everyone would go home pleased with himself. That was the point of a soirée. Everyone had the chance to make a successful or unexpected remark. The guests were usually happy if they thought they had learned something, and they could always take away a funny story.

Although many people complained during the July Monarchy that Parisian salons had lost much of their former quality, Madame de Girardin could still count at least twenty interesting political, diplomatic, or literary salons in Paris in 1844.[106] Foreigners were often eager to go to one of them, and it was easy enough to find a hostess who wanted a foreign aristocrat or writer at the party (workers, of course, did not normally see this side of city life). The visitors who managed to get invited frequently decided that Parisian conversational skills were superior to those of other cities. Catherine Gore compared French "deportment" to English shyness and concluded that French courtesies were more "soothing." "The readiness of the French in conversation," she explained in a very English sentence, "their communicativeness of disposition, and aptitude in seeking to please and be pleased, are certainly productive of the happiest results as regards the promotion of social intercourse."[107] Similarly, Charles Forster described French conversation as lively, colorful, and "full of charming variety."[108]

The passion for the *bon mot* carried its own risks, though, and the vigilant Karol Frankowski thought he had found one of the most important ones in the decline of religion. Egotistical Parisians, he reported, believed in nothing except knowledge and the cult of intelligence. "It is the religion, it is the faith, it is the God of France! And for Paris, it is the only God, the only faith, the only religion."[109] Frankowski was concerned enough to call for a religious revival that might counter the bad effects of French paganism.[110] Other foreigners, lost in the repartee of a French conversation, may have reached the same conclusions about Parisian values. There was not much space for ignorance among those courteous guests—or for people who did not speak French.

The French language was of course a central part of every foreigner's experience in Paris; it gave power and defined social hierarchies as regularly as the police or the press. Although writers such as Heine and Mickiewicz remained especially sensitive to linguistic differences, every visitor was likely to feel the language problem somewhere, and a Paris salon was one place where language established the hierarchy most clearly. Even Frances Trollope, who found plenty to admire in the social graces at Parisian soirées, was dismayed by the invariable necessity of speaking French. She complained that French people would never say a word in English, though many of them knew the language well. They would tolerate some very serious mistakes on the part of foreign visitors, but they would never allow the conversation to move into another language in which *they* would make the errors. The fear of mistakes was an important consequence of French manners, and it could put foreigners in an awkward spot when either their language or their information was not up to standard.[111] Trollope herself ran into one of those spots when Chateaubriand told her that no foreigner could fully understand French literature because the nuances of language were inaccessible to nonnative speakers. Despite her doubts about that assertion, there was no way for her to convince Chateaubriand otherwise. She was on the wrong side of the language line that ran through even the most hospitable French salon.[112]

To be successful on the salon circuit, a guest needed information and intelligence as well as the right words. (This was the "cult" that Frankowski disliked.) According to Trollope, the French talked incessantly about new books, new songs, new musicians, or new preachers to show that they had the requisite supply of well-used intelligence. These subjects were interesting to the English but "indispensable" for a Parisian. "To meet in society and have nothing new for the *causette*," she explained, "would be worse than remaining at home."[113] The French nevertheless managed to handle these conversational pressures with all the ease in the world.

> I know not how it is that people who appear to pass so few hours of every day out of sight continue to know so well everything that has been written, and every thing that has been done, in all parts of the world. No one ever appears ignorant on any subject. Is this tact? Or is it knowledge,—real, genuine, substantial information respecting all things? I suspect that it is not wholly either the one or the other....
>
> This at least is certain, that whatever they do know is made the very most of; and though some may suspect that so great display of general information indicates rather extent than depth of knowledge, none, I think, can refuse to acknowledge, that the manner in which a Frenchman communicates what he has acquired is particularly amiable, graceful and unpedantic.[114]

But Parisians did not all pass their evenings in the salons, and so the foreigners who described them needed more than salon knowledge. To find out how they really looked and behaved, the serious observer had to go back out on the street.

Class and Gender

Descriptions of July Monarchy Parisians indicate how the city's population divided along social lines. The relatively small wealthy and educated class kept mostly to itself, entertained in style, sheltered its single women, and was hard to meet without the right credentials. The much larger laboring class worked or loitered in dirty, crowded streets, amused itself noisily, tended toward violence, and was hard to avoid. Both groups had their share of foreign admirers and detractors.

The upper classes of course attended the city's soirées and had those conversations that foreigners wrote about with considerable appreciation. There was, however, both an inner and outer circle within salon society itself. Charles Forster sought to explain the distinction for unwary foreigners who wanted to join the group.

In the first place, he noted, there was a select society that presented "extreme, nearly insurmountable" obstacles for any would-be member without the proper letters of recommendation. Forster assured his readers that the apparent inhospitality of this inner group resulted from the dangers of city life rather than from an antisocial attitude; nonetheless, this class of people were likely to "keep their distance during the first moments of an acquaintance made by accident and give themselves the time necessary to judge anyone who wants to be received at their home." Once a newcomer passed these formalities, the "ice" melted, the "national sincerity" reappeared, and the visitor was soon welcomed like a member of the family.[115]

The other part of Parisian society did not demand recommendations. To be sure, even this group would not open its doors to just anyone, but a prospective guest with the right appearance—fine black coat, light yellow gloves, polished boots, and the ribbon of an order—could usually be admitted to the salons of widows and politicians. Once inside, it was easy enough to meet people and, with discretion, to seduce the ladies.[116] At least this was how it seemed to Forster, whose own experience as a foreign man among the Paris bourgeoisie must have been largely successful. Like those of many observers, his account suggests the important role of women in this society, though his own male interests did not take him very far into the characteristics of this role.

Frances Trollope's interests, however, led her to talk about French women in some detail. She called the Parisienne an "exquisite mosaic-work" who had never been adequately described; then, after denying her own competence to write the missing description, she offered some impressions. To begin with, she thought French custom denied single women their freedom and effectively barred them from any real participation in the social life of the community. Young women sat quietly and almost out of sight in French society until they were married according to the wishes and arrangements of their parents. Trollope found nothing to envy in either the social restraints or the arranged marriages, all of which seemed very strange to her.[117]

The married French woman, by contrast, enjoyed altogether different rights and a measure of respect that English women did not have. Married women in Paris danced and talked to men with as much liberty as did single women in London.[118] Moreover, they played a "very distinguished part" in all aspects of French social life, in setting style *and* in leading conversation. English women often believed that ignorance protected a social reputation better than knowledge, but "happily for France, there is no *blue* badge, no stigma of any kind attached to the female possessors of talent and information. Every Frenchwoman brings forward with equal readiness and grace all she knows, all she thinks, and all she feels on every subject that may be started; whereas with us, the dread of imputed blueism weighs down many a bright spirit."[119] Because it was safer in England to "be thought an idiot than a BLUE," English women simply did not talk about literary or political subjects in the way that French women did. Indeed, Trollope concluded that the female mind was more honored in France than anywhere else. Madame de Staël's high reputation was one example, and the willingness of French women to debate politics was another. In short, "the women of France have more power and more important influence than the women of England."[120]

Moreover, the influence of poor women among their social peers seemed to rival that of wealthy women among theirs. The women in Les Halles (the famous "fishwomen") had always played a major part in Parisian history. They were active in revolutions, received by kings, and honored in poetry and song. These women had authority at home and political force in the streets.[121] It was a role that the otherwise conservative Mrs. Trollope respected. The influence of women was in fact almost the only characteristic of the Parisian crowd for which she expressed admiration.

Many English visitors thought the Parisian lower classes were better off than the poor people in London. James Grant, for instance, reported that the Parisian poor wore better clothes, drank less, and seemed more content than the English working class.[122] Frances Trollope also concluded that the Parisian "thriftless" were less wretched—though more full of scorn—than their English counterparts. Still, she expressed a common bourgeois attitude when she wrote about the dangerous idleness in the French capital and when she complained about the "greasy citizens" who felt free to go wherever they pleased. She was especially upset at the Louvre, where some of the "rubbish" from the "Parisian mob" wandered through the halls in very old clothes, apparently convinced that the revolutionary efforts of 1830 gave them the privilege to be dirty in front of their social superiors.[123]

Despite such complaints, English responses to the Parisian crowd were mild in comparison to the reports of many other Europeans. While the English had seen their share of poor people in the cities at home, some visitors from the East had had little contact with modern urban poverty, and their encounter with the Parisian crowd was a dramatic and startling introduction.

Nobody was more shocked than the Polish writer Karol Frankowski, whose recorded personal impressions often provide the most extraordinary rhetorical description of what all foreigners tended to notice as they explored the French capital. Like Marx and Heine and many others, Frankowski uncovered that dark, brutish side of Parisian life that accompanied the glitter and gaiety, the underside of Paris that produced many of the goods and much of the anxiety to be found everywhere in the city. He described streets in Paris, even whole *quartiers*, where generations of "dirty, loathsome, filthy, alcoholic" people were born, raised, and brutalized. They looked stupid; they were "yellow with misery"; they were "green with envy" whenever they saw wealth or comfort; they were savages with bad blood, raging dispositions, implacable hates, and a passion for homicidal fights:

> It is among them that disputes sometimes degenerate into murder without swords or firearms; it is among them that for want of a knife in the hand, the tooth bites into the ear, the tooth bites into the lip, and bites everywhere; that the fingernail digs into naked flesh, that the wrist squeezes the throat and tears out the hair, that the finger goes into the eye.... These are not the French, these are not Europeans, nor even the wicked bimanes. It is in the veins of this wretched breed that the blood of *sans-culottisme* attains its final purity.[124]

Although the civilized world of Paris was constantly changing, the opinions and ideas of the "Seminoles of Paris" were forever fixed. They were a "race" rather than a caste, and they served as the workhorses of Paris.[125]

Usually about five feet tall, the "race" had lean muscular limbs and pale long faces with aquiline noses. Their voices were "hollow and cracked"; their backs were slightly humped; they kept their eyes on the ground, laughed rarely, grunted when they spoke, and gestured clumsily.[126] Thus, as Frankowski described them, the Parisian poor were half horse, half ape. They showed an "animal apathy" for everything around them. "Ugly in their gay moments and [like] bears in their jokes between friends, their simple amusements are ordinarily summed up by the familiar thump, the amiable punch or the facetious dirty trick. If they are not a pretty sight when they are happy, they are horrible to see angry."[127] Fortunately, noted Frankowski, these blustering fellows were less menacing than they seemed because they usually disappeared whenever there was real danger. "They are like oxen; as long as they have something upon which to graze, the world can turn as it wants." Even so, these creatures were dangerous enough for Frankowski to advise that visitors should avoid their neighborhoods at night because murders and robberies were common there.[128]

The violence Frankowski described was animallike rather than politically motivated. If the former variety seemed normal for workers, the latter could only be an aberration. This was also Charles Forster's perspective when he warned against giving political newspapers to workers. Forster found the lower classes less prone to "grazing," however; he believed that the natural curiosity of Parisians attracted them to every disturbance they saw. Once assembled, these crowds took on a highly active character. They would listen to orators or see a bloody incident and suddenly become a violent, aggressive force. Such crowds might be controlled if they were dispersed as quickly as they formed, but aroused mobs were deaf to all appeals for law and order, and no sensible person would want to be among them.[129] Although riots were an exception, Forster thought a visitor needed courage to enter working-class districts even on quiet days. The dirty streets, the nauseating odors, and the poorly clothed, hungry people were enough to turn any stomach. Forster nevertheless assured foreigners that these hungry people did not want charity. They were proud, he explained, and they wanted to work.[130]

They were also remarkably friendly to foreigners. Guidebooks promised visitors that the "humble worker" was no less willing than the businessman to welcome them to the city and to extend every courtesy.[131] This claim was borne out in the stories of many foreigners, the working-class reputation for bestiality notwithstanding. James Grant reported that a poor Parisian cobbler responded to his bad-French request for street directions with far more courteous help than he would have received at home.[132] French politeness to strangers seemed altogether extraordinary to Grant, who concluded that some Parisians actually reveled in the opportunity to answer inquiries: "I feel assured that the Frenchman . . . would feel much happier at having an opportunity of furnishing you with the information you desire than if you were to patronize him in whatever line of business he may happen to be." In Grant's account, this *politesse* was typical of the humblest laborer, the artisan, and the educated classes alike.[133]

Forster likewise believed that French people were exceedingly helpful to foreigners, though he cited mostly upper-class examples. The French, he explained, did not humiliate foreigners; they excused linguistic errors, helped a newcomer find the right words, and never laughed at mistakes. This was unique in Europe; the English and the Germans were neither as sympathetic nor as helpful. Indeed, this French tolerance was one reason for the near universality of their language.[134] Forster stressed that the French welcome extended to finances as well. Many foreigners who lacked resources or work benefited from French government aid—nearly unheard of in Germany or England. Most striking of all was the French "political generosity":

> There is no country in the world where a foreigner, an émigré, will find hearts that are warmer or more compassionate to his suffering. ...as soon as he touches French soil, he becomes, as it were, a citizen of the country; because, not only does he find the most cordial hospitality, but also the most effective protection. No one demands of him an accounting of his opinions or his nationality. He is an exile and that is enough. And if he does not have everyone's sympathy, he at least enjoys the esteem that is accorded to genuine convictions and for which he suffers. In this respect, as in its most chivalrous assistance, France will always be the purest, most noble model for the universe.[135]

Forster decided that this "extreme tolerance of opinion" deserved the highest possible praise and that France was the only nation in which persons with different opinions could maintain such mutual respect and politeness.[136]

Of course, there were exceptions. Catherine Gore, for example, found Parisians cautious in the way they welcomed the "heterogeneous" and "fluctuating" crowd of foreigners forever arriving in the capital. The French could not possibly receive all of this "mob" with open arms, yet anyone who gained acceptance in French society was securely established there for life.[137]

Most foreigners did not stay in France for life, but many did stay a long time. Some were able to move rather easily into French society (as Heine and Mickiewicz entered literary society); others kept mostly to themselves either because they wanted to or because they lacked the necessary *entrée* to the circles that welcomed the rich and the influential (Marx, for example, was always a complete outsider). Those foreigners who stayed on the outside managed to create a number of institutions and meeting places that gave expatriate society a flourishing life of its own. The French tolerance that Forster praised—limited as it was in some respects—provided an opening for the development of political and cultural groups that facilitated contact among foreigners and sometimes achieved influence both in their home countries and in France.

Emigré Communities

There were many ways for foreigners to meet each other in Paris during the years of the July Monarchy. Because the various nationalities formed their own communities in the capital, new arrivals could usually find compatriots if they knew the name of a restaurant, bookshop, or workplace where they congregated. Also, many newcomers—whether they came for work, politics, or pleasure—arrived with the name and address of someone who already lived in Paris and who could help integrate another person into the expatriate groups. This is how immigrant communities usually operate, and there is no reason to assume that the German, Polish, and Italian groups in nineteenth-century Paris were different.[138] A young artisan from Germany, a political writer from Russia, a wealthy visitor from England were all likely to have contacts or letters of introduction that would open the first doors.

Even with few contacts or none at all, the émigré was almost certain to meet other foreigners in his work, in exile organizations, in certain cafés and salons, in the universities and reading rooms, or through the foreign newspapers. In fact, Parisian expatriate life brought together people who might never have met at home. German intellectuals met German workers, for example, and Russian socialists met Polish nationalists. Although many nationalities had opportunities to meet and organize in July Monarchy France, the German and Polish associations were most active and prominent.

German political émigrés took up manual labor in order to survive in Paris and soon met artisans who had come to France for economic reasons. Each group was at first reticent toward the other, but the necessity of cooperation in the French environment encouraged a new social and political perspective, which became manifest in the formation of mutual aid societies and discussion groups. The goals of these groups changed rapidly; they often evolved from artisan associations into political societies favoring radical change in Germany. Once Prussian spies and the French police noticed the political emphasis of the German associations, they were subjected to close surveillance and to legislation that restricted them to nonpolitical activities. Nevertheless, these developments introduced many German intellectuals to working-class conditions and many workers to new social theories, thereby contributing significantly to the emergence of modern German political theory and practice.[139]

The political stance of the German groups evolved from liberal republicanism in the early 1830s to communism in the mid-1840s. The first important organization in Paris, the "German Patriotic Association" (*Deutscher Volksverein*), was founded in the spring of 1832; it began as a constitutionalist society favoring liberal principles and a free press, but its artisan members soon moved to a more radical neo-Babouvist position. It was dissolved after new laws (1834) restricted the rights of associations in France. The most active members carried their Babouvist ideology into a new clandestine organization called the "League of the Outlaws" (*Bund der Geächteten*), which was followed in turn by the "League of the Just" (*Bund der Gerechten*).[140]

The League of the Just became the most influential of all the German émigré societies in Paris during the July Monarchy. Founded in the winter of 1836–37, it was essentially the creation of dissidents in the League of the Outlaws and of recently arrived exiles from a "Young Germany" group that had been suppressed in Switzerland. The German tailor Wilhelm Weitling became one of the group's early leaders and gave it a socialist theory in his work *Humanity such as It Is and as It Should Be* (1838). The league pursued its political goals among German workers in Paris who went back across the Rhine with word of the group's objectives: a socialist economy in a democratic German republic. The league also established branches in Switzerland and England, and it maintained correspondence with worker groups elsewhere. This led to affiliation with the Committee of Communist Correspondence in Brussels—led by Marx and Engels—and finally to assimilation into the "Communist League" (1847).[141] The activity of the League of the Just in Paris and its connections abroad attracted attention from the French police. Despite surveillance, expulsions, and miscellaneous harassments, however, the league remained in Paris until the Revolution of 1848, offering an important point of contact for the German workers and radicals who were continually passing through France.

Like their German counterparts, Polish exiles also organized social and political groups in the French capital. They began forming a "Polish Committee" in 1831 to give direction to the rapidly grow-ing émigré community that fled to France after the collapse of the revolt against Tsar Nicholas I and the Russians. Although the ref-ugees were welcomed to France, this committee soon alienated the French government by defining itself as a kind of government in exile and by publishing belligerent manifestos against German, Austrian, and Russian regimes that French authorities did not want to antagonize. French police watched the group closely and even-tually (1833) expelled the leaders upon the request of government ministers.[142] Thereafter, the aristocratic exile Adam Czartoryski undertook the formation of an unofficial Polish "government," whose diplomatic and political initiatives were generally unsuc-cessful. The Poles in fact lacked an effective unifying organization for their movement, though they gathered in churches, divided into radical and moderate factions, and debated the ways in which Poland might best recover its freedom.[143]

The absence of institutional structures in the exile community added extra importance to the mass meeting that Poles held each November in Paris to mark the anniversary of the 1830–31 revolt. This was the one annual event (it was sanctioned by the French government) that united all factions of the Polish emigration and gave the exiles a moment of public attention.[144] During the rest of the year, the Poles met in the small circles that surrounded their often mystical leaders and carried on their intragroup disputes. In addition, fund-raising events on behalf of poor exiles brought Poles together with many French people. And the Pole in search of fellow exiles could always go to one of the four Polish bookshops, the Polish library, or one of the several Polish weeklies that were pub-lished in Paris between 1831 and 1848.[145]

There were also meeting places for foreigners who shied away from political meetings and secret committees. Some of the famous salons in the city belonged to foreign hostesses and served as places for expatriate contacts. The weekly soirée of the Italian Princess Cristina Belgioioso was probably the best-known social rendezvous for foreigners in Paris (Heine and Franz Liszt were two of the famous regulars). Belgioioso herself became something of a legend. She welcomed writers, artists, politicians, and conspirators with-out much regard for rank or wealth; this tolerance attracted a great many guests—sometimes as many as six hundred on Saturday nights—and made her salon a good source of information on all the liberal causes in Europe. Her own favorite cause was Italian nationalism. The Belgioioso home thus became the Parisian meeting place for Italian exiles, many of whom benefited from the charitable events she organized on their behalf.[146] Russian hostesses also presided over well-known salons during these years. Marie Kalergis welcomed foreign writers and artists to her salon in the rue d'Anjou. Madame de Lieven, Madame Svetchine, and the Countess de Circourt hosted salons for diplomats, conservative monarchists, and the religious-minded.[147] There was, in short, a salon for almost any foreigner who wanted social contacts and who arrived with money or intellectual ambitions or political plans.

For the rest, there were cafés and restaurants that served a large foreign clientele. The English were almost certain to find their compatriots in the cafés of the Palais-Royal and in the restaurants at the English-owned Bedford or Victoria hotels. Germans went most often to the Mulhouse and to the Café de la Porte-Montmartre, which was popular because it always had a good selection of German newspapers. Other cafés appealed to foreigners because of their political reputation (Café National, Café de Foi, Café de Buci) or their literary fame (Café du Divan, Café de Suède).[148] Foreigners in search of real intellectual fare, however, were likely to move from the cafés to the universities.

Many people went to Paris specifically to hear lectures at the Sorbonne or the Collège de France. The American socialist Albert Brisbane and the Polish theorist August Cieszkowski, for example, regularly attended academic lectures on economics and history; there they came upon new theories and other foreigners.[149] University lectures were free, and they were open to all foreign men who wished to attend.[150] This open-door policy apparently drew many expatriates. A report prepared in the French Foreign Affairs office noted that scholars in science and literature often spoke to more than 1,200 people in Parisian lecture halls and that the audience came from everywhere. "It is not unusual," wrote an anonymous official, "to see in the same amphitheater, English from the three kingdoms, Germans, Russians, Poles, Danes, Swedes, Italians, Spaniards, and Americans, so that in the same place, on the same benches one hears all the languages of the civilized world."[151]

It may have been difficult for these people to communicate, but they were together, and foreigners with initiative and perseverance might meet expatriates and French scholars alike if they went to the lecture halls regularly. August Cieszkowski, for example, met a remarkable number of French professors and Polish émigrés by attending discussions at the Académie des Sciences Morales et Politiques and by having a well-placed Polish friend among the academic economists.[152] Although he may have cultivated his opportunities more assiduously than most foreigners, Cieszkowski's experience suggests that an outsider could find contacts through the universities as well as in the less official institutions that were organized by the émigrés themselves. Meanwhile, those few foreigners who received university teaching positions (Mickiewicz is perhaps the most famous example) usually had more access to French society than even the most enterprising foreign students.

Expatriates in search of their compatriots might also find them in a reading room. Reading rooms, usually associated with bookshops or private libraries, provided newspapers, journals, and books for persons who paid a small fee. The Galignani brothers operated one of the most popular reading rooms for foreigners at their bookstore in the rue Vivienne near the Bibliothèque Royale. William and John Anthony Galignani were Englishmen of Italian origin who managed the shop their father had founded in 1800. They also published English language books (*Galignani's New Paris Guide* was well-known) and an English daily newspaper, *Galignani's Messenger*, for which they borrowed articles from the London press or translated pieces from other European journals. According to their own guidebook, the Galignanis' reading rooms were spacious, well-lighted areas offering the best selection in Paris of American and European newspapers, magazines, pamphlets, maps, and books. They had more than thirty thousand volumes in English, French, German, Italian, and Spanish, and a garden where subscribers could take their reading material on warm days—all for the price of ten sous per day, four francs a fortnight, or six francs a month.[153] The English went there more than anyone else, but it was almost equally popular with others. The bookshop of Heideloff and Campe, also in the rue Vivienne, served in a similar way as a meeting place for the German community in Paris.[154]

Apart from *Galignani's Messenger*, which had a daily circulation of almost five thousand,[155] the most important foreign publications were the German newspapers that were published in Paris to serve the large German community there or to avoid the strict censorship across the Rhine. The fast-growing colony of German workers offered an audience for any journal that could provide news from home, carry useful information about France, and appeal to the group's social or political interests. There were always expatriate German writers with an eye on this audience and a plan to publish for it. Because German laws required government approval for all publications of less than 320 pages, much important German political writing between 1830 and 1848 first appeared in France. Not content with its control inside Germany, however, in 1844 the German diet banned the sale of all German periodicals, newspapers, and books that were published outside the country. This made Paris even more important as one of the few places where disaffected Germans could print or sell their publications.[156]

Many tried to do both. Germans edited fifteen different newspapers and journals in Paris during the July Monarchy.[157] Although a few were in French, most were published in German, and most had political objectives. Some were designed for Germans in France, some were for people at home, and some sought to encourage Franco-German cooperation. None of them survived for long. They suffered from lack of funds, poor sales *(Vorwärts*, for instance, had only some two hundred subscribers in June 1844), and frequent Prussian efforts to have them suppressed. Some of their writers were expelled from France, and the editor of the most prominent newspaper, *Vorwärts,* ended up in a French jail. The subsequently famous *Deutsch-Französische Jahrbücher* appeared only once. No German journal lasted more than three years. The hardships of exile politics and journalism were apparent in the short history of every publication. It was hard to find an audience, hard to prevent personal conflicts among the members of even a small staff, and hard to avoid political disagreements that could destroy the fragile cooperation upon which each journal depended.[158]

Despite their many problems, these short-lived publications played a significant role in expatriate life. Several were closely connected to worker organizations and served as forums for their members and sympathizers. *Der Geächtete* (1834–36), for example, was linked with the League of the Outlaws, whose artisan members contributed to the costs of publication. As the editors changed (the first, Jakob Venedey, was expelled from Paris at the request of the Prussian government) and as the league evolved, the journal became more radical. The more famous *Vorwärts* (1844), which came into the hands of the most radical German socialists, began publishing in affiliation with the Parisian Aid Association for Needy Germans (before that association was taken over by the Prussian consulate). Similarly, the League of the Just financed the *Blätter der Zukunft* (1845–46), another short-term newspaper that carried a wide range of socialist positions. *Der Deutsche Steuermann/Le*

Pilote Germanique (1844–46) had close political and financial ties to the Prussian embassy.[159] Less well-known journals appearing on behalf of other political groups disappeared just as quickly.

The German press in France evolved through two phases during the July Monarchy. The early publications (1834–39) reflected the liberal, republican perspectives of the first wave of German émigrés. The prominent republican critic Ludwig Börne was perhaps the most typical and most important figure in the period before his death in 1837. (Although Börne wrote many articles in France, his own journal, *La Balance*, appeared only three times in Paris in 1836.)[160] Emigré attitudes changed rapidly in the early 1840s, however, and the second phase of the expatriate press (1843–47) was more radical and more theoretical. Publications in this period reflected the development of Hegelian criticism in Germany and the evolution of socialism in France. Radical theorists such as Arnold Ruge, Karl Marx, Friedrich Engels, and Moses Hess were typical of this younger generation of exiled writers.[161] Their work and the ties between German publications and worker associations helped to make the exile press more important than its instability and small circulation figures would suggest. Though often an outlet for disagreements, it served as another means of meeting and interaction (in addition to workplaces and political gatherings, salons and reading rooms) for disconnected foreigners.

There was no shortage of correspondents for the expatriate publications or for newspapers abroad that wanted reports from Paris. The city was full of poets, journalists, political theorists, philosophers, and travelers who were looking for ways to publish their latest criticisms, solutions, and observations. The German-edited journal *Revue du Nord* (1835–38), for example, drew upon a whole community of now-forgotten German émigrés as well as the works of Poles and Frenchmen to fill its columns with translations, reviews, and articles.[162] Meanwhile, the popular "Paris letters" by such writers as Börne and Heine inspired a crowd of imitators to describe Paris for newspapers at home. One observer reported in 1843 that more than fifty German "correspondents" had taken up residence in the French capital to write about the city for the German press; it was common for large German papers to have several correspondents dispatching articles on culture, society, and politics in France.[163] Literary travelers from England, America, and Russia frequently wrote about French life and French books for their hometown newspapers. Indeed, those assuming the title of "Paris correspondent" constituted a minor European industry supplying material for journals in cities from New York to St. Petersburg.

Contact with Parisian life introduced foreigners to a new social environment and to new ideas that helped to bring new awareness of the contradictory tendencies that coexist in all modern cities. It was an experience that affected Karol Frankowski, Margaret Fuller, Frances Trollope, Charles Forster, August Cieszkowski, James Grant, P. V. Annenkov, and many lesser-known or unknown foreign travelers and residents. It also affected some of the most influential writers and thinkers of the nineteenth century, including Heinrich Heine, Karl Marx, and Adam Mickiewicz. Living for various periods within a complex, rapidly changing society that fascinated contemporaries and exemplified increasingly modern patterns of population, immigration, commerce, journalism, entertainment, crime, housing, and social anonymity, these three writers worked out political and cultural theories that became important in their home countries and in France itself. The goal of the following chapters is to examine the significance of exile and the role of France in shaping their intellectual values and to suggest how their ideas evolved through the experience of living amid the crowds, institutions, social movements, intellectual culture, and émigré communities that made Paris what it was during the reign of Louis-Philippe—the center of European culture and the meeting place for many of the persons who contributed most to the development of international literary culture, socialism, and national political movements.

Chapter 2

Heine in Paris: Exile as Literary Identity and Career

> Paris is the capital not only of France, but of the entire civilized world; it is the rendezvous of its intellectual notables. Here is assembled all that is great in love or in hate, in sentiment as in thought, in knowledge or in power, in happiness as in misery, in the future or in the past. When one considers the collection of distinguished or famous men that one finds here, Paris appears like a Pantheon of the living. They are creating a new art here, a new religion, a new life; it is here that the creators of a new world are happily at work.
>
> Heinrich Heine, *Conditions in France*

Heinrich Heine arrived in Paris on May 19, 1831, and lived there until his death in 1856. In the course of those twenty-five years his place in the world evolved from that of a young German poet (aged thirty-three) to the status of an internationally known literary figure and cultural critic. He became the best-known contemporary German writer in France and perhaps the best-known interpreter of France in Germany. His works were published in German and in French; he knew most of the prominent French writers and German intellectual émigrés of his era; he wrote about Parisian politicians, artists, and musicians; he married a French woman; and he took upon himself the role of Franco-German cultural mediator. His literary projects and his fame grew directly out of his position as a German émigré in Paris. Indeed, Heine's pen and interests won him a place in Parisian intellectual culture that became an envied model for foreign literati in search of a French (and therefore European) reputation. No other émigré managed to achieve the ironic wit or self-dramatization that characterized his descriptions of France and of himself. Heine cast himself in the

58

role of exile hero and lived out the plot of his drama with the nuances and insights of an actor who has written his own script. Both the text of the play and the actor's interpretation of his leading role were distinctive enough to attract appreciative audiences in his own time and to win applause (as well as criticism) in many places long after the hero had left the stage. Exile in Paris thus gave Heine an opportunity to act out (and project) the tensions and contradictions within himself through literary works that established his reputation as a major European writer.

This exile success was nevertheless marked by its share of exile woes—lack of money, personal disputes, native country censorship, bad health, isolation, homesickness—and it began about as obscurely as the stories of countless other German immigrants who entered France during these years. The question of why Heine went to France in the first place can never be completely answered, though a great many Heine scholars have contributed their research and speculation to the search for an explanation. There were in fact a number of personal and public reasons for the poet to leave Hamburg (where he lived from 1829 to 1831) and to settle in Paris, but most scholars emphasize the personal. His biographer Jeffrey Sammons summarizes the motives for Heine's departure from Germany in terms of a "deteriorating personal situation": he did not have a job; his writings brought him into conflict with suspicious government authorities; he had quarreled with a wealthy uncle; his training in law had not led to a career; and his status as a converted Jew was highly ambivalent.[1]

The choice of Paris as a destination, however, reflected a more general historical context. Heine had grown up in Düsseldorf under the influence of the Napoleonic occupation, an experience that may have been especially significant in giving the young man an image of French liberalism versus German repression (a common perception in many German Jewish communities). The Revolution of 1830 reinforced the image and made France seem even freer in comparison with the constraints Heine felt at home. Having already traveled in and written about Italy and England, he was not disposed to return to either of those countries; furthermore, he had learned French as a student and had long talked of visiting France. Paris, in short, seemed the most appealing and sensible destination for an unemployed German writer escaping personal problems and looking for new adventures to write about. The adventure evolved into a lifetime's work, in part because in 1835 the Federal German Assembly banned the publication and sale of Heine's books in Ger-

Heinrich Heine in 1842. Lithograph following the design by Samuel Friedrich Diez, January 1842, with facsimile signature. Heinrich-Heine-Institut, Düsseldorf.

many.[2] France therefore became both a personal refuge and a place where he could make a living as a writer.

Heine's own accounts of his move to Paris emphasized his political motives and his sympathy for the more liberal order in France after 1830, passing over the personal unhappiness that modern scholars have discussed.[3] In 1833 he explained that he left home because the political force of events was too strong to resist. "It was not in the joy of my heart that I left all the dear things that bloomed on me in the Fatherland," he wrote. "My mother loved me dearly, for one. I went, I know not why; I went, because I must. Later I was sad at heart; and before the revolution of July I had been so long a prophet that I was almost consumed by the fire within me"[4] He wrote that justification soon after his arrival in France, when he was eager to establish himself as a spokesman for German liberalism. In his *Confessions* (1854), however, he attributed his departure from Germany to a chance encounter with a French wine merchant who told convincing stories of the merry life and the political *esprit* in post-1830 Paris. This promising mix of amusement and politics, combined with a deep fear of Prussian prisons, was enough to send Heine on his way.

> He [the wine merchant] told me that at every street-corner was the inscription, "Liberty, Equality, Fraternity." He likewise recommended the champagne of his firm, and gave me a large number of business cards. He also promised to furnish me with letters of introduction to the best Parisian restaurants, in case I should visit Paris. As I really did need recreation, and as Spandau [prison] was at too great a distance from the sea to procure oysters, and as the fowl-soup of Spandau was not to my taste, and as, moreover, the Prussian chains were very cold in winter and could not be conducive to my health, I determined to go to Paris, the fatherland of champagne and the "Marseillaise," there to drink the former and to hear the latter sung.[5]

The second explanation suggests a less dramatic sense of historical urgency than his earlier pronouncement. In this version, Paris offered escape from a German prison rather than an outlet for revolutionary passion. In any case, whether his dominant motivation for leaving Germany was personal frustration or political idealism, it seems certain that Heine felt himself so blocked and alienated within German society that his move to France might be described as a transition from implicit exile to explicit exile.

If Heine's reasons for leaving Germany were complex and somewhat obscure, his initial response to Paris was comparatively simple: he found it "charming" and remarkably open to newcomers like himself.[6] At least that was how Heine remembered his earliest impressions of the city he entered for the first time on a bright day in May 1831:

> I awoke at St. Denis from a sweet morning sleep, and heard for the first time the shout of the driver, "Paris, Paris!" Here we already inhaled the atmosphere of the capital, now visible on the horizon.... In twenty minutes I was in Paris, entering through the triumphal arch of the Boulevard St. Denis, which was originally erected in honour of Louis XIV, but now served to grace my entry into Paris. I was surprised at meeting such multitudes of well-dressed people, tastefully arrayed like the pictures of a fashion-journal. I was also impressed by the fact that they all spoke French, which, in Germany is the distinguishing mark of the higher classes.... The men were all so polite, and the pretty women all smiled so graciously.... I found everything quite charming. The skies were so blue, the air so balmy, and here and there the rays of the sun of July were still glimmering.... But at the street-corners the words "Liberté, égalité, fraternité" had already been erased.[7]

Paris clearly gave Heine the sense of personal and social freedom that he had never felt in Germany, and by the fall of 1832 he was summarizing his new enthusiasm in a frequently quoted letter to a German friend. "If anyone asks you how I am enjoying myself," he wrote, "say, 'Like a fish in the sea.' Or, better still, say that when one fish asks another how he is enjoying himself, the fish replies, 'Like Heine in Paris!' "[8]

This enthusiasm never entirely disappeared, even after Heine had lived in the city for many years and the early mystery had vanished. It was always a pleasure to breathe again the "delicious and civilized air of Paris," he explained as he returned to the city after a month-long trip to the provinces in 1842. Indeed, he compared the pleasure to the intoxicating sensation of a return to the soil and the accents of his native country. Paris was unique because there was "no place in the world where the German could feel more at home."[9] The French capital was in this respect altogether different from England. Heine detested the habits, language, and aristocratic pretensions of English people who, he declared with unconcealed scorn, lacked manners, heart, and all appreciation for true liberty.[10]

The Parisians, on the other hand, won Heine's admiration for their cheerfulness, their *politesse*, and their language. Paris had been the scene of great dramatic tragedies, and yet no tragedy ever overwhelmed the city's merry spirits: "All wounds heal far more quickly in Paris than anywhere else; its air has something as generous, as charming, as benign as the people themselves." Heine learned about the cure firsthand: "How my wounded spirit revived, that had suffered so much in Germany from the smell of tobacco, sauerkraut, and the roughness of life!" The French language seemed to give all French people an "air of distinction" and to make Paris more polite than any other city Heine had ever visited. "Such politeness almost frightened me, accustomed [as I was] to German digs in the ribs without a word of excuse," he wrote later. "In the first week of my stay I sometimes got jostled on purpose, only for the pleasure of hearing musical apologies."[11]

But Paris was for Heine much more than a city of jostling, polite pedestrians. In 1831 he called France the homeland of the world's new religion—which was liberty—and he regarded the French as the chosen people of the faith: "It is in their language that the first gospels and the first dogmas are transmitted; Paris is the new Jerusalem, and the Rhine is the Jordan which separates the holy land of liberty from the country of Philistines."[12] When Heine praised the "holy land" of the new religion, however, he was really referring to the capital. He traveled to other parts of the country and knew its resorts well, but Paris represented to Heine everything of real importance in France.

> [France] is only the great suburb of Paris. Except for its beautiful countryside and the amiable qualities of its inhabitants, in general all of France is deserted, at least deserted in an intellectual respect. All those who distinguish themselves in the provinces soon emigrate to the capital, the source of all light and of all brightness. France resembles a garden in which they have cut the most beautiful flowers to make a bouquet, and this bouquet is called Paris. It is true that its perfume is not as strong today as it was after the flowery days of July, when all the peoples [of Europe] were made giddy by it. However, it is still beautiful enough to stand out like a fiancée's bouquet in the midst of Europe.[13]

Heine gathered his share of the Parisian flowers by exploring the streets, restaurants, shops, and then the salons in the city. He ate in places that had been recommended to him and found a friendlier welcome than he had ever met at home. Wandering through the Palais-Royal, he sampled the spicy food in the two-franc restaurants and was flattered by the warmth of café owners and the glances of young *grisettes*.[14] He made his way into the crowds and into the life of the city. "[I] am drowning in the whirlpool of events," he wrote to a friend, "in the daily tide and in the roaring foam of the revolution." He likened himself to a "phosphorous" burning within a "furious ocean of men."[15] When he entered salon society, the people reminded him of a "curiosity shop," and everyone seemed extraordinarily gracious. Even enemies talked politely in this setting, a phenomenon different enough from German custom to attract Heine's attention at once. It was not long before he decided that women determined reputations in Paris and that their "charm" set the tone in every salon.[16]

When there was neither salon nor restaurant nor political event to distract him, Heine took refuge in the simple pleasures of street-watching (he lived at seventeen different addresses during his twenty-five years in Paris).[17] Parisian streets became the perfect antidote for sickness and depression: "I read nothing, I write nothing, I do nothing," he wrote to a friend during one illness, "other than look at the streets of Paris, the only thing that gives me some pleasure. I love this city of Paris like a sick child loves his mother, and merely looking at it makes me feel better already."[18] As he watched those streets, listened to salon conversations, read the newspapers, and met new people, he thought himself qualified to describe French society, and he set out to do so in letters and articles that were published in the German press throughout the 1830s and 1840s.

The most important outlet for Heine's Parisian articles was the Augsburg *Allgemeine Zeitung*, one of Germany's most prestigious newspapers in these years. He also published pieces on French art and culture in other German journals, including a series of letters on the French theater in the *Allgemeine Theater-Revue*. Almost all of the articles on France were eventually published in two books, *De la France* and *Lutèce*, (translated as *Conditions in France* and *Lutetia*), thereby bringing together Heine's changing reflections on French society over a fourteen-year period (1831–44). Although he continued to praise Paris in his articles, the experience of living in the capital gradually transformed the first impressions and sympathetic generalizations that shaped his early writing about France. As the visitor became a resident, the descriptions of French life changed too.

A sense of personal and political disillusionment began to appear in some of his reports during the later 1830s and the 1840s, notably in a series of letters on the French theater which were written in

1837 to August Lewald, the editor of the *Allgemeine Theater-Revue*. (The letters were published there and in subsequent editions of *De la France*.) The France that Heine described in these letters and in later articles for the *Allgemeine Zeitung* was a society increasingly characterized by materialism, deep class divisions, and a general breakdown of authority, all of which threatened the country's internal and external security. He offered neither flattery nor much optimism in these accounts, and he described the drama of French society as an unsettling combination of permanent comedy and haunting tragedy. His reports suggested that he had found a good place from which to watch the show but that he was a little nervous whenever he actually became involved with the lives and problems of the various actors.

The dominant party in the French social order was a newly risen aristocracy of wealth that had displaced the former aristocracy of birth. The old regime's nobility was bad, Heine wrote to Lewald, but the new aristocrats were even worse. Social rank now depended on stock certificates as it had once depended on birth certificates, and Heine did not think the resulting "coarseness without polish" brought France much honor; on the contrary, the great thinkers of the eighteenth century would be ashamed if they were to see how the postrevolutionary aristocrats of wealth ignored all values except personal interest and the pursuit of money.[19] "France is the country of materialism," Heine asserted. "It is manifest in all the acts of public and private life." He went on to compare France to a vast pot of milk into which millions of flies had fallen. The flies were trying to extricate themselves by climbing on the backs of other flies, but all the flies were drowning except for a lucky few who managed to reach the rim of the pot and crawl to safety with wet wings.[20]

Heine expressed considerable contempt for the wealthy "flies" who controlled this society and set the rules for everyone else. He blamed the *nouveaux riches* for destroying France's former heroic values: "This shrinking of all grandeur, and this radical destruction of heroism," he wrote, "are especially the work of this bourgeoisie that has acquired power in France through the fall of the aristocracy of birth, and which has imposed its narrow, cold shopkeeper ideas in all spheres of life. It will not be long before every sentiment and all heroic ideas become ridiculous in France, if they do not disappear completely."[21] French society was becoming "bourgeois society," and all the spontaneous energy and gaiety of Heine's idealized France seemed to be threatened. He complained that railroad magnates were a fast-evolving "surveillance committee for all of our bourgeois and industrial society" and that high society balls were decadent, false, and evil—a trap for unwary Germans who might be swept into their "wretched whirlpool."[22]

His hostility toward the "aristocracy of wealth" did not keep Heine away from wealthy people, however. The Baron de Rothschild and his family were close friends who gave Heine money, encouraged his literary projects, and received high praise in the same article that warned about the growing power of railroad magnates. Heine even expressed sympathy for Rothschild's problems with a public that was forever asking the banker for more money. Heine also had family connections in the Parisian financial community (he helped his wealthy cousin Carl Heine marry into a Paris banking family), and he knew other German and French bankers in the city.[23] In short, despite his harsh criticisms of the rich, Heine had some very rich friends. Moreover, he himself speculated a good deal on the Paris stock market, thereby accumulating an estate of 45,000 francs by the time of his death.[24] There was, to say the least, some contrast between his complaints and his behavior in this regard.

His tendency to be more critical of French capitalism and capitalists in theory than in practice thus reversed his relationship to the French proletariat, which consisted of much abstract sympathy for the plight of the poor and considerable fear of real-life working-class violence and disruption. Heine never had much real appreciation for "proletarian consciousness." He sympathized, for example, with working-class misery during the Parisian cholera epidemic in 1832, yet he thought the poor were exceedingly naive to believe that the disease was actually spread through the machinations of Carlist plotters.[25] Even worse, these suffering people were prone to violence, as Heine learned for himself when he watched an outraged mob kill suspected "plotters" in the Parisian streets. "No spectacle is more horrible than this rage of the people when they are thirsty for blood and when they slaughter unarmed victims," he reported. "At those moments, a sea of men rolls through the streets in black waves...[and] white-shirted workers foam here and there like white waves that crash against one another; all this rumbles and roars without a word of mercy, like the damned or like demons."[26]

True, these people might have listened to reason if they had ever been addressed in a reasonable way, but they did not hear much reason. They were caught between excessive police surveillance and mistreatment on the one hand and the harangues of radicals on the other. Abused by the authorities and confused by revolutionaries, the Paris workers were coming to believe in the dangerous notion of absolute equality. "There are 400,000 brutal hands in Paris," Heine wrote in 1841, "which await only the command in order to achieve the idea of absolute equality that is incubating in their unkempt heads."[27] Despite his manifest discomfort with those "unkempt heads," Heine believed that history was on their side. They were the carriers of communism, and they talked in a communist language of "hunger, envy, and death" that could be understood wherever it was spoken in the world.[28] It was, though, a language that left Heine in an ambiguous position: he recognized the problems of the Parisian poor, criticized the way they were policed, and condemned their bourgeois employers and landlords; but he feared their violence, disliked their ideas of social or economic equality, and distrusted the emerging communist movement that hoped to lead their new revolution. There was not much space for a German poet in their crowd.

Part of Heine's problem with both the bourgeoisie and the proletariat in Paris was that these new classes had no heroes, at least none like the dominant figures who had once commanded respect and carried such authority among the French people. The whole nation had of course shown itself to be a towering historical presence, and so it was difficult for individuals to stand above the heroic crowd. France had produced more than its share of heroes during the Revolution and the Napoleonic period, but that heroic era had left a difficult legacy. For one thing, a French person in search of heroes tended to look in the past instead of the present.[29]

Even more problematic was the legacy of radical equality, which had destroyed the French respect for authority. Heine's comments on authority sound remarkably conservative. Although he regularly praised French enlightenment and condemned German reaction, he was frankly distressed that "republicanism" was eliminating all authorities in French culture. This modern disrespect for authority had emerged, he explained, in the course of the great Revolution: the French first killed their king, and then they killed all the "popular heroes of liberty" because they feared the influence of those new leaders.[30] This was for Heine the essence of republicanism: respect the laws instead of the leaders and prosecute anyone who elevates himself above the people. "From the most majestic person to the very lowest, there are no longer any authorities here," he wrote from Paris in 1832. "From Louis-Philippe I to Auguste, head of the paid clappers in the theaters, from the great Talleyrand to Vidocq [a famous criminal], from the celebrated Gaspard Deburau to Lamartine, from Guizot to Paul de Kock, from Rossini to Biffi, no one, whatever his profession may be, enjoys here an uncontested respect; and this is the case not only for belief in persons, but for everything that exists."[31]

The skepticism extended to God, the church, traditional morals, and maybe even death. France was ostensibly a Catholic country, yet Heine found little evidence of religion anywhere. The Catholicism that maintained its place in the provinces, Heine suggested, might be simple consolation for people who could not live in Paris! In the capital itself, he asserted, Christianity had not really existed since the Revolution, save for the average Frenchman's baptism and funeral.[32] Otherwise, Christianity had lost its authority as completely as kings and heroes had lost theirs (Napoleon representing perhaps the only exception).

All this French disdain was in stark contrast to the attitude of the Germans, who continued to believe in authorities of every kind and to produce dominant figures who towered above the rest of the nation.[33] As Heine explained it in his articles on the French theater, the contrasting notions of authority and heroes were apparent in both the political life and the literature of the two countries. He argued that French playwrights no longer produced great tragedy because they could not affirm heroism in a country ruled by representative government, the bourgeoisie, and a free press.[34] Although the destruction of heroes precluded modern tragedy, it left an open field for comedy and satire, which were for Heine the principal modes in modern French theater and theatrical forms that owed a great deal to the French Revolution:

> We stand here on ground where the great despot, the Revolution, has exercised its tyranny for fifty years, tearing down this, sparing that, but everywhere shaking the foundations of social life. And this rage for equality, which could not elevate the low, but could only level off the elevations; this dispute between the present and past jeering at each other, the quarrel of a madman with a ghost; this overthrowing of all authorities, spiritual as well as material; this stumbling over their last vestiges; and this stupidity in awesome hours of destiny when the necessity for an authority is perceptible and when the destroyer takes fright at his own work and begins to sing out of fear and finally bursts into a loud laugh—This is terrible, yes, even horrifying, but for comedy it is very good.[35]

The comedies that delighted French audiences were therefore part of a deep historical transformation that had followed upon the French Revolution (the modern challenge to authority), and their humor was neither naive nor innocent. But the French willingness to laugh at those farces also reflected important traits in the French character.

Heine believed that a national literature was the product of national conditions and characteristics.[36] Accordingly, he often observed the Parisian theater more like an anthropologist than like a literary critic. He wrote about the theater as a microcosm of French culture and frequently contrasted its attributes with those of the theater (culture) in Germany. His arguments rested upon a number of temperamental oppositions that provided the analytical framework for much of his cultural criticism: material/spiritual, passion/constraint, present oriented/past- or future-oriented, light-hearted/serious. Heine used these oppositions to generalize about national character, attributing the first trait in each case to the French and the second trait to the Germans.

The French were almost all materialists, for example, because their education encouraged materialist philosophy and their commercial society made material interests a cult. Hence, they avoided the dreams, reveries, and intuitive speculations that were so common in German poetry and theater (culture). Where the French believed in reflection, passion, and sentiments, Germans cultivated "the secret language of the soul." French sentiment could seem shallow to a German, Heine explained, because it often served as little more than compensation for the inadequacies of materialism; it simply covered a few of the gaps that materialism could not quite fill.[37] His attitude toward French materialism had changed over time. In the beginning he had praised the "healthy common sense" of the French and appreciated their skepticism toward traditional Christianity. Within a few years, however, he was complaining about the "moral death" that resulted from pervasive materialism and writing somewhat nostalgically about the dreams, emotions, and spiritual insights of German literature.[38]

French theater (culture) emphasized passion as well as materialism, and here, too, the contrast with Germany was significant. Whereas German life changed little (it was quiet like deep water), French life was an unending story of dramatic agitation. Thus, French theater—a "mirror of life"—presented almost nothing except passion and action. "Passions which appear completely exaggerated to us when we read or see a French drama in some peaceful corner of tranquil Germany are perhaps the sincere expression of real life [in France] and that which disgusts us as false in the theatrical form happens every day at every moment in Paris in the most bourgeois reality. No, it is impossible in Germany to have an idea of this French passion.... People who live at the north pole of the human species cannot imagine the facility with which hearts become inflamed in the burning climate of French society."[39] Life itself was theater in France; it was no wonder, then, that French audiences hissed whenever a play slowed down for philosophical discussion, as commonly happened in Germany. The French saw more drama in the streets than Germans could tolerate in a play.[40]

It was precisely this passionate nature, Heine suggested, that made French people live solely for the moment and enabled them to profit from the fleeting situations of daily life. Once again, they were entirely different from the careful Germans, who thought only of the past and future. A Frenchman tried to grasp whatever passed within reach—in love as in politics. The slow-acting German, by contrast, might well exchange glances with his beloved for years before he ventured his first cautious touch. The French did not understand such hesitation because they always acted in the present, leaving the past and future to the dreamy Germans.[41]

Heine soon decided that German dreams interfered all too often with German pleasures. They were an unhappy people, more interested in the other world than in the here and now. Indeed, Germans were most compatible with ghosts. "In the word 'ghost' there is so much that is lonely, morose, German, taciturn," Heine explained. A "French ghost," on the other hand, would be a blatant contradiction. "In the word 'French' . . . there is so much that is sociable, polite, French, loquacious!" Proper (that is, German) ghosts would never survive in Paris: "Between twelve and one, the hour that has been allotted to ghosts from time immemorial, the full stream of life is still roaring through the streets of Paris . . . and the boulevards are thronging with rollicking, laughing, bantering crowds, and everybody goes to the soirées. How unhappy a poor walking ghost would feel amidst this animated multitude!" French ghosts would never maintain appropriate solemnity in the atmosphere of irrepressible Parisian gaiety. Nevertheless, wrote Heine, "I am convinced that ghosts would have far more fun here in Paris than the living do in Germany. As for me, if I knew that one could exist this way in Paris as a ghost, I would no longer fear death."[42]

Heine's ghost stories reflected his early (1833) enthusiasm for the amusements and values in French culture. Like many of his initial perceptions, however, this notion of the jovial French personality changed after more contact with French people, soirées, and public dances. By the time he published his letters on the French stage (1837), he had decided that the French were by no means the merry folk who once seemed so alien to ghost life. "The French are not at all a gay people," he announced; and the notion of innate French gaiety appeared to be "completely erroneous."[43] Traditional French gaiety had in fact disappeared after the Revolution of 1830, he advised German readers, in part because the anachronistic objects of French humor had disappeared. Meanwhile, they had learned somber habits from the Germans:

> Their faces are elongated, their mouths drawn; they have learned from us how to smoke and to philosophize. They have undergone . . . a great metamorphosis and they no longer resemble themselves. Nothing is more pitiful than the twaddle of our fanatic Teutons who, when they rail against the French, still think of the French of the Empire, whom they saw in Germany. They do not consider that these changing people, whose instability they continually attack, could not remain immutable in their ideas and sentiments for twenty years.
> No, the French are not gayer than we are.[44]

One reason there was less to laugh at in France than in Germany was that French society tended to eliminate exceptional stupidity before it could fully develop. Here was yet another difference between the two countries: if the Germans could not imagine French passion, the French could not imagine the colossal scale of German stupidity.

Heine's speculations on these questions of comparative national character could be provocative, but they did not evolve from text to text with much consistency. The object under discussion, France, was constantly changing; so was the reporter. When one finds him calling the French jovial in 1833 and serious in 1837, or arguing that France had reason to ridicule its leaders before 1830 and no respect for authority afterward, one suspects that the changes in French society may in fact have been outpaced by changes in Heine himself. Although he continued to describe the changing object, he was describing the changing writer as well, and the instabilities or contradictions that he found in French society almost certainly reflected instabilities or contradictions that he found within himself.

Heine's theories about the French character also appeared in his discussion of sex roles and language in France. He believed that

French materialism affected marriage and the relationship between the sexes as much as it influenced other institutions in French life. The resulting desanctification of marriage was apparent in the theater, where the majority of French plays turned on subjects of marital conflict and adultery. The themes came directly from French society itself, that "mountain of debris" which French dramatists faithfully portrayed with a sneering laugh. Domestic warfare was unique in France, Heine reported, because the two sexes commanded equal force on the marital battlefield. Plays about this sex war amazed German audiences insofar as they depicted something remote from German life. It was a different story, though, and a less humorous one, when one lived in the place where these battle scenes were enacted in daily life. Heine complained that there was nothing funny in these adulterous tales; on the contrary, so-called comedies of illicit love pained his "German heart" and nearly made him cry.[45]

French sexual mores seemed to bother Heine because the patriarchical order was somewhat less secure in France than in Germany or England. It is impossible to say exactly how this anxiety may have reflected his own tempestuous affair with the young French woman Crescence Eugénie Mirat (he always called her Mathilde), whom he met in 1834, with whom he lived after 1836, whom he married in 1841, and against whom he did battle in his own domestic wars. His jealous attention to her behavior, however, indicated how much he doubted the power of marital allegiances in Parisian society. He once called Paris "the devils' Eden, the angels' Hell," an assessment that no doubt reflected some of his attitude about the city's sexual order (or disorder).[46] Like Frances Trollope, Heine was much impressed by the freedom of married women in French society. While single women stayed almost entirely out of sight, married women dominated salon life and became "objects of love" in real life and the theater alike. It was an arrangement that fostered Heine's own anxieties about Mathilde, and he saw it as one more example of the general breakdown of authority in French society: "Just as in all relationships in life, all bonds in the French family have also been loosened and all authority broken down. It is easy to understand that the respect of son and daughter for their father has been destroyed if you consider the corrosive power of that criticism which emerged from materialistic philosophy. This lack of reverence is expressed far more harshly in the relation between man and woman, in marital as well as in extramarital unions, which here take on a character that makes them particularly suitable for comedy."[47] French materialism was merciless. It left no place for mystery, and without mystery there could be no authority.

The demystification that affected politics, morals, literature, and family life in France was also apparent in the French language. Three centuries of interminable conversation in French society had drained away the magic and mystery of words (and of life). "The French language, like the French declamation and like the people themselves, is suited only to the present, to the need of the day," Heine argued. "The hazy regions of memory and presentiment are forbidden in this language. It thrives only in bright sunlight, and from this derives its clarity and warmth. The night, with its pale moonlight, its mysterious stars, its sweet dreams and frightful specters is strange and inaccessible to it."[48] If something could not be said clearly, the French preferred not to say it at all.

Here, then, were a people, a culture, and a language that rested upon materialism. The French resisted mystery and authority, demanded clarity and passion, remained suspicious of all idols and reputations, and acted out their lives and loves like characters in a play. At least this was how Heine described them in reports that combined fascination and respect with detachment and dissatisfaction. He could use French materialism and realism to attack German otherworldliness, yet he could ridicule French superficiality with the weapons of German nuance, history, and irony. His description of French society (and of his own place within it) mixed praise with occasional contempt, an ambivalent combination that also emerged in his discussion of French politics.

Constitutional Monarchy

Heine's Parisian articles provide a great deal of specific information about French political history, the leading figures in contemporary political life, and the major political issues of the day. Like other aspects of French society, the political culture that Heine encountered in Paris offered alternatives to what he had known in Germany and a political system with which he could identify, though he also criticized many of the government's policies.

The principal source for his political journalism was the French press, which he read regularly and through which he kept himself informed of French opinion and public debate.[49] He had not followed the debates long before he decided that the parties and issues in French politics stemmed almost entirely from the revolutionary decade (1789–99), and so his account of contemporary affairs led him back through that revolutionary tradition. France and its revolution could not be separated: the materialism and breakdown of authority in France derived in large part from the ideology and practice of that period, as did the nation's role in European history. "Despite its nationalism," Heine wrote in 1840, "France still remains the representative of the revolution, and the French are only fighting for this common cause of all people, even when they fight out of vanity, egoism or folly."[50]

Heine's notion of revolution always stressed long-term historical transition rather than the dramatic events of a week or a year or a simple change in the national leadership. As he explained in 1832, revolutionary upheavals resulted from structural conflicts, and they could continue long after societies regained a superficial peace.

> When the intellectual culture of a people, and the habits and needs which are derived from it, are no longer in harmony with the old political institutions, there arises an inevitable combat against these institutions which causes them to change and which is called revolution. As long as the revolution is not completed, as long as this transformation of institutions does not accord entirely with the intellectual culture of the people, with its habits and its needs, the illness in the social body is not completely cured. The people who are prey to this over-excitement may well fall into the quiet flask of despondency from time to time; but soon raised again by feverish attacks, they will tear the most firmly tied bandages from their sores . . . they will throw the most noble-hearted guardians out of the window and will roam here and there, suffering and ill at ease until they find themselves placed amid institutions which suit them best.[51]

This early idealist description of revolution took on an increasingly economic dimension as Heine followed the conflicts in France during the 1840s. By then he had decided that in the next revolution, class conflict might be even more important than the disjunction of political institutions and intellectual values.

Although the bourgeois class that initiated the revolution in 1789 had finally—in 1830—won the power and equality it wanted, Heine believed that the "Revolution" had not yet run its full course in Europe or in France itself. The lower classes remained on the side, ready to resume the struggle that had begun and failed in the 1790s. Now they were better organized, more certain of their goals, and armed with new doctrines to justify their power. Thus, the historical conflicts between the revolution of 1789 (which established legal equality) and the revolution of the early 1790s (which was intended to lead to equal possessions) were still the central political reality of modern France. If Louis-Philippe's regime should fall, Heine warned in 1840, the political revolutions of 1789 and 1830 would give way to a social revolution more formidable than anything that had come before.[52]

That future revolution, like the upheavals of 1789–94, would be the work of anonymous people. Leaders had become almost incidental to the forces of modern historical change; here, too, the heroes had disappeared, and the drama featured new actors. "Modern tragedy [history] differs from ancient tragedy in that now the choruses act and play the chief roles, whereas the gods, heroes, and tyrants who used to be the acting characters now sink to representatives of the will of the party." The crowd and unknown martyrs in the street were taking history into their own hands. "The modest death of these unknowns," he wrote after Parisian riots in June 1832, "has the power not only of inspiring in us a melancholy sympathy, but also of raising our spirits as testimony that many thousands of people whom we do not even know are ready to sacrifice their lives for the sacred cause of humanity." It was this French willingness to die for the higher cause that terrified the despots of Europe and made France—"the crimson earth of liberty"—an enemy for fearful tyrants everywhere.[53] No despot could ignore what happened in France, for it was the place where modern revolution had been created and where the new revolutionary heroes (the masses) had come into existence.

The great "indivisible" revolution appeared in 1789 and again in 1830. According to Heine, this second appearance was one of the turning points in his life because it revived in him the revolutionary faith and prompted him to go France. Many scholars now doubt, however, that Heine's initial response was as passionate as he portrayed it in the letters he published to document his early emotional reaction to news of the July Days. Circumstantial evidence suggests that Heine actually composed these letters in 1839–40 and dated them 1830, perhaps to help establish his credentials as a lifelong revolutionary enthusiast.[54] Whatever the exact dates, Heine's letters on the Revolution of 1830 are interesting for what they show about his concept of a good revolution and his understanding of the French revolutionary tradition.

In the first "post-revolution" letter (which he dated August 6, 1830) Heine hailed the French people as carriers of liberty who had repeated the triumph of their revolutionary ancestors while avoiding the excesses. In this model revolution the people shed blood only for "the just defense of their rights" and then dressed the wounds of their enemies. The presence of General Lafayette established a living connection between these moderate defenders of liberty and their grandfathers. Indeed, the very name of Lafayette reminded Heine of inspiring revolutionary stories from his childhood, and the reappearance of that far-off dream on horseback was a profoundly moving experience.[55]

Calling himself a "son of the revolution," Heine defined the revolutionary tradition in his own moderate terms and then pronounced the 1830 upheaval the direct and proper descendant of the real thing. The Revolution of 1830 held an honored place throughout his political writing; though scholars have often argued that he became disillusioned with it after he arrived in Paris, his admiration for the events of 1830 in fact remained one of the most permanent features of his political outlook.[56] To be sure, he was disappointed when French leaders moved away from the objectives and values of the revolutionary program, yet he never turned against the revolution itself. Heine considered Delacroix's famous painting *Liberty Leading the People* the appropriate symbol for the July Days; his description of that painting in an early report on French art became an excuse for praising the recent revolution's extraordinary contribution to world history: "Sacred Days of July! You will be an eternal sign of man's original dignity, a dignity which can never be completely destroyed. Anyone who has seen you no longer mourns on the tombs of the past; he joyfully believes henceforth in the resurrection of the people. Sacred Days of July! Your sunshine was beautiful!"[57] The rhetorical excess disappeared in later reports, but the sympathy endured. The July Days seemed to embody for Heine all that was best in France's revolutionary tradition.

By any reckoning, that tradition was a vital part of French political life. It had created the nation's three major political factions—republicans, Bonapartists, constitutional monarchists—and provided inspiration for the party of the future, radical socialism. Heine observed each of these contending factions and then affirmed his sympathy for constitutional monarchy, the government that had in fact emerged from the Revolution of 1830. He feared republican guillotines and Bonapartist nationalism enough to oppose republics and empires alike. In spite of his self-defined status as a "son of the revolution" and his "high respect" for the republican heroes of 1793, Heine confessed that he could never live under a government of Robespierres and Saint-Justs.[58]

He nevertheless conceded that tendencies in French culture and politics were leading the country toward both republicanism and Bonapartism. The French respect for law (rather than royal personages) and general suspicion of authorities pointed to the probable reestablishment of republican government in France, but Heine doubted that a republic could survive on French soil. He first suggested (in 1832) that the French enjoyed life's pleasures too much to accept the conditions of republican austerity. Later (in 1840), he decided that a French republic would perish quickly because republicans were too jealous of one another, too suspicious of leaders, and too divided among themselves to hold power for long. The republican passion for equality and debate would doom a republic as soon as energetic aristocrats or oligarchs, led by strong individuals, rallied to reassert their power.[59]

Moreover, Heine thought that anachronistic republicans actually threatened the true revolutionary legacy as much as conservative legitimists did. "It is madness to revive the language of 1793, as the *Amis du Peuple* is doing," he wrote in 1832. "This group, without knowing it, acts in a sense that is as retrograde as that of the most ardent champions of the old regime. Whoever collects the red flowers of springtime after they have fallen in order to reattach them to trees is as mad as another one who replants the withered lily branches in the sand. Republicans and Carlists are plagiarists of the past."[60] Heine compared the meetings of these nostalgic groups to gatherings in a "house of fools." Although they aspired to very different roles, both sides had lost touch with reality.

Republican attacks on Lafayette in the early 1830s were for Heine a typical example of that side's unrealistic views. Charging that Lafayette had abandoned the Revolution of 1830 when he embraced Louis-Philippe, many republicans condemned the old general for being the naive dupe of scheming royalists. Heine did not agree; he continued to call Lafayette the "purest character of the French Revolution" and, except for Napoleon, the most popular hero of the revolutionary epoch. These two figures represented the two practical poles of the French revolutionary tradition and hence the two real alternatives in contemporary French politics. Lafayette, the man of peace and constitutionalism, was the inspiration for constitutional monarchy. Napoleon, the man of war and nationalism, was the inspiration for Bonapartism. Realists had to choose between these two inherited possibilities, and Heine chose constitutional monarchy.[61]

He realized, however, that many French people preferred empire and that another change in France would likely lead to Bonapartism. Heine was certain in 1832 that the French loved the dead Napoleon more than the living Lafayette. "Napoleon is their god, their cult, their religion. . . . Lafayette, on the other hand, is venerated much more as a man or as a protecting angel."[62] Heine accounted for Napoleon's deification by calling him a "Saint-Simonian Emperor" whose willingness to promote individuals according to merit instead of social rank and whose desire to protect the well-being of the poor made him the most beloved of all leaders in the peasant villages and working-class *quartiers*. Significantly, his picture still hung in almost every peasant home as a reminder, Heine said, of the glory France had known and of the dead son who might have become a general.[63]

The poor may have loved him most, but Napoleon remained popular with practically everyone in France. In an age of unheroic leaders, Heine noted, he was the only "sovereign hero" in whom the French believed. For this reason alone, the emperor's legend continued to be a political force and the most popular theme in French drama.[64] The French, moreover, were "Bonapartist by nature," for they loved war. Daily life in France was filled with combat and noise, and the whole nation seemed enamored of drums and gunpowder and glory. The love of Napoleon, though, was far more than simple militarism. Heine believed that the emperor represented the energy and aspirations of "young France" against "old Europe" and that the French rejoiced when Napoleon's remains were brought to Paris in 1840 because his career was so linked to the experience of France itself. Glorified and respected in victory, humiliated in defeat, Napoleon became the embodiment of modern French history. In his brilliant way, he transformed the prerevolutionary Bourbon claim of royal sovereignty into postrevolutionary Bonapartism: *Le peuple, c'est moi*. The French accepted that change, and so the celebration at his tomb was in fact a celebration of themselves.[65]

Still, Heine was eager to stress the peaceful element in both contemporary and historical France. He argued that although Bonapartist legend and nationalism remained important, most of the "imperial spirit" had disappeared. The new era was bourgeois and industrial rather than imperial, and its favorites were men such

as James Watt and Lafayette.[66] Indeed, Lafayette had always been
a better leader than Napoleon for the bourgeoisie. He was more
accessible, more orderly. "The idol of these [bourgeois] men,"
Heine reported in 1832, "is Lafayette creating order. They revere
him as a kind of providence on horseback, a guardian of the public
safety and a genius of liberty, who at the same time is careful to
see that in the struggle for liberty he does not commit himself to
theft and that each person conserves his precious little possessions! . . . Yes! he is the Napoleon of the *petite bourgeoisie*."[67] Heine
did not much like the petty bourgeoisie, but he clearly shared their
respect for Lafayette. He heard the veteran "hero of two worlds"
participate in debates at the Chamber of Deputies and found him
to be easily the most important orator there. Here was a man with
a "pure heart" who, like a compass pointing always in the same
direction, invariably supported the principles of liberty and the
rights of man. Lafayette was a messenger from the revolutionary
past, arguing in 1832 for the ideas he had supported in 1789.[68]

According to Heine, it was this continuity of principle that
formed the basis of constitutional government. A constitutional
monarchy differed significantly from absolutist monarchies in that
it depended upon "immutable political principles," institutions,
and the needs of the people rather than upon the whims of princes.
The constitutional system was far superior to absolutism because
it could respond to popular opinion (for example, in the appointment of ministers) and because it enabled the people to express
their disapproval without resorting to revolution (the only recourse
in absolutist states).[69] This was the kind of government that Lafayette endorsed and that Heine thought France had given itself
in the Revolution of 1830. It promised both liberty and order, a
combination that won Heine's strong support. "Monarchist by natural inclination," he wrote soon after his arrival in Paris, "I am
becoming one even more in this country by conviction."[70] Heine
expected his kings to respect principles, though, and his support
for the July Monarchy presupposed the regime's adherence to constitutionalism and its origins in the will of the people.

The Prussian monarchy, by contrast, functioned in the absolutist
manner. King Frederick Wilhelm III could ignore his subject's
wishes because he was not bound by constitutional constraints.
The fact that Prussians had no constitution was itself evidence of
the king's absolute power; he had promised a constitution which
he now refused to grant. Other princes followed his lead, and the
German people were left without the "human and divine right" of

constitutional protection.[71] Heine wrote angrily about the Prussian king's absolutist prerogatives; indeed, many of the articles in *De la France* carried implicit criticism, which the preface to the German edition made explicit, of political arrangements in Prussian-dominated Germany. The French system provided constitutional alternatives to Prussia that much of Heine's political writing from July Monarchy France sought to explain.

He also wanted Germans to understand the principles and the daily practice of French politics, for he assumed that what happened in France affected political culture everywhere. Whatever their military or diplomatic power in world affairs, the French maintained their influential role as the innovative center of world politics: "The other peoples merely form the honorable public that goes as spectators to the comedy of state played by the French people," Heine wrote in 1841, with his typical reliance upon metaphors from the theater. "It is true that this public sometimes feels the temptation to express somewhat loudly its approval or its reproach, or even to go up on stage and play a role in the performance; but the French, the usual actors for the good Lord, always remain the principal actors of the great universal drama."[72] The French play had now reached the point of constitutional monarchy, and Heine applauded the plot and the themes. But what did he think of the actors who played the leading roles? How well were they following the script?

The most important part was of course the one assigned to Louis-Philippe. As king, he had the greatest responsibility for seeing that the constitutional monarchy actually functioned in accordance with the revolution and the theory that had brought him to power. Although Heine criticized some of the king's actions, he seemed to decide very early that Louis-Philippe was a good man for the job. Most of his references to the monarch were sympathetic and most of his criticisms friendly. He simply wanted Louis-Philippe to be a better king: that is, a king who more nearly conformed to Heine's own definition of constitutional monarch. Unlike most radicals in France, Heine did not advocate overthrow of the regime or ridicule the personality and appearance of Louis-Philippe; on the contrary, he commended the king as a "man of perfect integrity," a family man of high character, and an honorable person. He praised the king's character in these terms both at the beginning of his reign and after he had been in power more than ten years.[73]

He did note, however, that Louis-Philippe demanded "blind obedience" from those around him, resembling in this respect an angry despot rather than a legitimate citizen-king.[74] Heine's main criticism of Louis-Philippe always focused on this gap between his absolutist inclinations and his citizen-king mandate. In truth, Heine conceded in 1840, the king "has not had the most sincere intentions toward his trusting supporters, the heroes of July, who raised him to power." To be sure, these July heroes had not been entirely sincere either. They had assumed that the Duke of Orléans would be their puppet, easily controlled by their powerful string-pulling. But Louis-Philippe was a clever leader who managed to pull his own strings, and the radical victors of July soon passed into the opposition again.[75]

Heine seemed to have more sympathy for Louis-Philippe in the 1840s than in the 1830s, perhaps because the increasing radicalism of the opposition left a liberal monarchist with nowhere else to go.[76] During his early years in France, however, Heine frequently criticized the citizen-king for favoring kings over citizens. In fact, he complained about Louis-Philippe's royal pretensions in his very first article on French politics:

> I do not think Louis-Philippe is an ignoble man. He certainly does not have evil intentions and merely has the defect of failing to recognize the principle that governs his own individual life. He can be ruined by this....Louis-Philippe has forgotten that his government rose through the principle of the sovereignty of the people, and in the most wretched delusion he would now like to try to maintain it by means of a quasi-legitimacy, by an alliance with absolute princes, and by a continuation of the Restoration period. This is the reason why the spirits of the Revolution are now angry at him and feud with him in all sorts of ways....Louis-Philippe, who owed the people and the July cobblestones his crown, is an ungrateful man whose defection is all the more insulting since one realizes more and more every day that one has been grossly deceived. Yes, every day visible retrogression occurs.[77]

This early analysis summarizes much of Heine's permanent political perspective, inasmuch as it establishes the Revolution of 1830 as the political event against which subsequent developments should be measured. The critics of Louis-Philippe's policies at first seemed closer to the July spirit than the king himself, and so Heine could share their complaints. By the 1840s, though, Heine recognized that the opposition had acquired a new idea of revolution—a radical, socialist, republican outlook that would make the next revolution very different from the last one. Now it was Louis-Philippe who seemed closer to the values of 1830, and Heine became more sympathetic to the king. In short, Heine consistently supported his choice of constitutional monarchy, never moving very close to the alternatives (Jacobins, Bonapartists) even when he criticized the king.[78]

Apart from Louis-Philippe, the two most prominent official actors in the July Monarchy political drama were François Guizot and Adolphe Thiers, who exchanged leading roles in the regime.[79] Heine called Guizot the "loyal servant of the bourgeois reign" and its "inexorable" defender against aristocratic and proletarian enemies who threatened it from above and below. Guizot's defense of the bourgeois right to govern was not doctrinaire, but he believed that this class was best suited to lead the state and to protect the interests of all people. If aristocrats became more willing to consider the public welfare or workers better educated, Heine explained, Guizot would make a place for them in the nation's political life. The proletarian passion for equality threatened all that was beautiful, however, and so Guizot's exclusion of the lower classes was understandable; at least Heine understood and accepted it.[80]

It is possible that Heine's personal connection with Guizot influenced his generally sympathetic accounts of the minister's policies. The men were not friends, but they did meet once in the fall of 1840, when Guizot informed Heine that he would continue to receive the annual pension of 4,800 frances that the French government had previously established for him. According to Heine's account of their meeting, Guizot demanded nothing in return for this money, explaining in very simple terms; "I am not a person to refuse a German poet who lives in exile a bit of bread."[81]

Modern research indicates that the pension began in 1840 while Adolphe Thiers was first minister in Louis-Philippe's government (March–October).[82] Heine and Thiers had met several years earlier at the salon of Princess Cristina Belgioioso and had become friends, in part through the mediation of the historian François Mignet, who was close to both men and also a regular at Princess Cristina's soirées.[83] "I hope that you have not forgotten to tell M. Thiers that I admire him and that I like him more than ever," Heine wrote to Mignet after Thiers lost his post as head of the Ministerial Council in 1836. Though he disliked Thiers's nationalistic foreign policy and his opposition to revolutions abroad, Heine respected the way Thiers successfully combined his literary and political careers: "He has had the unprecedented good fortune to prove himself as historian and man of action at the same time. Future historians will be grateful to him for having shown to the public that a great historian can also become a great minister."[84]

Heine praised Thiers in his newspaper articles, too. For example, he dismissed charges that Thiers's policies were motivated by egotism, arguing instead that Thiers was simply a loyal French patriot who, like Napoleon, identified himself entirely with the French national spirit. Thiers was thus less connected than Guizot to bourgeois attitudes. He was a true son of the revolution (though he also feared his parent) whose love of country accounted for all his policies: the return of Napoleon's remains, the fortification of Paris, the saber rattling whenever French honor seemed to be challenged. Thiers was in these respects close to the Bonapartist legacy that emphasized national glory over national liberty.[85]

The whole question of Heine's attitude toward Thiers and other French leaders is somewhat complicated by the government pension, which may have encouraged Heine's already expressed sympathy for the July Monarchy. Thiers and Guizot surely assumed that Heine's articles would improve France's reputation in Germany and that his pension (which came out of secret funds in the Ministry of Foreign Affairs) was therefore a well-justified expenditure. The ministers themselves left no explanation for the Heine payments, but the strategic thinking behind such arrangements can be found in a report prepared in Frankfurt during 1843 by a French consular attaché named Alexis de Gabriac; his "Studies on Journalism in Germany" argued that France should use the German press to create a favorable image for itself in German popular opinion. Significantly, Gabriac singled out the Augsburg *Allgemeine Zeitung* as the most important political newspaper in Germany and urged that the French government facilitate the publication of moderate, pro-French articles in that journal by giving money to sympathetic German correspondents. Gabriac apparently did not know that the Foreign Ministry already had the *Allgemeine Zeitung*'s star Paris reporter on the payroll. In any case, his recommendations must have encouraged government officials to believe that Heine was a good investment, for they continued the payments as long as they held power.[86]

The public learned of the pension when a French newspaper published documents from the July Monarchy archives after the Revolution of 1848. Heine responded with the claim that his pension was merely another example of French generosity toward foreigners whose revolutionary zeal forced them to seek asylum "at the hospitable hearth of France." He also argued that the payments became necessary because the German ban on his writings in 1835 ruined him financially.[87] These justifications failed to impress his critics; he was compelled to defend his integrity in the *Allgemeine Zeitung*, and the new government immediately canceled the pension. As he explained in a letter to Edouard de la Grange, the revelation left him feeling isolated and unappreciated on all sides.

> It has hurt my pride to say in the pages of the *Allgemeine Zeitung* and in front of all Germany that I asked the French for alms like all the other destitute refugees; and I made this humiliating confession without adding the remark that in the aid the French government granted me the renown of my name was worth a lot and that France clearly owed some recognition to an author who was at all times its most loyal ally and who has so valiantly fought for her against all these France-haters whom you know. This pension, which has brought me so many perfidious reproaches from my enemies across the Rhine, was fully owed to me here in France.[88]

Heine never really doubted that he deserved the money. His friend Alexander Weill wrote many years later of a conversation in the fall of 1843 during which, according to Weill, Heine assured him that everything he wrote was his own opinion. "I am *constitutional*," Heine explained. "I am not exactly republican or monarchist. I am for liberty."[89] For this reason he favored republics governed by monarchists and monarchies governed by republicans, a balance that French leaders had managed to achieve in the July Monarchy. He had come to France, Heine said, to live freely and to write against the enemies of liberty and humanity. Since he did not have the luxury of a French birth or the livelihood of a French literary man, it was French government money that enabled him to pursue this work. Thus, unlike Ludwig Börne, he had never sought alliance with radical French republicans, he told Weill:

> Even if I were a radical republican, I think that I would have to be ungrateful as well as stupid to attack the government which protects me and to join its most violent adversaries in Paris....I have demanded nothing from the July Monarchy. I did not go to it, it came to me. It has not converted me nor corrupted me, it allowed me complete liberty....Before getting my 6000 francs, I praised all the statesmen in Paris; since they gave me the pension, I have not dared to say a word in their favor, for fear of feeling bought.[90]

Although Weill's report must be taken with caution (he could hardly have quoted the conversation verbatim from memory), it provides a plausible description of how Heine could justify his pension and how he might have tried to avoid the appearance of pro-French partiality. He was happy enough with the French regime to accept its money without betraying either himself or the revolutionary tradition as he understood it. The pension did not really change Heine's politics, but it may have helped him to focus his political wrath on German leaders rather than French ones; his radicial complaints from Paris in the 1840s were directed against bad kings on the other side of the Rhine.[91]

There were many critics and unknown actors in France, however, who did not share Heine's respect for the leading characters in the national drama and whose disrespect stemmed from neither Jacobin nor Bonapartist nostalgia. Heine called this opposition "communism," by which he meant all of the gathering historical forces that threatened to overturn the reigning social and political order in western Europe. These forces were highly developed in the Parisian crowds, though they were usually ignored by the journalists who wrote about the political disputes of deputies and cabinet ministers. Ministry disputes were surface activities, Heine explained to his readers in 1842, which scarcely touched the political actors—communists—whom he expected to see on the French stage very soon.

> For our part, we know only that communism, though it may be seldom discussed at present and though it may continue its sickly existence in hidden garrets on its miserable straw bed, is however the somber hero for whom an enormous role is reserved, however brief, in the modern tragedy, and who only awaits the cue to enter the scene. We must never therefore lose sight of this actor, and we will report from time to time on the secret rehearsals by which he prepares himself for his debut. Such information will perhaps be more important than all the reports on electoral campaigns, party quarrels and cabinet intrigues.[92]

Heine later compared the communist movement to first-century Christianity, which defied repression and gained converts with moral appeals that its enemies could not refute. All members of the social opposition (for example, Saint-Simonians and Fourierists) eventually joined the movement's ranks, thereby placing the future in communist hands.[93]

Those hands were dirty enough to frighten a monarchist poet.

Heine confessed that he would have washed himself immediately if the "sovereign" masses had ever actually touched him. "The people are not pretty," he explained. "On the contrary, they are ugly." They were in fact so filthy that Heine's abstract sympathy for their plight could never overcome his physical aversion to their appearance and their smells. "I love the people," he wrote in his *Confessions*, "but I love them from a distance."[94] He was not at all sure he would enjoy the show after these "ugly" poor people took over the stage. Their callused hands were frightening because they threatened to destroy the beautiful along with the unjust, leaving the world without poetry and poets and without the work to which Heine was devoting his life.[95]

Despite this unwelcome prospect, Heine professed a certain admiration for the rising communist movement. He acknowledged that the forces threatening his *oeuvre* could also claim a place in the revolutionary tradition with which he identified, and he recognized that the communists opposed those groups in Germany that he opposed, too. The claim of the new revolutionaries—all people have the right to eat—seemed no less legitimate than the earlier established rights of liberty and equality. Having accepted the justice of this new claim, Heine felt obliged to accept what he took to be its real-life consequences. Even more important, however, was the communist hatred for narrow-minded German nationalism. This hatred alone, Heine wrote, was almost enough to win his support; indeed, he suggested that internationally minded communists were more Christian than the so-called Christian patriots in Germany, a perspective that offered him some consolation near the end of his life.[96]

Once again, it was his identification with a French alternative to German politics that gave Heine a position upon which to build some sense of security and legitimacy. The thought of a French socialist revolution terrified him and reassured him at the same time. Since the rapidly emerging political force that rejected his political vision of the world (based on July 1830) also rejected the vision of his xenophobic German enemies, Heine would give his ambivalent sympathy to the enemies of his enemies and take a chance with those callused communist hands.

Besides, not all communist hands were really dirty. Many belonged to radical intellectuals whom Heine once compared to the fathers of the church.[97] That church, though, was actually only a sect within the larger intellectual culture that flourished in Paris, welcomed Heine soon after his arrival in France, and helped him to define his role as a writer and an exile. Heine never quite became an inner-circle member of any sect, but he knew leaders in almost all of them, and he mastered their collective cultural network well enough to make himself the most noted German writer in Paris.

A German in the Culture Network

Parisian intellectual society may have been more important than Parisian politics in shaping Heine's French experience. While the July Monarchy offered a model for moderate revolution and constitutional politics, Parisian intellectual life—with its ideologies, prominent authors, and well-known publications—offered him the means to create a distinct literary identity. He described this intellectual community to an audience abroad and used its prestige to establish his French and European reputation as a *German* working and publishing in France; in fact, his enduring cross-cultural reputation is an excellent example of how the exile experience contributed to modern European literature.

Heine made first contact with Parisian intellectual life at Saint-Simonian meetings in 1831. The followers of Henri Saint-Simon (1760–1825) sought the creation of a new society wherein science and technology would alleviate all problems of material need, and social leadership would be entrusted to scientists and economic managers who, in turn, would be chosen according to ability rather than inheritance. Meanwhile, a "New Christianity" would emerge to give this society an appropriate, nonsectarian ethical and moral dimension.[98] The Saint-Simonian movement therefore called for both a new social order and a new religion, a combination that attracted the attention of dissidents and authorities alike. Reports of esoteric and unconventional "religious meetings" added to the notoriety of the group's doctrines, so that Saint-Simonians soon acquired a reputation for danger and absurdity. In Germany extensive press coverage of Saint-Simonian activities made the group almost as famous and as feared as it was in France itself, although a few Germans defied the academic establishment and almost everyone else by embracing Saint-Simonian doctrines and recommending the creed to their compatriots.

Heine was one of this small minority, for he studied Saint-Simonian publications, discussed the movement with German sympathizers, and pronounced himself a follower of the "new gospel."[99] By the time he reached Paris he knew a good deal about Saint-

Simonian ideas and had expressed his intention to become a "priest" of the new religion. Indeed, his interest in the movement may have been one reason for his decision to go to France.[100] He began attending Saint-Simonian meetings in the rue Taitbout as soon as he arrived in Paris and was first mentioned in the group's newspaper, *Le Globe*, on May 22, 1831.[101] In the months that followed he went regularly to Saint-Simonian assemblies, read *Le Globe*, and met such leaders as Prosper Enfantin and Michel Chevalier. The influence of these contacts remains obscure, however, because Heine wrote practically nothing about the Saint-Simonians after he arrived in Paris. The most direct indications of his involvement—references in a few letters and the dedication of *De l'Allemagne* (1835) to Enfantin—do not suggest that Heine ever developed much religious passion or became a "priest" in the movement. He assured one of his German friends in May 1832 that Saint-Simonianism was still important to him, but a year of first-hand experience with the movement in Paris had clearly tempered the enthusiasm he first expressed in Germany:

> I am working a great deal on the history of the French Revolution and of Saint-Simonianism. I intend to write books on those, but there is still a lot for me to study. However, during this last year, in seeing the political parties and the Saint-Simonians at work, I have come to understand many things, including the *Moniteur* of 1793 and the Bible. . . . What you write me about Saint-Simonianism is in complete accord with my views. Michel Chevalier is my very good friend and one of the most noble people I know. It might perhaps be advantageous for the doctrine itself if the Saint-Simonians retired from the scene; the doctrine will fall into more prudent hands. The political part especially and the question of property will be better worked out. As for myself, I am only interested in the religious ideas which needed only to be expressed in order to be sooner or later realized. Germany will fight most vigorously of all for its spiritualism; *but the future belongs to us.*[102]

This is one of the fullest statements Heine ever made about his relationship to the Saint-Simonians. The doctrine offered an appealing view of the future, if it could survive the eccentricities of its present representatives. Heine nevertheless maintained his friendship with some Saint-Simonian leaders into the 1840s, by which time he had decided that the future really belonged to communism and that most true Saint-Simonians would end up in that movement.[103] The others, Heine explained, were making their greedy accommodations with existing society.[104]

One of the compromisers was Prosper Enfantin, the Saint-Simonian leader to whom Heine dedicated the first edition of his book on German literature and philosophy *(De l'Allemagne)* in 1835. Enfantin responded to that book with a long letter that criticized Heine for failing to sympathize with hierarchy, order, and religion—which Enfantin believed to be essential traits of the German spirit—and for overlooking the true, progressive significance of Austrian-German religion and politics; in short, Heine showed too much sympathy for an Enlightenment, liberal, French tradition in opposition to an organic, truly religious, Austrian-German tradition.[105] These criticisms must have displeased Heine (he never responded to them directly), but he could perhaps take some satisfaction from the fact that Enfantin acknowledged his special role as Franco-German cultural mediator. In this respect, at least, the Saint-Simonian community helped Heine begin his career as a German expert on France and a Paris-based expert on Germany.

Enfantin's concept of that work, however, was different from Heine's, in part because Enfantin's concept of Germany seemed to ignore the German culture that Heine was trying to describe. This became clear when Enfantin told Heine how he should work for the unity of German and French youth:

> It is your task to unite their hands and to place on their head a sign that might make them recognize one another. It will no longer be history that you will do, it will be living politics, it will be religion. ...Leave the benches and chairs of philosophy; that is not where you must resume and continue the work of Madame de Staël. Make us understand the German heart and not the mysteries of its thought; dare to say out loud the virtues of these hard-working, economical, good, enlightened people whom Napoleon and our liberals have so long taught us to regard as ignorant automatons, brutalized by despotism. Speak to us of its beautiful river, its rich earth, its tranquil villages, its mores—so simple, so patriarchical—from the emperor down to the peasant.[106]

Enfantin, in other words, wanted Heine to describe again the Germany of Madame de Staël, a medieval nation which was "one of the two crowns of the Christian world," which survived the interventions of Luther and Napoleon and "conserved its old faith."[107] This was in fact the Germany Heine did not like (he much preferred Luther and Napoleon). In any case, it no longer existed in the era of modern German nationalism and Prussian absolutism; he did not believe in Madame de Staël's imaginary Germany.[108] Enfantin thus misunderstood or rejected the substance of Heine's project, though he supported the formal objective—cultural mediation— and affirmed Heine's preeminence in the task.

Heine may have taken much more than his cultural mediation role from the Saint-Simonians, but his textual silence on the group presents interpretive problems for critics who try to explain how Saint-Simon's doctrines actually influenced his thought. The ambiguity of the relationship has encouraged considerable speculation among modern Heine specialists. Some scholars have argued that Saint-Simonian notions did not have much effect on Heine because he found there merely confirmation of ideas he had already worked out for himself. Those who deemphasize the importance of Heine's Saint-Simonian contacts stress that his Enlightenment-style liberalism was incompatible with what they see as the anti-liberal, reactionary tendency of the Saint-Simonians and that the movement did not significantly influence Heine's politics or religion.[109]

Another scholarly tradition, however, argues that the Saint-Simonian movement affected "the whole trend of his life and thought" and provided the "only intellectual experience which resulted in creative thought."[110] More specifically, they suggest that it gave him a conception of harmony between the conflicting demands of sensualism and spiritualism. Resolution of the flesh/spirit tension produced exceptional coherence in *De l'Allemagne*, which is the most systematic philosophical work that Heine ever produced. In order to achieve that coherence, he may have drawn upon Saint-Simonian doctrine for a philosophy of history (especially a doctrine of progress), a theory of art (its historical attributes and social functions), and a critical view of traditional (as opposed to "New") Christianity. Even those who see Heine's Saint-Simonian experience as decisive nevertheless recognize that his silence on the group and his own independently developed doctrines indicate that he was by no means an uncritical convert.[111]

This scholarly debate, like many others, seems to call for the common pluralistic solution that recognizes some truth on both sides. In this case, the unique status of French Saint-Simonianism for the German cultural critic makes the bland pluralistic perspective more acceptable. If Heine had already developed a Saint-Simonian outlook on his own in Germany, he nevertheless wanted and needed the reassuring confirmation of those views that he could find more readily in the rue Taitbout than in the streets of Hamburg. At the same time, if the doctrine became influential in his writing, it became useful primarily as a historical perspective for interpreting his own culture to readers outside that culture or to compatriots for whom the perspective of an outsider (Saint-Simon) was inaccessible. Whatever the importance of specific Saint-Simonian doctrines in Heine's thought, the fruitful, confident use of those doctrines depended to a great extent upon his status as a German interpreter of Saint-Simonianism who was living in Paris. Drawing upon a doctrinal framework that was never explicitly acknowledged, Heine used his special position (close to and separated from Saint-Simonians in both Germany and France) to begin describing French conditions to Germans and German culture to the French. The importance of Saint-Simonianism in his outlook and literary projects was therefore closely linked to his expatriate position. Saint-Simonians offered an intellectual and semiinstitutional starting point from which he began developing a literary identity as cultural interpreter. By the time he had secured that identity in the 1840s, the Saint-Simonians had lost their importance in France and in the social movements of the day. Heine continued to discuss France and those movements, however, without having to overcome the stigma of a discredited Saint-Simonianism. It was altogether a good example of the way his independent outsider status could work to his advantage, for he took from the movement what he needed without becoming its victim.

Heine also put his outsider status to good use when he discussed other members of the French intellectual community by name. Most of the prominent figures in July Monarchy culture received their share of comment and criticism in articles suggesting, among other things, that the dissidents in France were themselves an establishment.[112] In fact, Heine seemed to like well-established dissidents (George Sand, Edgar Quinet, Honoré de Balzac) more than either the intellectual establishment (Académie Française, Victor Hugo) or the marginal dissidents (Louis Blanc, communists). But he could find a good word and a bad word to say about almost all of them, thereby placing himself in the middle as he wrote for an audience that was on the outside.

He praised Louis Blanc's knowledge and his identification with the people, for example, in an article that also warned readers about Blanc's extreme antiindividualism, his passion for material equality, and his invariable seriousness. Blanc mixed republican virtue with what Heine saw as the typical vanity of a short man; he resembled a latter-day Robespierre whose character and abilities attracted Heine's attention and some of his respect but none of his sympathy.[113] Similarly, Heine admired Pierre Leroux's ability to write about difficult philosophical issues while staying close to the physical suffering of the lower classes. Here was one of the impoverished church fathers actively elaborating a socialist religion for future generations. Yet Leroux, like Blanc, was humorless, ascetic, prone to building castles in the sky, and merciless toward his opponents.[114] It all added up to the kind of radicalism that Heine could not support: puritanical, unpoetic, uncompromising. There was no way to accommodate aristocratic values in such a view, and so there was really no way to accommodate Heine.

The French intellectual establishment, on the other hand, acknowledged the importance of those elite, poetic values and granted a place to Heine himself. Thus, although he had no love for the intellectual hierarchy in his own country, Heine was on good terms with some of the leading establishment intellectuals in France. His sympathy for Victor Cousin and François Mignet was not unlike his sympathy for Thiers and Guizot. He preferred their outlook and values to those of their opponents.

Cousin was a professor of philosophy at the Sorbonne and a member of both the Académie Française and the Académie des Sciences Morales et Politiques. From these various positions, he served as a semiofficial philosopher for the July Monarchy *juste-milieu*. His "eclecticism" joined Kant, Hegel, and Descartes in a kind of pantheistic synthesis that achieved prominence as the most popular French theory of the period, though it did not leave much of a mark on European philosophy.[115] His lectures attracted enormous audiences as well as the withering scorn of such radicals as Pierre Leroux and of conservative Catholics (who attacked his pantheistic notions). Heine may have doubted Cousin's stature as a philosopher,[116] but he was certain that Cousin's conservative and radical enemies were much more dangerous than any of the philosopher's eclectic lectures: "In this combat all our support is for Cousin; because although the privilege of the university has its inconvenience, at least it keeps all education from falling into the hands of those persons who have always persecuted men of science and progress with inexorable cruelty." Cousin was animated by the "spirit of liberty," Heine maintained, which was more than could be said for his enemies.[117]

Moreover, Cousin expressed deep sympathy for German philosophy and the German people, to which Heine responded by calling him a philosopher in the "German sense" of the word—someone "who occupies himself more with the human spirit than with the needs of humanity." (Leroux was a "French" philosopher in that he worked mainly on social questions.)[118] There may have been an ironic twist in that compliment, and yet Heine wanted Cousin to know that he was praising him in the German press. He forwarded a copy of his pro-Cousin article to the historian François Mignet and asked Mignet to show the piece to Cousin. "I have defended him against the slanders of my virtuous friend Leroux," Heine explained in a cover letter, which also suggested that Cousin might be the most important philosopher in France since Descartes.[119] The observation must have pleased Cousin and, along with Heine's eagerness to get the praise into Cousin's hands, shows how diplomatically the German critic went about cultivating the French establishment.

Mignet himself was a prominent figure in that establishment through his role as permanent secretary of the Académie Française and his membership in the Académie des Sciences Morales et Politiques. Heine attended public meetings at these academies and wrote approvingly of Mignet's orations in his newspaper articles, one of which he enclosed in the packet with his piece on Cousin.[120] The Académie des Sciences Morales et Politiques was in Heine's view the only lively section in the otherwise senile Institut Royal, but he also liked to watch the stodgy members of the Académie Française. He especially enjoyed the youthful appearance and the historical presentations of the "handsome permanent secretary." Mignet regularly delivered the eulogy at the death of an academician, a common event in an association whose members were mostly old men. Indeed, these gray-headed, limping members of the French intellectual aristocracy became targets for Heine's sarcasm. Both their appearance and their awareness of living people in the streets outside seemed utterly unimpressive, and the greatest moment in their lives came at death: "How happy they are, these French academicians! Seated there in the calmest spiritual peace on their solid benches, they can die in tranquillity, because they know that however perilous their actions may be in life, the good Mignet will nevertheless curl their hair, praise them, and exalt them after their death."[121] Heine clearly respected Mignet's reputation-making skills far more than he respected the dead academicians whom Mignet eulogized. He understood the powers of a reputation-maker, inasmuch as he could help bring a French name to prominence through his own articles in the *Allgemeine Zeitung*. Accordingly, he took care to see that French reputation-makers knew he was on their side. One good reputation deserved another.

Heine's contacts with the French intellectual community were by no means limited to the representatives of official culture, however. His closest literary friends were George Sand, Balzac, Théophile Gautier, and Gérard de Nerval, all of whom played reputation-maker roles in the unofficial intellectual hierarchy of July Monarchy France. At the same time he had enough contact with Victor Hugo, Alfred de Musset, Jules Michelet, Edgar Quinet, and influential literary editors to have opinions about both their work and their personalities. These connections were more important for his reputation and his place in Parisian culture than his friendships within the academic hierarchy because the most famous figures among them were known to readers throughout Europe, whereas many academicians were best-known to themselves.

George Sand may have been the most famous French writer in Europe during the 1840s, partly because she wrote novels that appealed to romantic readers everywhere and partly because she was a woman with a scandalous reputation. She was also one of Heine's best Parisian friends after they met in 1834 and began sharing dinners, soirées, friends, literary opinions, and advice about love.[122] Although most scholars doubt that they ever became lovers, their friendship was clearly more than mere professional cooperation (they called each other "cousin" in their correspondence). "I love you very much, with all my heart, with every part of my heart," Heine wrote in one consoling letter about Sand's love life. "If you are free rejoice in your liberty.... Never cry; tears weaken the eyes. What beautiful eyes you have!"[123] Sand, for her part, advised Heine that love was the "highest possible moral value" and the best support in times of physical or mental pain.[124]

They also promoted each other's literary projects and friendships. Sand urged Heine to attend a dinner in the spring of 1840, for example, because "it is advantageous for you (you know in what sense I am speaking) to cultivate the sympathy of Sainte-Beuve. He is dining with us."[125] While Sand helped him to circulate in the inner circle, Heine was helping her in useful ways, too. He sent assurances that her enemies were "fleas" and little people; he gave her translations of his prose; he praised her work, her personality, and her beauty in the German press.[126] "George Sand, the greatest writer in France, is at the same time a woman of remarkable beauty," he wrote in an article that also characterized her as the "champion of the social revolution" and as an "ardent genius who had dared the most extreme things in her writings." Sand's willingness to question religion and marriage, Heine explained after the performance of her play *Cosima* (1840), displeased audiences and the mediocrities who dominated the French theater. Heine, though, favored genius over mediocrity, and all his sympathy went to Sand. In passages that indicated close acquaintance and high respect, he also emphasized her maternal skills, her interesting conversations, and her fine voice.[127] The theme in all of this was straightforward: George Sand was France's greatest writer, and Heinrich Heine was one of her friends. It was a portrait that flattered both subjects (and both artists).

The only major flaw Heine found in Sand's work was a tendency to preach about obscure issues. That flaw came directly from the unhappy influence of Pierre Leroux, who led Sand away from the real source of her art; "he induces her to enter into sterile abstractions instead of abandoning herself to the serene joy of creating living and colorful forms and of practicing art for the sake of art."[128] Fortunately, other men in Sand's life did not share Leroux's antiartistic bias. This was especially the case with her composer friend Frédéric Chopin, whom Heine called a genius and a "tone poet." Indeed, Chopin was so absorbed in his artistic universe that the idealistic Sand seemed worldly by comparison.[129] Her friend and former lover Alfred de Musset was in Heine's view the greatest poet in France, which meant that the best poet and the best novelist had also been a couple. At least Heine believed that no one in France wrote as well as Musset and Sand; he found even the self-proclaimed "great poet of France," Victor Hugo, inferior to them.[130]

Heine was not fond of Hugo. To be sure, he respected some of Hugo's work—he once called him France's "greatest poet" (1837) before granting that honor to Musset—and he appreciated Hugo's ability to produce art that avoided political moralizing.[131] But he did not like Hugo's personality, and the flaws in Hugo's character eventually became for Heine the flaws in Hugo's art; he saw both as egotistical, tasteless, and ultimately lifeless. This was not a hasty judgment. Heine at first cultivated Hugo's friendship by visiting his home, expressing admiration for his work, and introducing him to appreciative German critics.[132] Perhaps Heine saw himself as a German Hugo ("greatest poet") or Hugo as a French Heine, parallel roles that Hugo chose not to accept. In any event, the friendship did not develop, and Heine joined the Hugo critics, apparently "offended by that egoism which is very advantageous in creating masterpieces but is a great disadvantage in social intercourse."[133] He decided that Hugo was "false" and "cold" and altogether lacking in passion.

The contrast with Sand was instructive. Sand's work and life showed all the qualities that Hugo lacked: naturalness, taste, truth, beauty, enthusiasm, and harmony. She was in these respects a French genius, while Hugo had the bad taste and clumsiness of a German. Heine was explicit about this dichotomy: French taste and natural vitality versus German tastelessness and coldness.[134] One suspects that the attack on Hugo became Heine's attack on the Germany he had fled. If Hugoism was threatening at home, it was monstrous in France. Heine in fact reported gleefully that Hugo suffered from a hump on his back, thus establishing to his own satisfaction the enemy's physical, spiritual, and moral coherence.

> There is in him [Hugo] more hardness than force, and his forehead is the most brazen bronze. Despite all of his imaginative and spiritual talents, we see in him the clumsiness of a *parvenu* or of a savage who makes himself ridiculous by dressing up in streak-colored finery, by overloading himself with gold and precious stones or by using them at the wrong time; in a word, everything in him is baroque barbarity, glaring dissonance, and horrible deformity! Someone has said of Victor Hugo's genius: it is a beautiful hunchback. The word may be more profound than its inventor might suppose.
>
> In repeating this word, I do not have in mind merely M. Victor Hugo's mania for burdening the principal heroes of his novels and plays with a material hump; I especially want to suggest here that he is himself afflicted with a moral hump which he carries in his spirit.[135]

Hugo clearly became some kind of a scapegoat. He was perhaps the barbarous, upstart, deformed Germany with whom Heine could never feel at ease. Perhaps, too, he was Heine himself, the Heine who felt deformed in Germany or like an upstart in Paris, the Heine who feared that all of his imaginative talents amounted to hardness rather than force, the Heine who feared a "moral hump" in his own spirit, the Heine whom Heine did not like. Whatever this Hugo scapegoat may have been, he was not French. Heine's French intellectual friends were supposed to be *French;* that was their role and that was a reason for him to be in France. So he chose Sand over Hugo and became a good friend of Balzac.

Heine and Balzac respected each other's work, laughed at the same stories, enjoyed eating together, and did not threaten each other—all of which contributed to an amiable relationship. Heinrich Laube saw them together at a dinner of French literati in 1839 and reported that Heine joked with Balzac more than with anyone else in the group. Despite their different styles—Heine was impeccably dressed while Balzac was almost intentionally slovenly— they were extremely compatible in conversation.[136] And it was also a friendship that lasted: the two men continued to meet for dinner into the late 1840s, when Heine's health was keeping him away from most Parisian social life and when some of his other friendships (including the ties with Sand) were beginning to lapse.[137] Yet Heine did not write about Balzac as he wrote about other French authors. He complained privately to Sand that drama critics treated Balzac unfairly because of one weak play ("It's like eunuchs who scoff at a man because he fathers a deformed child"), but he did not choose to discuss the play or its critical reception in his newspaper articles.[138]

In the long article that praised Sand and condemned Hugo, however, Heine did commend Balzac for describing French actresses with "the most frightening fidelity"; such descriptions, he said, were the key to Balzac's narrative skills. "He describes them [the actresses] as a naturalist describes a species of any animal, or as a pathologist describes an illness, that is to say without intending to moralize and without predilection or repugnance." Balzac thus refused to embellish or to rehabilitate the phenomena he described, a literary temptation that "would be as contrary to art as to morality."[139] Although Heine preferred this frank depiction of unpleasant realities to Sand's moralizing, he did not pursue the point; he would not choose between Balzac and Sand as he had chosen between Sand and Hugo.

Still, he seemed to understand what Balzac was trying to do and to sympathize with the project. Balzac, for his part, returned the favor by dedicating his short novel *Un Prince de la Bohème* (1844) to Heine and by affirming the cultural identity Heine had carved out for himself:"My dear Heine, this study is for you, for you who represent in Paris the spirit and poetry of Germany, as in Germany you represent the sharp and witty critical spirit of France. I dedicate it to you, who know better than anyone what it contains of criticism, of jokes, of love, and of truth."[140] Balzac got it right, and Heine surely appreciated the gesture. These old dinner friends understood each other well enough to have a good time and to help each other get their respective messages to the public. Along with its warm personal dimension, therefore, it was also a friendship that showed how writers in Paris enhanced literary reputations by writing about people whom they knew.

Another friend who often joined Balzac and Heine at dinner was Théophile Gautier, whom Heine may have known longer than any other writer in France. Gautier was an extremely loyal friend, serving as a witness at Heine's wedding, a mourner at Heine's funeral, and an advocate for all of Heine's work. He introduced a French edition of *Reisebilder* (1856) with a eulogistic essay that called Heine "Germany's greatest lyricist," compared him to Goethe and Schiller, and affectionately stressed the complexity of his character: "He was at the same time gay and sad, skeptic and believer, tender and cruel, sentimental and sarcastic, classical and romantic, German and French, delicate and cynical, enthusiastic and full of *sang froid;* everything except boring."[141] Gautier did as much as anyone in France to build and defend Heine's reputation. A younger friend, Gérard de Nerval, also contributed his share of reputation-enhancing services by translating many of Heine's poems into French. The two men worked closely on these translations: "I sometimes experience great difficulties," Nerval explained to Heine, "less in understanding than in translating, and I have left a number of ambiguous meanings [*sens douteux*] in order to submit them to you."[142] The collaboration produced successful French editions of Heine's poems—Gautier, for one, called the poetry "magical"— and introduced his work to a much wider audience.

After Nerval's suicide in 1855, Heine described their extraordinary rapport and found much to praise in his friend's character and talent alike. "It was a highly sympathetic soul," Heine recalled, "and without knowing much of the German language, Gérard divined the spirit of a German poem better than one who had passed his life in the study of the language. And he was a great artist. . . . Yet I found nothing of the artist's conceit in him."[143] Heine's opinions sometimes changed quickly, but he remembered the people who helped him and stood by him and admired him. In contrast to his many conflicts with German friends and literary rivals, Heine managed to maintain most of his French friendships over many years. Much like French society as a whole, French writers offered him a place in which he could achieve the distinction and independence that eluded him in Germany; and he protected that place by conforming to the customs of French cultural life. He was usually willing to praise those who praised him, a practice that worked

to his own literary advantage and that reflected conventions in the
close-knit Parisian intellectual community. Heine flourished there
in part because he had some creative and influential French friends
and because he described them as sympathetically as they described him.

The same pattern appeared in Heine's relationship with Jules
Michelet and Edgar Quinet. Heine traded private compliments
with these historians in the 1830s and praised them in print in the
1840s.[144] He called Michelet a writer of brilliant, even poetic history
(sometimes marred by disorder or excess) and described Quinet as
one of the most imaginative and original poets in the world.[145]
Quinet was in fact more important than Michelet in Heine's Parisian career, for he was both a rival and an ally. Quinet took on
the task of describing German culture to France in essays and
articles that might well have threatened the position that Heine
had staked out for himself. But the two men remained friends
because they held similar views of Germany (that is, anti-Staël)
and because Quinet facilitated Heine's career in France.

Shortly after Heine's arrival in Paris, Quinet recommended him
to France's literary elite in the *Revue des Deux Mondes* by reporting
that Heine wrote about German convictions and hypocrisies with
"entirely French" abandon.[146] Later, after Heine's prose had begun
appearing in the *Revue*, Quinet characterized Heine's laughter and
satire as weapons against ancient, musty, self-important, idealist
Germany. Indeed, Heine was one of the socially conscious, new-
generation poets who understood the poet's mission in the world
as a labor of lonely mediation between nations and generations:
"He must endure the rain and the wind, the cold and the heat, the
love and the hate of foreign climates; because his heart is henceforth too big for either the city or the village to contain it. His
religious calling is to be the mediator with the people to come. His
voice no longer belongs to anyone. In the interregnum of political
powers, he alone becomes sovereign again. He is already the leg-
islator of the great European federation which does not yet
exist."[147] Quinet situated Heine in the position he wanted: as a
poet-mediator who understood and attacked the stultifying traditions that oppressed modern Germany, and who did so from an
internationalist perspective that pointed to the future. Quinet thus
provided the kind of immediate status that no foreign writer could
achieve in Paris without French support, and his praise helped
Heine as Heine could never have helped himself.

Quinet also served Heine through his assistance with translations, his contacts with editors, and his belief that the French should know more about Germany,[148] all of which may have encouraged Heine's sympathetic description of Quinet's work in an 1843 article for the *Allgemeine Zeitung*. Heine ascribed to Quinet a German character in which a German spirit flourished—even his appearance was more German than French—yet Quinet's German spirit did not produce the clumsiness and barbarity that made Hugo so reprehensible for Heine. On the contrary, his "Germanness" enabled him to understand and criticize problems in Germany (like Heine) and to create poetry with German sensitivity and imagination.[149] Quinet was the "good German," Hugo was the "bad" one, perhaps because Quinet's acknowledgment of Heine's international literary role contrasted all too clearly with the unresponsive Hugo's indifference.

Quinet's sympathetic treatment in the *Revue des Deux Mondes* was only one example of the help that Heine received from that journal. The editor, François Buloz, took an interest in Heine's works and began publishing extracts from *Reisebilder* and *De l'Allemagne* in 1832–34.[150] This was an extremely important entrée for Heine because it enhanced his reputation in Germany as well as in France. Parisian intellectual prestige was such that a writer who published there achieved international legitimacy that he might never acquire at home. The relationship between Paris and foreign readers resembled the relationship between capital cities and colonies. A good reputation in Paris provided the mark of approval that was likely to improve a reputation at home. Heine won that mark from the prestigious *Revue des Deux Mondes* and from the early French publication of works such as *Conditions in France* (1833) and *De l'Allemagne* (1835).[151]

He also came to know Victor Bohain, publisher of a journal called *L'Europe Littéraire*. Bohain wanted to reach an international audience with articles on all European literatures, including the series "Etat actuel de la littérature en Allemagne" that Heine wrote in early 1833 (the articles eventually became part of *De l'Allemagne*).[152] *L'Europe Littéraire* did not survive for long, but before it disappeared, Heine met many of the people who mattered in Parisian literary life—people whose approval could make a reputation. Bohain invited Heine to staff dinners, served him champagne, and granted him the freedom to write whatever he wished about Germany.[153] All of this helped establish Heine's position in Parisian culture and gave him a certain influence among other Germans, as he suggested in soliciting one of his old German friends for a contribution to *L'Europe Littéraire*. "I am very active here," he explained, "and I hope to make you known soon to the French also and to illuminate, from Paris, your laurels with a light bright enough to make your enemies cry."[154] Heine clearly appreciated the opportunities that Parisian publishing connections provided for him and for other Germans. In fact, the value of Heine's personal contacts with editors, translators, and the rising generation of Parisian literati can hardly be overestimated. They were mostly acquaintances rather than confidants.[155] Yet these acquaintances and the institutional support of their publications contributed decisively to Heine's European reputation: they confirmed his place in Parisian intellectual life and explicitly recognized the role of "German émigré mediator" that he had chosen to play.

Heine once wrote that all French people were natural actors who understood instinctively the role that each situation required of them. French society was therefore very much like French theater, and successful people in France were much like successful actors in that they chose their parts carefully and played them brilliantly.[156] Germans, by contrast, could not play such varied parts: "We are honest people," wrote Heine, "and the roles of honest people are the ones we play best."[157] And that was the German role he wanted for himself—an émigré speaking honestly to French people about the Germans and to Germans about the French. The Paris network of literature, politics, and publications made the role possible and gave him audiences he never reached at home. True, his performance did not impress everyone. Alfred de Vigny, for example, may have spoken for more than one Frenchman (and some Germans, too) when he wrote of Heine: "I find him cold and offensive. He is one of these foreigners who, having failed to achieve fame in their own country, want people in another country to believe they are famous."[158] Vigny's view, however, did not become Heine's public reputation. Instead, he established his mediator role in print and in salon society and came to be regarded as a witty and important German intellectual.[159] One enthusiastic reader assured him, "You are the German Cervantes, the modern Rabelais."[160] It was a big part, but Heine's dramatic sensibilities made him entirely willing to play it. The role offered a unique opportunity to perform in the theater of French and international literature, and it helped Heine to express the personal contradictions (elitist democrat, aristocratic Saint-Simonian, sensual moralist, converted Jew, political poet, French German, and so on) that he could never act out to his satisfaction in Germany. It was also a role on the margin that led Heine toward his own complex center.

Cultural Mediator: The Outsider as Insider

Although it was never easy to be both German and Rabelaisian, that dual identity—and the cultural reconciliation it suggested— provided the narrative perspective for much of the prose Heine wrote in Paris. He believed that France and Germany should be allies and that his books should facilitate understanding and co-operation between the two countries.[161] This reconciliation de-manded all of Heine's talents as a cultural mediator. He had to point out both the similarities that made national cooperation seem plausible and the differences that impeded cooperation and justified his own mediating role. His discussion of French char-acter, society, politics, and culture, for example, often carried ex-plicit or implicit references to Germany that could make the French case more comprehensible to readers across the Rhine. Similarly, he drew upon parallels and contrasts in French history when he wrote about Germany for the French. The strategy on both sides was to make the alien more familiar even while stressing that it really was different.

Heine's exile status was extremely important in this project be-cause he could write for the French audience as a German "insider" (someone who could be trusted to unravel German mysteries with French wit and clarity) and for the German audience as a Parisian "insider" (someone who lived there and knew the leading French figures). One of the remarkable features of Heine's life and work in France is that he was a perennial outsider who made his rep-utation by writing as an insider. To be sure, this "outsider as in-sider" status placed him in a somewhat ambivalent position, yet he was able to exploit that position in his prose and to create a career and an identity out of the very characteristic (being an outsider) that had blocked his career and satisfaction in Germany. Paris was probably the only place where he could have turned all of this to advantage, where he could find a place for himself as an outsider and write insider books. Thus, Heine used his "German-ness" in France as often as he used his "Frenchness" in the articles he sent to Germany. His reputation and mediation depended on both parts of this identity, though Heine himself never forgot that he was a German.

He was a German who sympathized with France, however, and he wanted the French public to recognize that fact. As he emphasized in an 1840 letter to a Paris newspaper, "Everything that I have written about France during the last ten years in German newspapers or in special publications has had but one goal: to react against certain correspondents who, for reasons of their own, never stop slandering the men, the affairs and the entire social life of the French people."[162] Here, then, was a trustworthy German friend who defended France abroad and who, in the spirit of friendship, sought to explain German culture to the French in works such as *De l'Allemagne*. The two parts of this book ("The Romantic School" and "On the History of Religion and Philosophy in Germany") were designed to correct what Heine saw as widespread French misconceptions of modern Germany stemming from Victor Cousin's inaccurate descriptions of German philosophy and especially from Madame de Staël's influential study *De l'Allemagne* (1813).[163] Heine thus referred explicitly to her precedent in his title but rejected her account of a Germany that remained essentially medieval, romantic, and idealist. This misrepresentation, Heine suggested, resulted from the bad influence of her friend August Wilhelm Schlegel and from her desire to criticize French materialism and realism with a highly distorted German alternative.[164]

His own objective was quite different. Where Madame de Staël stressed the otherness of Germany, Heine wanted to indicate its similarities to France. More specifically, he wanted to show that both countries had broken with the medieval past, though they had done so in different ways. What Heine described, therefore, were the progressive, radical elements that constituted the German revolt against medievalism (the point that the Saint-Simonian Enfantin misunderstood or rejected) and that coincided with the evolution of materialist philosophies in seventeenth- and eighteenth-century France. This historical perspective became a major part of Heine's alliance-making project; he wanted to show that a German philosophical revolution ran parallel with the French political revolution and that this dual revolution could be the starting point for future cooperation. He believed the French might understand and respond to this history if it were explained without the distorting romantic mysticism of Madame de Staël, and he reported with satisfaction that this had happened. "My revelations excited the greatest surprise in France," he wrote later, "and I remember that leading French thinkers naively confessed to me that they had always believed German philosophy to be a peculiar mystic fog, behind which divinity lay hidden as in a cloud, and that German philosophers were ecstatic seers, filled with piety and the fear of God."[165]

Heine conceded that it was easy for the French to overlook the German revolt against medievalism, because its form differed a great deal from the French revolt. The French got rid of Gothic ideas and Gothic behavior at the same time; Germans waged war against Gothic ideas, but Gothic behavior and the interests that supported it (for example, a conservative Catholic Church) continued to exist.[166] Despite the difficulty of shedding external medievalism, the German attack on the medieval past had been as radical and decisive as had the French. Heine described the German attack as a three-pronged assault that began with the Lutheran Reformation, widened into German pantheism, and culminated in the philosophical revolution of Kant and Hegel.

The Reformation was for Heine the turning point in German history. Indeed, it was a crucial event in the long struggle between spiritualism and sensualism that Heine viewed as perhaps the central conflict in all of human history: the dispute between Plato and Aristotle, between Christians and pagans, between spiritualists and materialists in every generation. Medieval Christianity had achieved a solution to this ongoing conflict when it found a place for God and the devil, the spirit and the body.[167] The synthesis could not last, however, and medieval Catholicism ultimately fell to attacks from both sensualist and spiritualist positions. This anti-Catholic campaign owed its success to an effective division of labor: French critics launched the materialist attack on the spiritual demands of Catholicism; German critics provided the spiritualist attack on the sensual concessions of Catholicism. The French attack led eventually to Enlightenment materialism and the French Revolution. The German attack, after its own brief moment of sensual exuberance, evolved gradually into idealism and the philosophical revolution.[168]

The hero of this story on the German side was Luther, who managed to create in himself a new historic synthesis. "He was a complete man," wrote Heine, "I might say an absolute man, in whom matter and spirit are not separate. To call him a spiritualist, therefore, would be just as wrong as to call him a sensualist." He was that rarest kind of historical figure, "both a dreamy mystic and a practical man of action."[169] Luther's successors could not maintain this difficult balance, though, and his Protestant synthesis soon faced a new challenge in the philosophy of Descartes, the starting point of modern philosophy. Descartes's philosophical synthesis, like that of medieval Christianity and of Luther, brought together the idealist and materialist components of human thought and experience. The French again chose the materialist side of the synthesis, supplemented Descartes with John Locke, and became the most sensualist nation in Europe. The Germans developed the idealist component of Cartesianism through the mediation of Leibniz and became the most spiritualist nation in Europe.[170] The implicit message throughout Heine's spiritualist/sensualist analysis was that some synthesis or harmony between these forces was desirable. One senses here a Saint-Simonian perspective (as well as a vague Hegelianism) in which Franco-German reconciliation is a crucial step in the development of a higher historical synthesis. The next Luther would have to be French and German.

Heine did not follow the French materialist evolution past its early deistic, Lockean phase; as he saw it, the French materialist world view had established itself by that point, and all that ensued was merely a working-out of its consequences.[171] In Germany, however, the "history of religion and philosophy" continued to develop by moving away from both deism and the system of Leibniz. German challenges to both parts of the Cartesian inheritance appeared in pantheism and then in the philosophy of Immanual Kant.

Heine liked the pantheists and their favorite philosopher Spinoza because he believed that they had achieved a new synthesis of spirit and matter. Unlike the deists and almost everyone in France (except some of the Saint-Simonians), the pantheists saw that God was present in everything that exists. The French materialist tradition did not welcome such beliefs, and so Germany became the center for modern pantheism. Like their ancient ancestors who saw spirits in all of nature, modern Germans understood how the spiritual might also exist in the material and how divinity might exist in humanity.[172] "In man the deity attains self-awareness and reveals this self-awareness again through man." According to Heine, this was the pantheistic insight that overthrew deism in Germany. "This is the religion of our greatest thinkers [and] of our best artists," he wrote. "Pantheism is the clandestine religion of Germany."[173] Such a creed did not foster passivity or romantic dreams or Madame de Staël's medievalism; on the contrary, it was a faith that encouraged belief in action, in change, and in the modern political values that were so influential in France.

> The political revolution that is based on the principles of French ma-
> terialism will find in the pantheists not opponents, but allies, allies,
> however, who have drawn their convictions from a deeper source,
> from a religious synthesis. We promote the welfare of matter, the
> material happiness of the peoples, not, like the materialists, because
> we despise the spirit, but because we know that the divinity of man
> is also revealed in his corporeal form, that misery destroys or debases
> the body, God's image, and that as a result the spirit likewise perishes.
> The great maxim of the Revolution pronounced by St. Just, *"Le pain
> est le droit du peuple"* is translated by us, *"Le pain est le droit divin de
> l'homme."*[174]

German pantheism, in short, was a real-world, radical, foreign ally
of the French revolutionary tradition.

The same could be said for the German philosophical revolution
that began with Immanuel Kant. Here, too, German culture had
produced useful weapons for attacking tradition; here, too, the
radical French might find a history to parallel their own and a
distinctly German ally for their revolutionary heritage. The philosophical revolution was for Heine entirely equal to the French
Revolution in both its radical break with the past and its radical
consequences for the future. He made the comparisons explicit:
Kant was a German Robespierre, the bourgeois radical who attacked old-regime dogma (deism) with merciless Jacobin effi-
ciency. When he had finished his work in the *Critique of Pure
Reason,* the Robespierre from Königsberg had destroyed all proof
for the existence of God, introduced a radical "critical spirit" to
German thought, and thrown German culture into turmoil. As
Heine described it, this philosophical revolution reached a climax
in 1789, thereby creating a remarkable historical symmetry during
that momentous year: "We had riots in the intellectual world just
as you had in the material world, and we became just as excited
over the demolition of ancient dogmatism as you did over the
storming of the Bastille."[175] Kant later tried to assert that "practical reason" guaranteed the existence of a God that theoretical
reason had destroyed, but the battle was already over, and deism
in Germany lay as shattered as the Bastille in France.

The revolution entered its imperial phase in the person of Johann
Gottlieb Fichte, who argued for the existence of a universal or
transcendent Ego, the Ego that creates and comprehends all. In
Fichte's doctrine, wrote Heine, the world and all individuals are
only expressions of a "universal world Ego awakened to self-awareness."[176] It became the fullest expression of German idealism—

"things have reality only in our minds"—and the Napoleonic moment in German history: "After the Kantians had completed their terroristic work of destruction, Fichte appeared, just as Napoleon appeared after the Convention had demolished the whole past, and like the Kantians by using a critique of pure reason. Napoleon and Fichte represent the great inexorable Ego in which thought and action are one, and the colossal structures successfully created by both testify to a colossal will."[177] But the Fichtean triumph, like Napoleon's empire, did not survive (though it continued to affect German thought), and the philosophical revolution fell into the hands of Friedrich Schelling.

Schelling took German philosophy back to nature, reviving the pantheistic tradition in a new guise of nature philosophy. Heine suggested that Schelling's work might be compared to that of the French Restoration, insofar as he provided the inevitable reaction to Kant's Jacobinism and Fichte's Napoleonic empire. He restored nature to its rightful autonomous place and then attempted a new reconciliation between matter and the mind, all of which Heine respected as important, pantheistic work. In the end, though, Schelling deserted the promising possibilities of his own early doctrine by reverting to Catholicism and going over to the reactionary enemy camp.[178] The great revolution meanwhile achieved its final synthesis and scientific order in the work of Schelling's student Georg Hegel, whom Heine called "the greatest philosopher Germany has produced since Leibniz."[179]

Hegel's systematic accomplishment closed the "great circle" of the German philosophical revolt and marked the starting point for all that would follow in Germany.[180] Yet Heine ended his history without describing this culminating Hegelian event, much as he wrote about French materialism and politics without explicitly discussing the Revolution of 1789. Although Heine saw both Hegel and the French Revolution as decisive historical turning points (originative events that were also culminations), he never wrote about either of them except by allusion. They were always material for other books that Heine said he intended to write (but did not), the *great* events that stayed just outside his insider reports while they influenced his perspective on almost everything he wrote about both France and Germany.[181]

Even without Hegel, however, Heine had made his point about the radical strains in German thought from Luther to Schelling. Now the philosophical revolution had run its course, and Germany might soon turn to deeds that even the activist French would find appalling. When the Germans set aside their books, warned Heine, the drama of world history would move across the Rhine, and everyone else should look for cover.

> When you hear crash and the clashing of arms, watch out, you neigh-bor children, you French, and don't meddle in what we are doing at home in Germany. It might cost you dearly. Take care not to fan the fire; take care not to put it out. You could easily burn your fingers in the flames. Don't smile at my advice, the advice of a dreamer who warns you against Kantians, Fichteans, and nature philosophers. Don't smile at the visionary who expects in the realm of reality the same revolution that has taken place in the realm of the intellect. The thought precedes the deed as lightning precedes thunder. German thunder is of course truly German; it is not very nimble but rumbles along rather slowly. It will come, though, and if some day you hear a crash such as has never been heard before in world history, you will know the German thunder has finally reached its mark.... A play will be performed in Germany compared with which the French Revolu-tion might seem merely an innocent idyll....
>
> As on the steps of an amphitheater, the nations will gather around Germany to witness the great contests. I advise you, you French, keep very quiet, and for Heaven's sake, *don't* applaud. We might easily misunderstand you and in our rude fashion, might somewhat roughly shut you up. If in times past, in our servile, discontented state, we could sometimes overpower you, we could do so far more easily in the elation of our intoxication with liberty.[182]

This was the concluding advice in "On the History of Religion and Philosophy in Germany," advice that draws again on theatrical metaphors and that suggests a certain discomfort with the actors who would do the deed in Germany. Despite Heine's hatred for reactionaries and his support for the long-developing Franco-Ger-man assault on the medieval foe, he anticipated "German thunder" with some apprehension. A German political revolution would not replicate the July Revolution in France. It might preclude the Franco-German alliance that he desired (the two countries could collide if they began to fight the medieval enemy with the same political weapon), and it might leave him as much on the outside as before. Heine could not in fact find much consolation in a Ger-man future that might conform to the ambitions of German rad-icals in Paris, because the political and personal opinions of most German émigrés he knew there differed significantly from his own.

Heine's German contacts formed an important and complicated

part of his life in Paris. Ideological affinities and a common sense of German identity drew him into the exile community, but the similarities were never strong enough to win him a comfortable niche—and he seemed to want it that way. Still, he shared important concerns with his exiled compatriots: for example, the common radical interest in French politics, and the inspiration that enlightened Germans had always found in the French revolutionary tradition.[183] Furthermore, he accepted the radical belief that Germany might soon experience major political changes, precipitated in part by the example of the July Revolution in France. The cannons of that week awoke the German people, Heine explained in 1832, and the authorities could not make them sleep again.[184] This awakening extended even to German writers, who now rejected the oppressive abstraction of German literature. Tired of "annotating the classics," a new generation plunged into the real-life concerns of political power, political freedom, and modern social movements. Heine found this new outlook especially notable in writers of the "Young Germany" movement "who wish to make no distinction between life and writing, who never separate politics from science, art and religion, and who are simultaneously artists, tribunes and apostles."[185] Germany had produced writers believing in progress and in a Saint-Simonian vision of economic prosperity, and Heine wanted French readers to know about them. (It was Heine's own reputation as a "Young Germany" writer that led to the 1835 ban on his works in Germany.)

This support for politically conscious literature linked Heine with most German radicals in France. Similarly, his criticism of German xenophobia reflected typical expatriate attitudes insofar as radical republicans favored internationalist politics over narrowly defined German nationalism. Like many German radicals, Heine wanted a German state that would embrace the universalist principles of the French Revolution. He therefore condemned the Prussian state, the ruling regime, and the effects of German patriotism. "A German's patriotism," he complained, "means that his heart contracts and shrinks like leather in the cold, and a German then hates everything foreign, no longer wants to become a citizen of the world, a European, but only a provincial German."[186] Here was a judgment of German reaction which most radicals could accept and which, combined with the praise for France and the support for a German political awakening, brought Heine close to the political values of many German émigrés. Yet he always kept his distance from these would-be allies, criticizing them almost as readily as he criticized the Prussian state and expressing considerable animosity for both their politics and their personalities.

In the first place, Heine did not like their obsession with republicanism, partly because he preferred monarchies and partly because he believed that German republicans suffered from a serious misperception. "The principal error of these German republicans," he wrote, "comes from the fact that they do not take correct account of the difference between the two countries when they call for Germany to have this republican form of government which might perhaps be suitable for France."[187] French character and culture had become essentially republican, whereas Germany remained essentially royalist, a dichotomous formula by which Heine meant that French people expressed a pervasive republican disrespect for authority, while Germans still showed a pervasive royalist respect for authorities and princes of all kinds. It was this cultural difference that made the German republican movement seem inappropriate, often irrelevant, and, according to Heine, more or less doomed to failure. The republican *idea* was nevertheless a powerful concept, and for that reason alone the Germans would explore its possibilities to the final consequences, no matter how absurd or irrelevant it might become in the actual historical context.[188]

Heine's objection to the republicans was more than a simple case of politics, however, for he also disliked their asceticism. Radical republicans seemed to presuppose the necessity of personal sacrifices (not to say repressions) that were incompatible with his own pantheistic notions of revolution. Heine's revolution called for fine taste and pleasure as well as political justice, and so he had no tolerance for the self-denial of puritanical revolutionaries: "You demand simple dress, austere morals, and unspiced pleasures, but we demand nectar and ambrosia, crimson robes, costly perfumes, luxury and splendor, the dancing of laughing nymphs, music and comedies. Don't be angry with us because of this, you virtuous Republicans. To your censorious reproaches we will respond in the words of one of Shakespeare's fools: " 'Dost thou think because thou are virtuous, there shall be no more nice cakes and sweet champagne in the world?' "[189] Heine wanted a bounteous revolution that left a place for his poetry and that would fit what he took to be the character and needs of Germany. Many of his émigré compatriots had a different idea, and it was not long before his opinions and behavior were arousing criticism in much of the exile community.

Although most republican expatriates expected Heine to be a useful literary ally, he refused from the beginning to play the role they wanted him to take. He would never join the exile associations or conform to the republican lifestyle favored by leaders such as Ludwig Börne, choosing instead to promote his political causes and to pursue his pleasures in his own way. He nonetheless signed manifestos, gave money to needy exiles, and occasionally intervened with the French government on behalf of those who were expelled from France. When the French expelled Jakob Venedey from Paris in 1835, for example, Heine responded to Venedey's appeal for help by asking Thiers to rescind the expulsion order; when that request was turned down, Heine gave Venedey money.[190] Venedey, who was active in the German League of the Outlaws and editor of the newspaper *Der Geächtete*, was only one of the many exiles asking for Heine's assistance in one form or another. There was in fact a whole network of needy people that caused Heine the greatest aggravation. The "Young Germany" writer Karl Gutzkow later described the 1830s as a time in which "never a day passed without an attempt to dethrone some prince by means of a manifesto, or in which some new subscription list was not opened. At every other moment he [Heine] found himself called upon to take his pen and sign his name, and it exasperated him."[191]

Indeed, Heine seemed to resent his solicitous republican "allies" as much as he resented Prussian spies. "The Germans whom I meet in Paris," he wrote to Heinrich Laube, "have kept me from being homesick. [They are] rabble and beggars who threaten you when you don't give them anything. . . . [They] speak continually of honor and of the fatherland—liars, thieves."[192] Acting upon this perception, Heine decided to avoid the republican exile community whenever possible and to write about the misery of sharing exile with such unpleasant people.

> He's heard to complain: Bad company
> Is the worst plague in exile that can be.
> We have to consort with vermin and slugs
> And even a swarm of dirty bugs,
>
>
> Who treat us as comrades, brothers in blood,
> Because we're wallowing in the same mud—
> Thus Virgil's disciple, too, wailed erstwhile,
> The poet who sang of Hell and exile.[193]

As it happened, this contempt for exiled republican "vermin" extended from the most bothersome "beggars" to the most prominent leader, Ludwig Börne.

Heine's conflict with Börne, the most important dispute of his exile years, developed because the two men were close enough to be rivals but too different to be friends. They first met in Germany in the late 1820s and formed a congenial relationship as political and literary dissidents, which Börne expected to continue in France.[194] Börne moved to Paris shortly after the July Revolution and began writing articles in which he advocated a German republican revolution. Heine's liberal monarchist sentiments and his notion of the German "royalist" character (and perhaps also his personal pride) precluded the cooperation that Börne had anticipated. As he became aware of Heine's attitudes, Börne decided that Heine's politics and character were both seriously flawed, and by 1833 he was attacking Heine in print for dilettantism, lack of serious conviction, poetic aestheticism, and sympathy for aristocrats.[195] Börne's Heine, in short, was an immoral, insincere character who could not be trusted.

In addition to commenting on republican irrelevance to the German situation, Heine defended his own radicalism. He noted in the preface to a French edition of *Reisebilder* (1834) that the charges of moderation and of excessive contact with aristocrats resulted from an out-of-date radicalism that understood nothing except the language of 1789, a primitive radicalism to which he himself had once adhered. "But I have moved much farther along the road of progress since then," he explained, "and my simple Germans, who, roused by the cannon of July, have followed in my tracks and now speak the language of 1789 or even of 1793, are still so far away from me that they have lost sight of me and believe that I am behind them."[196] These Saint-Simonian claims failed to silence the Börne faction's criticisms, however, and after Börne's death in 1837 Heine published a bitter anti-Börne book titled *Heinrich Heine über Ludwig Börne* (1840).

Heine used the book to defend art against a republican revolution that might destroy all beauty and to characterize Börne as a puritanical, repressive "Nazarene." In other words he returned to the theme of the recurrent struggle between spiritualism (Nazarenism) and sensualism (Hellenism) and then declared himself to be the advocate of a new stage in historical development: where Börne defended one-sided ascetic puritanism, he, Heine, defended the higher pantheistic synthesis. He thus aligned himself with the cause of art, freedom, and progress, relegating Börne to the camp of uncomprehending levelers and repressors. To make the attack conclusive, he added virulent criticisms of Börne's personal character, his close friends, and his working-class associates.[197] The book by no means destroyed Börne's reputation, however. Instead, its bitter personal tone caused almost all radical Germans at home and in France to turn against Heine. Ironically, the anti-Börne campaign ended in another victory for the enemy it was supposed to destroy and left Heine more isolated than ever. After nearly a decade in exile, he had managed to achieve the unique status of *persona non grata* among Prussian monarchists and radical republicans alike.

It was therefore fortunate for Heine that a new wave of more radical German exiles began arriving in Paris during the early 1840s. In their new émigré community Heine could overcome some of his isolation, and their publications offered an outlet for the radical political poetry he had started to write. Although Heine and the Young Hegelians differed in important ways, they shared common enemies on both the right and the left, and that was reason enough to form an alliance. They also needed each other. Heine needed new friends, and he wanted to encourage the development of new exile publications. The younger émigrés needed the prestige of a famous writer; they wanted sympathizers who could provide contacts in the unfamiliar French community; and their idea of Franco-German cooperation was of course one of Heine's perennial themes.

So Heine came to know a number of the exiles who wrote for *Vorwärts* and the *Deutsch-Französische Jahrbücher*. He had long favored the creation in France of a German press using the techniques of French political journalism; in fact, he once planned to publish a German newspaper of his own in Paris because, as he explained to a friend, a Parisian-based journal could carry European political information that was not otherwise available in Germany.[198] Heine soon abandoned his plan (citing the likelihood of Prussian confiscation and financial collapse),[199] but he remained interested in the idea and agreed to work with Marx and Ruge on the *Deutsch-Französische Jahrbücher*. He told his German publisher that the "Ruge coterie" deserved support, though he intended to keep his distance from the inner circle. "I never belong to a coterie like that," he explained, "but I support everything which seems to me good and worthy of praise. Thus, I have already written something for Ruge's Review."[200] Heine contributed to the *Jahrbücher* three satirical poems about King Ludwig of Bavaria. They were the first in a series of political verses that he published during 1844, mostly in the radical *Vorwärts* (the most famous, "The Silesian Weavers," appeared there in July 1844), and they coincided with the most radical phase of his career.

Among all the collaborators at *Vorwärts*, Heine formed the closest association with Karl Marx, whom he met in late 1843. Their friendship has attracted considerable scholarly attention, inasmuch as it united for about a year the most important German social theorist and the most famous German poet of the period. The two men shared a rigorous critique of the existing European order, an interest in the French revolutionary tradition, and a considerable mutual respect—all of which must have contributed to their friendship.[201] They apparently spent a good deal of time discussing their work and sharing the vicissitudes of exile life (Heine reportedly saved the life of Marx's infant daughter by treating her severe convulsions with a warm bath). They also came under attack from the same enemies. Prussian government officials, for example, tried unsuccessfully to have Heine expelled from France while they were arranging for Marx's expulsion in early 1845.[202] Yet the friends did not really share the same notion of history, nor did they have equivalent faith in the beneficial consequences of a proletarian revolution. Although Heine believed that the future probably belonged to the Hegelian "doctors of revolution" and to communism, his fear of the working class and his spiritual interests (which deepened as he grew older) precluded wholehearted participation in the radical Hegelian "coterie."[203] He was less radical than most of the Young Hegelians; he had a much greater stake in French society; and he remained more interested in artistic values than in the rigorous logic of radical politics.

All of this became more evident in the late 1840s as Heine gradually lost touch with Marx and the communists, expressed dissatisfaction with the 1848 revolution, and then turned increasingly toward Judaism and personal religious concerns during the last years of his life. To be sure, he never broke with Marx so dramatically as with Börne, but his insider contact with the rapidly developing German communist movement proved ultimately to be a brief and passing phase of his Parisian career. Heine was in this respect the true "poet in exile," living on the edges of both French society and the German émigré community, even as he became a prominent member of both. Despite important connections with the French and Germans alike, he always kept a certain distance from all of them. There was in Heine an enduring sense of otherness that somehow made exile the only comfortable position for him and made the French experience central to his career and identity. Paris enabled him to use his exile status to achieve recognition and some measure of satisfaction, to become celebrated for his otherness. He would never sacrifice that position by becoming simply another republican émigré or a member of the Hegelian "coterie." His role, his identity, required that he remain the perennial outsider—the sympathetic or critical observer on the margins of every circle.

Still, perpetual exile was not an easy existence, as Heine indicated repeatedly over the course of his twenty-five years in France. This was true even though he never forgot the unhappiness of his life in Germany. Within weeks of his arrival in Paris, Heine was describing that former life as one of "struggles" and "miseries" and his native country as a place "where they poisoned all my vital sources."[204] That memory of discomfort did not diminish; he could still evoke the pain and nightmares when he was composing his *Confessions* in the 1850s. He recalled there the bad dreams that had disturbed his sleep and the melancholy that had hastened his emigration to France.[205] Heine did not detail the causes of his German misery (anti-Semitism, pressure to find a suitable career, family, political alienation?), but the experience produced in him a lifelong sense of separation from his homeland and a fear of persecution.[206] As he reminded himself in one of his exile poems, the German tribunals seemed always to await his return: "You wrote some lines for which / you could be lined up, they say, / It would be discomforting, / to be sure, if I were shot."[207]

In spite of that lingering fear, however, Heine's German identity remained central to his self-perception and to his role in France. Significantly, he never renounced his German citizenship or applied for French naturalization.[208] He wrote in German rather than French (though he worked closely with French editors and translators in order to publish in both languages); he depended on a German publisher and the German public for much of his income and reputation; and he described himself as a German patriot. Indeed, he informed his compatriots in 1833 that expatriate life actually fostered his patriotic pride.

There is a strange thing about patriotism—the real love of one's country. A man may love his country and live to be eighty years old in it, and yet not have learned to know it; but then he must have stayed at home. It is in winter that we learn of spring, and the best May carols are written by the fireside. Love of liberty is a dungeon flower, and the worth of liberty is best learned in prison. So love of the German lands begins at its frontiers, and, above all, at sight of the woes of Germany in a foreign country.[209]

Heine attributed this exile patriotism to a new appreciation for the people, the language, and the culture from which he came. An encounter with German emigrants in Normandy, for example, aroused in him the greatest compassion for "blond Germany, with her earnest eyes, her sad and thoughtful face and . . . that troubled look of constraint that used to tease and anger me, but now moved me sadly." Heine described the meeting as an instant of reconciliation with the "whole fatherland" and as an expression of his "nobler" patriotism, which differed entirely from the crass nationalism of so-called German patriots across the Rhine.[210] It was a moment of genuine contact with home, a moment when he and his wandering compatriots spoke freely to one another in German.

This German linguistic identity was extremely important to Heine, and it was one of the most significant barriers to his thorough assimilation into French culture. "Everything I write and think has to clothe itself laboriously in foreign expressions," he once complained. The language problem may in fact have affected Heine as much as any other aspect of his exile life. "No doubt you have some idea of what bodily exile means," he told his German readers, "but only a German poet condemned to speak and write French the whole livelong day, and even to sigh in French on his loved one's breast at night, can have any idea of what spiritual exile means! Even my thoughts are exiled, exiled into a foreign tongue."[211] This sense of linguistic isolation no doubt contributed to the nostalgia for Germany that became a theme in some of Heine's work during the late 1830s and early 1840s. He had by then seen enough Parisian gaiety to make him wish for the tranquility of German life and the sobriety of German women. "In Paris, reason, cold, unfeeling, / Reigns, full of wit and indiscreet," he lamented in verse ("Anno 1839"), concluding, "Our German rudeness, though vexatious, / It added to my happiness."[212] The exile adventure became an exile life, and Heine came down with a typical case of exile fatigue.

The nostalgia for Germany culminated in two visits to Hamburg (in 1843 and 1844) and in the poem that grew out of these trips, *Germany, A Winter's Tale* (*Deutschland, Ein Wintermärchen*). The

poem satirized contemporary German political life, but it also re-
affirmed his German cultural and linguistic identity: "And hearing
the German language I / Felt strange beyond all measure; / It was
as if my heart began / To bleed away with pleasure."[213] *A Winter's
Tale* expressed considerable affection for German culture (in contrast to German politics) and described an idealized German nation
that might one day exist, a future Germany that would take up the
progressive cause of the French Revolution and thereby win the
support of all the world. It was to this ideal Germany that Heine
pledged his patriotic support. He knew, though, that the real Germany of 1844 was by no means ready to promote the universal
work of the French Revolution and that his own higher patriotism
might be most prudently advocated from Paris. "I love the fatherland just as much as you do," he wrote in the preface to *A
Winter's Tale*. "Because of this love I have lived in exile for thirteen
years, and because of this same love I return to exile, perhaps
forever."[214] Accordingly, he lived the rest of his life in France as a
permanently displaced "patriot."

Heine thus staked out his position on the high ground of exile,
true patriotism, and creativity. He would make a virtue (sacrifice)
of what others saw as fault (flight), and he would make a place for
himself within the broad cosmopolitan tradition that "Paris" represented. Paris was also a real place, however, and the higher life
within the cosmopolitan tradition meant also a daily life on the
margins of an alien culture. "You see my dear friend," he wrote
to Lewald, "it is the exile's secret curse that we cannot really feel
at ease in the atmosphere of a foreign country; with our opinions
and our own national sentiments we are always isolated amid a
people who feel and think very differently from us. We are continually offended by moral or rather immoral actions to which the
natives have long since become accustomed and which custom
even prevents them from noticing. . . . Alas, the moral climate of a
foreign country is even more unhealthy for us than the physical
climate."[215] Here was the difficult isolation of exile which Heine
exploited with much creativity, but which, as he said elsewhere,
"pours night and poison into our thoughts."[216]

Heine's chosen literary role called for continuing mediation between "French" and "German" parts of himself as well as the
mediation between national cultures, and it helped him to recognize some of the instability in his exile position. "My opinions
[French?] are in contradiction with my sentiments [German?]," he
explained to Princess Belgioioso in 1836. "I carry a wreath of roses

on my head and pain in my heart. I am thirsty for moral unity to make my opinions and my sentiments harmonious."[217] This notion of harmony appears in much of Heine's work—the harmony of spiritualism and sensualism, harmony between poetry and the conditions of life, harmony between France and Germany, personal and material harmony in a Saint-Simonian future. One senses that feelings of displacement or otherness in Heine fostered a recurring desire for oneness. The desire may also have owed something to the Hegelian vision in which ancient harmony had been destroyed by an era of disharmony, alienation, and conflict; there remained however the dream of future harmony and the end of exile and separation.

As A. I. Sandor has suggested in a very fine critical study, Heine managed to elevate his own alienated position into a general theory of history, politics, and art by identifying his quest for unattainable harmony with the universal movement toward reconciliation. Thus, he could see his own unrequited desire for harmony as part of the "Exile of the Gods" (the title of a Heine essay) and his literary work as a contribution to a higher historical synthesis.[218] Although the achievement of this synthesis seemed remote if not impossible, Heine found a certain transitional harmony by linking himself with human exile in its broadest sense. Indeed, his mediation role presupposed the continuation of exile and difference, even as he advocated harmony and reconciliation.

Heine's exile in France must therefore be seen as a decisive aspect of his life and work; it is impossible to understand either without exploring the significance of his French experience. France offered an escape from the confinement he felt in Germany and gave purpose to his lifelong outsider status. In Paris he discovered the complexities of modern society—the "crisis of authority," the developing capitalist economy, the urban proletariat, and radical social movements—all of which he discussed in his articles for the German press. In Paris he found also a political tradition (Enlightenment and revolution) and a political model (July Revolution and constitutional monarchy) with which to compare and criticize German political life. Moreover, the Parisian cultural network gave him valuable contacts and the opportunity to publish in journals that created for him a European reputation. He became more famous in Germany because he was well known in France. Finally, Heine's position in France provided an identity and a role to play in international literature, for he assumed the task of cultural mediator. Paris enabled Heine to draw upon the conflicts within himself

as he described conflicts in France or Germany, and it gave him
ways to use his marginal status to great advantage: he would become the outsider upon whom insiders must rely for knowledge of
other insiders, the marginal contact who facilitated understanding
between otherwise uncomprehending rival insiders.

It was of course a task that precluded completion, but it gave
Heine a series of creative projects and a relatively satisfying way
to exploit his exile status. His literary projects and exile prominence depended to a great extent upon the specific context of July
Monarchy France. Although Heine obviously brought much German experience (and alienation) to France, his mature interests
were transfused with the concerns of the social, political, intellectual, and émigré communities that constituted Paris. Heine's life
and work evolved with the alternatives, the models, the subjects,
the opportunities, and the status that France provided.

Chapter 3

Marx in Paris: Exile
and the New Social Theory

When all the inner conditions are met, the *day of the German resurrection* will be heralded by the *crowing of the Gallic cock*.
Karl Marx, "A Contribution to the Critique
of Hegel's Philosophy of Right"

Karl Marx went to Paris at the age of twenty-five, in late October 1843, and lived there until the French government expelled him from the country in February 1845. His stay in Paris was thus much shorter than Heine's; nevertheless, the French influence played a significant formative role in his life and thought. Isaiah Berlin is not the only scholar to see the Parisian period as "the most decisive in [Marx's] life," bringing about his "final intellectual transformation" from Hegelianism to communism.[1]

Marx went to France partly to explore the French tradition of politics, economics, and revolution, which offered alternatives to the German philosophical tradition he had studied at home. Although his Parisian study demonstrated to him materialist inadequacies in the German tradition, it soon suggested weaknesses in the French intellectual tradition as well. Responding to French conditions and texts with the critical perspectives of his own philosophical and historical heritage, Marx opened a new analysis of political culture and material reality in France. At the same time, he turned the tools of French materialism upon German Hegelianism to produce extremely harsh criticism of the philosophical school from which he had come. Marx also seemed to draw from his French sojourn a new interest in Germany and the German proletariat; his entry into French society and his withdrawal from it both seemed to stimulate reassessments of the German situation.

120

In the interval, however, he devoted himself to extensive study of French history, economics, and socialism.

The Franco-German interaction in Marx's Parisian texts suggests the importance of the specifically Parisian component in those works. It suggests, too, that this "decisive" transition in his life and work evolved as Marx's creative response to exile—that Paris itself made a significant contribution to what came to be known as Marxism. His response to France was more abstract than that of Heine and most other exiles, but his abstractions drew on the conditions of French society as well as the books of French writers. Although he did not follow Heine's script for the role of literary exile, Marx, too, exploited his position between national cultures to develop a critical analysis of the theory and practice in both Germany and France. Marx's first months in exile therefore helped to stimulate some of the most imaginative, synthetic work that he ever produced.

Marx decided to go to France in 1843 because strict censorship made it impossible for him and his Young Hegelian allies to publish in Germany. His career in political journalism ended abruptly in March of that year when the Prussian government suspended publication of the newspaper, *Rheinische Zeitung*, that he had been editing in Cologne. This action followed upon the earlier suppression of the *Deutsche Jahrbücher*, a "Young Hegelian" journal that Arnold Ruge had been publishing in Dresden.[2] Marx already knew Ruge through mutual Hegelian friends, and now they came together with the shared frustration of censorship and a plan to expand the *Deutsche Jahrbücher* into an international publication that would stress Franco-German political and philosophical cooperation. The idea of such an intellectual alliance was not new (Heine, for one, had argued for it in *De l'Allemagne*), but the tightening restrictions on German publications made the cooperative idea more appealing and a Paris base almost essential for the critical work that the radical Hegelians wanted to continue. Although the collaborators also considered publishing in Zurich, Strasbourg, and Brussels, those alternatives all proved to be less practical for financial or political reasons. Hence, Ruge established himself in Paris during August 1843 and began arranging for publication of the new journal with funds he provided himself.[3]

Ruge held a typically romantic view of the French opportunities and milieu: "We are going to France, the threshold of a new world," he explained as he set off for Paris. "May it live up to our dreams! At the end of our journey we will find the vast valley of Paris, the

Karl Marx in 1836. From a lithograph of Trier students at the University of Bonn by D. Levy-Elkan. Internationaal Instituut voor Sociale Geschiedenis, Amsterdam.

cradle of the new Europe, the great laboratory where world history is formed and has its ever fresh source."[4] Marx approached Paris with a much more cautious assessment of the possibilities there, stressing the obstacles in Germany rather than the liberating prospects of France as justification for the move: "In Germany everything is suppressed by force, a veritable anarchy of the spirit, a reign of stupidity itself has come upon us and Zurich obeys orders from Berlin. It is becoming clearer every day that independent, thinking people must seek out a new centre. I am convinced that our plan would satisfy a real need and real needs must be satisfied in reality. I shall have no doubts once we begin in earnest."[5] Marx's decision to emigrate grew out of his practical desire to publish freely and to extend the philosophical and political work he had begun in Germany, rather than out of the sentimental enthusiasm for Paris expressed by Heine, Ruge, and other expatriates.

Marx at first moved into the building in which Ruge was living on the left bank (rue Vaneau), but this arrangement offered more togetherness than he and his wife, Jenny von Westphalen, needed or wanted. Eventually they settled at 38 rue Vaneau, where they lived until the expulsion order in 1845.[6] Marx apparently kept mostly to himself and his work during his early months in Paris; at least there is no evidence of social contact with French radicals until he attended a banquet for the socialist writers of *La Réforme* in March 1844.[7] The public relations work thus fell to Ruge, whose solicitations in Parisian socialist circles failed to produce a single contribution for what was to be called the *Deutsch-Französische Jahrbücher*. Meanwhile, Marx worked on the articles that were to appear in what turned out to be the only issue of the *Jahrbücher* ever published (February 1844).

Marx had explained his view of the new journal's purpose in letters he wrote to Ruge and Ludwig Feuerbach before he left Germany in the fall of 1843. He wanted the *Jahrbücher* to expose the mystifications by which dominant ideologies and political leaders maintained their power and to clarify the criticism of that ruling power. As he summarized the task in his letter to Ruge, demystification required *"ruthless criticism of the existing order, ruthless in that it will shrink neither from its own discoveries nor from conflict with powers that be."*[8] Radical criticism formed the negative aspect of the dialectical work that Marx expected to undertake in Paris. Along with this negation, however, he believed that the *Jahrbücher* could serve the positive, creative function of showing the world "why it is struggling" and how it might develop "new prin-

ciples from the existing principles of the world." These objectives
encouraged Marx to envision a major historical role for the Young
Hegelian writers converging on Paris and for the journal they
planned to publish: "We are therefore in a position to sum up the
credo of our journal in a *single word:* the self-clarification (critical
philosophy) of the struggles and wishes of the age. This is a task
for the world and for us. It can succeed only as the product of
united efforts."⁹ The clarification process would call for political
criticism as well as philosophy, and it would depend upon the
critical insights of French and Germans alike.

Marx especially stressed the cooperative goals of the project
when he wrote Feuerbach to request an article on Friedrich Schelling for the first issue. This appeal in fact differed significantly
from his earlier letter to Ruge in that Marx seemed to assure Feuerbach that international cooperation might well be *the* principal
characteristic of the new review: "You were one of the first writers
who expressed the need for a Franco-German scientific alliance,"
he told Feuerbach. "You will, therefore, assuredly be one of the
first to support an enterprise aimed at bringing such an alliance
into being. For German and French articles are to be published
promiscue in the *Jahrbücher.* The best Paris writers have agreed to
cooperate."¹⁰ If the Franco-German alliance alone would not entice
Feuerbach to contribute, Marx hoped that the freedom to say what
could not be published in Germany would attract his attention.

Criticism of Schelling provided one good example of what a
Paris-based journal could offer. The Prussian government had
made Schelling its official philosopher, Marx reminded Feuerbach,
and so attacks on Schelling became also attacks on the Prussian
regime. Moreover, since the French did not yet understand Schelling's true position, an exposé in Paris would serve useful political
and philosophical functions at home and abroad: "Just imagine
Schelling exposed in Paris, before the French literary world! His
vanity will not be able to restrain itself, this will wound the Prussian government to the quick, it will be an attack on Schelling's
sovereignty abroad, and a *vain* monarch sets much greater store
by his *sovereignty abroad* than at home."¹¹

Although these persuasive efforts did not bring a Feuerbach contribution to the new review, Marx's arguments for the value of the
Jahrbücher project—along with the outline of critical objectives he
sent to Ruge—indicate how much he expected from the cooperative, analytical journal he planned. Like many of his more ro-
mantically minded contemporaries, Marx arrived in France with

the idea that Paris offered access to the widest possible literary and political audience in Europe. In the end, though, the *Jahrbücher* project collapsed, partly because the French refused to contribute their share to the alliance-building program the German radicals had developed and partly because the German collaborators soon fell into disagreement among themselves.

Marx told the dream rather than the truth when he assured Feuerbach that the "best Paris writers" would be contributing to the *Jahrbücher;* Ruge's appeal to French socialists such as Louis Blanc, Pierre Leroux, Alphonse de Lamartine, Etienne Cabet, and Victor Considérant elicited little interest and no articles.[12] Apart from a general French reluctance to join a project organized by Germans, the French hesitation resulted in large part from intellectual suspicions about the consequences of the Young Hegelian hostility to religion. German criticism of Christianity reminded French radicals of Enlightenment-era atheism and materialism, doctrines that such writers as Louis Blanc perceived as the ideology of the bourgeois liberals who triumphed in the French Revolution and who continued to block the creation of a true democratic society. Blanc and others preferred to use a religious model when they wrote about the aims of the French radical party, whereas Marx and the radical Hegelians wanted to eliminate all religious justifications and referents from social criticism and action. "Like Feuerbach's critique of religion," Marx wrote to Ruge, "our whole aim can only be to translate religious and political questions into their self-conscious human form."[13] This emphasis differed enough from that of July Monarchy French radicals to preclude any significant cooperative theoretical work.

Blanc responded to the Ruge-Marx proposal for collaboration with an article in the socialist journal *La Revue Indépendante.* After acknowledging that a Franco-German alliance would be a good thing, he went on to assert that the Germans might well learn important lessons from French history and especially from the social history of the Enlightenment. The secular materialism of the eighteenth-century French philosophes, Blanc argued, produced individualist theories to justify bourgeois rule during and after the French Revolution. French democracy, on the other hand, grew out of a Rousseauistic legacy that opposed the materialistic (individualist) philosophe tradition and favored unity, liberty, and the fraternal principles of the Christian gospels. The revolution of 1789 brought France under the control of an atheistic liberal party that directed the nation away from the true democratic (Rousseauistic) system and established a new bourgeois order. Blanc warned the Hegelians that they were likely to contribute unwittingly to the same process in their own country unless they moved away from what he took to be the anachronistic, eighteenth-century philosophical stance of militant atheism.[14] Although he by no means rejected the idea of French and German cooperation, Blanc in effect suggested (somewhat arrogantly) that the Germans would gain more than the French from such cooperation and that the alliance would become possible only if the Germans abandoned their aggressive anti-Christian campaigns.[15]

The socialist newspaper *La Réforme* immediately endorsed Blanc's argument and recommended its principal points to the organizers of the *Deutsch-Französische Jahrbücher*. The French seemed unable to separate religious criticism from the discredited Enlightenment or to see the Hegelians as anything other than latter-day philosophes. Atheism meant liberalism to French socialists, and they wanted no part of it. "It is certain," *La Réforme* editorialized, "that through our internal struggles and through our terrible revolutions, reddened with our blood, we French have bought the right to teach foreigners everything about liberalism that is narrow, tempestuous, and oppressive. M. Louis Blanc has indicated exactly . . . the difference which exists between the liberal school and the democratic school. But this experience which has cost us so dearly . . . is one the Germans have not had, and the example of our misfortunes can be of use to them."[16]

Whatever the historical validity of these claims for French insight, this vaguely patronizing, anti-Hegelian attitude became influential enough in Paris to keep all would-be French contributors out of the *Jahrbücher*. The collaborative project that Marx and Ruge had planned therefore evolved into another journal of the German émigré community; as such, its publication failed to achieve the international critical impact that the editors originally anticipated for it. Indeed, except for one sympathetic review in *La Revue Indépendante*, the French press ignored the *Jahrbücher*, and its appearance went virtually unnoticed in the French intellectual community.[17]

The Germans did not take much note either. Heinrich Börnstein published a review article in *Vorwärts*, which condemned the *Jahrbücher* for poor quality (Heine's poems received special criticism on this score) and for simple "negation of everything that exists," but most émigrés remained unaware of the new journal.[18] Börnstein's review showed that the *Jahrbücher* aroused little support among intellectuals who did know about it, and its difficult, the-oretical essays effectively precluded much response from the German workers in Paris. Meanwhile, the Prussian government banned the journal and confiscated hundreds of copies at the border when the editors tried to send the first issue into Germany. One of the German backers of the project, Julius Froebel, soon withdrew his financial support. As a result Marx and Ruge found themselves without public interest, French contributors, sympathetic reviews, financial backers, or an audience in Germany. All of these obstacles contributed to the demise of the *Jahrbücher* project; it fell apart completely when the editors themselves began to disagree about politics, philosophy, and friends.[19] Marx and Ruge stopped speaking to each other by summer, and the journal that Marx hoped would clarify the "struggles and wishes of the age" disappeared after a single obscure issue in February 1844.

The defunct project was nevertheless an important event in Marx's life: it brought him to Paris; it encouraged his analysis of the Hegelian tradition; and it initiated his study of the French political alternatives to German philosophical criticism. The letters and articles ("On the Jewish Question" and "A Contribution to the Critique of Hegel's Philosophy of Right") that he published in the *Jahrbücher* indicated ways in which his thought was evolving toward political and economic perceptions of historical change and ways in which France provided a reference point in the development of those perceptions. The French contrast to German thought and society had attracted radical Hegelians to France in the first place, and Marx, like many other radicals, now began a careful investigation of the French tradition as he moved from the *Jahrbücher* to other critical projects.

Most Young Hegelians accepted the common dichotomy that portrayed France as the nation of politics and Germany as the nation of philosophy. Thus, when the left Hegelians looked for revolutionary precedents, they turned to the French Revolution to find philosophical allies and Jacobin political theory.[20] It was this revolutionary history and theory that established France as *the* political center of Europe. Marx himself typified the radical Hegelian outlook on these matters, inasmuch as he shared the strong interest in the French Revolution and accepted the French (political)–German (philosophical) dichotomy. The distinction appeared clearly in the articles he wrote for the *Jahrbücher*. In his essay "On the Jewish Question," for example, Marx argued that Germans always approached this issue as a theological question, whereas in France, "the *constitutional* state," the same issue became politicized and emerged as "a question of the *incompleteness of political emancipation*."[21] This emphasis on the political aspect of French life had of course formed a major theme in Heine's comparative study *De l'Allemagne*, but other writers had followed his work with books that developed the theme in more detail and brought French social thought into the debates of the Young Hegelians. The most influential of the new interpreters of France were August Cieszkowski, Moses Hess, and Lorenz von Stein.

Significantly, these writers all lived in Paris during the 1830s, and they all stressed French social activism in books that encouraged German Hegelians to move from philosophical criticism toward economic and political criticism. Although Cieszkowski was the only one to publish before he went to France, his *Prolegomena to Historiosophy* (1838) introduced the notion of *praxis* (social acts) to Hegelian circles and drew heavily on French historical theory and social utopianism, especially that of Fourier.[22] Cieszkowski's work was followed by Moses Hess's *Europäische Triarchie* (1840). Hess, who first lived in Paris in the early 1830s, emphasized the historical role of French socialism as a social counterpart to German philosophy and called attention to the importance of economic forces in social development.[23] Finally, Stein's *Socialism and Communism in Contemporary France* (1842) provided a detailed account of recent socialist thought and again stressed France's role as the active social initiator in European life. According to Stein, all study of modern social and political questions would have to begin there. "The history of France is the best justification for the emergence of the science of society," he explained in a passage that summarized the views of most German radicals in Paris. "Therefore, historical research dealing with society will first turn towards France and her revolutions.... Everything that has been said and thought during the last half-century with reference to the great questions of our future may be found there in embryonic form."[24]

Stein's book made it clear that recent French contributions to "the great questions" showed up most prominently in the development of socialism, a development that (along with the revolutionary tradition) offered further justification for the radical German interest in France. The emerging socialist movement attracted the attention of almost everyone who wrote about France, so that Hegelians who first turned to France for its revolutionary political tradition soon came upon the extraordinary profusion of French socialist theory and criticism that appeared throughout the

1830s and 1840s. Hence, the newly politicized Hegelians added the work of French socialist writers to their reading on the revolution and thereby discovered new ways to interpret and understand the revolutionary history they studied.[25] If French socialism seemed utopian, it nonetheless addressed social questions that German philosophy had overlooked, and it pointed the Hegelians in new directions. Cieszkowski may have expressed the Hegelian starting point for this new critical project best when he summarized the achievement and failure of Fourier: "One can say that Fourier is the greatest but also the last utopian. In general, the main defect of utopia is not to unfold with reality but *to want to step into* reality. It can never do this as long as it is utopia, and thus an unbridgeable gap arises between utopia and reality."[26] Other Hegelians, taking up the problems Cieszkowski raised in his *Prolegomena*, were soon working through the history of revolution and socialism in France to find an unfolding reality rather than utopias or philosophical abstractions, and nobody joined the search more diligently than Marx.

Once settled in Paris, Marx undertook some of the most intense historical and economic study of his life. He began with an investigation of the French Revolution and then went on to the classical French and English economists, working virtually non-stop for days at a time. Arnold Ruge's famous description of Marx's work habits in Paris suggests that the search for non-Hegelian historical explanations helped to generate extraordinary intellectual energy:

> He reads very much; he works with uncommon intensity, and has a critical talent, that sometimes degenerates into arrogant dialectics; but he finishes nothing, he breaks everything off and always plunges himself again into an endless sea of books .... he works himself sick and does not go to bed for three, even four nights in a row. Marx wants to write a history of the Convention and has gathered the material for it and worked out some very fruitful points of view. He has put aside the critique of Hegel's philosophy of law.[27]

The influence of this reading began to appear in the texts Marx was writing in Paris: the *Economic and Philosophical Manuscripts*, *The Holy Family*, and the various journal articles. Indeed, Ruge's account and the number of manuscripts Marx produced during 1844 seem to indicate that his Parisian life consisted almost entirely of reading and writing.

Actually, there was more to it than that; Marx's personal contact with the Parisian milieu may have been as important as the books he read in shaping his new views. In addition to Heine, he came to know the writers at *Vorwärts* (Carl Bernays, Heinrich Börnstein, Georg Weber) who took that journal steadily to the left during the summer and fall of 1844. He participated in discussions at the *Vorwärts* office and apparently influenced what the editors wrote and the articles they chose to publish. At the same time, he met Mikhail Bakunin, Cieszkowski (whom he found boring), and French socialists such as Blanc and Pierre-Joseph Proudhon.[28]

The most important new friend, however, was Friedrich Engels. Marx and Engels met in late August (1844) at a café in the Palais-Royal and began a conversation on history and economics that lasted (with breaks) about ten days. Their close agreement on the proper approach to these matters initiated the collaboration that proved to be the most enduring personal consequence of Marx's time in Paris.[29] Engels first earned Marx's respect with a critique of political economy, which appeared in the *Jahrbücher*, but their Paris meetings expanded a budding intellectual alliance into the closest friendship of Marx's life.

Meanwhile, Marx found even more in Paris than new books and new friends: he discovered there the vital activity of anonymous French people. Although he scarcely resembled the typical German visitor in search of Parisian pleasures, Marx clearly noted the city's sensual dimension and judged it superior to the interminable critical reflections of German philosophers. He argued, for example, in one attack on the naive otherworldliness of the German critic Szeliga, that Parisian dance halls were more real than all of the "categories" ever described in the Hegelian *Allgemeine Literatur-Zeitung*. Hegelians in Berlin could not imagine the men and women who danced in Paris without the slightest reference to the abstractions of German philosophy; their pleasures were specific and immediate, completely alien to the self-absorbed thinkers across the Rhine: "The reverend parson [Szeliga] speaks . . . neither of the *can-can* nor of the *polka*, "Marx wrote from Paris," but of *dancing* in general, of the *category* Dancing, which is not performed anywhere except in his Critical cranium. Let him see a dance at the Chaumière in Paris, and his Christian-German soul would be outraged by the boldness, the frankness, the graceful petulance and the music of that most sensual movement."[30] Of course the poor German critic would have no way of understanding the "frank human sensuality" of these French dancers because his "categories" would not encompass that reality. Indeed, if a German theorist such as

Herr Szeliga actually encountered the people at a Parisian dance, he would no doubt try to prove why "of necessity [they] cannot and must not be frankly sensual human beings!!"[31]

This sensual, material element of Parisian life must surely have caught Marx's eye when he was not reading books at home in the rue Vaneau—even if he did not become one of the dancers at the Chaumière (it strains the historical imagination to think of the bookish Marx doing the polka in a Parisian dance hall). True, he did not write about this side of French life in the way he wrote about French politics or economics, yet, as his wife seemed to understand, this other Paris also formed part of Marx's life in France.

Jenny Marx revealed her perspective on this other Paris when she described her concern about leaving Marx alone there while she visited Germany after the birth of their first child in the summer of 1844. "And then in the background are dark feelings of anxiety and fear," she wrote, "the real menace of unfaithfulness, the seductions and attractions of a capital city—all those powers and forces whose effect on me is more powerful than anything else."[32] She had seen enough of Parisian life to convince herself that her husband was living in a very special environment, a sensual environment that Marx too perceived as different from that of Germany. It is more difficult to evaluate the "seductions and attractions" of material Paris in Marx's thought than to trace the influence of French authors, and many scholars have understandably emphasized Marx's sleepless nights with books as the definitive aspect of his French experience. It should be stressed, however, that his contact with Parisian people—the crowds, the workers, the dancers—also affected him and that his Parisian texts grew out of his response to the "frankly sensual" aspect of Parisian life as well as from the synthesis of German philosophy, French socialism, and English economics. It therefore seems important to consider Marx's reaction to France as part intellectual, part social, though the two components in fact overlapped in almost all the texts he wrote there.

History, Politics, and Political Economy

Marx's intellectual response to France turned primarily on issues of history and economics. His study of French history and French economics led him toward materialism, a new analysis of revolution, and a critical view of classical economic theory—the modern history of all of which began in the eighteenth century. That century represented for Marx the beginning of critical social theory insofar as the Enlightenment developed a materialist outlook that speculative German philosophy never achieved. This Enlightenment philosophy, which Marx traced to Locke and Descartes, first served the needs of the new bourgeois interests, but its long-term implications pointed toward socialism. Locke held more importance than Descartes in Marx's history of materialism because Locke provided theory for social science, whereas Cartesian physics became the source of modern natural science. The Lockean tradition thus served as the point of departure for the earliest Marxist interpretation of the Enlightenment.

As Marx explained it, French philosophers adopted Locke because his antimetaphysical viewpoint coincided perfectly with the material interests of eighteenth-century France. Traditional religion and philosophy simply failed to accommodate "the practical nature of French life" after the seventeenth century. "This life," Marx wrote in *The Holy Family*, "was turned to the immediate present, to wordly enjoyment and worldly interests, to the *earthly* world. Its anti-theological, anti-metaphysical, materialistic practice demanded corresponding anti-theological, anti-metaphysical, materialistic theories."[33] Lockean empiricism therefore justified the new materialism and encouraged the (bourgeois) Enlightenment intellectual transition that Marx found so important for the history of his own critical work. By bringing analysis and debate to the level of the "earthly world," French materialism opened the way to a human (as opposed to metaphysical) understanding of knowledge and society.

Marx believed that the epistemology of Locke, Condillac, and Helvétius, with its emphasis on the material and sensory origin of all knowledge, made possible a revolutionary and socialist conception of historical development. As he began to define his own notions of socialism during the fall of 1844, Marx explicitly situated communism in the tradition of eighteenth-century empiricism and materialism.

There is no need for any great penetration to see from the teaching of materialism on the original goodness and equal intellectual endowment of men, the omnipotence of experience, habit and education, and the influence of environment on man, the great significance of industry, the justification of enjoyment, etc., how necessarily materialism is connected with communism and socialism. If man draws all his knowledge, sensation, etc., from the world of the senses and the experience gained in it, then what has to be done is to arrange the empirical world in such a way that man experiences and becomes accustomed to what is truly human in it and that he becomes aware of himself as man. If correctly understood interest is the principle of all morality, man's private interest must be made to coincide with the interest of humanity.[34]

A material understanding of human conditions must therefore precede all efforts to make those conditions more human.

After Enlightenment writers had established the importance of materialism in European philosophy and social theory, the revolutionaries in France (1789–94) attempted to implement those materialist principles, thereby providing the great historical example of modern revolutionary practice. The study of that revolution became the starting point for Marx's analysis of revolution, and it convinced him that political revolutions were insufficient for creating a world in which "private interest" might coincide with "the interest of humanity." Marx returned to this theme whenever he discussed the French Revolution in his Parisian texts—notably in the essays "On the Jewish Question" and "Critical Notes on the Article 'The King of Prussia and Social Reform,' " and in the book *The Holy Family*.[35] The reiterated point in all these discussions was that a political revolution and the state it creates cannot overcome the social contradictions that produce poverty, class distinctions, and religion and preclude the equality that political revolutionaries proclaim as their objective.

In order to stress the limitations of political revolution, Marx pointed to the fact that even highly developed political states had found no way to deal with pauperism, a pervasive social condition that showed how much structural inequality remained in nations ostensibly committed to political equality. England had clearly failed to eliminate the problem, and even the French Revolutionary Convention, which "represented the *maximum of political energy, political power* and *political understanding,*" found itself utterly incapable of transforming beggars and paupers into equal members of French society.[36] Marx concluded that political leaders (and the states they controlled) could not resolve social problems such as rampant pauperism because they did not recognize the non-political aspects of their historical situation: "The more powerful a state and hence the *more political* a nation, the less inclined it is to explain the *general* principle governing *social* ills and to seek out their causes by looking at the *principle of the* state, i.e. at the *actual organization of society* of which the state is the active, self-conscious and official expression. *Political* understanding is just *political* understanding because its thought does not transcend the limits of politics. The sharper and livelier it is, the more incapable it is of comprehending social problems."[37] Therefore, the modern political state inevitably failed to achieve real political equality because it was itself an outgrowth of a social system whose dominant characteristic, unequal distribution of wealth, depended on inequality. Hence, among the many historical lessons of the French Revolution, Marx found decisive evidence for the inadequacy of political revolutions and for the enduring inequalities within political states.

To be sure, he said, the French Revolution had made major contributions to the process of political emancipation—what Marx called "the last form of human emancipation *within* the prevailing scheme of things"[38]—yet this political emancipation managed only to elevate the behavior of egotistical, self-interested man to the status of universal rights. The "Rights of Man," in short, offered theoretical justification for an alienated, individualistic way of life that political will alone would never overcome, and revolutionary leaders largely succeeded in making bourgeois man the universal (natural) man. "Therefore," Marx wrote, "not one of the so-called rights of man goes beyond egotistic man, man as a member of civil society, namely an individual withdrawn into himself, his private interest and his private desires and separated from the community. In the rights of man it is not man who appears as a species-being; on the contrary, species-life itself, society, appears as a framework extraneous to the individuals, as a limitation of their original independence."[39]

The "rights" that generally misconstrued man's relation to society also misconstrued the nature of freedom in all its particulars. The political revolution did not free people *from* property or religion or the egoism of trade. Instead it gave them "freedom of property" and "freedom of religion" and "freedom to engage in trade," so that activities embodying man's alienation from the social community (species-being) received their fullest sanction in the program of the political revolution.[40]

These theoretical flaws, though, formed only one of many shortcomings in the French Revolution, for the radical leaders failed to understand important practical conflicts in their program as well.

The Jacobins, for example, did not see the contradiction in their effort to rally France to a vast collective campaign of national unity while asserting "universal" principles of radical egoism. Leaders such as Robespierre and St. Just soon fell from power because they tried to build an ancient, democratic republic in a modern bourgeois society and to justify collective sacrifice for that republic with the individualistic "Rights of Man." This highly unstable situation did not last for long, however, because their successors quickly abandoned the part of the Jacobin program which did not fit a modern society (the notion of communal sacrifice, an ancient idea for an ancient society), and post-Thermidorian France entered the era of unabashed bourgeois rule.[41] The "Rights of Man," as the ideological justification for that rule, achieved the status of universal principles, thus obscuring the egotistical base upon which they rested.

The bourgeois victory did receive major challenges from Napoleon, whose imperial war policies frequently ignored the material interests of the bourgeoisie, and from the restored Bourbons, whose aristocratic sympathies impeded bourgeois access to political power. But Marx passed over these challenges quickly on his way to an examination of 1830 and the revolution that finally consolidated the social order for which the bourgeoisie had been working since 1789.[42] In the process, the long-developing bourgeois victory also produced the class and many of the ideas by which the political revolution would eventually give way to social revolution. The earliest representatives of this emerging revolutionary class and its ideas—which Marx called communism—were Parisian radicals such as Jean Leclerc, Jacques Roux, and especially Gracchus Babeuf. Though suppressed by bourgeois political leaders in the 1790s, these early radicals managed to create a nascent communism, which Marx called "the *idea* of the *new world order*"; the idea reappeared in France after 1830 in the person of Babeuf's aging friend Filippo Buonarroti. In the course of his Parisian sojourn Marx began to expect that a future communist revolution would bring about the human emancipation that political revolution alone could not achieve.[43] Thus, although the political revolution seemed almost complete in France after 1830, Marx decided that the more significant social revolution had scarcely begun.

The political revolution did not lead to true emancipation because it represented a particular class rather than universal human interests. It merely broke civil society into its parts without "revolutionizing" those parts, and then it defined "man" as an "egotistic individual" and an "abstract citizen."[44] The social revolution, on the other hand, would revolutionize all components of society, criticize rather than sanctify the alienating characteristics of bourgeois society, and transform the relationship between real people (not abstract citizens) and the community from which (as egotistic individuals) they had become separated.

> A social revolution possesses a *total* point of view because...it represents a protest by man against a dehumanized life, because it proceeds from the point of view of the *particular, real individual,* because the *community* against whose separation from himself the individual is reacting, is the *true* community of man, *human* nature. In contrast, the *political soul* of revolution consists in the tendency of the classes with no political power to put an end to their *isolation from the state* and from power...In accordance with the *limited* and *contradictory* nature of the political soul a revolution inspired by it organizes a dominant group within society at the cost of society.[45]

The French Revolution, therefore, failed to emancipate the French people because it altered the relationship between the bourgeois class and political power without transforming the relationship between individuals and society; in fact, it diminished that social relationship by encouraging the alienation and separation that were embodied in bourgeois practice and ideology.

Whatever the exact truth of this argument, Marx's analysis of the political revolution provided an answer for the question that haunted almost every radical, liberal, and conservative of his generation: Why had the French Revolution failed to establish the equality that its radical leaders had expected it to produce? Marx concluded that the political revolutionaries were simply unwilling to attack the social causes of inequality and alienation and thus unable to achieve true equality or freedom.

Despite these limitations, Marx never doubted the importance of the French Revolution; he saw that it carried extremely significant social consequences. It opened the way to further expansion of bourgeois trade and the bourgeois economic system, but at the same time it produced the first examples of the social revolutionary program that would one day transform societies as well as states. Of course, the bourgeois revolution had eliminated the primitive "communists" who advocated such social revolution but not before these radicals had laid the path for a subsequent revolutionary step in the historical movement toward human emancipation.

Marx described what this future social revolutionary process would entail in one of his articles for the *Deutsch-Französische Jahrbücher:* "Only when real, individual man resumes the abstract citizen into himself and as an individual man has become a *species being* in his empirical life, his individual work and his individual relationship, only when man has recognized and organized his *forces propres* as *social* forces so that social force is no longer separated from him in the form of *political* force, only then will human emancipation be completed."[46] The French Revolution, then, convinced Marx that the struggle for emancipation would have to move from politics to other social activities and especially to economics. Accordingly, he began to study economics in Paris—only to discover that classical political economy was as inadequate for understanding economics as political theory was for understanding (or completing) revolutions.

Throughout the spring and summer of 1844, Marx devoted himself to a careful reading of the most prominent classical economists. His notes in the *Economic and Philosophical Manuscripts* (written between April and August) refer repeatedly to Adam Smith, David Ricardo, Jean-Baptiste Say, and Simond de Sismondi, and the text itself includes long paragraphs quoted verbatim from these economists. In addition, he was reading works by Eugène Buret, Constantin Pecqueur, and the German Wilhelm Schulz, all of whom stressed the social consequences of the real-world activity of modern industrial capitalism.[47] Marx accepted a number of the classical economists' descriptions of how capitalism functioned. He took from Smith, for example, the assumptions that workers were a commodity, that the normal wage would always be the lowest possible wage with which the worker could survive, and that all capital and all value came from labor.[48] Capitalist prosperity was therefore built upon worker misery, a state of affairs that classical economists took to be the natural and universal operation of economic relationships: "It goes without saying that political economy regards the *proletarian,* i.e. he who lives without capital and ground rent from labour alone, and from one-sided abstract labour at that, as nothing more than a *worker.* It can therefore advance the thesis that, like a horse, he must receive enough to enable him to work. It does not consider him, during the time he is not working, as a human being. It leaves this to criminal law, doctors, religion, statistical tables, politics and the beadle."[49] Political economy thus stripped workers of their humanity; in the guise of a "science", it justified material misery as the inevitable consequence of the modern economic system. Marx, for his part, accepted such assumptions as valid for capitalism, but denied that they must apply to all systems of production.[50]

While affirming the necessity of worker misery, classical economists tended to ignore or to endorse the extraordinary alienation of labor that accompanied the expansion of capitalist production. Marx discussed this problem at length in his Paris *Manuscripts*, charging that the economists refused to describe the alienating process which modern capitalism created and upon which it depended. "Political economy," he complained, *"conceals the estrangement in the nature of labour by ignoring the direct relationship between the worker* (labour) *and production."*[51] Specifically, the economists did not investigate the way in which the worker became alienated from the product of his labor. Capitalists took from him the objects he produced, so that the products of his work became wholly external to him; indeed, they became a power (in the form of capital) that was actually used against him. The more labor a worker put into objects, the poorer he became, for an ever increasing part of himself was expropriated by the capitalist: "The *devaluation* of the human world grows in direct proportion to the *increase in value* of the world of things."[52]

The daily operation of this process carried an enormous cost for workers because it meant that their productive activity met the needs of the capitalist rather than their own needs. Productive activity itself and the results of that activity increasingly alienated laborers from their own work, from one another, and from themselves, a severely debilitating social reality that classical economists chose not to explain or criticize. Here was a mental and physical analogue to the wage misery that economists also passed over as a "natural" function of the modern economic system. The consequences of alienated labor were as disastrous as low wages for the worker who "does not confirm himself in his work, but denies himself, feels miserable and not happy, does not develop free mental and physical energy, but mortifies his flesh and ruins his mind."[53] Instead of studying this process of estrangement, however, the classical economists simply raised to the status of "universal standard" what was in fact the *"worst possible state of privation* which life (existence) can know."[54]

Marx concluded that political economy often served as little more than an apology for capitalism; he could think of no other way to account for a "science" that took misery, alienation, and private property to be the natural, unquestioned presuppositions of its analysis. Its practitioners steadfastly refused to recognize the

historical particularity of capitalism or to open their founding assumptions to criticism (as the Young Hegelians demanded in their
critical projects). Lacking this critical rigor, the classical economists mistakenly described the laws of an alienating economic
system as the "true" condition of human economic experience in
the same way that theologians described man's alienation from
himself (God) as the "true" basis of meaning and order in the
world.[55]

There was in fact for Marx a remarkable similarity between the
self-denial preached by theologians and the self-denial preached
by economists, and in both cases the needs of people lost out. Thus,
when Marx launched his attack on the French and English economists, he did so with the language, imagery, and fervor of a left
Hegelian attack on Christian theologians:

> Political economy, this science of *wealth*, is therefore at the same time
> the science of denial, of starvation, of saving, and it actually goes so
> far as to *save* man the *need* for fresh *air* or physical *exercise*. This
> science of the marvels of industry is at the same time the science of
> *ascetism*, and its true ideal is the *ascetic* but *rapacious* skinflint and the
> *ascetic* but *productive* slave ... Self-denial, the denial of life and of all
> human needs, is its principal doctrine. The less you eat, drink, buy
> books, go to the theatre, go dancing, go drinking, think, love, theorize,
> sing, paint, fence, etc., the more you *save* and the greater will become
> that treasure which neither moths nor maggots can consume—your
> *capital*. The less you *are*, the less you give expression to your life, the
> more you *have*, the greater is your *alienated* life and the more you
> store up of your estranged life. Everything which the political econ-
> omist takes from you in terms of life and humanity, he restores to you
> in the form of *money* and *wealth*, and everything which you are unable
> to do, your money can do for you.[56]

One hears in this attack the echoes of that antitheological campaign
which so dominated German radical discussion during Marx's
youth and formed the critical tradition that he brought to his reading of classical political economy. While German theologians had
workers saving for the eternal reward of heaven, the French and
English economists had them saving for the earthly reward of capital, neither of which left workers with anything in the historical
world they actually inhabited.

Marx decided that the alienation as well as the justification for
it were a consequence of historical forces rather than universal
laws. Drawing upon Hegelian theories of dialectical change and

alienation, Marx approached his study of revolution and economics with German philosophical and historical perspectives that differed from those of most French and English writers and that helped him to recognize the mutability of what other theorists took to be universals.[57] Meanwhile, he was also living in the urban culture of mid-nineteenth-century Paris, a material setting that encouraged him to investigate the historical inadequacies of the economists, the philosophical errors of the Hegelians, and the revolutionary mistakes of the Jacobins. Whatever these traditions might claim in the realm of theory or practice, Marx could see that they had not overcome the alienation of Parisian crowds; they had not led to a community where people might fulfill their needs as species-beings. Indeed, these traditions tended to declare the problem insoluble or to ignore the situation altogether or to seek political answers for a social condition.

Of course, Marx did not discover the theoretical and practical limitations of these traditions all at once. He moved from book to book in search of explanations for a social condition he could see (misery, alienation) and of proposals for changing it (social revolution in history). When the books failed to explain the reality or to offer a comprehensive perspective for transforming it, Marx responded to both the books and the social reality with an analysis of his own. That analysis, "Marxism," began to appear in the texts he wrote during his fifteen productive months in Paris.

People and Animals: Historicizing Materialism

Marx's Paris writings grew out of his contact with the life of the city as well as his reading and study of new books. In its social aspect, his Parisian period consisted mainly of meetings with radical intellectuals and of contacts with French and German workers. Marx did not share Heine's interest in salon life or his friendships among the Parisian literary elite. He was looking for theoretical insights and personal contacts that the establishment could never provide, and so Marx took his search into the milieu of the Parisian proletariat. He did meet French and émigré intellectuals as well, but these acquaintances too were persons who wrote about and represented the working class. The radical intellectual community in Paris was small enough to provide Marx a means of meeting many influential figures of the era, including Leroux, Blanc, Proudhon, and Bakunin, in addition to the German radicals associated with the *Jahrbücher* and *Vorwärts*.[58] Among non-German intellectuals in France, however, only Proudhon and Bakunin had much influence on his life or thought, and even that was eventually negative; they represented the kind of radicalism that Marx rejected.

Marx and Proudhon had direct personal contact only between October 1844 and early February 1845. Neither man left a record of how they met, how often they talked, or what they discussed, though Marx claimed to have instructed Proudhon on the subject of Hegelian philosophy.[59] Some scholars have argued that Proudhon was more important for Marx in this period than Marx was for Proudhon, but each seems to have drawn on the other to work out new perspectives on history and economics. Analysts of the elusive influence problem suggest that Marx's Hegelian lessons may have affected Proudhon more than he explicitly acknowledged (he never mentioned Marx in his correspondence or notebooks during this period). Scholars who argue for Marx's influence point to a letter of October 1844 in which Proudhon stressed the necessity of looking for objective laws in social and economic relations rather than accepting the subjectivity of philosophers and legislators.[60] Marx was only one of several "Hegelians" whom Proudhon knew, however, and the influence of Karl Grün and Bakunin may have been more significant in shaping the dialectical notions that ultimately appeared in Proudhon's book *The Philosophy of Poverty* (1846).

It seems somewhat more apparent that Marx drew upon Proudhon to a considerable extent during the months they knew each other. There is no better evidence for this interaction than *The Holy Family*, a work Marx was writing during this period and a work that uses Proudhon as ammunition in an all-out attack against the German Hegelians (see the following section of this chapter). The importance of Proudhon, explained Marx, lay in his willingness to examine critically a phenomenon that traditional political economy took for granted: "Proudhon makes a critical investigation— the first resolute, ruthless and at the same time scientific investigation—of the basis of political economy, *private property*. This is the great scientific advance he made, an advance which revolutionises political economy and for the first time makes a real science of political economy possible."[61] This demystification of private property (along with his antireligious views) made Proudhon the most important French socialist for Marx and established the intellectual context for a personal relationship between the two men in Paris.

At the same time, though, Marx began to express the reservations about Proudhon that led to a complete break two years later: for Marx, Proudhon's critique of property did not move far enough beyond the assumptions of political economy or beyond a reformist attitude that failed to understand the nature of total revolution. He called Proudhon's work a "criticism of *political economy* from the standpoint of political economy" and predicted that it would be surpassed by a more complete critique (such as his own).[62] The definitive attack came in Marx's anti-Proudhon work, *The Poverty of Philosophy* (1847), but critical comments in the Paris *Manuscripts* set the tone for the later assault. Marx noted, for example, that Proudhon's demand for wage equality "would merely transform the relation of the present-day worker to his work into the relationship of all men to work. Society would then be conceived as an abstract capitalist."[63] Such criticisms contributed to the later characterization of Proudhon as an apologist for the petty bourgeoisie; hoping to make his own class interests into a general social system, Proudhon was simply unable to break with capitalism in ways that a communist revolution would require (see the final section of this chapter).[64] Marx chose not to make the anti-Proudhon case in public, however, until after he had worked out his own socialist position in 1845–46. Meanwhile, the Proudhon he knew in Paris clearly helped to stimulate the critical evaluation of political economy which was ultimately turned on Proudhon himself.

Marx's other links with intellectuals in Paris consisted primarily of contact with German and Russian émigrés. The most important members of this group were those who worked with him on the German publications, notably Ruge, Heine, Engels, Hess, and George Herwegh. Except for Engels, none of these friendships lasted much beyond the French years or had much influence on the evolution of Marx's social theory (though one might include Hess in a list of influences on Marx's early study of economics and money).[65] The German expatriate writers seemed to affect Marx less than his reading in economics or French history or French socialism because they came from the tradition he already knew best. As for the Russians, he came to know mostly aristocratic émigrés such as the radical Mikhail Bakunin.

Marx's friendship with Bakunin, like his contact with Proudhon, later culminated in a significant political and personal dispute. The break with Bakunin did not come until the early 1870s, however, and the Parisian contacts seem to have been amicable enough. Bakunin, who originally knew Ruge in Dresden, moved to Paris around the time of the Hegelian migration and entered enthusiastically into the émigré community he found there. Although Ruge soon tired of his dilettantism, financial requests, and extreme radicalism, these qualities by no means precluded relationships between Bakunin and other radicals in Paris. He became especially close to Proudhon, with whom he shared a vaguely anarchist tendency that differed significantly from the more "scientific" socialist views of Marx. Bakunin and Marx nevertheless moved in the same circles—from Ruge to *Vorwärts* to Proudhon—and met somewhat regularly during 1844, the year they both lived in France.[66]

Bakunin wrote his account of that period after he had broken with Marx on issues of organization and theory in the First International, but he remembered their Paris encounters as congenial and frequent despite (or perhaps because of) a certain superficiality.

> At that time I understood nothing of political economy, and my socialism was purely instinctive. He [Marx], though he was younger than I, was already an atheist, an instructed materialist, and a conscious socialist. . . . We met fairly often because I very much admired him for his knowledge and for his passionate and earnest devotion to the cause of the proletariat, although it always had in it an admixture of personal vanity; and I eagerly sought his conversation, which was instructive and witty so long as it was not inspired by petty spite—which, unfortunately, happened very often. But there was never real intimacy between us. Our temperaments did not allow it. He called me a sentimental idealist; and he was right. I called him morose, vain, and treacherous; and I too was right.[67]

Though Marx left no report of his Parisian friendship with Bakunin, this description probably offers a clear view of what happened between them. While Bakunin may have taken some insights from Marx, it seems unlikely that Marx learned much from Bakunin. The Russian connection, then, like the contact with other intellectuals in Paris, provided Marx with new acquaintances rather than influential new ideas. His Paris texts do not carry many references to the writers he met there, except for Proudhon and Engels, and one senses that the Parisian intellectual community never became especially interesting or important to him.

The Paris of anonymous workers and émigré artisans attracted Marx's attention as much as the intellectual community and stimulated his analytic efforts as much as the books on history and economics. France had not achieved the level of industrial or urban development which characterized England in the 1840s, but the economic activity and urban density of Paris exceeded that of German cities in these years. Hence, Marx found a social class structure that was defined more clearly in France than in the developing social classes of the smaller German towns. The experience of revolution and political conflict had given French social classes a stronger sense of their relationship to one another and a vocabulary with which to describe their roles and objectives in the social order.[68] Though Marx had begun reading socialist texts (for example, Fourier and Saint-Simon) before he went to France,[69] he did not observe socialist worker meetings until he settled in Paris. This material encounter with the Parisian proletariat coincided so closely with Marx's transition from Hegelian theory to communism that it seems entirely plausible to argue (as many scholars have) that contact with the Parisian working class helped to bring about changes in Marx's thought.[70] It was not a simple conversion; rather, Parisian social life offered an experience to which Marx brought Hegelian theoretical insights, which were in turn transformed by the experience of meeting an urban proletariat. The social text of Paris, in other words, significantly extended his understanding of other texts that he had read before he went to France.

Marx apparently went to a number of working-class gatherings in Paris. He observed both French groups and the reunions of German émigré artisans, especially the League of the Just.[71] Though he never actually joined any organizations, the meetings he attended must have impressed him. He began praising the German proletariat ("On the Jewish Question," "Critique of Hegel's Philosophy of Right," "Critical Notes on 'The King of Prussia'"), and his explicit references to the French proletariat were extremely favorable, not to say idealized. A well-known passage in the *Manuscripts* summarizes his opinion of Parisian workers and suggests as well as anything else how Marx liked to pass his evenings when he put aside the books:

> When communist *workmen* gather together, their immediate aim is instruction, propaganda, etc. But at the same time they acquire a new need—the need for society—and what appears as a means has become an end. This practical development can be most strikingly observed in the gatherings of French socialist workers. Smoking, eating, and drinking etc., are no longer means of creating links between people. Company, association, conversation, which in its turn has society as its goal, is enough for them. The brotherhood of man is not a hollow

phrase, it is a reality, and the nobility of man shines forth upon us from their work-worn faces.[72]

Marx was not often sentimental, but those workers in Paris clearly held more than an abstract interest for him. He reported the same exceptional sensation in a letter to Ludwig Feuerbach: "You would have to attend one of the meetings of the French workers to appreciate the pure freshness, the nobility which burst forth from these toil-worn men."[73] The people whom Marx was beginning to view as the universal class were also beginning to exhibit for him an appearance commensurate with their historical role.

Another aspect of the working-class community, which Marx by no means ignored, was the degradation and misery that often struck visitors and residents alike in the crowded, lower-class *quartiers* of the city. This was the "physiological" character of Parisian life to which the Polish writer Karol Frankowski devoted his account of the city (1840) and to which he referred in calling the workers a half-animal, half-human "leprous caste" that lurked in the narrow, stinking streets of the faubourgs Saint-Antoine and Saint-Marceau.[74] The same images appeared commonly in popular French literature of the period, encouraging a fearful perception of the working class among most of the Parisian bourgeoisie. Indeed, bourgeois public opinion tended to equate the laboring classes with the dangerous classes and to view poor people as a biologically distinct species living like precivilized savages amid the otherwise modern society of July Monarchy Paris.[75]

The memoirs and novels of nineteenth-century French writers, including well-known works by Balzac, Hugo, and Eugène Sue, suggest that the theme of "savages" shaped most contemporary accounts of the Parisian laboring class. As Sue explained in the beginning of his immensely popular novel *Les mystères de Paris* (1842–43), these classes shared no more with respectable Paris than did the savages on the frontier:

Only, the barbarians of whom we are speaking are in our midst; we can brush elbows with them if we venture into the dens in which they live, where they meet to plot murder and robbery and to share out their victims' spoils. These men have manners of their own, women of their own, a language of their own, a mysterious language replete with baleful images, metaphors dripping blood. Like the savages, these people usually address each other by nicknames borrowed from their energy, their cruelty or certain physical qualities or defects.[76]

Sue's novel repeatedly referred to working-class brutality and became part of a general mythology. The most prominent feature in the stories and drawings of this mythology was the ugliness of the lower classes, a beastlike physical repulsiveness that reflected what bourgeois writers took to be the beastly character of their behavior and the biological inferiority of their "race."[77]

Upper-class observers who attributed the savagery of this lower-class "species" to inherent flaws sought ways to insulate themselves from the "barbarians" in their midst, but they rarely tried to find other causes of the misery. Balzac was in these respects typical of many contemporaries:

> One of the most horrifying sights is certainly the general aspect of the Parisian population, a people of ghastly mien, gaunt, sallow, weather-beaten...whose contorted, twisted faces exude at every pore of the spirit the desires and poisons teeming in their brain; masks, not faces; masks of weakness, masks of strength, masks of misery, masks of joy. ...At the sight of this exhumed people, foreigners, who have no obligation to look into the causes, at once experience a feeling of aversion to this capital, this vast sweatshop of pleasure, but soon they are incapable of quitting it again and stay on, deliberately settling down to their perversion.[78]

Balzac seemed no more willing or able than the foreigners to whom he alluded "to look into the causes" of this "horrifying" situation. Ironically, it was a foreigner, the German émigré Marx, who initiated the most thoroughgoing new theoretical search into the nature and causes of Parisian working-class conditions.

Marx, too, recognized the "savagery" that Balzac and others noticed but did not explain. In fact, the problem of animalized people emerges as a major theme in the *Economic and Philosophical Manuscripts*, where Marx described dehumanized workers in language remarkably similar to that of descriptions of the "subspecies" in many French texts of the era. But Marx developed a nonbiological explanation for lower-class bestiality: whereas many French observers attributed it to bad blood or bad character, Marx saw it as a consequence of historical forces. He brought to the material context of Parisian life a German philosophical tradition that provided the theroretical framework for describing working-class "savagery" as something other than a problem of biological destiny. Marx traced the social problem to capitalism through a creative investigation of conjunctions in philosophy and social life; more specifically, he used the philosophical notion of alienation (in idealist Hegelian terms, the Spirit became separated from itself) to explore the material misery of the Parisian poor (who, in materialist, social terms, became separated from their labor and the realization of their needs).

The Parisian encounter with books and crowds provoked Marx to set down in his notebooks a number of ideas about the characteristics of human activity and about the nature of life in modern, capitalist society. Although he did not imagine the existence of a Rousseau-like utopia in some early golden age, Marx clearly believed that modern society took from modern people many of the traits that distinguished them from animals or machines. His project therefore became in part the search for a social system and theory that might establish more human activity in modern society and might use productive forces to meet human needs. This search informs several important sections in the *Manuscripts*, a text that discusses the differences between human activity and animal activity and situates much capitalist production and interaction on the level of the latter.

Marx defined man as an "*active* natural being" who possesses "*vital powers*," capacities, and drives that act upon objects outside himself. Despite the external quality of these objects, they are essential to man because they are objects of man's needs and, as such, "indispensable to the exercise and confirmation of his essential powers."[79] In other words, man's active, sensuous being can express itself only in relation to real, sensuous objects. Man's actions thus resemble those of other animal species, though human activity is distinguished by a consciousness of the activity, by reflection, and by the fact that it takes place in society. Man is always a social being or, to use the term Marx often employed, a *species-being*. Human powers must be used in a social context or they lose their human attributes, he believed; hence, the liberal dichotomy between the individual and society rested upon a serious misperception of the individual's inescapable social existence. "The individual *is* the social being," wrote Marx. "His vital expression—even when it does not appear in the direct form of a *communal* expression, conceived in association with other men—is therefore an expression and confirmation of *social life*."[80] While this social dimension was for Marx an essential trait of all human activity, it constituted only one aspect of the most important characteristic of man's productive life—the consciousness of his activity.

As Marx described it, man's awareness of his productive ac-

tivity allows him to act upon objects in accordance with a mediating will, something that animals cannot do. This difference
in reflective will power creates the human/animal distinction:
"The animal is immediately one with its life activity. It is not
distinct from that activity; it *is* that activity. Man makes his life
activity itself an object of his will and consciousness. He has
conscious life activity. Only because of that is he a species-
being. Or rather, he is a conscious being, i.e. his own life is an
object for him, only because he is a species-being. Only because
of that is his activity free activity."[81] It is consciousness that en-
ables man to produce whatever other species can produce (that
is, he produces "universally"), whereas animals "produce only
according to the standards and needs of the species to which
they belong."[82] In short, man shares with animals a sensuous
existence and a need for objects, but his relationship to those
objects, his social life, and his consciousness all separate his life
activity from that of animals.

The modes of production in capitalist society, however, were
breaking down the human/animal distinctions and stripping human activity of the traits that made it human. This process
touched almost all aspects of human activity. In the first place,
it was causing man to lose control over the objects he produced
and needed for the exercise of his human powers and capabilities. This was of course a major tendency in what Marx called
the alienation of labor—the capitalist process that takes from
workers the objects they produce with their creative capabilities
and places these products outside the control of workers "as
something alien, as a *power independent* of the producer."[83] Instead of manipulating objects in accordance with his human
needs, the worker himself becomes an object, a commodity to
be bought and sold and used like any other. This operation re-
verses the proper relationship between man and object, so that
production controls man rather than serving man's needs. The
whole process carries the direst consequences because it reduces
man to "a *mentally* and physically *dehumanized* being" and
leads to the "immorality, malformation, [and] stupidity of
workers and capitalists."[84]

At the same time that it overturns the proper relation between man and object, alienated labor under capitalism destroys man's life as a species-being. It destroys the social
component of productive activity by dividing the species-beings
into competitive individuals who confront one another as aliens

rather than as cooperative social beings.[85] As man loses his identity as a species-being, he also loses the consciousness of real needs and the ways in which those needs are connected to social existence. He sinks to the animal level of work without consciousness, and the productive life becomes a desperate necessity for physical survival instead of a productive process in the socially integrated life of a species-being: "Life itself appears only as a *means of* life."[86] People respond to this alienated condition by regressing toward animalism (that is, loss of consciousness) as rapidly as the capitalist economy progresses toward material productivity. "The result is that man (the worker) feels that he is acting freely only in his animal functions—eating, drinking and procreating, or at most in his dwelling and adornment—while in his human functions [such as work] he is nothing more than an animal."[87]

Marx returned to this theme at several points in the *Manuscripts*, as if to reformulate Rousseau's famous pronouncement on the human condition—"born free, but everywhere in chains"—with a latter-day description of proletarian conditions in urban capitalism: Man is born human but is everywhere an animal. Indeed, Marx attacked the capitalist harm to workers with the kind of vehemence and syntax that Rousseau used to discredit the achievements of modern culture: "It is true that labour produces marvels for the rich, but it produces privation for the worker. It produces palaces, but hovels for the worker. It produces beauty, but deformity for the worker. It replaces labour by machines, but it casts some of the workers back into barbarous forms of labour and turns others into machines. It produces intelligence, but it produces idiocy and cretinism for the worker."[88]

The recurring theme in all of this argument was that modern capitalism was generating a new savagery (or "cretinism") along with its other new products. The new savages lived, among other places, in the crowded, stinking side streets of Paris. True, even these savages sometimes acquired a kind of Rousseauistic nobility ("the nobility of man shines forth upon us from their work-worn faces"); nevertheless, they were the underside of an emerging capitalist civilization whose material progress seemed to Marx dependent upon the *regression* of the workers who made it possible: "Man reverts once more to living in a cave, but the cave is now polluted by the mephitic and pestilential breath of civilization."[89] The "capital of the nineteenth century" suggested to Marx a clear relation between wealth at the top and misery at the bottom, between the monuments of capitalism and savagery in the back streets.

Significantly enough, his analysis of the cavelike working-class conditions in Paris turned to a large extent on the philosophical notion of alienation. That was the analytical tool with which he arrived on the scene and the theoretical base upon which his social theory began to take shape. Hegel had described the alienation of the Idea from itself as a major theme of world history, and Feuerbach had described the alienation of man from himself as a central characteristic of religion. Marx was now describing the alienation of man from his labor and from his needs as a principal characteristic of capitalism and therefore of modern life. The material product of this alienation, private property, increased in value and quantity commensurate with the increasing alienation of the worker who produced it.[90] Marx explicitly compared this economic process to the religious alienation that Feuerbach and the German critics had described: "The more man puts into God, the less he retains within himself."[91] Although the economic alienation of workers repeated the religious pattern, it carried more severe material consequences in that it gave to products what rightly belonged to people. "The worker places his life in the object," Marx argued, "but now it no longer belongs to him but to the object."[92] Thus, where alienated religious societies granted all power to God, alienated capitalist societies granted all power to money, and the tribute that went to both deities diminished human life. Money in capitalist societies became "the alienated *capacity of mankind*," acquiring the power to do what individuals could not do for themselves. Like God, money was the inversion of human creativity, and its victims—those whom it punished—were also its producers.[93]

It was the condition of these victims/producers that Marx analyzed in the *Economic and Philosophical Manuscripts* from the standpoint of his German concept of alienation. His recognition of both the material conditions and the alienating processes that produced them became, moreover, the decisive justification for Marx's communism—as that which must historically transcend capitalism—to which he adhered for the first time in Paris. He explained his conception of communism in the *Manuscripts* as an overcoming of the alienating capitalist process that produces private property and separates man from his labor and himself: *"Communism* is the *positive supersession* of private property as *human* self-estrangement, and hence the true *appropriation* of the *human* essence through and for man; it is the complete restoration of man to himself as a *social,* i.e. human being."[94] The practice of communism would thus replace alienated labor with human labor (by superseding private property) and thereby transform the degraded proletarian condition under capitalism into a more human social existence. Communism became for Marx the theoretical solution for the alienation that French materialists had not understood historically and the material solution for a problem that German philosophers had tried to resolve abstractly. As Marx explained in one of his most famous claims for communism, "It is the solution of the riddle of history and knows itself to be the solution."[95] It was also what Marx called the negation of the negation (private property, alienation) and, as such, the next necessary step in history—though not the end of history.[96]

The *Manuscripts* show more clearly than anything else he wrote in Paris how Marx's thought evolved while he was there. One might say that what Marx did in his Parisian texts was to historicize materialism and to materialize history. The *Manuscripts* achieved the first part of this project by bringing philosophical-historical perspectives (notably, theories of alienation and dialectical change) to classical economics and to an analysis of the working-class conditions he encountered in Paris. Stressing both the process of dialectical historical evolution and the alienating characteristics of proletarian life in capitalist society, Marx developed a critical *historical* explanation for what most contemporaries took to be the universal characteristics of economic life and the biological characteristics of working-class people. Then he proposed a historical solution (communism) to overcome alienation in the economic system and to transform the conditions of proletarian life. Marx's critique of life in capitalist society and of the assumptions in capitalist economics thus depended to a great extent upon intellectual traditions and insights that he brought from Germany. After using those insights to help explain and criticize French economics and material life (in the *Manuscripts),* however, he set about explaining and criticizing the German philosophical tradition with the perspectives and values of French materialism (in *The Holy Family*). In the end, he settled his score with the Hegelians by materializing their history and philosophy as he had worked upon the French by historicizing their materialist theories and the conditions of their social life. It was a two-sided project that reflected on both sides the creative interactions of a German intellectual in a French context.

Philosophers and Society: Materializing History

While Marx's response to the social and intellectual life of France clearly reflected the Hegelian tradition from which he had come, his work and experience in Paris encouraged him to begin the critical evaluation of German philosophy that led eventually to *The German Ideology*. In fact, his mode of analysis as well as his early ideas incorporated so many Hegelian tendencies that the development of his critical projects in Paris seemed to require a confrontation with his German past. That confrontation began in the critique of Hegel that appeared in the *Deutsch-Französische Jahrbücher*, continued in the *Economic and Philosophical Manuscripts* and culminated in the polemical pages of *The Holy Family*. The mounting urgency of these anti-Hegelian attacks suggests how important that tradition was for Marx and how much his own thought evolved as a dialogue with Hegelianism, even as he was moving away from it. French culture served Marx's intellectual needs in this period of transition by providing critical alternatives to the German traditions he wanted to challenge. Writing in Paris, Marx repeatedly turned to French thought and society to support his critique, so that the dialogue with Hegel became also a dialogue between France and Germany.[97]

Marx stated the central motivation for his critical investigations in the *Jahrbücher* article that was intended to serve as an introduction to his never completed "Critique of Hegel's Philosophy of Right." Although he argued in that article that Germany's emancipation would come through the actions of the proletariat rather than the theories of philosophers, Marx emphasized that this emancipation also required some theoretical work that German criticism had not yet undertaken. "It is the immediate *task of philosophy*, which is in the service of history, to unmask human self-estrangement in its *unholy forms* once the *holy form* of human self-estrangement has been unmasked," Marx explained. "Thus the criticism of heaven turns into the criticism of earth, the *criticism of religion* into the *criticism of law* and the *criticism of theology* into the *criticism of politics*."[98] This view of the modern critical task formed the starting point for Marx's increasingly angry assault on the otherworldliness of German philosophy, which (like many historians of German culture) he traced to Luther and Hegel. Those two figures embodied for Marx the German penchant for making revolutions in the realm of theory instead of the realm of political action. Luther's theological revolution had been an important challenge to traditional religious authority, but that earlier Protestant transformation would soon be surpassed by the material revolution of the German proletariat.[99] The theoretical imperative for Marx was therefore to anticipate the real-world proletarian emancipation with a real-world philosophy. This project carried him rapidly out of the Hegelian community he had left in Germany, a point that Marx himself frequently stressed in his Parisian texts.

The first step out, however, depended on a careful critique of Hegel; it appeared, among other places, in the *Economic and Philosophical Manuscripts,* in which Marx's treatment of Hegel went back to the problem that influenced so much of his discussion of classical economics and working-class conditions: alienation. Unlike the economists, Hegel had recognized the problem of alienation and attempted to analyze its characteristics. But, Marx said, his analysis rested upon two decisive errors: he first located alienation on the level of abstract thought, and then he accepted this alienation as the "absolute" and "final expression of human life."[100]

These idealist notions of course provided an inviting target for the developing materialist thrust in Marx's thought. The target in fact became all too conspicuous in the light of the materialism and economic life that Marx encountered in Paris. From that perspective, Marx described Hegel's limitations with some extraordinarily forceful summaries in his Paris *Manuscripts.* "The entire *history of alienation* and the entire *retraction* of this alienation is therefore nothing more than the *history of the production* of abstract, i.e. absolute thought, of logical, speculative thought."[101] Having situated history and alienation in the mind alone, Hegel could ignore the material basis of alienation and see its transcendence as a problem of pure abstraction. The objects in man's world, man's needs—even man himself—seemed to disappear in Hegel's work: "The object [for Hegel] appears only as *abstract* consciousness and man only as self-*consciousness,*" Marx complained. "The various forms of estrangement which occur are therefore merely different forms of consciousness and self-consciousness ... [and] the result is the dialectic of pure thought."[102]

Hegel's abstract notion of alienation, moreover, offered no way for humans to transcend it because he described the supersession of alienation (as well as its creation) without reference to the concrete activity of a real-world alienated subject. Indeed, Marx asserted, man loses his status as an autonomous subject in Hegel's formulation and becomes merely the "predicate" for some universal Subject that separates from itself and then rejoins itself in a kind of self-referential abstract cycle. There is no way for *man* to overcome or transform this process, which seems to go on pretty much without him. "Real man and real nature become mere predicates," Marx wrote, "symbols of this hidden, unreal man [Subject or God] and this unreal nature. Subject and predicate therefore stand in a relation of absolute inversion to one another; ... the *absolute subject* [exists] as a *process*, as a *subject* which *alienates* itself and returns to itself from alienation, while at the same time re-absorbing this alienation, and the subject as this process; pure, *ceaseless* revolving within itself."[103] Hegel's theory of alienation thus denied man a role in its creation or transcendence and thereby mystified or ignored the historical, material, human processes to which the concept might properly refer.

Marx's criticism of Hegelian errors by no means destroyed the importance of Hegel's work for him. He acknowledged, for example, that Hegel recognized the "self-creation of man as a process," that he saw man "as the result of his *own labour*," and that he understood man as a "species-being" who realizes his powers through collective, cooperative efforts.[104] To be sure, Hegel developed all of these insights (like the notion of alienation) in a one-sided, abstract way, but they nevertheless provided a beginning for the critical project that Marx had set for himself. "The *Phenomenology* [of Hegel]," Marx wrote in his *Manuscripts*," is therefore concealed and mystifying criticism, criticism which has not attained self-clarity; but in so far as it grasps the *estrangement* of man—even though man appears only in the form of mind—*all* the elements of criticism are concealed within it, and often *prepared* and *worked out* in a way that goes far beyond Hegel's own point of view."[105] Thus, however strongly Marx might attack his abstractions, Hegel simply offered too much insight to be dismissed with the contempt or satire that Marx directed at the second-generation followers and imitators who formed the school of "Critical Criticism" in Germany and extended the abstract inclinations in Hegel to extremes that Marx found altogether absurd. The relatively moderate critique of Hegel in the *Economic and Philosophical Manu-*

scripts therefore evolved into the scathing ridicule of the "Critical Critics" in *The Holy Family*.

Although that book was the first project upon which Marx and Engels collaborated, Marx actually wrote almost the entire text. The work grew out of their long conversations in late August 1844 and their mutual desire to discredit the reputed radicalism of the Berlin Hegelians who were publishing a journal *(Allgemeine Literatur-Zeitung)* and meeting for philosophical discussions under the leadership of Bruno and Edgar Bauer. Even before his conversations with Engels, Marx had begun to define his opposition to the Bauer group by arguing that they acknowledged only the theoretical, intellectual components of human experience and needs. "This criticism therefore lapses into a sad and supercilious intellectualism," Marx complained in a letter to Feuerbach. *"Consciousness* or *self-consciousness* is regarded as the *only* human quality."[106] His complaint reappeared in harsher language throughout the anti-Bauer text he and Engels soon produced, and it served as the starting point for some of their harshest polemic.

The Holy Family is not a well-known work, partly because its long digressions on people and books seem unimportant to modern readers, and partly because many of its arguments received fuller treatment in *The German Ideology*. Despite its comparative obscurity, however, *The Holy Family* is essential to any assessment of Marx's work and thought in France; it was the longest text he wrote there, the only book from his Parisian period to be published at the time (February 1845), and the Parisian work in which he explicitly attacked his German contemporaries with arguments that reflected his contact with the theories and social conditions of France. Two recurring themes suggest the extent to which Marx was drawing upon his French base to confront his German rivals: first, Berlin Hegelians were utterly irrelevant to the real radical movement because they ignored the material base of human needs, and second, they completely misunderstood French thought and society. After a year in France, Marx was more than willing to correct his compatriots on these points by means of insistent, even redundant, examples in *The Holy Family*.

Engels set the rhetorical tone for Marx's assault in a short introductory section that ridiculed the "Criticism" of the "Critical Critics" as a pathetic anachronism lacking interest or appeal for modern Germans: "It is and remains an old woman—faded, widowed *Hegelian* philosophy which paints and adorns its body, shrivelled into the most repulsive abstraction, and ogles all over Germany in search of a wooer."[107] Marx went after the Critics in somewhat more philosophical terms, mocking their preoccupation with the Spirit, their tautological explanations for its failure to realize itself in the world, and their hostility for the masses (whom they viewed as adversaries of the Spirit).[108] According to Critical Criticism, wrote Marx,

> the whole evil lies only in the workers' "thinking"....But these *mass-minded* communist workers, employed, for instance, in the Manchester or Lyons workshops, do not believe that by *"pure* thinking" they will be able to argue away their industrial masters and their own practical debasement. They are most painfully aware of the *difference* between *being* and *thinking*, between *consciousness* and *life*. They know that property, capital, money, wage-labour and the like are no ideal figments of the brain but very practical, very objective products of their self-estrangement and that therefore they must be abolished in a practical, objective way for man to become man not only in *thinking*, in *consciousness*, but in mass *being*, in life. Critical Criticism, on the contrary, teaches them that they cease in reality to be wage-workers if in thinking they abolish the thought of wage-labour; if in thinking they cease to regard themselves as wage-workers and, in accordance with that extravagant notion, no longer let themselves be paid for their person. As absolute idealists, as ethereal beings, they will then naturally be able to live on the ether of pure thought. Critical Criticism teaches them that they abolish real capital by overcoming in *thinking* the category Capital, that they *really* change and transform themselves into real human beings by changing their "abstract ego" in consciousness and scorning as an un-Critical operation all *real* change of their real existence, of the real conditions of their existence, that is to say, of their *real ego*.[109]

This long passage brings together many of the major themes in *The Holy Family:* it attacks the abstractions of the Bauer-circle Hegelians, their ignorance of social conditions in industrial societies, and their naive view of historical change. It also suggests how Marx believed that his own work—based upon acquaintance with economic and social realities and with "mass-minded" workers in France—could recognize and overcome the limitations of the idealist Hegelians; they would never transcend their one-sided abstractions because they had no experience whatsoever with the working-class people who would lead the modern historical transformation.

It was this social naiveté that separated the Germans from all other modern nations—especially the French and English, who, for all their shortcomings, at least acknowledged and thought about social forces instead of spiritual categories. Marx may have overstated French and English "realism" as much as he devalued German "idealism," but the extreme contrast served his polemical purposes and showed how useful a foreign alternative could be in the exile assault on home-country values. "The criticism of the French and the English is not an abstract, preternatural personality outside mankind," Marx explained. "It is the *real human activity* of individuals who are active members of society and who suffer, feel, think and act as human beings."[110] Such criticism achieved its concreteness through a direct relationship with the social experience of the French and English masses, an experience that altogether exceeded the abstract labors of German theorists, but one with which Marx himself could claim some firsthand contact.

Indeed, he made a point of assuring his German readers that his own critical positions were partly rooted in his familiarity with real-world workers and the social movement they represented. "One must be acquainted with the studiousness, the craving for knowledge, the moral energy and the unceasing urge for development of the French and English workers," Marx explained, "to be able to form an idea of the *human* nobleness of that movement."[111] Without this knowledge of the masses, the "Critical" efforts of the Berlin Hegelians took them right out of history and the revolutionary processes that workers (and those who supported them) knew about from their own experience. "Were *Criticism* better acquainted with the movement of the lower classes of the people it would know that the extreme resistance that they have experienced from practical life is changing them every day. Modern prose and poetry emanating in England and France from the lower classes of the people would show it that the lower classes of the people know how to raise themselves spiritually even without being directly *overshadowed* by the *Holy Ghost of Critical Criticism.*"[112] The recurring point in all these anti-Criticism statements was of course that Marx himself identified with the relevant historical position of French materialism (the basis of "mature communism")[113] and with the worker movement and writings that went unnoticed in Berlin.

Marx found the German Critics as mistaken about French writers as they were about French workers. Accordingly, long sections in *The Holy Family* showed how the Bauer-circle Hegelians had misunderstood both the classical works of French materialism and contemporary texts by authors such as Eugène Sue and Proudhon. Marx wanted to refute Bruno Bauer's contention that the whole tradition of French materialism and the Enlightenment amounted to a French "Spinozism," which Romanticism eventually displaced in French culture. Writing his own materialist history of the Enlightenment, he charged that the Berlin Hegelians were naively repeating what Hegel had written about materialism without bothering to read the French texts themselves. Whatever the Hegelians might say, French materialism was something besides Spinozism—its real origins could be traced to Bacon and Locke in England and to material changes in western Europe—and its insights had by no means disappeared from French life but continued to flourish among modern communists and socialists.[114]

This history of materialism offers a good example of the way in which Marx could cast himself as the correct interpreter of French authors, but it was relatively brief and vague in comparison with his detailed attacks on the Berlin Hegelians' views of Sue and Proudhon. Sue's *Les mystères de Paris* was the most popular fiction in France when Marx arrived there in the fall of 1843. It was attracting attention from foreign readers, too, including the Bauer-circle Critic who wrote a sympathetic review under the pen name Szeliga. Marx attacked Szeliga for all the abstractions that he attributed to Hegelians throughout *The Holy Family* and went on to ridicule the poor Critic's glaring ignorance of the Parisian conditions that Sue depicted in his novel. Although Szeliga tried to fit the realities of Paris into his speculative categories, Marx explained, the realities and categories would never coincide—and so the Critic simply ignored reality. Marx drew upon his own knowledge of Paris to show that Szeliga knew nothing about the behavior of porters or servants or police agents or aristocrats at balls; he also mocked Szeliga for his "spiritual" responses to Sue's descriptions of Parisian sensuality, calling the German reviewer an "inexperienced, credulous *Critical country parson!*"[115] Marx's two chapters of detailed textual analysis portrayed the Hegelian Critic as a naive simpleton who had misconstrued the real Paris and created irrelevant fantasies out of his Critical imagination. Once again, Marx clearly identified himself with Parisian sensuality in opposition to German abstraction and used his contact with contemporary France to discredit the mistaken interpretations of the Berliners. (His condemnation took on the special vehemence of someone who was attacking his own past—or the always-present dangers in his own theoretical projects.)

His sympathy for French sensualism did not mean that Marx especially admired Eugène Sue. On the contrary, though he found Sue's depiction of Paris more concrete than anything in the German Critics, he dismissed the novelist as a naive reformer who failed to perceive the underlying causes of the poverty and crimes he described. Sue's suggestions, for example, that Parisian social problems might be rectified through reforms in legal practices, penal codes, education, and sanitation policies elicited from Marx the contempt that he reserved for all unreal solutions to real-world conditions.[116] Sue shared Critical Criticism's inclination to change social injustices with passages in books rather than with social actions in cities: "A part of the city complains of the shortcomings of preliminary education," Marx noted at one point. "He [Sue] promises a reform of preliminary education for that district of the city in the tenth volume of *Juif errant*."[117] Thus, while Sue provided plenty of material for an attack on Szeliga, he also functioned in some ways as a French counterpart to the Critical Critics; and he was not much more dangerous to the ruling order.

If Szeliga's reading of Sue enabled Marx to ridicule Hegelian ignorance of Parisian social conditions, Edgar Bauer's response to Proudhon gave Marx an opening to describe Hegelian ignorance of economics. Proudhon, like Sue, had important limitations for Marx, and yet the French socialist seemed so superior to the German Critics that Marx felt compelled to write a strong defense. Bauer had worked out the "Critical" position on Proudhon by translating the famous treatise "What Is Property?" and providing an interpretation of that text for German readers. Bauer's reading of Proudhon seemed to Marx utterly beside the point; it took Proudhon completely away from his real, "mass-type" explanations of society and property and transformed him into what "Critical Criticism" thought he should be. Provoked by this transformation, Marx assumed the task of describing for Germans the "mass-type" Proudhon who was distorted beyond recognition in Bauer's translations and who disappeared altogether from Bauer's account of the "Critical" Proudhon.

This misinterpretation may have angered Marx more than anything else he found in the Critical Critics' works, for in *The Holy Family* he plunged into the Proudhon question with page after page of examples to show how Bauer had mistranslated key passages in Proudhon's work and how he had misread almost all of Proudhon's theoretical arguments.[118] The "Critical" Proudhon, for example, scarcely dealt with economic relations or property at all; instead, he was a theological writer who concerned himself primarily with justice as the Absolute in history. Having removed the economic issue from Proudhon's theory, the German Critic could attack the Frenchman for his "theological" misconceptions and for taking up the cause of the Absolute—a cause that Critical Criticism had already reserved for itself. By ignoring the economics in Proudhon's book, "Herr Edgar" kept the discussion on the abstract level he knew best but missed both the point of Proudhon's argument and the importance of Proudhon's historical contribution. Marx's account, by contrast, stressed an "economic" Proudhon who first examined the private property that political economists regarded as an unquestioned fact and who discussed the misery and the human consequences of the economic system that economists overlooked when they wrote about capital. These two achievements were rooted in the French "mass-type" language and perspective that the German Critics could neither understand nor tolerate.[119]

Proudhon's examination of private property led him to recognize that "private property as such and in its entirety" was responsible for the inhuman realities in capitalist economies that traditional economists always explained away as a consequence of some *particular* aspect or practice of private property. At the same time, he correctly showed that labor determined the value of a product, thereby making human activity rather than capital the decisive factor in his economics. "Proudhon," Marx wrote, "reinstates man in his rights;" he helped to demystify the power of capital and landed property that political economists regularly described without further reference to the people who created them.[120] These insights, which constituted Proudhon's significance in modern economics, grew out of the historical experience of workers that German Criticism entirely ignored.

It was this historical base that made the "mass-type" Proudhon important for Marx and incomprehensible for Critics such as Edgar Bauer: "He [Proudhon] does not write in the interest of self-sufficient Criticism or out of any abstract, self-made interest, but out of a mass-type, real, historic interest, an interest that goes beyond *criticism*, that will go as far as a *crisis*. Not only does Proudhon write in the interest of the proletarians, he is himself a proletarian, an *ouvrier*. His work is a scientific manifesto of the French proletariat and therefore has quite a different historical significance from that of the literary botch work of any Critical Critic."[121] Proudhon's mass-based French perspective thus advanced for enough beyond "Herr Edgar's" categories ("Critical Criticism sees nothing but categories everywhere")[122] to allow for action that might change the relations of property, work, and wages.

To be sure, Marx also stressed that Proudhon continued to operate within the context of many traditional economic assumptions; that these limitations affected both his critique of classical economics and his solutions for the maldistribution of wealth, which amounted mainly to a proposal for a new form of *"equal possession"* to replace the traditional unequal ownership of private property; and that the very notion of possession still reflected the alienated presuppositions of political economy ("Proudhon abolishes economic estrangement *within* economic estrangement").[123] Although these criticisms would eventually escalate into the full-scale assault of *The Poverty of Philosophy*, Proudhon served as a most useful ally in the anti-Hegelian attack that was so central to Marx's Parisian period. The "mass-type" Frenchman provided far more to that campaign than anything the Bauer brothers could produce in Berlin, and so Marx went to his defense—claiming all the while a superior understanding of French writers as well as French conditions.

The Proudhon-Bauer contrast offered Marx one of the best cases for the analysis of French-German differences that ran through all parts of *The Holy Family* and gave him a position from which to discredit the Germans. It seemed in fact that the contrast between French social and political concreteness and German abstraction informed the discussion of virtually every substantive issue Marx addressed. Take, for example, the problem of equality:

If Herr Edgar compares French *equality* with German self-consciousness for an instant, he will see that the latter principle expresses *in German*, i.e., in abstract thought, what the former says *in French*, that is, in the language of politics and of thoughtful observation. Self-consciousness is man's equality with himself in pure thought. Equality is man's consciousness of himself in the element of practice, i.e., man's consciousness of other men as his equals and man's attitude to other men as his equals. Equality is the French expression for the unity of human essence, for man's consciousness of his species and his attitude towards his species, for the practical identity of man with man, i.e., for the social or human relation of man to man.[124]

Marx of course had a good deal to say about the mistaken view of equality in French political revolutions and in Proudhon's work, but it was nevertheless the practical, "mass-type" French perspective that facilitated Marx's break with the Hegelians at home and helped him confirm for himself the superiority of his own views. The same stance—as the correct interpreter of French writers, of French conditions, of German Hegelians, of German conditions—became part of his relations with other émigrés and part of the reason for disputes with exiles in Paris as well as with the Critical Critics in Berlin.

Marx's emphasis on the "mass-type" social movement and his adherence to communism soon separated him from many of the Hegelians with whom he had come to Paris. As he immersed himself in economics and met workers in the city, his *Jahrbücher* colleagues seemed increasingly remote from the social conditions he wanted to explain, and so he broke from the Ruge circle with decisive polemical arguments that resembled those of the anti-Bauer campaign. The argument in both cases charged that Hegelians misunderstood social reality, but since it was difficult to criticize Paris-based exiles for ignorance of France, the anti-Hegelian project there reproached other émigrés for ignorance of conditions in Germany. As it happened, the harshest blows fell on Arnold Ruge, Marx's first and closest collaborator during his early months in France.[125]

Although the two men had drifted apart after the collapse of the *Jahrbücher*, the break became final when Marx published a scathing criticism of Ruge in *Vorwärts* (August 1844). In an article on the Silesian weavers' revolt, Ruge had argued, essentially, that the revolt had little significance and aroused few fears among the German ruling class because Germany was still an unpolitical country; lacking political consciousness, the weavers could be easily suppressed and easily forgotten. Ruge's argument seemed to Marx both naive and dangerous, perhaps all the more so because Ruge had published his article as the anonymous contribution of "A Prussian." Marx thus wrote his "Critical Notes on 'The King of Prussia and Social Reform' " to show Ruge's errors and to make sure that no reader mistakenly identified him, Marx, as the "Prussian."

The response included a great many complaints about the style as well as the substance of Ruge's analysis. Marx charged that the "Prussian" suffered from an "illogical mind," that he wrote with "*rare naivety*," and that he discussed the Silesian revolt from the standpoint of a German schoolmaster. It all added up to "ready-made phraseology saturated in an overweening love of oneself" that reflected an appalling ignorance of the masses.[126] Like the Hegelians at home, this "Prussian" abroad had no insight into the historical development of the worker movement. He failed to see, for example, that the Silesian weavers actually recognized their real class enemies (industrialists, bankers) with more clarity than had workers in England or France. The German workers *knew* what they were doing when they acted, and they conducted themselves with exceptional courage and foresight—though theoretical prejudice prevented the "Prussian" from seeing what had happened. Even the German bourgeoisie realized that something significant had taken place in Silesia, as anyone would learn from reading accounts in the bourgeois press.[127]

Such glaring ignorance of both the German proletariat and what they had achieved was bad enough, but Ruge also repeated the common misconceptions about the relation between politics and society. That is, he assumed that political maturity must precede social reforms and that the Germans would not deal with poverty until they had arrived at the necessary *political* consciousness. Marx found in this view another example of the naiveté that attributed autonomy to the political spirit and state. In fact, Marx argued, the political state represented the social order and could never be expected to make substantive changes in the social system upon which it rested; after all, the politically mature English state showed itself utterly incapable of dealing with pauperism. Nothing, then, could be more "foolish" than to hope (as Ruge did) that political thought might discover and root out the causes of social misery in Germany.[128] The only real solution would be a social revolution led by a socially conscious proletariat, a total revolution of the sort that Marx had earlier described in his *Jahrbücher* essay "On the Jewish Question" and in his "Critique of Hegel's Philosophy of Right." Ruge failed to understand that the Silesian weavers had taken an important first step in that social revolution and that the German worker movement far exceeded the theoretical categories to which it was consigned by ill-informed Hegelians.[129]

Assuming that his own article set all of this straight, Marx concluded with a self-justification and some advice for Ruge that effectively assured the end of their relationship. "Such lengthy perorations," Marx wrote of his own essay, "were necessary to break through the *tissue* of errors concealed in a single newspaper column. Not every reader possesses the education and the time necessary to get to grips with such *literary swindles*. In view of this does not our anonymous 'Prussian' owe it to the reading public to give up writing on political and social themes and to refrain from making declamatory statements on the situation in Germany, in order to devote himself to a conscientious analysis of his own situation?"[130] Marx had, in short, discovered Bauer-brother faults in his erstwhile Parisian colleague, and he wasted no time in revealing those faults to the "reading public."

The attack on Ruge became a declaration of independence from the Hegelians with whom he had come to France, much as *The Holy Family* was a declaration of independence from those he had left in Germany. Both attacks reflected the rapid evolution in France that led Marx to view materialism, the working class, and communism as the proper sources of historical understanding. Those critics who were unwilling to follow him into this "French mode" of analysis were rapidly dismissed as irrelevant and uncomprehending theoreticians of the "German philosophical mode," and they soon disappeared from Marx's life. Significantly enough, Marx formed his closest friendships in Paris with Heine (the "French" German) and Engels (the "English" German).[131] The rest of the German exiles he knew there—Ruge, Hess, Herwegh, and others—did not retain much interest for him, perhaps because in a certain intellectual sense they were too German.

Yet Marx himself by no means forgot that he too was German. Indeed, the attack on Ruge represented another step in the changing relation to Germany that became an important aspect of his experience in France. Living outside his native country, Marx seemed to discover the German proletariat—the "mass-type" Germany—and to redefine for himself what it meant to be German.

A German Abroad

Much of what Marx wrote about Germany from his base in Paris emphasized the uniqueness of his native country. This uniqueness derived from both its history and its philosophy, and it was something that Marx discussed with considerable ambivalence. The harsh attacks on Hegelian abstractions, for example, were somewhat mitigated in other Parisian texts that expressed a certain pride in German theoretical superiority vis-à-vis the other nations of modern Europe. Marx never quite extricated himself from the tradition of Critical Criticism, for that tradition involved part of what he admired in Germany even as he condemned it. Similarly, the question of Germany's role in modern history seemed highly important to Marx; it was a question that prompted considerable analysis from the perspective of French history, fueled much of his anti-Hegelian ardor, and finally reappeared as he broke away from the "French" phase of his life and work in the late 1840s. The Franco-German contrast could haunt Marx as deeply as it haunted Heine, and, like Heine, he never became a German who simply followed (or completely identified with) the French. As he explained from one angle after another in France, Germany was a special case that always demanded its own special analysis.

It was special because its history was so different from that of other nations. The German political culture was for Marx a glaring anachronism, a peculiar relic of the old regime, forever relegating Germany to a passive role amid the political upheavals of modern Europe. "Indeed, German history prides itself," Marx wrote, "on having travelled a road which no other nation in the whole of history has ever travelled before, or ever will again. We have shared the restorations of modern nations without ever having shared their revolutions. We have been restored firstly because other nations dared to make revolutions and secondly because other nations suffered counterrevolutions.... With our shepherds to the fore, we only once kept company with freedom, on the *day of its internment*."[132] Marx favored action against the political status quo, but he warned that the simple negation of Germany's present would still leave the nation at least a half-century behind modern history—corresponding perhaps to French conditions in 1789—because German economics, politics, and society lagged so far behind the historical development in other countries.[133]

Despite its political and economic backwardness, however, Germany had achieved exceptional modernity in its philosophy and theory. This theoretical accomplishment constituted the unique German contribution to modern Europe, and it seemed to arouse in Marx a bemused combination of pride and irony. "We are the *philosophical* contemporaries of the present without being its *historical* contemporaries," he once noted. Lacking a modern social history with which to contend, German theorists had worked out a remarkable critique of an ideal Germany that did not yet exist, thereby creating a radicalism that was almost entirely philosophical. "What for advanced nations is a *practical* quarrel with modern political conditions is for Germany, where such conditions do not yet exist, a *critical* quarrel with their reflection in philosophy."[134]

Although the "critical quarrel" had made its greatest advances in the area of religion, it was now turning to law and political theory, as Marx himself announced in "The Critique of Hegel's Philosophy of Right."

Germany had something to offer other nations in this project (as in its religious criticism) because the one-sidedness of German development brought the defects of modern politics into clearer focus. The Germans had *thought* what other nations had *done;* that is, they had left the whole man out of their philosophy of law and state in the same way that modern liberal states excluded the whole man from participation in the body politic. Thus, a German critique of political philosophy, equivalent to French or English critiques of political states, was a necessary first step in the process of true emancipation ("You cannot transcend philosophy without realizing it").[135] Theoretical weapons could never overthrow the material forces of the modern state (you cannot "realize philosophy without transcending it"), yet critical theory could become materially significant once it was sufficiently radical and once it had "gripped the masses." In fact, theoretical weapons were essential for the material revolution that would ultimately raise Germany to a social level that could be more human than the "official level" of other modern states.[136]

The superiority of German theory, combined with the political peculiarities of the German state, made Marx believe that Germany's future might be as unique as its past. Germans had the critical tools to attack an anachronistic state that united the deficiencies of the old regime (absolutism) with the deficiencies of a modern state (whole person excluded). Radical criticism would help Germans see that their revolution must be total in order to challenge the debilitating contradictions of *both* the old regime and the new. They could spare themselves the mistakes of France, where revolutions had been partial and where political changes had resulted in nothing more than a transfer of power to the bourgeoisie. By recognizing and averting that French mistake, Germany might lead all of Europe toward true emancipation. "It is not *radical* revolution or *universal human* emancipation which is a utopian dream for Germany," Marx argued. "It is the partial, *merely* political revolution, the revolution which leaves the pillars of the building standing."[137] A German revolution could thus begin with the social lessons of the French Revolution before it, and the transcendence of the German political state would facilitate transcendence of old and new regimes alike. Ironically, the most backward political nation might become the agent of the most advanced social liberation and achieve what no other revolution or state had yet accomplished.

The vision rested upon a kind of radical patriotism, a German exceptionalism:

> *Germany, as a world of its own embodying all the deficiencies of the present political age,* will not be able to overcome the specifically German limitations without overcoming the universal limitation of the present political age. . . .
>
> Germany can emancipate itself from the *Middle Ages* only if it emancipates itself at the same time from the *partial* victories over the Middle Ages [such as the French Revolutionary model?]. In Germany *no* form of bondage can be broken without breaking *all* forms of bondage. Germany, which is renowned for its *thoroughness*, cannot make a revolution unless it is a *thorough* one. The *emancipation of the German* is the *emancipation of man.*[138]

Unique possibilities for universal emancipation existed in Germany because the "thorough" Germans could link their theoretical superiority and historical insight with a rapidly developing universal class that would lead the revolution—the German proletariat, which Marx began to describe with such admiration in his Parisian texts. While radical philosophy became the "head" of emancipation, the proletariat was becoming its "heart."[139]

Marx began to discuss the general characteristics of the proletariat in his early Paris writings, especially in his critique of Hegel. The proletariat was the universal class, he wrote, in that it was the class excluded from all particular interests in civil society. It was a class with a "universal character because of its universal suffering," and it claimed "no *particular right* because the wrong it suffers is not a *particular wrong* but *wrong in general.*"[140] Thus, the proletariat was the only social class that could lead the revolution for universal emancipation. Marx conceded that the class was not yet well formed in Germany, but he also emphasized that the German proletariat seemed better-positioned than the working class in France to move directly into its universal role.

Since French classes defined themselves more clearly than their counterparts in Germany, they possessed a much stronger consciousness of their social and political roles within the French state. Each French class therefore claimed its powers by negating the class that preceded it in power—the bourgeoisie overthrew the nobility as workers would overthrow the bourgeoisie—and each step in this process represented a partial emancipation of man. In Germany, where class interests were less defined, social changes were more likely to come all at once.

> In France partial emancipation is the basis of universal emancipation. In Germany universal emancipation is the *conditio sine qua non* of any partial emancipation. In France it is the reality, in Germany the impossibility, of emancipation in stages that must give birth to complete freedom. In France each class of the people is a *political idealist* and experiences itself first and foremost not as a particular class but as the representative of social needs in general. The role of *emancipator* therefore passes in a dramatic movement from one class of the French people to the next.[141]

German classes, however, lacked the audacity to claim that their own interests represented the interests of society in general. Hence, the German bourgeoisie never really negated the old aristocracy and never viewed itself as the proper ruling class—and German society never achieved the class order that characterized France. "Thus," explained Marx, "princes struggle against kings, bureaucrats against aristocrats, and the bourgeoisie against all of these, while the proletariat is already beginning to struggle against the bourgeoisie."[142] It was precisely this historical disorder in Germany and the weakness of the bourgeoisie that offered the German proletariat such exceptional opportunities; the revolution there could be the dissolution of an entire society rather than the simple negation of another ruling class. In short, Marx found a way to turn the backwardness of Germany into a unique precondition for true emancipation by arguing that the social and political anachronisms of Germany made possible a thoroughgoing social revolution led by the German proletariat.

The other German advantage (as compared to France) was that the proletariat could draw upon the critical insights of German philosophy for intellectual weapons to complement its own material strengths. Philosophical perspectives (the "head" of emancipation) would enable German workers to become aware of their position in German society and to negate the existing social order through class-conscious actions.[143] This emphasis on the theoretical insights of the German proletariat became one of Marx's recurring themes in the Parisian texts and the basis for much of his attack on Hegelian ignorance of "mass-type" realities. The point emerged most forcefully in the anti-Ruge article (in *Vorwärts*) on the Silesian weavers' rebellion, an event that confirmed for Marx what he had been saying about the true revolutionary potential of the German workers. He believed that the weavers had shown remarkable understanding of their class status and established themselves as the theoretical vanguard of the European social movement:

> The Silesian rebellion *starts* where the French and English workers finish, namely with an understanding of the nature of the proletariat. This *superiority* stamps the whole episode. Not only were machines destroyed...but also the *account books*, the titles of ownership, and whereas all other movements had directed their attacks primarily at the visible enemy, namely the industrialists, the Silesian workers turned also against the hidden enemy, the bankers....
>
> It must be granted that the German proletariat is the *theoretician* of the European proletariat just as the English proletariat is its *economist* and the French its *politician*. It must be granted that the vocation of Germany for *social* revolution is as *classical* as its incapacity for *political* revolution.[144]

These claims for the theoretical achievement of German proletarians surely contributed to Marx's contempt for such armchair theorists as Ruge or the Bauers (his opinion of intellectuals went down as his opinion of workers went up), and they may also have contributed to his evolving criticism of French socialism. In the *Vorwärts* article, for example, Marx suggested that the insights of Weitling, the German tailor, clearly surpassed "from a theoretical point of view" the writings of the French worker Proudhon.[145] The vaguely ironic point in all of this was that Marx increasingly praised the philosophical acumen of German workers while he ridiculed the Hegelian theorists to whom much of their theoretical insight (and his own) might be traced. The proletariat, though, had emerged as Marx's universal class, and he had no patience with Hegelians who failed to understand this decisive, material transformation of their own philosophical tradition.

It is impossible to know exactly why Marx discovered the German proletariat with such enthusiasm in Paris. Perhaps his study of French history and his encounter with the French working class directed him to look for parallels in his home country. Perhaps, too, the contact with French socialism alerted him to the importance of a socially conscious proletarian class. At the same time, Marx came to know a number of German workers through meetings of the League of the Just, and he clearly became interested in the significance of these socially active proletarian expatriates.[146] The

contact with German artisans differed from his intellectual contacts at home and set him to investigating and instructing the
people he met. "I must not forget to emphasize the theoretical
merits of the German artisans in Switzerland, London and Paris,"
Marx wrote to Feuerbach; several hundred German workers in
Paris, he said, were enthusiastically studying Feuerbach's works
in sessions that met twice a week throughout the summer of 1844.
True, the Germans still showed too much of the artisan (as opposed
to proletarian) spirit, "but in any case it is among these 'barbarians' of our civilized society that history is preparing the practical
element for the emancipation of mankind."[147]

His new firsthand contact with proletarian writers and activists
almost surely encouraged Marx to see all of German politics, society, and philosophy with a new eye and to place home-country
developments in a new framework. It may have been easier, after
all, to situate the Silesian weavers' revolt in world-historical perspectives from a desk in Paris than from a village in Silesia itself.
The French experience pushed Marx toward a comparative assessment of French and German conditions, enabling him to find
the positive as well as the negative in Germany. The prospects and
achievements at home often looked better from abroad. Marx could
use his theoretical categories in Paris to explain why German history provided revolutionary opportunities that even the French
could not duplicate. His view of Germany therefore evolved with
considerable optimism through national comparisons that stressed
both the uniqueness and the universal significance of his native
country.

Meanwhile, his view of France evolved, too, as he began to find
problems in French socialist thought and as he got into trouble
with the French government. Whatever hopes he may have had for
Paris had clearly diminished by the time the French police served
notice of his expulsion from the country. Having discovered that
German intellectuals misunderstood the world, that French radicals clung to religion, and that French authorities could be as
intolerant as the Prussian police, Marx seemed to find some consolation in an idealized German proletariat that he believed would
lead the way to true human emancipation. In Paris, that consolation and belief became fundamental to his thought.

The French government informed Marx on 25 January 1845 that
he was to be expelled from France, and he left Paris a week later.
The expulsion came in direct response to pressure from the Prussian government, whose representatives had for many months been

urging Guizot to suppress *Vorwärts* and to expel its émigré writers. Prussia's ambassador to Paris, the Count von Arnim, repeatedly informed Guizot of his government's displeasure with articles in *Vorwärts* that supported the Silesian workers' revolt, spoke approvingly of an assassination attempt on the Prussian king, and criticized the German social order.[148] Guizot nevertheless hesitated to move against *Vorwärts*, explaining to von Arnim that foreign newspapers in France could publish freely so long as they abided by French press laws.[149] By late August 1844, however, Guizot had become willing—for diplomatic reasons—to honor the Prussian request and to begin legal action against the editor, Carl Bernays, despite strong protests in liberal French newspapers.[150]

The press complaints apparently slowed the prosecution, but in December 1844 Bernays was sentenced to two months in prison and fined three hundred francs for violating the law that required all periodicals to pay a security deposit to the French government. *Vorwärts* ceased publication at the end of the month.[151] With Bernays in prison and the newspaper out of business, the interior minister, Charles-Marie Duchâtel, fulfilled the other Prussian request by ordering the expulsion of Heinrich Börnstein, Ruge, and Marx. Börnstein and Ruge were ultimately granted permission to stay in France, and French authorities ignored Bernays once he had served his time in jail; thus Marx was the only member of the *Vorwärts* group to leave the country.

It is curious that Marx made no effort to protest the explusion. Bernays wrote an impassioned open letter (published in *La Réforme*, 14 February 1845) to express his disappointment in the way France—"the foyer and refuge of European liberty"—had treated *Vorwärts* and the people who wrote for it;[152] Ruge and Börnstein, for their part, successfully petitioned to remain in the country. But Marx quickly packed for Brussels, leaving without protest or petition of any kind. One suspects that he had begun to feel isolated or blocked in Paris by February 1845. The publications with which he associated had failed; the Germans he knew there were no longer important to him (except Heine perhaps); and he had few French friends. He had taken all that he needed from French history and social theory and worker meetings and the streets of Paris. In *The Holy Family* he had worked his way through the French Revolution and French socialism back to German philosophy, where his interests would generally focus until he settled things to his own satisfaction in *The German Ideology* (1845–46). Perhaps his intellectual preoccupations led him to assume that French society had yielded to him all that it could offer. In any event, the experiential component of Marx's Paris came to an end, and within a couple of years he had broken most of his intellectual links as well.

The intellectual break appeared most clearly in the harsh attack on Proudhon that he published in 1847. Indeed, Marx seemed to feel the need to break with French socialists as decisively as he had broken with the German Hegelians. The anti-Proudhon work (written in French for a French public) thus became another of Marx's vehement declarations of independence. Proudhon may have been the most important and influential living French socialist when Marx wrote the critique; Marx himself had earlier praised Proudhon's work and in May 1846 had even asked him to be the French correspondent for the international communist association with which Marx was working in Brussels.[153] Proudhon declined the request, however, in a cordial letter that combined praise for Marx's work with warnings about the dangers of intolerance.[154] That exchange marked the end of the friendly relationship that the two men had established in Paris. When Proudhon soon thereafter published *The Philosophy of Poverty*—a work that utilized Hegelian dialectics in ways that Marx found absurd—Marx decided it was time to discredit Proudhon as a bad philosopher, a bad economist, and a bad socialist, all of which he sought to prove in his ironically titled study *The Poverty of Philosophy*.

In the first place, Marx explained, Proudhon misunderstood the notion of dialectical movement as Hegel and others used it. The dialectical process was one in which two contradictory tendencies coexisted, entered into conflict, and ultimately fused into a new category; but Proudhon, who did not grasp the dynamic *interaction* of the two tendencies, naively assumed that one need merely remove one side of the dialectic (evil) to produce a new synthesis. This was philosophy to suit the needs of a "petty-bourgeois" reformer because it dispelled much of the inevitable conflict in the historical process. Proudhon's "good side" in history was the side of equality, and so he simply assumed that this could become the historical synthesis by negating the "bad side," which was inequality (in wages, property, rights, and so on).[155]

Marx dismissed Proudhon's view as wholly idealist and ahistorical: "In short, [Proudhon's] equality is the *primordial intention*, the *mystical tendency*, the *providential aim* that the social genius has constantly before its eyes as it whirls in the circle of economic contradictions."[156] Proudhon's dialectical imagination, in other words, ignored the long-developing historical process whereby economic relations (not a misdirection of providential aims) produced inequality, and opposing forces entered into conflict (not simply disappeared). Ironically, it seems that Marx had come to accept much of Critical Criticism's description of the "theological" Proudhon. Having denounced that view of Proudhon to the Germans in *The Holy Family,* he seemed now to use part of that very analysis to expose Proudhon's mistakes to the French.

Simple-minded dialectics (Marx said that Proudhon "never got further than sophistry")[157] and idealist history were only part of Proudhon's failure, however. Marx maintained that he was also a very bad economist: he did not understand labor or value or property, and he ignored most of the details that constituted modern political economy. Marx laid out Proudhon's failure in a summary that left him no place among either the economists or the socialists:

> M. Proudhon flatters himself on having given a criticism of both political economy and communism: he is beneath them both. Beneath the economists, since, as a philosopher who has at his elbow a magic formula, he thought he could dispense with going into purely economic details; beneath the Socialists, because he has neither courage enough nor insight enough to rise, be it even speculatively, above the bourgeois horizon.
>
> He wants to be the synthesis—he is a composite error.
>
> He wants to soar as the man of science above the bourgeois and proletarians; he is merely the petty bourgeois, continually tossed back and forth between capital and labour, political economy and communism.[158]

Lacking a clear critical stance of his own, Proudhon received from Marx a label that clarified his position for generations of hostile Marxist critics: petty bourgeois. Behind all the jargon about dialectics and economics, Marx claimed to have found a typical bourgeois moralist, seeking his share of the property, harping on the traditional French theme of equality, and longing sentimentally for hearth and conjugal love.[159]

These tendencies convinced Marx that Proudhon ultimately wanted no more than those wrongheaded socialist reformers who called for adjustments in the system without recognizing the necessity for thoroughgoing social revolution. His naive diagnosis of the social problem led to prescriptions for curing it that went no further than a petty-bourgeois ideal of equal shopkeepers.[160] Like the German reformers, and like many radicals in the French tradition, Proudhon did not understand that true equality and human liberation required the overthrow of all existing economic relationships rather than the simple reorganization of the wage system, better opportunities for craftsmen, or the creation of new theoretical categories.

Indeed, as Marx explained to the Russian critic Annenkov, Proudhon's faults bore remarkable similarity to the Bauer brothers' errors: "The solution of present problems does not lie for him [Proudhon] in public action but in the dialectical rotations of his own mind. Since to him the categories are the motive force, it is not necessary to change practical life in order to change the categories. Quite the contrary. One must change the categories and the consequences will be a change in the existing society."[161] Marx finally dispatched Proudhon, therefore, with the list of errors he had ascribed to the Hegelians, calling him idealistic, ahistorical, unaware of productive forces, and naively reformist. Even worse, perhaps, Proudhon offered France a fuzzy, mistaken imitation of the German philosophical tradition, making his other errors all the more irksome to Marx. The whole attack thus carried the explicit multinational purpose of showing the French that Proudhon was a misinformed philosopher and the Germans that he was a misinformed economist—and suggesting to everyone that he would best be ignored.[162] As it happened, Marx's work attracted practically no attention in the Parisian socialist community at which it was directed.[163] Yet this attack, like many others Marx had written between 1843 and 1847, served the important function of defining his own position in opposition to French or German alternatives and hence enabled him to enunciate further the philosophy, economics, and socialism of his emerging social theory.

The critique of Proudhon may be seen as the completion of Marx's intellectual affair with France. To be sure, he continued to write about French politics and society *(The Eighteenth Brumaire of Louis Bonaparte* is one notable example), but he turned increasingly to England—where he would soon settle for the rest of his life—for his research and examples. To put the pattern in very simple terms, the French experience had helped Marx to confront both the German philosophical legacy and the history of French politics, materialism, and socialism. Now he would focus increasingly on the economic issues—the English tradition—that formed much of his theoretical concern thereafter and led to such major works as *Grundrisse* and *Capital*.

But that is another subject. The argument here is that the time in Paris marked the crucial transition from philosopher to social theorist (with an important economic component), that Marx became "Marx" in the course of his social and intellectual encounter with France. True, he might have reached many of his conclusions by other means and in other places, yet it is important to stress that he did so in Paris in the 1840s. The experiences and perspectives of that time and place reappear in significant ways throughout his mature thought, so that the young exile in Paris leads directly toward the old exile in London.

It was French history that encouraged Marx to think about the nature of revolution, the limits of political reform, and the importance of economic forces in the process of historical change. It was in Paris that he studied the materialist tradition and found philosophical weapons to turn upon his Hegelian compatriots; it was there that he read and criticized the classical texts of political economy; it was there that he met the "bestial" French urban proletariat, a class that he approached with insights from his own philosophical tradition and described in ways that the French themselves had not yet considered; it was there that he discovered the German proletariat and patriotically announced its special role in the international revolutionary future; it was there that he found the most advanced socialists, whom he defended to the Germans and then criticized to the French. It was in Paris that Marx materialized the philosophical problem (dialectics, alienation) and brought philosophy and history to the material problem (economics, poverty).

Marx's theoretical work in France was therefore an extraordinary multicultural synthesis, a project that drew upon the social and intellectual context that Paris provided and a process that evolved through the special insights and position of exile life. Paris, in short, offered a great deal of material to help a German philosopher become a European social theorist.

Chapter 4

Mickiewicz in Paris:
Exile and the New Nationalism

One of the qualities of our epoch is the mutual affection which causes people to come together. It is recognized that Paris is the focus, the spring, the instrument of this tendency: by the intermediary of this great city, the peoples of Europe get to know one another and sometimes to know themselves. It is glorious for France to possess such a powerful attraction, it is a proof of the development which it has attained; because this attraction is always a direct proof of the force of the internal movement, of the mass of spiritual warmth, and of the light which produces it. The superiority of France, as the oldest daughter of the church, as the trustee of all the inspirations of science and of art, is both so evident and of such a noble character, that the other peoples do not feel humiliated to acknowledge its preeminence in this respect.

Adam Mickiewicz, Lecture at
the Collège de France (1840)

Adam Mickiewicz arrived in Paris in August 1832, at the age of thirty-three, and lived there the rest of his life except for brief periods in Switzerland, Italy, and Turkey (where he died in 1855). Mickiewicz's life in France resembled that of Heine more than that of Marx: he spent most of his mature years in Paris (almost exactly the same years Heine was there); he came to know many writers in the French intellectual elite; he made a name for himself by describing his home country to the French and France to his fellow Poles; he transformed himself from a poet into a journalist, historian, and political analyst; he received income from the French government; and he became increasingly religious, even mystical, in the course of his long exile. Mickiewicz differed from Heine, however, in many of his political interests, his literary values, his extreme emotional identification with his home country, and his style of life; external similarities in their French experience should therefore not obscure their important differences. Moreover, despite the overlapping aspects of their personal biographies, the two famous exile poets never became friends. Indeed, they seem never to have known each other at all, though they shared so many common friends in the close-knit Parisian literary world that each must surely have known about the other, and they almost surely met somewhere through mutual friends during their long years in Paris (though neither of them ever reported such a meeting).

Mickiewicz did not share Heine's attraction to Parisian pleasures or Marx's interest in the Parisian proletariat. He preferred instead to stay among the Polish exiles whose intense nationalist concerns set them apart from the diversions of salon life and from the historical or theoretical projects of exiles such as Heine and Marx. Mickiewicz was entirely typical of this Polish émigré community in that national salvation overshadowed every other literary or social issue for him. His French experience thus became a twenty-year effort to define the Polish national identity, to defend the uniqueness of that identity against the West (and East), and to mobilize France in the campaign to restore Polish independence. Although he never moved the French to act, he probably did more than anyone else to create an image of Poland in French society and to construct a messianic self-image for the Poles themselves. It all added up to an exile story of occasional success, frequent frustration, and enduring alienation.

Mickiewicz's journey into exile was by no means a simple passage from Poland to Paris. When he settled in France, he had already lived eight years as an exile in Russia, Italy, and Germany. The Russian government had banished him from Poland in 1824— because of his participation in a Polish nationalist youth organization—and compelled him to move to Russia, where he lived for various periods in Saint Petersburg, Moscow, and Odessa. This first phase of exile life was important for Mickiewicz's development as a poet because he met Russian intellectuals, became acquainted with the broader characteristics of Slavic culture, and wrote his first epic poem, *Konrad Wallenrod* (1828). He also began to think about Poland's unique position in Europe and the difficulties of achieving true independence from the enormous Russian empire, themes that first appeared in *Konrad Wallenrod*. The Russian phase in Mickiewicz's exile ended in 1829 when he received permission

Adam Mickiewicz in 1842. Anonymous daguerreotype. Société Historique et Littéraire Polonaise, Paris.

to leave for western Europe. His travels thereafter took him through Germany and Italy to Rome, where he stayed for several months during the winters of 1829–30 and 1830–31. The Roman phase became important, too, inasmuch as it brought about a religious conversion that gave Mickiewicz a lifelong commitment to spiritual values and a strong inclination to mysticism. Thus, by the time of the Polish uprising in November 1830, Mickiewicz had considerable knowledge of Slavic cultural traditions and Christian mysticism, which he would eventually bring together in the theories of history and politics that he developed in France.[1]

The Polish revolt against Russia in 1830–31 became the most important historical event in the formation of Mickiewicz's view of the world. It began while he was living in Rome, where he hesitated for several months before he left to join the struggle. Traveling by way of Paris (his first visit to the French capital), he finally reached the Prussian-controlled city of Poznań—only to meet Poles who were beginning to flee from the rapidly collapsing revolt (August 1831). With the Russian army now blocking all entrances to Warsaw (the city surrendered in September), Mickiewicz was forced to drift about eastern Prussia until he settled into the growing refugee community at Dresden in March 1832. His contact with exiles there revealed to him the details of Poland's defeat and apparently provoked him (perhaps because of guilt over his nonparticipation in the great revolt) to begin writing his response to the recent events in *Forefathers' Eve*.[2] The Polish Emigration had begun, and much of it was passing through Dresden en route to the West. Although Mickiewicz had missed the revolt, he became immediately connected to its consequences and to the debates about what Poles must do to regain their freedom. Many émigrés anticipated help from France, but Mickiewicz had seen enough of Paris to doubt that Poland's salvation would come from that direction. He thus began urging Poles to take strength from their own heritage (a theme of *Forefathers' Eve*) and to avoid the consoling hope for salvation in France.

This early skepticism toward France apparently kept Mickiewicz in Dresden a long time. He explained why he expected so little from the French in a letter from Dresden (March 1832) to the Polish historian Joachim Lelewel, who had been working in Paris since the previous fall.

Some [Poles] seem to me to have faith in the French government, others in the nation as a whole or in the members of the movement.

As for me, I consider these two French parties as a herd of demoralized egotists and count upon them not at all. France is, to my way of thinking, what Athens was at the time of Demosthenes; the French will shout, will change orators and leaders, but they will never be cured, for they have a cancerous heart. I have great hopes in our nation and in the help of events which no diplomacy could forsee. . . . I have only to suggest that we must impress on our tendencies a religious and moral character different from the financial liberalism of the French, and that we must choose as our basis Catholicism. . . . Perhaps our nation is called to preach to the peoples of the world the gospel of nationalism, morality, religion, and scorn of budgets—that single basis for present-day policy, which truly smells of the customhouse. The most learned of the French feel no patriotism, no enthusiasm for liberty; they content themselves with arguing about it.[3]

Even before he had settled in France, therefore, Mickiewicz was stressing that the Polish nation must follow its own course in the campaign for freedom and that Polish values must necessarily differ from those of the rhetorical, materialist French. To be sure, he too joined the Emigration and returned to Paris in the summer of 1832, but he did so because it offered the most practical base for Polish activity rather than because it offered salvation. Poland must save itself—with the aid of Providence. Yet Mickiewicz soon became one of the most outspoken and prominent advocates for French aid to the Polish cause. He went to Paris without illusions; he stayed there with extraordinary hope for more than two decades. And unlike most émigrés who arrived in July Monarchy France, he went as a veteran exile who had already learned a great deal about his native country from the outside and about displacement as a way of life.

The Polish Emigration was well on its way to becoming institutionalized in Paris by the summer of 1832. The first members of the Polish community in France (it would grow to almost 10,000 people by the late 1840s) had established themselves in the capital and created the Polish National Committee, which sought to organize new Polish legions, secure French aid for Polish independence, and coordinate a multinational European campaign against the Russians.[4] Mickiewicz's liberal friend Lelewel became president of the committee, whereupon the movement quickly divided into the conservative and radical factions that constituted the Emigration during all the years that followed. Meanwhile, French liberals led by Lafayette organized the Franco-Polish Committee, which collected funds to aid destitute Poles, distributed news on

Polish affairs, encouraged widespread popular sympathy for be-
leaguered Poland, and tried to win official support for the Polish
movement.[5] All of this activity attracted the attention of the press
and government authorities, but it failed to produce any substantive pro-Poland response from Louis-Philippe or his ministers. Polish exiles and their French sympathizers thus became part of the
opposition to July Monarchy policies, and Polish independence
took its place as one of the major causes in the radical European
movements of the era.

As the Polish community grew and its leaders established links
with liberal and radical critics within French society, government
distrust of the refugees evolved into increasingly severe policies of
regulation and control. Reports of suspicious Polish activity appeared frequently enough in police files to convince the prefect,
Henri Gisquet, that conspiratorial French radicals had misled the
whole Emigration into opposition to the French government. "In
the eyes of the majority among them [the émigrés], the *juste-milieu*
was therefore the tyrant of France," Gisquet explained in his memoirs, "[and] it deserved their hatred as much as the other tyrants
of Europe."[6] The exiles' hostility to their French protectors might
seem inexplicable, Gisquet suggested, unless one remembered that
exile groups included a great many "individuals with ardent passions, amateur troublemakers, [and] habitués with violent emotions; others [in the groups were] animated by fanaticism,
contemptuous of notions of right and wrong, and disposed...to
drown themselves in blood in order to serve their dreadful ambition!"[7] It is not surprising, of course, to find that such perceptions
on the part of French officials helped to shape government policy
toward the émigrés who continued to stream into Paris.

The official attitudes became apparent in a series of regulatory
actions during 1832–33. First, the refugees were removed from the
jurisdiction of the War Department (where they might have formed
their legions as part of the French army) and placed under the
control of the Interior Ministry (April 1832). This transfer indicated
that the French subsequently viewed the Poles as an internal problem for the police rather than as an aspect of foreign policy or
military policy—a shift in status that restricted the social and
political freedom of the exiles. Second, the government devised a
decentralization program designed to move Poles out of politically
turbulent Paris and disperse them in isolated provincial centers.
Although the program met with considerable resistance, most exiles had no choice but to live where they were assigned, because

the government would not grant money to refugees unless they went to the *dépôts* (refugee centers) in cities such as Avignon, Besançon or Lyon, and most refugees had no income except the benefits they had begun to receive from the government. Once they were assigned to a *dépôt*, it was illegal for Poles to live in Paris or even to visit the capital without permission and special passes from the police. (The system of control resembled somewhat the restrictions on French workers, who were obliged to carry a *livret* when they changed employers or cities.) Finally, whether they lived in Paris or the provinces, Poles were subjected to regular police surveillance and to tight controls on all forms of political activity. Whenever French authorities believed that such activity exceeded tolerable limits, they could expel Poles from the country—as they did Lelewel and other leaders of the Polish National Committee in 1833.[8]

The government regulations produced considerable disillusionment among Poles who had expected sympathy and support in France. True, most refugees were allowed to remain in the country, and many did receive financial help, but the isolation and limitations that resulted from French policies gradually caused the Emigration to turn in upon itself and to consume much of its energy in internal disputes that led nowhere.

The exiles divided broadly into conservative and radical factions reflecting the contrasting views and strategies that had earlier emerged in the revolt itself. Conservatives supported Adam Czartoryski's effort to win support for the Polish cause through diplomatic channels and his belief that Poland could be saved through the intervention of sympathetic Western governments. Radicals doubted that other governments would ever act on Poland's behalf or that negotiations would produce results, and so they hoped for broad revolutionary changes that would eventually sweep Poland into a liberated new world. Conservatives tended to be aristocratic and to support the traditional Polish social system; radicals favored social reforms (such as the abolition of restrictions on the rights of peasants) that would create a new Polish society. Although a strong religious motivation seemed to influence almost all members of the Emigration, conservatives were also likely to be more staunchly Catholic.[9] Both groups naturally assumed that their own plans would lead most directly to Polish liberation, and they argued bitterly among themselves. Meanwhile, the French predictably turned to other concerns, and Poland began to lose its prominence and special appeal amid the welter of competing causes, fads, factions, and events that passed through the Parisian press and salons.

All of these tendencies—government surveillance, dispersion to *dépôts*, expulsions, internal dissension, diminishing French interest—had become characteristic of the increasingly demoralized Emigration into which Mickiewicz settled after reaching Paris in August 1832. The continuity of the Emigration was in fact the only settled aspect of his life in France, for he lived at fourteen different addresses in Paris, followed several "careers," and moved through at least three groups of French friends over the next two decades.[10] Throughout all of the dislocating changes in his French life, however, he held resolutely to the *unity* of Polish identity. When other émigrés divided into conservative and radical camps, Mickiewicz stressed the essential similarity of all Poles; when the French turned to other concerns, Mickiewicz stressed that Poland was not just another problem in diplomatic affairs but the central issue of modern European history. Threatened on all sides by extreme separations, discontinuities, and fragmentations, he sought to bring about harmonious reconciliations between conservative and radical Poles, between the cause of the Emigration and the cause of France, between Poland and Europe, between history and heaven.[11] His literary projects in France expressed extreme faith in the uniqueness of Poland, a faith sustained and intensified through his critical response to the social and cultural characteristics of Louis-Philippe's Paris.

The intensity of this faith soon made him a leader in both the Polish Romantic politics and the Polish Romantic literature that flourished in France when Russian power blocked political and literary expression at home.[12] It was a dual role in an exile community that encouraged a multiplicity of overlapping political, religious, and literary projects. Mickiewicz knew something about all of them and enough about France to establish his special political-literary identity at the intersection of the Polish Emigration and July Monarchy society.

In the beginning he devoted himself to the immediate needs of the disparate and disoriented Polish community he found in Paris. He came to France with a theory about the unique destiny of the Polish Emigration which he wanted his fellow exiles to understand and to accept. Accordingly, his first project was to publish *The Books of the Polish Nation and of the Polish Pilgrims* (1832), which he intended as a guide for émigré values and behavior. He explained there in biblical prose that Poles must see themselves as

representatives of a higher mission—the redemption of mankind—
and that they must prepare themselves for this mission through
cooperative unity and a rigorous moral superiority in all aspects
of their exile lives. It was therefore essential for Poles to overcome
the conflicts that divided conservatives and radicals, a goal that
both sides might achieve if they remembered their common Polish
destiny. He tried also to practice what he preached by working
with different exile factions, giving money to some of the poorest
refugees, and opening his home to Poles of all persuasions.[13]

Thus, despite his frequent moves around Paris, his financial problems, and the unsettled external circumstances of his own life,
Mickiewicz soon became a remarkably stable and uncompromising
reference point for the evolving Polish movement. After issuing his
manifesto on the Emigration he went on to write the epic poem
Pan Tadeusz (1834), in which he described, among other things,
Polish traditions and society in some of the most lyrical passages
in Slavic literarture.[14] Meanwhile, he was publishing political articles in an exile newspaper called the *Polish Pilgrim*, articles that
explained the unique attributes of Poland and also advocated unity
among all European people—Poles, French, Germans, Italians,
everyone. "What is today the first, foremost, most vivid desire of
peoples?" Mickiewicz asked in one essay. "We do not hesitate to
say that it is the desire of reaching an understanding, uniting,
combining their interests; without this it would be impossible to
comprehend the general will . . . [or] this great tendency of the spirit
of the age."[15]

The desire to encourage "the spirit of the age," to further the
cause of unity, and to publicize Poland's plight gradually led Mickiewicz from his more specific Polish preoccupations into wider
contact with French culture. He came to know French intellectuals
who embraced both the cause of European cooperation and the
special Polish role in promoting the cause. This widening participation in French society, though, was never a simple process. He
wrote plays for the French stage, but they were never produced;
he lectured on Slavic literature at the Collège de France, but his
courses were suspended; he returned to journalism after the Revolution of 1848, but the newspaper for which he worked (*La Tribune
des Peuples*) was closed by the government; he was employed as
librarian at the Bibliothèque de l'Arsenal, but he departed for Turkey to organize a Polish legion. He was, in short, forever moving
into and out of institutions in French society; always participating
as the *Pole* with a larger view of Europe, of politics, of literature,

of destiny, of unity; always working with France insofar as doing so served the greater cause and leaving whenever the cause might be better served in another way or another place. There seemed always to be some element of incongruity in these processes. In fact, during all his years of exile, Mickiewicz, the cause, and France came together only once with much success, and even that conjunction did not last long. As professor of Slavic languages and literature at the Collège de France between 1840 and 1844, Mickiewicz managed in his own way to unite literature and politics, Poland and France, the cause and the public. But the incongruities, which never disappeared, soon took over again and sent him back to the exile margins from which he seemed unable or unwilling to escape.

French Friends

The French government established the chair in Slavic literature in the summer of 1840 and chose Mickiewicz to be the first professor. Minister of Education Victor Cousin and his associate Léon Faucher actually created the position expressly for Mickiewicz, to whom they suggested that the post might offer exceptional political and patriotic opportunities. "It is a question of naturalizing Poland in France," Faucher explained to Mickiewicz. "This is the mission entrusted to you. The chair to which you are named has a political character. We want to create a center, at least literary, of the Polish nation in exile."[16] A bill to establish the chair was introduced in the Chamber of Deputies in April and brought to debate in June 1840. There was little dissent—perhaps because the Polish cause remained fashionable in liberal circles, and a professorship seemed a safe way to acknowledge it.[17]

Cousin clearly aimed his recommendation for the new chair at the patriotism of the deputies, for he justified the professorship as an appropriate manifestation of France's special mission in Europe:

The Collège de France, like all our *grandes écoles* in Paris, in our century as in the Middle Ages, is attended by foreigners from every nation, and one can say with truth and legitimate pride that the audience at the Collège de France is recruited in the whole of Europe. There is at this moment in all the countries of the Slavic race a sort of renaissance movement wherever there is free scholarship....All that would form the subject matter for a professorship that [it] is fitting to endow at the Collège de France....

The new instruction would put France in intellectual communication with a race that numbers 60 million people....It is worthy of France to be acquainted with everything in order to appreciate everything; it is rich enough not to fear any comparison. It is necessary that France have all the great literatures appear before it in order to judge them with its reason [and] to spread them with the aid of its universal language over the surface of Europe and the world, so that it may continue the noble role that belongs to it as the propagator of enlightenment and civilization.[18]

The paternalism and pride in Cousin's argument offer a curious revelation of the French attitude toward the foreigners who lived among them and suggest how the French could use the foreign presence as confirmation of their own importance in the world. The speech convinced the deputies to endow the chair without delay. As it happened, Mickiewicz's financial problems had forced him to move to Switzerland, where he was teaching language and literature at a school in Lausanne (1839–40). The new academic appointment, however, brought him back to Paris and enabled him to rent a comfortable right-bank apartment in the rue d'Amsterdam. He began his lectures at the Collège de France in December 1840, settled into a relatively stable phase of his exile life (he lived almost five years at the same address), and entered the career of a Parisian intellectual celebrity.

The lectures became a weekly event that attracted prominent French writers as well as other exiles and the public at large; Poland was *à la mode*, and Mickiewicz became "Poland." The position at the Collège de France gave Mickiewicz an opportunity to trace the development of Slavic culture for a Western audience and to stress the qualities that made Poland different from the rest of Europe. These themes gave his courses an important political dimension (as the government noted by suspending them in 1844) and made the lectures popular enough to justify later publication of the entire series in a five-volume collection, *The Slavs*. Mickiewicz's assessment of his academic role stressed the extraordinary responsibility he felt as the representative of Slavic culture in France. "You would not believe what hopes the Slavs attach to the establishment of this chair," he told his audience at one lecture. "They regard it as a tribune, as a flag and almost as a military post."[19] He seemed to believe that his professorship was in fact what Faucher had said it might become: a center for the Polish nation in exile.

It was of course a center whose power depended on words and literature rather than military weapons, but Mickiewicz emphasized that the public word itself inspired Poles and carried power in the world. "The Slavs, who have not yet misused the word, suppose it is still a primitive force. They think that it suffices to pronounce a word for the thing to be done.... They believe that it is only necessary to whisper softly a single word to the French genius for this formidable genius to put it immediately into action."[20] This faith in words was one to which Mickiewicz himself adhered; he expected that his lectures at the Collège de France might encourage French support for the Polish cause as well as a new respect for Slavic literature. Although the French government showed little interest in the cause, French intellectuals responded by giving Mickiewicz a prominent place in Parisian intellectual society—the Polish poet for a community enamored of Poland and poets. Thus, the professorship offered Mickiewicz and his cause exceptional visibility, an advantageous point he stressed to Cousin as he wrote to accept the position. The new chair placed Slavic "in the ranks of the scholarly languages," Mickiewicz noted with considerable optimism, and it established eastern European literature at "the most famous university in Europe." Here was a literary and political opening that led Mickiewicz to the center of Parisian intellectual life, and for once he confessed to feeling "extremely flattered."[21]

Mickiewicz did not reach his position through mere chance, however. The chair came to him in large part because he had long before made his way among the French literary elite. Indeed, the appointment at the Collège de France simply initiated a new phase in a cycle of contacts which had already taken Mickiewicz through several influential groups in July Monarchy Paris. He first moved into the circle of religious radicals which surrounded Félicité Robert de Lamennais and Charles Montalembert and then (in the late 1830s) associated with novelists and poets such as George Sand and Albert de Vigny. He was thus no stranger to French writers by the time he joined the academic society of Edgar Quinet and Jules Michelet in the 1840s. Each of these circles met some of Mickiewicz's most pressing needs in that they facilitated his attempts to make Poland known in France, publicized different aspects of his work, and contributed to the development of his French reputation; at the same time, these contacts with the elite of French national culture seemed to expand his conception of Poland as a distinctive national culture in modern Europe.

Mickiewicz arrived in Paris with religious sentiments and political attitudes that made the radical Catholic community the most congenial place in which to begin his search for new friends and allies. He had read in Rome the works of Lamennais, whom in 1832 he believed to be the most loyal friend of Poland in all of France. "He is the sole Frenchman who has sincerely wept over our fate," Mickiewicz wrote Lelewel from Dresden. "His are the only tears I have seen in Paris."[22] Despite this high opinion, however, Mickiewicz did not meet Lamennais until early 1833, when the two men were brought together by Montalembert. Mickiewicz had met Montalembert in September 1832 and quickly formed a friendship that rested firmly upon a shared commitment to the cause. Montalembert devoted himself to Poland with exceptional enthusiasm, learning Polish, writing articles on Polish developments for the French press, and assembling a Franco-Polish group every week at his home to plan pro-Polish work in France. Mickiewicz joined the meetings and became an exile hero for Montalembert, who soon undertook the task of translating the *Books of the Polish Nation and of Polish Pilgrims* into French.[23]

Montalembert used that work to make a case for what he called in his translator's preface the "genius" of Mickiewicz. He explained to French readers that Mickiewicz wrote with "a piety so impassioned and so exalted that it might be said to have been borrowed from the legends of the primitive Church or from the choirs of celestial spirits."[24] This was a work that no French reader should overlook, Montalembert advised, for it combined the oldest Catholic traditions with insights into the most modern national problems. It was, moreover, accessible to the "most simple intelligence, while the substance of his work puts it on the level of the highest thoughts that have distinguished mankind."[25] Montalembert's description emerged as the popular view of Mickiewicz among the Catholic radicals, who became the first French audience for what he was writing about Poland, France, and the unique religious mission of the Great Emigration.

Even more important, perhaps, the translations and praise from Montalembert soon brought Mickiewicz to the attention of literary Paris, thereby proving again how important a first contact could be in the interlocking world of French literati. The critic Charles Sainte-Beuve, for example, wrote a sympathetic review of the *Books* (1833) and strongly recommended the work as a talented expression of both Slavic literature and Slavic politics. "We have seen, above all, in this [work] a thoroughly noble use of poetic genius in a time of national disaster," wrote Sainte-Beuve. "We have admired in it . . . the beauties of a thought that is serious and virile and quite naturally biblical. To tastes that are too often sated, it has been bread of a distinguished and acrid flavor, rather strange, kneaded in a Slavic manner."[26] This was the kind of review by which Sainte-Beuve regularly helped to make or break the reputations of would-be authors in July Monarchy France, and it helped an otherwise alien Polish name become familiar to Parisian readers who were always in search of a new book or a new cause.

Reputations in France, though, were a consequence of friendships as well as favorable reviews, and Mickiewicz undoubtedly gained something in this respect from his early connection with Lamennais. Scholars who have speculated on the mutual influences of this friendship usually suggest that the Pole ultimately gave to the Frenchman more than he took.[27] There is in any case plenty of evidence that Lamennais admired Mickiewicz and his work. His correspondence in 1833 carried frequent references to his Polish friend, discussed the religious theories in Mickiewicz's writing, and encouraged acquaintances to read the *Books:* "There will shortly appear a little volume entitled *The Books of the Polish Pilgrims,* by *Mickiewicz,* undoubtedly the first poet of our epoch," Lamennais wrote to a friend in the spring of 1833. "It contains enchanting things; without forgetting all the distance which separates the word of man from the word of God I should almost dare to say: this is as beautiful as the Gospel. Such a pure expression of faith and liberty joined together is a miracle in our age of servitude and disbelief."[28] This enthusiastic praise forms part of the justification for the scholarly notion that Mickiewicz significantly influenced the form, style, and content of Lamennais's famous *Paroles d'un croyant* (1834).

Whatever their exact stylistic influence on one another, the two friends in fact shared a number of important ideas: Catholicism could lead to reform and freedom; the "people" would move from present suffering to future harmony; nationalism must serve a higher internationalism; salvation would come from popular movements rather than from European monarchs; and social morality depended on private morality.[29] These ideological affinities, strongest in 1832–33, surely made their early friendship possible; however, they began to drift apart in the mid-1830s. Mickiewicz found the *Paroles* to be insufficiently spiritual, and Lamennais became increasingly skeptical of Polish messianism; as Mickiewicz became more mystical, Lamennais became more republican, more democratic, and more separated from the Catholic Church. The relationship between them declined accordingly.[30] Yet the early connections with Lamennais and his radical Catholic friends had given Mickiewicz his introduction to French intellecutal culture and brought his name to the French public. That introduction, in turn, became the starting point for the new contacts that constituted his French intellectual community over the next decade.

Mickiewicz needed money as well as a reputation to survive in Paris, of course. The French government had provided a small grant and a yearly pension of a thousand francs, but this had not been enough to support him in the capital.[31] Thus, like many writers in July Monarchy Paris, he had decided to enter the popular and sometimes lucrative world of French theater. He wrote a play depicting eighteenth-century Polish patriots which he hoped would produce a large profit, ease his financial problems, and open the way to other theatrical projects. In order to get it into a theater, though, he needed help from French friends, and so he appealed to Alfred de Vigny and George Sand for advice. Vigny read *Les confédérés de Bar* in the spring of 1837, recommended some revisions, and then introduced the new playwright to the director of the Theâtre Porte Saint-Martin. Despite the efforts of both Vigny and Mickiewicz, however, the director refused to produce the play, and the project collapsed. Its failure seemed also to end the friendship between the poets, though some critics maintain that Vigny's poetry reflects a clear and continuing interest in Mickiewicz.[32]

The theatrical venture led Mickiewicz into a much more enduring and important relationship with George Sand. She, too, offered advice on the play, praised it to her acquaintances, and urged an actor-friend to help bring the work to the stage at Porte Saint-Martin, but the failure of the project by no means ended her friendship.[33] On the contrary, she soon replaced Lamennais and Montalembert to become Mickiewicz's most loyal advocate in France. Although they first met in 1836 at the salon of Madame d'Agoult (another writer who befriended the Pole and facilitated his entrée into literary culture), Sand's significant connections with Mickiewicz did not begin until he sought her advice on *Les confédérés*. She responded with a friendly letter in which she said his work was as "beautiful" as that of the most talented French writers. Even her suggestions for stylistic changes came with such praise that Mickeiwicz must surely have felt encouraged; at the same time, however, she warned that the French public was extremely "stupid" in its choices and that quality therefore carried no guarantee of success on the Parisian stage. "I can only say that if beauty, greatness and depth should be honored, your work will be prized," she wrote Mickiewicz.[34]

Such encouragement provided the emotional support and enthusiasm that Mickiewicz always valued in his French contacts and to which he responded appreciatively. He reciprocated Sand's comments on his play, for example, with a round of praise for her insight and amiability and assistance.[35] The Sand-Mickiewicz connection thus evolved into another of those friendships between a foreigner and a Parisian in which each party embraced and supported the other with almost limitless enthusiasm and goodwill. (Perhaps it was easier for the French to praise foreigners than to praise their rivals in the French literary community.) Sand helped Mickiewicz carry his Polish message to the French public, clarify his French prose, and publish in *La Revue Indépendante*.[36] Mickiewicz, for his part, offered Sand a living example of the mystical "Eastern" genius, a vaguely idealized figure whom she wanted to know and describe for reasons of her own.

Sand's belief in Mickiewicz's mystical genius contributed to her exceptional interest in both the man and his work and formed the theme for articles about the poet that she published in French journals. Her journal essays may in fact have been the most useful service she provided, because she argued there for the unique historical significance of her friend's writing and Polish cause. Her "Essai sur le drame fantastique: Goethe, Byron, Mickiewicz" in the *Revue des Deux Mondes* (December 1839) ascribed to the Polish exile a place among the greatest poets of the century. Indeed, Sand suggested that Mickiewicz combined the real world and the dream world with more skill than either Goethe or Byron. "Real life is itself a vigorous painting, startling and tremendous, and idea lies at its center," she wrote. "The world of fantasy is not outside or above; it is at the bottom of everything, it moves everything, it is the soul of all reality, it lives in all facts. Each character, each group carries it in itself and shows it [in] its own way."[37] Other writers had never managed to represent this intricate combination as effectively as Mickiewicz. "Since the lamentations and denunciations of the prophets of Zion," Sand explained, "no voice has been raised with so much force to sing of an event so stupendous as that of the fall of a nation."[38]

She went on to quote extensively from Part III of *Forefathers'*

Eve (so that readers might be introduced to "the genius of Mic-kiewicz") and to compare Konrad, the hero of that work, with Goethe's Faust. Mickiewicz's character, Sand declared, was more clearly the *modern* man because he brought together belief and skepticism, vanity and anger, suffering and justice, ignorance and the vision of a better future.[39] Some readers may have questioned Sand's critical pronouncements, but there can be no doubt that her essay in the leading journal of the day gave Mickiewicz new status in European literature and helped to establish his reputation beyond the community of Polish exiles and French intellectuals in Paris. Here was another poet for all of Europe to acknowledge, a *Pole* whose characters possessed "savage energy" and the "stamp of the poetry of the North" and whose themes turned upon the universal problems of faith, suffering, justice, earth, and heaven.[40]

Sand reiterated the message in an article for *La Revue Indépendante* (1843), which analyzed and defended Mickiewicz's lectures at the Collège de France. Although the mystical enthusiasm in those presentations was beginning to alienate some intellectuals, Sand (who attended many of them herself) supported Mickiewicz's unorthodox academic style and explained it as a manifestation of Slavic genius and inspiration. "Adam Mickiewicz is not only a great poet, the first cousin of Goethe and the brother of Byron," she wrote. "He is the moral expression of Poland, he is the symbol of its being in the sphere of sentiment. In a word, he has long been regarded as the man of Poland, and this view has no opponents."[41] At his public lectures he spoke with eloquence, originality, and simplicity.[42] As for his mysticism, Sand argued that it was probably a necessary component of Polish religion and politics because Poles had no access to such means of expression as a free press, national assemblies, or open discussion. French critics who objected to Mickiewicz's mystical, religious outlook therefore simply failed to understand the particularities of Slavic culture:

> The Slavic race, younger in civilization and more naive in sentiment, will perhaps declare later than we the definitive death of Christianity. ...And perhaps Mickiewicz, endowed with a more profound view of the instincts and tendencies of the Slavic race than we can have, has discovered in the dogmatically religious idea that animates him and the race the direct route to a social regeneration for the Slavic family. If we dare to contest him from the point of view of general philosophy or universal religion, we would not venture to contest his personal inspiration nor the certitude of his mission.[43]

While others chose to mock the Polish faith, Sand would instead accept it as a legitimate vehicle for a resurgent people and as a welcome contrast to the tiresome rationalities of Western thinkers. She was not even especially concerned about the influence of a radical mystic named Andrzej Towiański whom Mickiewicz had embraced despite the ridicule that his teachings elicited from most Poles and Frenchmen alike. Sand was willing to respect Mickiewicz wherever he wanted to go; if he followed Towiański, he surely knew what he was doing.[44]

To be sure, important differences continued to exist at all times between the two friends, differences that Sand acknowledged but did not pursue in *La Revue Indépendante*. She doubted, for example, that Mickiewicz's faith in divine political interventions had any relevance for France, and she rejected his belief in messianic leaders—new Napoleons—who might save modern Europe and resurrect Poland. This seemed naive, even dangerous, because the "people" could and must save themselves without waiting for a great man.[45] Sand did not make an issue of these points, however, and her continual support for Mickiewicz stands out as one of the most significant and valuable consequences of his long residence in Paris. Indeed, among the many French people Mickiewicz knew, only Edgar Quinet and Jules Michelet were as important in his exile life, and even their friendships seemed more formal than the association with Sand.

Mickiewicz, Quinet, and Michelet worked together at the Collège de France, where they became for a time the most popular and celebrated lecturers of the day. Linked by common ideas and sympathies, they developed a public reputation that suggested the interlocking alliance of an intellectual triumvirate. There were in fact important differences among them, but their triangular friendship in the early 1840s emphasized similarities and gave each of them an entrée to another culture.

Although Mickiewicz met both men in 1837, it was Quinet who first expressed strong interest in becoming a friend.[46] He compared Mickiewicz to Heine ("the angel and the demon"), apparently drawn to both exile poets as the "two antipodes" of life and literature.[47] Quinet had been one of the first French writers to praise Heine's wit and understanding of German culture; now he praised Mickiewicz's religious inspiration and told the poet himself that he was "one of those virile souls with whom I ought to be associated the rest of my days." He asked Mickiewicz to be a mentor as well as a friend: "Your advice can be infinitely precious to me," Quinet explained in a letter, "and I ask for it in all sincerity of heart. I shall give you in return a heart yearning for truth and sympathy. I thirst for friendship and serious thoughts...Dear Friend, help me to emerge from my ignorance, or teach me how to bear it."[48]

Quinet admired Mickiewicz as the embodiment of Poland, yet he also found in his friend the qualities of a modern prophet whose mysticism and faith made him exceptional among the Poles and altogether unique among the French. In one of his own lectures at the Collège de France, Quinet called Mickiewicz the "foremost poet of the Slavs" and went on to describe the saintlike characteristics that set him apart from all of his contemporaries: "Who has ever heard words more sincere, more religious, more Christian, more extraordinary than those of this exile among a remnant of his own people, like the prophet under the willows? Ah, if the soul of the martyrs and saints of Poland is not in him, I do not know where it is. Above all, who has ever spoken of our country, of France, with such filial emotion, if it is not this child of Poland?"[49] Like George Sand, Quinet was eager to defend Mickiewicz's mystical pronouncements, but he also stressed his friend's loyalty to France, thereby arguing for Mickiewicz's legitimacy when French critics complained about his religious ideas and peculiar politics. Quinet's exceptional sympathy for the religious Mickiewicz separated him from almost all of his academic colleagues and provoked him to defend those prophetic traits with particular insistence when French authorities turned against Mickiewicz's course on Slavic literature. Like Sand, Quinet seemed to respect his friend's inspiration no matter where it led. Mickiewicz, in turn, relied upon Quinet for help in revising his French texts, for support against French critics, and for aid in his frustrating and futile dealings with the French bureaucracy.[50]

The friendship with Michelet differed somewhat, in part because Michelet looked to Mickiewicz for something besides the spiritual experience that Quinet admired. When Michelet, the great historian of France (the nation he believed to be the central reference point in modern European history), became interested in Poland as the "France of the North," Mickiewicz assumed the identity of representative Pole, the complement of France. It was "Mickiewicz the Slav" who intrigued Michelet, as he explained to the poet in a letter about their friendship: "You are for me a revelation in more than one sense. Your Orient illumines my Occident with unexpected flashes. I remain myself, but I am enlightened, and I

will be more fruitful because of it."[51] Mickiewicz seemed to function as a Slavic alternative whom Michelet needed for a better
understanding of France itself. He shared something of Mickiewicz's messianic outlook, though it was the French whom he saw
as the people with a special destiny and mission in history. Nevertheless, while the French Revolution was one sacrifice for humanity, the repression of Poland was another; in each case the
experience and suffering of a nation acquired universal historical
significance. Drawing upon this analytical analogy, Michelet became a staunch supporter of the Polish cause, wrote on Polish
politics and history, and discovered in the Polish story more evidence for his semimystical faith in the moral qualities of the "people" and the moral characteristics of each nationality.[52]

Michelet's emphasis on the similarities between France and Poland owed a good deal to the information and ideas he heard from
Mickiewicz. He used the poet's lectures, for example, when he
needed cultural details for his own works on Polish history, such
as *La légende de Kościuszko* (1851). More important, however, Michelet seemed to take from the lectures a new outlook on history and
nations. He came to many of these views through his own analysis,
of course, but the contact with Mickiewicz helped to clarify his
thought in "fruitful" ways. Mickiewicz's influence therefore contributed a Polish perspective to many of Michelet's principal concerns during the 1840s: the cooperation between peoples, the
special role of France in modern civilization, the importance of
inspiration and intuition in life and in historical research, the subjectivity of history, and the need for a new, unofficial religion.[53]

Mickiewicz also provided a supreme example of the intellectual
engagé: the writer who devoted his words to a vast, long-term
historical struggle. Michelet seemed to find in that example considerable encouragement to broaden his own work into the modern
movement of history. It was during the period of contact with
Mickiewicz that Michelet wrote his influential study *Le peuple* (1844)
and the *Histoire de la Révolution française* (1847), both of which
expressed themes close to those of the poet insofar as they described
the heroism of suffering people and the struggle to establish a new
society based on a new morality. There was in all of this a certain
mystical faith that distinguished Michelet from many of his contemporaries and from the French Enlightenment tradition, a faith
that many scholars have traced in part to Mickiewicz.[54] Indeed,
Michelet may have used Mickiewicz more than Mickiewicz used

him, though Michelet also helped his friend by defending his work
when French authorities intervened to suspend the lectures on
Slavic literature.

Michelet was more than willing to acknowledge his special relation and debt to the Pole. Describing the lectures of Mickiewicz
many years later, Michelet attributed to them a special Eastern
insight that was especially valuable to him and Quinet. "This
course [of Mickiewicz], Oriental in language and imagery, fitted
in intimately with ours, which were the work of two Occidentals.
It was a call to heroism, to great and noble desires, to unlimited
sacrifice."[55] Mickiewicz—the "Oriental" poet—therefore offered
precisely the figure that Michelet needed to complete the "Occi-
dental" project upon which he had embarked. The energy, sacrifice,
heroism, and imagery of the Pole coincided with the needs of
France and the desires of the historian who described it. Mickiewicz
recognized Michelet's interest and responded from his "Oriental"
position with considerable enthusiasm for the historian who represented the France to which Poles might look for sympathy and
aid. "Your method conforms with the needs of the epoch and the
universal movement of ideas," he wrote to Michelet in 1843. "To
support the *spontaneity of the soul* is to support the generative tenet
of French nationality and to support Poland."[56] Mickiewicz and
Michelet, in short, embraced each other partly because that embrace was for both men another way of affirming the ideal images
they had created to describe their native countries and the French-
Slavic connection in which they both believed.

This mutual support did not cover every point of view, however,
and the embrace of the other carried in each case a strong reas-
sertion of national self-identity. Michelet was in fact almost as
eager to note their differences as their similarities, since his conception of France also depended on the enduring contrast with the
Slavic East. As he read through the lectures of Mickiewicz, Michelet
decided that Polish nationalism rested upon assumptions significantly different from his own: the Slav believed in great men who
embodied the national spirit, whereas Westerners ascribed the national spirit to the people at large. Thus, despite their common
hope for a regeneration of nations, Michelet concluded that different assumptions about that rebirth would always separate him
from Mickiewicz. "The last hero who appeared is not Napoleon,
as people say; it is the Revolution," Michelet wrote in his journal.
"And its greatness consisted exactly in the fact that there was no
great man to absorb the fecundity of the movement in the phan-

tasmagoria of a new mysticism."[57] The West, he explained, was becoming "collective," an outlook that precluded all faith in saviors. Calling this view rational, Michelet suggested that the "great man" faith of Mickiewicz returned to the early Christian belief in a new messiah and hence departed from the tendencies of modern history. It all added up to a kind of "Oriental" mysticism that would never be appropriate for France, where the rebirth must necessarily begin with the masses at the bottom long before it reached the leaders above.[58]

Although Michelet wrote about these differences only in his journal, he did feel obliged to distance himself from Mickiewicz in public when a group of admirers struck a medallion carrying the portraits of Michelet, Mickiewicz, and Quinet with the message: *Ut omnes unum sint* (So that all be united as one). Michelet objected to the medallion and explained immediately to Mickiewicz the reasons for his discomfort:

> We are on very different paths, dear colleague and friend. As you know, I have just published a book [*Le Prêtre*] that is very rationalist and very hostile to mysticism. In my opinion, everything rises from the people.
>
> I am united with you in affection; when your course was threatened I went around for two days to inform all the newspapers and to prevent misunderstandings. Whoever loves me, loves you and whoever injures you, injures me.
>
> In spite of all that, our route is not the same. However glorious it might be for me to see myself on a medallion that links me to your immortality, I cannot, in frankness, let it be thought that our sentiments were the same on some of the most serious questions.[59]

Mickiewicz responded to this polite statement of differences with an apology for misunderstandings and a new assurance of friendship.[60] He did not discuss the issues of rationalism/mysticism or people/messiah that Michelet regarded as expressions of contrasting cultural attitudes; perhaps he did not feel the distinctions as acutely as Michelet did ("everything rises from the people" was actually a fine mystical formulation), or perhaps he did not wish to explore differences with one of his most loyal and sympathetic French friends. In any case, the friendship with Michelet, like those with other French acquaintances, rested upon differences as well as similarities, and it clearly did not overcome the deep-seated sense of exile in Mickiewicz's Parisian life.

That sense of isolation always remained part of his outlook, the beginning and end of much that he wrote in France. Indeed, one of the remarkable aspects of his long exile life is that all his contacts in Paris and all his cooperative efforts with French people in no way diminished his Polish identity. On the contrary, French friendships served to deepen his identification with Poland, perhaps because the French needed him to be different from themselves. He never became French, for he devoted his work and his life to an unending exploration of what it meant to be Polish. If his French friends used him as a source on "Polishness," it was a role he accepted without hesitation. While Heine and Marx manifested some ambivalence about their German tradition in France, Mickiewicz seemed extraordinarily comfortable with his heritage and identity as a Pole—unless one assumes that the militant affirmation of national identity is itself a compensation for ambivalence. But what did "Poland" mean to him?

The Messiah Nation

Mickiewicz became the best-known advocate of Polish messianism in France. He was one of the first exiles to formulate the doctrines of this messianic creed, and it emerged as the dominant theme in all of his writings about Poland. The creed asserted that Poland was the Christ of nations—punished, crucified, and buried but certain to rise again from the dead and to bring salvation to all of Europe. Despite the mystical aspects of the doctrine (or perhaps because of them), most Polish exiles accepted it as a legitimate and consoling explanation for Poland's unique historical role in the world.[61]

Mickiewicz first developed the messianic themes in the *Books of the Polish Pilgrims* and then returned to them often in his articles and lectures. The great powers of Europe could not allow Poland to exist, Mickiewicz explained, because it embodied the spirit of freedom and refused to worship the modern gods of money and interest. This was so unusual that the kings of Europe decided to divide Poland among themselves, destroy freedom, and thereby bring the Poles into their world of material interests.

> The Polish Nation alone did not bow down to the new idol [of material interest], and did not have in its language the expression for christening it in Polish, neither for christening its worshippers, whom it calls by the French word egoists.

The Polish Nation worshipped God, knowing that he who honoreth God giveth honor to everything that is good.

The Polish Nation then from the beginning to the end was true to the God of its ancestors....

And finally Poland said: "Whosoever will come to me shall be free and equal, for I am FREEDOM."[62]

Poland thus became unique in modern Europe as the land where ancient religion flourished, where freedom still existed, and where values other than self-interest still predominated. Like Christ himself, Poland was executed by the wordly authorities because of its adherence to higher values, and yet (also like Christ) its life did not end with this execution. "For the Polish Nation did not die: its body lieth in the grave, but its soul hath descended from the earth, that is from public life, to the abyss, that is to the private life of people who suffer slavery in their country and outside of their country, that it may see their sufferings."[63] If Poland must undergo humiliation and pain before its resurrection, this pain was nothing more (or less) than Christ had suffered for the redemption of mankind.

Poland's historical position in the 1830s therefore corresponded with the days Christ passed in the tomb. The darkness and death of those days became meaningful as the prelude to new life; similarly, the suffering of Poland would become meaningful if the exiles could understand the apparent death of their country as a preparation for both national rebirth and the salvation of Europe.

On the third day the soul shall return to the body, and the Nation shall arise and free all the peoples of Europe from slavery.

And already two days have gone by. One day ended with the first capture of Warsaw, and the second day ended with the second capture of Warsaw, and the third day shall begin, but shall not end.

And as after the resurrection of Christ blood sacrifices ceased in all the world, so after the resurrection of the Polish nation wars shall cease in all Christendom.[64]

Mickiewicz clearly wanted the biblical imagery and style in these messianic accounts to remind Poles that their patriotism formed part of a vast moral epic in which Poland played the role of chosen people and savior. No other people had been granted such a place in European history, but it was a place of responsibility as well as honor—a dual role that Mickiewicz was forever explaining to fellow exiles who seemed more eager for rewards than for sacrifices.

All other nations defended only themselves, he pointed out, and hated whoever contested their narrow self-interest. The Poles alone defended freedom and did so in a spirit of disinterested sacrifice that would win them support in heaven, even as it seemed to cause them unending misery on earth.[65] Although this transcendent destiny imposed enormous burdens on the Poles, Mickiewicz believed that Providence and history had prepared them for their duties and that exceptional suffering would lead to exceptional insight. "This [Slavic] race, which instead of using its soul in works of the intellect and industry conserves a pure and profound religious instinct, will certainly not be content with any of the political forms known until now," he argued in one of his lectures. The people who were to guide Europe into a new age would have to choose institutions that differed from those of all other nations. "It is therefore highly logical to conclude that the Slavic race and the Polish nation in particular are destined and prepared to form a completely new society."[66]

Mickiewicz did not suggest how this new society might function—his utopianism described past details and future abstractions—but he was sure it would rest upon messianic traits that appeared repeatedly in Polish literature, philosophy, and politics and that made Poland unique in world history: the necessity of sacrifice, the necessity of death and rebirth, the universal and humanitarian tendencies of the Polish people.[67] These prominent themes in Polish culture must necessarily form the framework for exiles who were preparing for the Polish future, and yet Mickiewicz would never explain what these themes meant in social or political practice. He preferred to describe Poland's messianic role in world history without reference to the demoralizing conflicts that emerged whenever Poles tried to work out their transcendent mission in specific policies. His own work always served the higher purpose of encouraging Polish *consciousness* and of helping the exiles of the Great Emigration see their Polish similarities amid the practical differences that divided them and the French differences that surrounded them. Ultimately, he made his greatest contribution to the Poles by discovering national virtue (the sacrifice of a savior nation) in their most obvious national weakness (oppression by a more powerful, alien state).

Mickiewicz chose to call the Polish émigrés "pilgrims" rather than exiles or wanderers because they were on a "journey to the holy land," a journey that led through France and through an abyss on a route that would eventually take the pilgrims back to Poland.

They did not simply wander, for they had a clear goal toward which they were always moving.[68] This Polish pilgrimage, like all religious movements, depended upon sacrifice and suffering; indeed, Mickiewicz stressed that the suffering was absolutely necessary, though he also recognized that it was not an easy thing to endure. "My name is million, for I love as millions," he wrote soon after the failure of the 1830–31 revolt. "Their pain and suffering I feel; / I gaze upon my country fallen on days / of torment, as a son would gaze / Upon his father broken on the wheel."[69] Since the pain seemed likely to continue for a long time, Mickiewicz offered a great deal of specific advice to help his fellow pilgrims withstand the many temptations and compromises that might ease the suffering but betray the soul.

Their most important task was to protect the traditions and integrity of Polish culture. Although the Poles who lived abroad would be tempted to embrace Western values, styles, manners, and beliefs, to do so would soon destroy the purity of the pilgrims and divert them from their special calling: "Ye have not to learn the civilization of strangers, but ye are to teach them the true Christian civilization."[70] To be sure, Poles should master whatever crafts or sciences they needed to support themselves in the wilderness, but the new crafts must not displace traditional Polish customs or values. "Strive not with foreigners in arguing and idle talk, for ye know that they are talkative and clamorous, like boys in school, and the wisest teacher will not outtalk one insolent and loud-tongued boy."[71] Pilgrims would teach by example and behavior rather than by the futile discussions that foreigners so admired. Their mission required, moreover, that they preserve their native dress, their festivals, their foods, their religion, and their ancestors' wisdom.[72]

Despite the ridicule to which they might be subjected, Poles must know that their own culture and traditions were more civilized than the cultures they were advised to emulate. "They say to you more than once that ye are in the midst of civilized nations and should learn civilization from them," Mickiewicz explained, "but know that they who talk to you of civilization, understand not themselves what they say."[73] Civilization once meant sacrifice, citizenship, and a commitment to higher principles, "but afterwards in the idolatrous confusion of languages they gave the name *civilization* to fashionable and elegant raiment, to savory cookery, comfortable inns, beautiful theaters, and broad roads. So not only a Christian, but a pagan Roman, if he were to rise from the grave and behold men whom they now call civilized, would be stirred with anger and would ask, by what right they call themselves by a title which cometh from the word *civis*, citizen."[74] Civilization had come to mean good food, good shelter, and good health, but even animals enjoyed these things. For man, civilization must be something else: "Christian."

Mickiewicz, in short, decided that truly civilized values had disappeared in the West and that if Poles were to preserve their "civilization," they must define themselves in *opposition* to the materialist, rationalist culture that they encountered in France and England and Germany. Christian Poland was different, but this difference gave strength rather than weakness. The West bought its progress by selling its soul, an exchange that Mickiewicz insisted Poland must never make. Poles would instead have to unite around their common inheritance, resisting both foreign ways and discord among themselves. There was no reason to make recriminations about the past or to dispute the details of Poland's future government. All of this became insignificant beside the higher goals that Poles were called to pursue: the sacrifices for civilization, Christianity, and rebirth. Whatever the internal differences might be, they were nothing when compared to the great distance that separated all Poles from other people. "Be mindful," wrote Mickiewicz, "that ye are in the midst of strangers as a flock among wolves and as a camp in an enemy country, and there will be concord among you."[75]

Mickiewicz carried this sense of Polish separation beyond the point of mere distinctiveness to a more general assertion about the superiority of Poles over all other people. "Ye are not all equally good," he explained to his fellow exiles, "but he who is worse among you is better than the good stranger, for each one of you hath the spirit of self-sacrifice."[76] To preserve this spirit, Poles could depend only on themselves; they must never rush to princes or representatives of the "civilized" West, who understood nothing except might, balance of power, and self-interest.[77] The messianic pilgrimage brought Poles together with Poles in a sacrificial crusade that self-interested Western leaders would never fully support and never really comprehend. Mickiewicz thus built his conception of the messiah nation upon specific characteristics that many Western critics blamed for Poland's problems—weakness, religion, isolation. Where others saw inferiority in these traits, he found the clearest signs of national greatness and spiritual justification for the suffering of his fellow exiles.

These notions about Polish destiny and the special responsibilities of Polish émigrés carried important consequences for Mickiewicz's views on literature and politics. If one discerned in Polish
history the expression of God's plan for Europe, then it became
apparent that Polish literature reflected divine influence from the
earliest days to the nineteenth century. All nationalisms require
some explanation of what makes the nation's literate culture
unique and important in the world, and Mickiewicz provided this
explanation for the Poles by emphasizing the religious component
in Slavic literature. His lectures at the Collège de France argued
that Polish poetry expressed religious continuity because it revealed God's role in the nation's past and pointed prophetically
toward Poland's future.[78] Polish literature therefore differed from
Western European literature as Polish history differed from Western European history.

Mickiewicz made this point repeatedly in his lectures and
stressed this Polish particularity in the most famous poem he wrote
in France, *Pan Tadeusz* (1834). That epic about life in Poland and
Lithuania during the Napoleonic era portrayed a world in which
nature, society, and noble individuals coexisted in remarkable harmony, a world for which an unhappy poet could yearn without
apology. As Mickiewicz suggested throughout *Pan Tadeusz*, it was
the half-mythic, half-historical place where all exiles wished to go
and where the poet too would one day return—God's country.
"Meanwhile bear my grief-stricken soul to those wooded hills, to
those green meadows stretched far and wide along the blue Nie-
men," Mickiewicz wrote at the beginning of his story, "to those
fields painted with various grain, gilded with wheat, silvered with
rye; where grows the amber mustard, the buckwheat white as
snow, where all is girdled as with a ribbon by a strip of green turf
on which here and there rest quiet pear trees."[79]

Such idealized images of a distant place and faraway time created a framework for *Pan Tadeusz* by reminding all Poles of the
world they had lost. It certainly served that purpose for Mickiewicz
himself as he wrote from his exile refuge in Paris. Furthermore, as
in all stories about a lost paradise, Mickiewicz had to account for
the "fall," and he did so in part through a description of the cor-
ruption that came into the idyllic world of old Poland from abroad.
The "fall" of Poland seemed to coincide with the appearance of
foreign ideas and manners—which, as it happened, arrived mostly
from France. Mickiewicz in fact wrote a good deal of anti-French
sentiment into *Pan Tadeusz*, a tendency that may have reflected some

of his personal discomfort in French society during his first two years in Paris when he was writing the epic. His complaints about French decadence resemble the themes that appeared in the descriptions of Paris by other Poles such as Charles Forster or Karol Frankowski. Like many eastern Europeans, Mickiewicz held French influence responsible for the loss of Slavic innocence and faith because France carried the germ of modernity that weakened or killed traditional values. Mickiewicz's encounter with modern Paris seemed to contribute both to the nostalgia for Poland and to the criticisms of French culture that appear in *Pan Tadeusz*. One of the characters in the epic, for example, discusses the loss of Slavic traditions in a speech that explicitly blames France for much of the crisis that eventually destroyed Poland's harmonious, virtuous world:

> I remember the times when on our fatherland there first descended the fashion of imitating the French; when suddenly brisk young gentlemen from foreign lands swarmed in upon us in a horde worse than the Nogai Tatars, abusing here, in our country, God, the faith of our fathers, our law and customs, and even our ancient garments. Pitiable was it to behold the yellow-faced puppies ... stuffed with brochures and newspapers of various sorts, and proclaiming new faiths, laws and toilets. That rabble had a mighty power over minds, for when the Lord God sends punishment on a nation he first deprives its citizens of reason. And so the wiser heads dared not resist the fops, and the whole nation feared them as some pestilence, for within itself it already felt the germs of disease. They cried out against the dandies but took pattern by them; they changed faith, speech, laws, and costumes. That was a masquerade, the license of the Carnival season, after which was soon to follow the Lent of Slavery.[80]

The xenophobic dislike for all things foreign that Mickiewciz expressed here and the fear of all alien influences on Polish literature and culture—which appeared early in the *Books of the Polish Pilgrims* and in *Pan Tadeusz*— influenced his lectures on Slavic literature and surely contributed some of the passion to his praise for the traditions of Polish prose, poetry, and politics. He may also have found that fear growing within himself as he settled into the uneasy position of an exiled Polish writer in the capital city of France.

Polish messianism affected Mickiewicz's politics as much as it did his literary views, for he believed that the Polish question was *the* issue in modern European history. Accordingly, the good or bad aspects of all political policies depended upon their likely consequences for Poland, the best policy of course being the one that might help liberate Poland most rapidly. He accepted the necessity of a revolutionary war that would redeem Poland through sacrifice and bloodshed, but he did not concern himself much with questions about how Poland might be governed after liberation. That was a matter best left to prayer and to spiritual meditation when freedom was actually at hand. These mystical inclinations did not mean, though, that he assumed Poland could free itself by prayer alone. Other nations (especially France) must be brought into an armed struggle, and even a general European war would not be bad, since the liberation of Poland would assure the salvation of the whole continent. Thus, despite the strong nationalism in all of Mickiewicz's pronouncements, he was also a firm internationalist insofar as he believed that the movement for Polish freedom would inevitably become part of the wider movement for international peace and freedom; indeed, it must serve as the vanguard of that movement because Europe could never achieve real freedom until Poland had completed its revolutionary Christian campaign.[81]

This hope for a French-led international movement on behalf of Poland obviously placed France in a pivotal position. It also caused repeated Polish disappointment: Louis-Philippe's government had no desire to enter a war for Polish liberation; by the all-important Polish standard, then, French leaders and policies were bad. Mickiewicz complained bitterly about the architects of those policies in his *Books of the Polish Pilgrims*, calling Prime Minister Casimir Périer a corrupt worshiper of the idol *Interest* and asserting that his name would be forever "accursed among the Slavic race."[82] But Périer alone was not the problem. Mickiewicz went on to condemn most of France for hypocrisy and cowardice in the face of despotism and closed with a warning to its leaders about the danger of refusing aid to the Polish freedom movement.

Rulers of France and ye men of France who call yourselves wise, ye who talk of freedom and serve despotism, ye shall lie between your people and foreign despotism as a tire of cold iron between the hammer and the anvil.

And ye shall be beaten, and the dross from you, and the sparks from you, shall fly to the ends of the earth. . . .

And ye shall cry out to the hammer, to your people: "O people, forgive thou and cease, for we have talked of freedom." And the hammer shall say: "Thou didst talk in one wise, but thou didst act in another." And it shall fall with new force upon the tire.[83]

In fact, among all the prominent political figures in modern France, Mickiewicz proclaimed that only Lafayette still embodied "the spirit of self-sacrifice, the remnant of the Christian spirit."[84] He alone refused to worship "Interest," that omnipotent force that caused almost every other French leader to betray the Polish cause. Nevertheless, there remained some possibility that the French people at large might be moved to the international actions their leaders so steadfastly avoided.

Apart from the aging Lafayette, however, France did not seem inclined to take the role that Mickiewicz had in mind or to fulfill the image he had created for it. Yet the image never quite went away. On the contrary, Mickiewicz devoted much of his political energy in Paris to reaffirming an optimistic image of disinterested French activism and then exhorting the French to live up to it. Thus, although the French role in European history always referred in some way to the Polish issue, France itself acquired a certain autonomous place in Mickiewicz's thought as the *other* nation with a mission in the world. Not surprisingly, therefore, France seemed to arouse in Mickiewicz a constantly shifting mix of skepticism and faith, disappointment and hope that made the Franco-Polish relationship both a torment and a necessity for him.

The French Spirit

Mickiewicz explained his perceptions of France while he was describing Slavic history and literature in the lectures at the Collège de France. This was his principal public forum, and he used it to remind the French of their unique history and destiny. Since the audience often included some of the most prominent Parisian writers of the era, he directed his pronouncements on French culture at influential French opinion-makers as much as at the students who came to hear him. According to one report in a German periodical, the typical lecture provided plenty of substance but very little style, a method of presentation that made the large audiences all the more remarkable. "His voice is hoarse," wrote the German reporter. "He pronounces French very harshly, almost brokenly.

There is no insinuation in his delivery, no expressive pantomine, no lively gesticulation."[85]

Whatever the quality of his French diction (even the admiring George Sand noted the "harshness" of the "Lithuanian accent" with which he achieved his unusual eloquence),[86] Mickiewicz's message was clear enough: France had a special destiny and duty in world history. The spirit lived in France, the true Christian spirit that burned as a sacred fire in the national character and set the French apart from all other people except, of course, the Poles. "The sacred fire is the result of thorough, internal work," Mickiewicz explained in one of his lectures. "And that is why France, which possesses the greatest quantity of this fire, is the nation *par excellence*, and why we have acknowledged the French spirit as more Christian than Rome."[87] Unfortunately, he said, the Spirit often disappeared from view in the capital, and yet it remained always present somewhere within the French nation.[88] Mickiewicz's idealized view of the French genius and character—as distinct from French leaders—led him to assume that this character would express itself if only it received proper direction and encouragement from above. The French who had brought the "sacred fire" to earth now asked simply to be used in its service. "Have you observed the fire in the eyes of these people?" he asked his audiences. "There is in the soul of this or that French worker enough fire to electrify and give energy to an entire Slavic region."[89] As it happened, though, nobody was willing to tap this energy by leading the French people toward their destiny in Poland or even within France itself.

Mickiewicz found enough evidence of the sacred fire in French history to sustain his perennial hope for a new flame in the French future. In his analysis of the past, for example, the French Revolution of 1789 became among other things an extraordinary manifestation of the Christian spirit in action. True, the revolutionaries expressed a great deal of explicit anticlerical sentiment, but Mickiewicz argued that critics who emphasized that feature of Jacobin language or practice missed the deeper Christian impulses that motivated the revolutionary movement. Dechristianization, in his view, was by no means a cause or a consequence of the revolution. "The French Jacobins, while murdering priests and destroying churches, gave to Jesus Christ the title of sans-culotte, an ignoble title to be sure, but the most noble of those that people held at the time, [and they] conferred upon him the title of citizen; the Jacobins recognized in him their brother."[90] Mickiewicz thus turned the common Catholic hostility to the revolution upside down, claiming the revolution as a triumph of the Christian tradition and keeping France firmly within the Catholic community.

The Christian "fire" that Mickiewicz preceived in the major event of modern French history encouraged his hope that the same fire might also inspire future French contributions to European development. He believed that the status quo in Europe would inevitably change, but that *progressive* change would have to come about in conjunction with the power and influence of France. "Yes, the force that will shake the future cannot emerge from any center except France," he explained to his lecture-hall audience. Catholic nations could develop the faith, and Poles could apply spiritual truths to daily life; France, though, could implement both faith and truth in ways that would truly "shake the future."[91]

Meanwhile, France's sacred fire—the fire of past and future— made the nation extremely valuable in the present because its sympathetic "Christian genius" had transformed the country into a haven for displaced persons from the rest of Europe. The Poles clearly depended on Paris for the survival of an autonomous national tradition, a theme Mickiewicz stressed in lectures whenever he described the characteristics of the unique Franco-Slavic relationship. Despite its reluctance to join the Polish liberation movement, France remained the major center for Polish liberty and the only territory where Slavs had managed to attain a bit of freedom. "The Slavic countries are indebted to France for the only refuge where the truth can be heard," Mickiewicz noted. "This hall is the only public place where the Poles, the Russians and the Bohemians can discuss their religious and moral affairs. France has emancipated the Slavic voice."[92]

While a free Parisian auditorium was in no way equivalent to a free country, France had at least helped the cause by allowing the Slavic word to be expressed there. The next contribution of the French "genius," however, would have to be more forceful. In fact, Mickiewicz suggested that it should be nothing less than active military intervention on behalf of the oppressed people in Europe. Since no other nation had both the mission and the power to carry it out, the French should embark on a campaign to light their sacred fire throughout the civilized world.

The France that Mickiewicz described in the 1840s differed considerably from the rhetorical ("cancerous heart") France he had first described to Lelewel in 1832. As he pointed out repeatedly in his literary lectures, France had become for Mickiewicz the place where the Spirit emerged in acts. "A word pronounced here is the beginning of action," he declared in one of his optimistic pronouncements on Franco-Polish relations.[93] It was precisely this genius for action that confirmed the nation's unique character. Some nations embraced principles but could never act; others acted but never supported higher principles. France alone managed to combine the two. "A principle proclaimed by the French people becomes a reality," Mickiewicz wrote after the Revolution of 1848.[94]

The special French genius for principle *and* action in turn justified the creation and support of a strong army. Mickiewicz argued that the moral task of liberation required the material force of arms, a necessary connection that made the military and moral force of France inseparable. He believed, moreover, that its role as protector of the sacred fire caused France to use its force in disinterested ways that distinguished its arms from those of all other powers and that posed no threat to the people of Europe. "The armies, fleets and arsenals of France belong to humanity," he explained. "Upon them rests the hope of nations." Anyone who could remain unmoved by the sight of a French flag must surely be incapable of understanding the source of true progress in the world.[95] Unfortunately, however, the French government itself failed to understand the nation's progressive mission in the world and neglected to tend the sacred fire inherited from French tradition.

The failure of French leadership clearly formed a central theme in Mickiewicz's analysis of contemporary France. Unwilling to alter his view of the French character, mission, or destiny, he placed the blame for real-world French indifference to Poland's problems on the government of Louis-Philippe.[96] The weakness of this modern, self-interested government appeared all the more glaring when Mickiewicz contrasted its policies with those of Napoleon, the most important single figure in all of French history. Napoleon fascinated Mickiewicz as the decisive, insightful, inspired leader who grasped the special French mission in world history and befriended Poland. With that image as his model, Mickiewicz became convinced that France needed a new Napoleonic figure to mobilize the national genius.

This messianic search may ultimately have isolated Mickiewicz from his radical French friends more than any other feature in his thought, for it caused him to favor "great man" solutions to French problems and prompted him to support Louis Napoleon's consolidation of power in the early 1850s. Ironically, his fervent praise for Napoleon may also have been the single most important factor in the decision of July Monarchy authorities to suspend his courses, because Bonapartism could threaten Orleanist liberals as much as it threatened populist radicals. But Mickiewicz refused to renounce his Bonapartist dreams; he seemed to hope above all that another great man in France might become another great man for Europe; then salvation would follow on all sides, "for friends and foes alike recognize that France is the moving spirit in Europe."[97]

This faith in Napoleon derived in part from the influence of the Lithuanian mystic Andrzej Towiański, whom Mickiewicz met in the summer of 1841. Towiański viewed himself as a prophet of God sent to complete the teachings of Christ and to initiate a new Christian era. Mickiewicz accepted the Lithuanian's self-described mission soon after they met—perhaps because he may have helped to cure Mickiewicz's wife of a serious mental illness—and thereafter devoted himself to the task of spreading "the Master's" messianic doctrines. Towiański saw Napoleon as a key historical predecessor who had played a major role in the divine plan to lead mankind from darkness to light and from conflict to political cooperation. Napoleon had of course failed to complete this work, but now the mission had fallen to Towiański, who claimed a special link with the deceased emperor (and whose followers often spent a night at Waterloo as part of their spiritual pilgrimages).[98] Responding to "the Master's" mystical vision, Mickiewicz embraced this spiritual interpretation of Bonaparte so enthusiastically that by the time of his final lecture at the Collège de France he was distributing lithographs that depicted Napoleon grieving over a torn map of Europe.

Napoleon's spiritual grandeur, as Mickiewicz described it, resulted from his embodiment of the French genius and character (the sacred fire). Chosen by God for his historical role, Napoleon had come to enact all that was good and progressive in the Enlightenment while refuting the excesses of reason and rationality that were bad. Indeed, his very existence was an inexplicable mystery, a living challenge to the false assumption that all phenomena may be explained through rational laws.[99] He represented the true objectives of the revolution (which, it is important to remember, were for Mickiewicz an expression of the Christian spirit) because he "put into practice the revolutionary ideals" and thereby proved himself to be the historical figure who "defended its ideals with the greatest and most fruitful determination."[100]

Yet even this enormous French achievement did not constitute the whole Napoleonic story, for he was truly a world-historical leader who belonged to progressive people everywhere. His character in no way restricted itself to Gaulish traits or to the outlook of the West: "There was in his genius," Mickiewicz argued, "something indefinably Eastern."[101] The East always appealed to Napoleon, partly because he believed that all great men in history had gone there, and partly because his Corsican heritage seemed to draw him away from Europe. The Egyptian expedition was only one of many examples showing just how strongly Napoleon felt this attraction in his life and military projects.[102] Ultimately, therefore, this Eastern dimension in his world vision contributed as much as his French genius to creating the Emperor's world-historical status, to shaping his aspiration to liberate and unify all nations, and to establishing his role as the inspiration for all those who continued to dream of a new era in human evolution. "The terrestrial life of Napoleon is finished," Mickiewicz explained in 1844. "As the head of a political party, as the leader of a dynasty, Napoleon no longer exists. But who here will deny the existence and permanent activity of his spirit? Religious men, military men and statesmen consult it by meditating upon his works and actions. Is not such meditation a true prayer? The mission of inspired artists is to raise themselves to the region in which this great spirit dwells, to evoke it and to make it visible to us. Napoleon is the archetype of the new art."[103] Napoleon thus became for Mickiewicz a symbol of transformation and, as such, a symbol whom all advocates of progressive change might legitimately claim as their own.

Nobody of course had a better claim to the symbol than the Poles and the French. These peoples understood Napoleon most profoundly because they were closest to the spirit he embodied, and they shared exceptionally close connections to his policies. Mickiewicz suggested in his lectures that this shared history with Napoleon formed the base for a shared admiration, which in turn justified future alliances between France and Poland.[104] Poles could look back to the Napoleonic era as one of relative independence (the Emperor's Grand Duchy of Warsaw was at least free of Russian control), and they could remember French armies fighting Russians. In fact, one of Mickiewicz's own early memories was the sight of Napoleon's French troops retreating across Poland after the disastrous campaign against the eternal Russian foe.[105] Here at least was a common hero and a common enemy—and the starting point for new Franco-Polish cooperation. "Napoleon initiated an evolution of Christianity," Mickiewicz declared, and launched the modern campaign for international fraternity.[106] That evolution and that campaign had now fallen to the Poles, who were more than willing to carry it forward if only the French themselves would respond to their Napoleonic heritage.

The ties with Napoleon, however, constituted only one aspect of the special Franco-Polish relationship to which Mickiewicz so frequently alluded in his lectures. History had established a commonality of experience and purpose that the future would surely confirm. The powers that opposed the French Revolution, for example, had also opposed Poland, so that the partition of Poland in the 1790s coincided exactly with the great events of the revolution. Unable to crush the "Spirit" in France, the reactionary interests of Europe decided to attack it in Poland.[107] Similarly, the two nations shared with each other a highly developed notion of treason. The French and the Poles condemned more traitors than all other nations because these spiritually linked peoples had higher ideals to betray. With their unique sense of national mission, they quickly recognized deviance from the ideal and then prosecuted traitors in the name of moral imperatives.[108] It was a painful and uncompromising task, but it was at the same time further evidence of the exceptional burdens that seemed forever to connect the destinies of the two countries.

Historical similarities fortunately prepared the way for contemporary cooperation and understanding, as Poles found when they emigrated to France after 1831. The émigrés needed to explain their cause in the West and to develop a new creed through which they might reconstruct their nation. France offered Poles the freedom and tolerance that the Russian occupation denied them at home and thus enabled Polish messianism to establish its place as a leading component of the progressive European movement. Since the messianic doctrines had to be introduced to the West as both a force and a science, Mickiewicz explained, France provided the indispensable base from which this project became possible. Establishment of the chair in Slavic literature was itself strong proof of French openness to Slavic culture and of the French desire to facilitate expression of the Polish message in the West.[109] Mickiewicz perceived a divine pattern in both sides of this cooperation inasmuch as he saw Poles as latter-day Israelites wandering in the wilderness with a providential message that France alone had been willing to hear. "Poland was destined to incarnate the new revelation; France is destined to be the first to receive it," he announced in one of his final lectures.[110] Building upon this divinely sanctioned intersection of missions and peoples, the two nations could move together toward the new age, united in belief and committed to common action.

The French responsibility in this partnership was of course to provide more of the action. French armies had twice come on to Slavic soil, and they managed each time to precipitate a revolution in Slavic culture: Charlemagne had implanted the idea of royalty; Napoleon brought ideals of liberty, fraternity, and universality. Slavs now anticipated a third French intervention to complete the work that Napoleon had begun, a final intervention that would bring about "the union of the races of the West and North around a universal idea, around a Christian idea that must find its representative."[111] The general reconciliation of people would emerge from French-Polish cooperation because these two nations embodied corresponding attributes of the eternal Spirit. Their unification would therefore establish the essential prelude to human cooperation, harmony, and full knowledge (the image here is thoroughly millenarian).

Mickiewicz used an astronomical metaphor to clarify his point: the history of the two nations resembled that of a remarkable planet whose bright side (France) had long been known in the West and whose dark side (Poland) was only now coming into view. The people on both sides shared remarkable *intuitive* abilities, though they utilized their abilities somewhat differently in response to the problems and events in their histories. Despite the contrasting shades of light on their respective sides of the planet, however, both peoples revolved around the same sun (Napoleon, for example) and expressed allegiance to the same Spirit.[112] Poland might therefore be described as the other side of France, a place where the approach to the Spirit took a more mystical form but where the Spirit itself existed and even flourished. The complementary aspects of this Franco-Polish planet reflected a number of interacting oppositions: West and East; French activism and Polish insight; French power and Polish suffering; French science and Polish spiritualism; French political tradition and Polish religious tradition.[113] If these opposing qualities could only be reconciled in an active French-Polish alliance, Poland would be liberated, the people of Europe would be united, and the whole "planet" would enter a new era.

Mickiewicz's call for Franco-Polish cooperation thus emphasized the common identity and values of the two countries. Poland was the France of the East; France—in its allegiance to the Spirit and universality—was the Poland of the West. For strategic reasons, Mickiewicz (like Heine) wanted to show similarities, yet he also believed that his native Polish side of the planet he described remained always different from the French side where he lived and worked. Lectures that developed themes of Franco-Polish commonality therefore carried enough reminders of divergence to keep alert listeners from forgetting that France and Poland were also very different nations. Like all thoughtful exiles, Mickiewicz seemed to recognize an unending dialectic of similarity and difference, so that his lectures in France suggested a kind of dialogic interplay between Poland's Western affinities and Poland's profound exceptionalism. But the Polish differences were ultimately more important.

Slavic Identity

After a decade of firsthand contact with French society, Mickiewicz was more certain than ever that Polish values, institutions, and ideas could never be like those of the West and that Poland's identity, which was Slavic, rested primarily on that difference. Slavic people were generous and disinterested rather than selfish and materialist; Slavic language was spontaneous and open rather than rigid and codified; Slavic society was agarian and cooperative rather than urban and competitive; and Slavic thought was spiritual and intuitive rather than rationalist and secular. Mickiewicz thus defined the Slavic identity for Parisians in opposition to the West, stressing that many Slavic virtues (and Poland's moral superiority) resulted from those social characteristics that were most unlike modern Western culture.

In fact, as he explained them, the differences went beyond social institutions to other traits such as race and national character. In one of his earliest lectures, for example, Mickiewicz enumerated the physical characteristics of Slavs and offered scientific evidence to show why they differed from all other European and non-European people. Slavs were on the margin of Europe, but modern science also set them apart from other non-Europeans (including Mongols, Celts, and Arabs) by proving that they had unusually strong arms, shoulders, chests, and hands. These exceptional attributes were in large measure responsible for the agricultural skills that supported Slavic society and separated Slavs from the mercantile or nomadic cultures that flourished elsewhere.[114]

Although Slavic society evolved out of certain physical traits and the agrarian system they helped to create, Slavic identity rested upon much more than strong arms and good hands. Slavic peasants—whose agrarian qualities meant that they embodied the Slavic character in its purest form—possessed exceptional moral strength to go with their strong bodies. "What especially distinguishes him," noted Mickiewicz in reference to the typical peasant, "is this spiritual warmth, this sentiment of love that we recognize so well in his morals, in his customs, in his taste for poetry and songs, and also in his hospitality."[115] Mickiewicz emphasized that this view of peasant virtue was not his alone; all ancient and modern observers alike agreed that Slavs were unusually generous and lively. Unfortunately, though, these good-hearted peasants were never governed by the values they expressed in their own daily lives, and no political movement had yet managed to mobilize this mass of agrarian people by appealing to the love that lay embedded in their character.[116] The responsibility and opportunity for all would-be leaders of these people was therefore to speak to them with the faith and love that derived from their own tradition. Indeed, no movement that did otherwise could ever succeed.

Despite the deep love and generosity in Slavic peasants, however, Mickiewicz recognized that the Slavic character had its share of faults, as the Poles themselves showed all too painfully in their propensity for envy and slander. Perhaps they inherited these traits from their ancestors, or perhaps they envied the virtue of others and wished to equal it, or perhaps there was merely "something in the air and the mysterious influence of climate and stars" that encouraged such unhappy tendencies. In any case, Poles missed no chance to chastise and correct one another, obsessively and with remarkable arrogance. "We are vain and fickle," Mickiewicz complained. "We mock our ecclesiastical leaders and our statutes, and ...we place ourselves in a situation that will one day end in some great catastrophe."[117] Such flaws might help explain the recent sufferings of Poland (inasmuch as God both punished and rewarded his people), and they might lead to even more pain in the future.

Meanwhile, the special qualities of Slavic character—good and bad alike—found expression in the Slavic folktales and literature that Mickiewicz sought to explicate in his lectures. This unique literary tradition, which reflected the unique Slavic character, remained almost wholly unknown to the French because translations failed to capture the important *daily* details of Slavic life that shaped most Slavic literature.[118] Nobody could really understand Slavic literature or the culture from which it derived without a thorough comprehension of Slavic languages, and so both the literature and the culture continued to be inaccessible to almost all western Europeans. Thus, while Mickiewicz wanted his lectures to make that Slavic world, that other realm, more familiar to the West, he felt himself forever stymied by linguistic limitations. Slavic identity also meant Slavic language, a linguistic difference that remained somehow irreducible for Mickiewicz and prevented him from accomplishing the deeper French-Slavic communication he had set out to achieve.

He believed that each nation created its own philosophical and religious attitudes through expressions that would always be distorted when translated into a foreign language.[119] This proved especially true of the Polish spiritual ideas that formed so much of the personal creed Mickiewicz wanted to convey to his Parisian audiences. When Western languages seemed to lack the expansiveness to accommodate the ecstatic, mystical insights Mickiewicz found in his own experience and linguistic tradition, he decided that this inadequacy revealed a major difference in the history of Western and Eastern languages. A language such as French, he explained, evolved according to the dictates of intellectual authorities who decided on proper phrases and then put them in dictionaries that established standard usage for everyone. People thus spoke or wrote French to conform with the comparatively rigid formulations of the intellectual tradition, all of which produced some beautiful phrases but very little spontaneity.[120]

Slavic languages, by contrast, offered the openness and spontaneous expression that Mickiewicz missed in French. "Of all languages," he argued, "Slavic, by its immensity, responds best to the immensity of nature."[121] A native Pole, for example, felt no obligation to study the phrases of great writers in order to learn good usage because Polish vocabulary and structure allowed exceptional flexibility. Poles freely rearranged or discarded words in the same way they erected buildings; that is, they used whatever material was at hand and then made changes whenever new materials became available. Tradition had almost none of the authority it enjoyed in France. Indeed, it was not uncommon for the elegant phrases of one generation to be forgotten by the next, so rapidly and spontaneously did the Polish language evolve.[122] Polish, in short, provided a perfect linguistic medium for the spontaneous activity and expression of the Spirit in human discourse.

Mickiewicz felt the constraints of the linguistic dichotomy throughout his time at the Collège de France, where his lectures repeatedly emphasized how thoroughly he identified his thought and his self-perception with a Polish idiom that could never be duplicated in another language. "I am a foreigner," he stressed in his first lecture, "and yet it is necessary for me to express myself in a language which in its origin, its forms [and] its character has nothing in common with that which serves habitually as the organ of my thoughts. Not only must I literally translate for you my ideas and sentiments into an idiom that is foreign to me; I must also completely transform the expression before translating the ideas." Although his French audience might well find this painful translation process to be a tiresome distraction, Mickiewicz could promise no way around the problem. "With each movement of my thought," he explained, "I feel the weight of the [linguistic] chain as you hear its noise."[123]

Mickiewicz's self-defined duty to describe Slavic culture to France and to serve as a "minister of the word [*parole*]" encouraged him to lecture in his Polish French during every week of four academic years, but it never enabled him to overcome his sense of linguistic isolation. "I speak your language badly," he noted in his final lecture. "I did not learn it except by usage.... I express myself with difficulty; often in an ordinary conversation my phrases become muddled and the proper word eludes me; and yet it was necessary for me to speak the most difficult language of those I know, to speak it in public at the Collège de France! But I had to talk to you about my religion and about my nation."[124] Since the gospel itself dictated his responsibilities, Mickiewicz concluded that he must never use the language barrier as an excuse for shunning his duties. Even the gospel, though, could not make him comfortable in French, and the problem of language remained for Mickiewicz a perpetual mark of his alienation from the culture in which he lived.

The sense of Polish uniqueness (or difference) that informed his discussions of national character and language extended also to Mickiewicz's account of Polish society. In contrast to Western societies, which revolved around the city, Slavic societies organized themselves around the agrarian village. The urban, commercial, centralized West thus created institutions and problems that did not exist in the rural, agricultural, decentralized East. Slavic villages, administered by wise old men, controlled the property and goods of the community as a communal trust and hence avoided the evils of private property. Each village was autonomous, meeting its own needs without recourse to central authorities or conquest. These ancient communes, which resembled the utopian *phalanstères* that Fourierists wanted to establish in the West, evolved naturally out of the agrarian Slavic genius and provided a structure wherein social equality flourished because everyone had a fair share of both the work and the rewards. Slavs therefore had resolved in practice the great problem of Western society and political economy (private property) long before Western radicals (Fourier, Saint-Simon) even began to address the problem in theory.[125] These communes were of course agrarian rather than industrial, but Mickiewicz made no apology for that; he believed that agricultural communities conformed with the nonmaterialist, cooperative Slavic character.

The future society in Poland must build upon this unique, communal tradition so that Poles would not become alienated from their own character or from what God wanted them to be. Mickiewicz insisted that Providence did not want Poles simply to emulate the West in their social development. But what exactly did God plan for Poland?

> Is it that which we see in the industrial countries, in the merchant countries or in the conquering countries? Or is it that which exists in our countries, among this people who in their mythology have no god of war? It is a question here of the rehabilitation of agriculture [and] of the agrarian life....
>
> It would be in vain therefore that we should want to involve these people in limitations by offering them European models.... When they speak of the barbarism of these peoples, it is necessary to return the question. It is the class that is called civilized, the class which reads and writes, that, among the Slavs, really approaches barbarism; and, on the other hand, in my deepest conviction, I regard the Slavic people as more civilized [and] as placed in the best position to receive the truth.[126]

It was Slavic agriculture that kept Poland close to God's design and revealed Christian truth to the Polish people—the truth of *duty*, which could never be learned through foreign theories or foreign customs. Once again, Mickiewicz developed his conception of Polish nationalism by praising a characteristic that others held responsible for Poland's problems—in this case, a premodern agrarian economy. He therefore attacked all those who urged Poland to become more Western or industrialized and explicitly rejected the hierarchy that equated industry with progress and agrarianism with backwardness.[127]

Instead of that hierarchy, he chose (like many nineteenth-century romantics) to emphasize the human qualities of agrarian life and to condemn industrial society for its antihuman misery. This misery seemed so obvious to Mickiewicz that he could not imagine why some "so-called reformers" were urging Slavs to imitate the West.[128] When Poles borrowed Western systems of ownership, contract, and property, for example, the effects upon traditional (that is, true) Polish society were disastrous. The Napoleonic era provided a good case history of the risk: Poles had at that time adopted the French legal code and thereby managed to destroy much of the trust, responsibility, and cooperation that made possible the informal legal relations of traditional Poland.[129] Such historical precedents offered Mickiewicz all the evidence he needed to pursue his campaign against "Westernizers" in the Polish movement. As he stressed repeatedly from his exile perspective in Paris, the salvation of Poland would not come about through any program that rejected Polish traditions and truths in favor of the materialist, capitalist values of the West. Even Napoleon could not negate that truth.

Barbarism for Mickiewicz thus tended to be modern rather than primitive, and it came more often from the West than from the East. This notion of course inverted the common Western view and placed Mickiewicz among those early nationalist radicals on the European margins who believed that European progress in their countries caused deterioration insofar as it destroyed traditional (and idealized) values and relationships. Mickiewicz's social radicalism therefore leaned toward the reactionary, locating the "golden age" in a past to be recovered rather than in a future to be gained.[130] Although his millenarianism looked forward to a new age in human history, he clearly yearned for a Polish world of religion, farms, social equality, cooperative relationships, and small villages that was fast disappearing (if it had ever existed at all). These distinctive social qualities suggested yet again the enormous distance that separated Polish society from the urban institutions of the West, a distance that Mickiewicz, for one, wished always to maintain.

The social distance between West and East was no greater, though, than the intellectual distance that Mickiewicz also wanted to describe and preserve. He believed that the insights of each nation resulted from unique historical circumstances and that "the philosophies of different nations must differ, if not in the kind of subjects they treat, at least in the number of truths they are capable of gaining."[131] According to Mickiewicz, French and Polish thinkers recognized this particularity of *national* philosophies more astutely than the philosophers of other nations. At least they avoided the mistake of the Germans, who naively assumed their own philosophy to be universal when in fact Hegelianism represented the Prussian outlook in much the same way that materialism represented the French.[132]

This criticism of German philosophical arrogance formed one theme in Mickiewicz's general critique of the way Germans thought and wrote about the world. For example, as he described them, Germans liked to work on theories that evolved from book to book without much reference to social conditions or much effect on real-world activity. This weakness became especially obvious when Germans tried to write about politics. Constrained by their own political inexperience, Germans had to borrow their politics from France, where people *acted* upon the problems that Germans merely discussed. German thought evolved always in the realm of theory; French and Polish thought evolved directly out of social experience and action. The experiential base in Franco-Polish thought made these nations less susceptible to Hegelianism because their own social-philosophical insights had already surpassed the abstractions of pure thought. Mickiewicz rejected the common assumption of German philosophical superiority on the grounds that other nations achieved greater insights through their social and political experience; he argued from this criterion that France possessed the most advanced philosophy in the world except, of course, for the special insights of the Poles. Despite the contemporary fashion of Hegel's philosophy, therefore, he doubted that German thought could ever have much real influence in France or Poland.[133]

Still, it seemed important to warn these nations against the Hegelian temptation, which he did by suggesting that Hegel was simply irrelevant to their own national experiences. The danger in Hegel for would-be Franco-Polish followers thus became in part the danger of losing contact with French or Polish experience and with the national identities deriving from that experience: "The man without a nationality is an incomplete man."[134] It was the uncompromising sense of national identity that prompted Mickiewicz to caution Poles against accepting Hegelianism; that acceptance would carry with it a necessary rejection of the Polish spiritual tradition. August Cieszkowski offered in this respect a good example of what Poles ought not to do. Even though his *Prolegomena to Historiosophy* won praise from Mickiewicz for its critical analysis of Hegel's limitations, the work clearly situated itself within the Hegelian movement and adhered all too closely to Hegelian methods, thereby indicating Cieszkowski's greater interest in an alien national philosophy than in his own Polish intellectual heritage.[135] Mickiewicz himself made every effort to avoid this mistake, choosing instead to stress the Polish characteristics in his own thought and to show how that Polish perspective differed from the systematizing theoretical tendencies of the Germans and from the intellectual values of the West in general. Even the French could not help the Poles in this realm.

As Mickiewicz explained the difference, Poles approached their problems through intuition and spiritualism rather than through the structure of Western analytic thought. This distinction meant to Mickiewicz that his own nation-enhancing work would inevitably require non-Western modes of thought and action and that he must feel in no way apologetic for his intuitive Polish insights. In order to achieve Polish comprehension, Mickiewicz explained, "I find myself obliged first to abandon the method which dominates all political and religious discussions in the West, the method of analysis, the terrain of customs and of habits taken from the school. ... We cannot accept the course that the doctrines and doctrinaires of the West present to us. The work whose title I have given you [*The Banquet* by Towiański] is a declaration of war against all rationalist systems."[136]

The Poles, in short, could not move into their future unless they ignored sterile (Western) intellectual formulations and adhered to the spiritual imperatives of their own national experience. Anyone might accept an intellectual doctrine, because it demanded nothing of the soul ("The West is withering away in its doctrines"), but the spiritual life demanded commitment.[137] It also resolved problems that rational analysis alone could neither explain nor transform. True philosophy for the Poles therefore depended upon the revelations of spiritual intuition and upon the actions that the Spirit encouraged.

This faith in the intuitive route to truth appeared in almost all of Mickiewicz's pronouncements on philosophy and art. It contributed, for example, to his distrust of systematic philosophy; it convinced him that Poles could learn more from Ralph Waldo Emerson than from Hegel; and it shaped his appreciation for literature and poetry. Since good literature reflected inspiration and a prophetic sensibility, literary works could often reveal truth in the form of unmediated, spontaneous expressions of the Spirit; as for poetry, its truth value surpassed philosophy in that it allowed more freedom for intuition and mystical visions.[138]

Nobody understood these truths about truth as well as the Poles. Rejecting Western theories that separated heaven from earth, they preferred to see the spiritual element in all of human history. Secular explanations for events and for truth invariably overlooked what Poles perceived to be the *real* historical forces and relationships. "The belief in the existence of immediate connections between the higher world and earth," Mickiewicz explained, "formed the moral and political foundation of Polish organization; and whenever one wanted to draw from that either a force of resistance or a force of action, one had only to make an appeal to this belief."[139] The extraordinary spiritual component in Polish history and the Polish recognition of a divine spark in literature and politics made Poland almost incomprehensible to people in the West and helped to explain why Polish politics and philosophy developed differently from the politics and thought of other nations. Here was a spiritual disparity that no worldly perspective or practice could ever abolish.

Mickiewicz's analysis of the contrasts between Poland and the West did not rest entirely on spiritual themes, however. Like some of the Western analysts he disliked, he could find secular, historical patterns to account for the East-West differences that had become so conspicuous in the modern period. Mickiewicz traced the historical origins of these differences to the consolidation of Protestantism in seventeenth-century Germany, which blocked Catholic Poles both geographically and intellectually from the centers of Western Catholic culture—especially Rome and Paris. This separation disoriented, isolated, and weakened Poland, but it also forced Poles to formulate political and religious principles for themselves and to search for their own course into the future. That Polish course steadily intensified the East-West distinction over the next couple of centuries, so that Mickiewicz could summarize Polish history by the 1840s as an inversion of the West. "The whole political and philosophical movement of Europe," he argued, "is diametrically opposed to the political and religious movement of Poland."[140]

The increasing Polish difference from Western development in the eighteenth century caused Western philosophers, historians, and politicians to lose interest in Poland during the Enlightenment and opened the way for Eastern powers to partition Polish territory according to their own interests. The major philosophes cared nothing for Poland, in part because their materialist, rationalist outlook precluded sympathy for a nonmaterialist, spiritual people such as the Poles, and in part because they decided that Russia was the true Slavic country. Voltaire, for example, distorted Polish history and even congratulated the Russians, Prussians, and Austrians for their first entry into Poland.[141] Thus, in contrast to Germans such as Heine and Marx, who supported the French Enlightenment, Mickiewicz expressed vehement religious and nationalist dislike for the philosophes. He concluded that the Enlightenment had somehow placed Poland on the side of darkness and Russia on the side of progress, thereby leaving Poles in the extremely difficult position of battling Russian power on the one hand and Western prejudice, ignorance, and indifference on the other.[142] (Napoleon again provided a special case for Mickiewicz by breaking with much of the Enlightenment and by opposing Russia.)

Mickiewicz acknowledged that many French people had challenged the eighteenth-century attitudes by supporting the Polish independence movement in 1831, and Franco-Polish contacts thereafter reduced some of the inherited ignorance about Poland. The cultural gap that had separated the philosophes from the Poles nevertheless continued to separate economic and social reformers from the Poles in the nineteenth century and to prevent either party from truly understanding the other. The "laws" of political economy were a typical example: Western economists could not account for the ways in which Polish forms of property, organization, and morality created a different, non-Western economic system.[143] At the same time, the radical prescriptions of Saint-Simonians or Fourierists carried little relevance for Poles, who had their own agrarian, communal traditions to protect and who, unlike most socialists, understood the importance of nationality in the creation of social institutions. Insofar as French socialists were eager to include Slavs in their new world, their cosmopolitan theories tended to see Russia as the natural leader of the Slavic people and to ignore other national distinctions.

Mickiewicz's own notion of international cooperation left a very large place for the unique Polish nation, of course, and it differed enough from the views of many socialists to keep him closer to nationalist radicals than to radical internationalists.[144] Since his real interests led him to spiritualism, literature, and Polish nationalism rather than to the economic concerns of socialism, in his view a radical socialist who misunderstood Poland could offer little more to the higher cause than could an uncomprehending conservative. Westerners of all political persuasions still had a great deal to learn about Poland, but—as Mickiewicz realized when the government suppressed his course at the Collège de France—the long-standing French ignorance of Polish needs and character could easily withstand and overwhelm all efforts to introduce Polish culture and ideas to France.

The police officially suspended Mickiewicz's course on 31 May 1844, following almost two years of government surveillance and deliberation. Mickiewicz's name had begun to appear in police documents as early as 1842, when agents first reported on the cult around the mystic Towiański and on the unusual religious ceremonies that were occurring in Mickiewicz's home. After the police expelled Towiański from France in July 1842, informers sent word that Mickiewicz had assumed leadership of Towiański's followers and that he intended to convert French students as well as Poles to the movement. The prefect of police, Gabriel Delessert, found this allegation especially troublesome because it meant that the French government was paying a lecturer whose pronouncements were likely to disrupt order and stability in the capital.[145] Delessert's concerns led to a police surveillance of Mickiewicz's course which had become quite thorough by the time he began his fervent pro-Towiański lectures in the spring of 1844. The reports from the Collège de France eventually convinced Delessert that Mickiewicz had abandoned literature for politics and that the government must intervene.[146] Although the agents assigned to cover the lectures seemed confused about what Mickiewicz was actually saying (one later government summary claimed that he advocated Saint-Simonian doctrines), Delessert sent their accounts to the Ministry of Public Instruction as part of an internal government campaign to inform officials about the disruptive effects of the Polish poet's course and to urge action that might end these "intolerable scandals."[147]

According to the police, the "scandal" in Mickiewicz's lectures resulted from his fanatic faith in Towiański, his attacks on the official church, and his incessant praise of Napoleon. The Towiański influence worried French authorities most of all, perhaps because the mystical doctrines seemed so alien or perhaps simply because Towiański's creed challenged church authority and deified Napoleon. In any case, the police portrayed Mickiewicz as a dupe of the latter-day Lithuanian messiah and warned that the whole mystical movement challenged the public order: "For a long time, M. Mickiewicz has made himself the active and devoted apostle of a M. Towiański, a kind of Visionary ... expel[led] from France to put an end to his schemes. Under the sway of this strange influence, this professor allows himself to issue the most reprehensible attacks against the social order, the government and the Catholic religion."[148] More specifically, these strange doctrines caused Mickiewicz to criticize the church for ignoring the Spirit, for encouraging passivity, and for obstructing the noble cause of progressive, forward-looking people—criticisms that guardians of the social order would not tolerate for long. When the doctrines produced also an extreme enthusiasm for Napoleon, government officials had all the justification they needed to stop the lectures.

Mickiewicz's final lecture became a kind of homage to the spirit of Napoleon; it included distribution of the emperor's portrait to an audience whose response gradually erupted in emotional frenzy. One woman rushed toward the platform, collapsed to her knees shouting, "Long live Adam! Long live Mickiewicz," and created a drama of such intensity that (according to the police) almost every woman in the hall began to cry. Previous lectures had already provoked repeated outbursts in the audience (this scene was only the most dramatic) and had led to several dangerous Polish political meetings. By the end, therefore, police agents saw Mickiewicz's course as simply a strange exile gathering that disrupted the "public tranquillity," aroused passions, and encouraged subversive activity through pronouncements on Towiański, the church, and Napoleon.[149] This threatening combination exhausted the official support that had created and protected Mickiewicz's position at the Collège de France, and he never lectured there again after the tumultuous finale on 28 May 1844.

Still, the authorities let him go with notable care and respect. Correspondence between Minister of Public Instruction François Villemain and Minister of the Interior Charles-Marie Duchâtel during the academic break in 1844 indicates that both men regarded the case as an especially delicate problem; they hoped that Mickiewicz might listen to "reason" (Duchâtel's phrase) and abandon the Towiański doctrines. Duchâtel suggested that Towiański was probably a Russian agent and emphasized to Villemain that the police were expelling foreigners who worked for him in France; Mickiewicz, though, differed from all other Towiański enthusiasts in that he worked for the French government, held a prominent public position, and could not simply be expelled. Villemain thus chose to warn Mickiewicz several times that he must change the tone and content of his course in order to resume his duties, but the poet resisted the advice and requested a leave (4 October 1844) for the 1844–45 academic year. The minister quickly agreed and then extended the leave through the following year. By that time Mickiewicz seemed to realize that his Collège de France career was definitely over; he agreed to surrender half of his income to the Slavic scholar Cyprien Robert, who took over the Slavic literature course and soon received appointment to the chair that had first belonged to Mickiewicz. Despite this change, however, in what amounted to a kind of prolonged severance pay, Mickiewicz continued to receive half of his former salary until 1848.[150]

Mickiewicz's public role in Paris thus ended with a bang in May 1844, followed by a long silence—which left him more or less as he had started, a freelance Polish poet struggling to proclaim a nationalist message and to survive in a Parisian milieu that sometimes responded and sometimes seemed not to hear at all. Alone in the "wilderness" again, he gradually moved away from Towiański (1846–47) and eventually decided to support more concrete programs for Polish salvation. He responded to the revolutions of 1848, for example, by attempting to organize a Polish legion that would march from Rome to liberate Warsaw, but the project dissolved before his tiny force could even get out of Italy.[151] Back in France, he helped found the short-lived radical newspaper *La Tribune des Peuples* (1849) and then became a strong supporter of Louis Napoleon. Although this support was entirely consistent with his steadfast faith in the Napoleonic spirit, it alienated almost all radicals in France and separated him from most other exiles as well. The sympathy for Napoleon nevertheless eased his financial problems because in 1852 the Second Empire government made him librarian at the Bibliothèque de l'Arsenal. He acquired French citizenship in order to accept that position, and so the Parisian experience of Poland's most famous exile ended somewhat obscurely. The outbreak of the Crimean War encouraged Mickiewicz to participate in the formation of yet another Polish legion, a project that worked no better in 1855 than it had in 1848. But the complex arrangements for the new legion took him to Constantinople, where he died of cholera in late November.[152]

His body was returned to France for burial, as perhaps befitted a French citizen who had spent most of his adult life in Paris, and yet there could be no doubt that Mickiewicz had always lived in France as a Pole.[153] The struggle to free Poland from Russian control and to define the Polish national identity dominated his Parisian career from beginning to end, even though this struggle also became at times almost inseparable from the policies and outlook of France. Describing Poles always as the chosen people of Europe, Mickiewicz explained how their historical role coincided with the historical mission of the French and how France might fulfill *its* destiny through an active intervention in eastern Europe. The clear spiritual affinity between France and Poland demanded that their actions should correspond too. Mickiewicz clarified his theories about Polish uniqueness and the special French-Polish relationship through both the isolation of his exile life and the long-term interaction with the French intellectuals he met in Paris: Montalembert, Sand, Quinet, Michelet. They in turn helped to make Mickiewicz the symbol of suffering Polish people and the representative figure of Polish nationalism. Mickiewicz became famous in Europe because (like Heine) he became famous in Paris.

Nevertheless, the sympathetic response of French intellectuals and their willingness to embrace Poland as the "France of the North" was never enough to overcome Mickiewicz's sense of alienation from French society. His encounter with an urban, industrializing, secular, Western culture in Paris seemed to encourage in him a steadily deepening faith in the traditional virtues of a rural, agrarian, religious, Slavic culture that made Poland forever different from France. He would never advocate Western values or methods to achieve Polish freedom or a new Polish society. Whatever France might be (and Mikciewicz found much to admire in its revolutionary, Napoleonic tradition and its well-developed national identity), it could never be Poland, and it could never be the social or intellectual source for Polish salvation. Still, July Monarchy Paris could provide Mickiewicz the institutions and contacts he needed in order to introduce Polish messianism to the European public and the alternative (Western) social milieu he needed in order to analyze (nostalgically) the distinctive Polish society from which he came and to which he hoped always to return.

To sum up, therefore, Paris played a decisive role in making Mickiewicz the symbol and theoretician of Polish nationalism, much as it enabled Heine to become the literary mediator between

France and Germany and provoked Marx to formulate new theories to describe the changing social conditions of modern capitalist society. The French experience intensified Mickiewicz's identification with Poland and helped to transform him into the most influential literary figure of the Polish Emigration.

Conclusion

Exiles in Paris and
Modern European History

The history of Heine, Marx, and Mickiewicz in July Monarchy Paris offers three notable examples of the common and influential experience of exile in modern European history. For all their significance as individuals, they may also be taken as a group to typify the difficult and creative processes that often follow separation from native cultures and traditions. Their lives and work in France contribute strong support for the broader argument that has informed this study: the connection between the exile experience and creative intellectual work is so common that it should be analyzed as a historical pattern rather than as a historical accident. Like many other influential figures in modern history, Heine, Marx, and Mickiewicz developed many of their priorities and interests, theories and texts, friends and enemies through the dislocating social and intellectual experience of exile. Although the details of this process varied, we may note by way of conclusion certain general characteristics of exile that these three men shared, as well as the significance of the specific French context in their lives and thought.

The common experience of exile in July Monarchy Paris united these intellectuals with other foreigners and to some extent with each other—despite their many important differences. Each of them came to some new identity and understanding through contact with the other culture, other tradition, other language, and other people he encountered in France. All three did so by working through French texts (Saint-Simon or Proudhon or Lamennais) and by coming to terms with the modern, urban civilization that had evolved in Paris after the French Revolution. At the same time, the exile position provoked in each man an extensive exploration of the national tradition from which he had come and an analysis of how his native country would or should develop in the future. They

229

rediscovered their homes and their origins by leaving home for good.

But that discovery, which contributed so much to the insight of other exiles and of compatriots who never left home at all, brought with it an enduring sense of displacement. All of these exiles experienced that modern intellectual phenomenon of estrangement, or what Marx himself called alienation (though he gave the term a more explicit economic meaning). All felt themselves to be alienated from the French culture in which they lived, alienated from their native countries, and also alienated from the general development of nineteenth-century European capitalist society. There was in each one a belief that modern people were losing something of what made them human—the appreciation for beauty, the products of labor, the spiritual truth of religion. One finds in their exile texts a recurring sense of loss, of separation, of difference, of change, of conflict, of crisis, and of death; one finds an especially acute sense of the anxieties and problems that seem to disturb people everywhere in the modern period.

Significantly, these exile writers all expressed some expectation of future harmony that might overcome the alienation they experienced and discussed in their works. Heine sought a reconciliation between poetry and life, art and politics, Germany and France, himself and history. Marx anticipated a more cooperative social order that would transcend the alienating contradictions of capitalism; if communism was not for Marx the end of history, it was at least the end of class conflict and the end of the dehumanizing consequences of capitalist production. Mickiewicz yearned for a harmonious unification of Poland and the subsequent "brotherhood of nations"; Poland's resurrection was for him the new millennium, the new Jerusalem, the new reconciliation.

The desire for harmony is of course very old in Western civilization, and it reappears whenever people feel disoriented, threatened, separated from the past, or cut off from traditions; that is, it reappears in almost every generation. Since exiles usually feel this dislocation even more acutely than others, their writings often become especially concerned with the losses they perceive and with the future reconciliations (with home, within nations, between peoples, with heaven) that might restore what seems to have disappeared. In this sense, the exile writers studied here may be typical of a collective Western consciousness that is extremely old and was highly characteristic of the century after the French Revolution and the Industrial Revolution. Heine, Marx, and Mickiewicz were by no means simple utopians, and their notions of harmony differed enormously. Yet their views of the future all suggested a world with less conflict, less division, and less separation; and while these aspirations could evolve in response to a number of nineteenth-century conditions and experiences, the alienating experience of exile seemed specifically to increase their sensitivity to modern losses and to encourage their visions of a more harmonious European society. Their exile may, in fact, be seen as a particular manifestation of broader alienating tendencies in European history (nationalist divisions, industrial economies, urbanization) that almost all modern people have experienced wherever they happen to live. The *explicit* estrangement of exile thinkers, however, gave them a highly conscious position from which to discuss what many other nineteenth-century Europeans may have known or felt *implicitly* but could not describe for themselves.

But it was not exile alone that produced new insights and new identities among these intellectuals. Indeed, as this study has argued, the society and culture of July Monarchy Paris affected the concerns and development of foreigners as much as the exile status itself. Drawn to the city by its historical reputation for culture and revolution, outsiders typically responded to the complexities and contradictions of Parisian life with the mix of fascination and discomfort that characterized the views of Heine, Marx, and Mickiewicz. Heine relished the boulevards and admired the constitutional monarchy but feared the social revolution of unwashed workers and the breakdown of authority that they represented. Marx found his universal class in the back streets of the city and borrowed from the French revolutionary tradition but condemned the bourgeois state and the religious-minded reformers who challenged it. Mickiewicz celebrated the Napoleonic genius and discovered the Spirit in the French people but attacked the secular, self-interested leaders of the *juste-milieu* and the urban, industrial society those leaders were creating. Like most foreigners who settled in Paris, they all found reasons to identify with France and other reasons to reaffirm their own national identities. It was the encounter with Parisian social and intellectual life, however, that facilitated both tendencies in this process of cultural, theoretical, and national identification. The French experience provided an opening, a threshold over which these people could cross into a new social or intellectual world.

To be sure, that world carried various meanings for everyone who went there: Heine's France, for example, represented personal

freedom and literary opportunity; Marx's France represented theoretical alternatives to German Hegelianism; Mickiewicz's France
represented the hope for Polish national liberation. Yet Paris, with
its culture industry, its class-conscious urban economy, and its
ideology of revolutionary nationalism, led all of its visitors toward
a new world—the modern world—and often became a transforming experience for anyone in search of different realities or different ideas.

Furthermore, exiles such as Heine, Marx, and Mickiewicz depended in important ways upon the institutions and social network
of July Monarchy Paris. They used its publications, its politics, its
cafés, its schools, its clubs, its streets, its crowds, its books, and its
language to develop their own views and to make those views
known to others. Their work became linked to the émigré communities they joined and to the French writers and theorists with
whom they associated. They found a base in the "capital of Europe"
from which to build reputations, clarify theories, argue with home,
and preach to the world. No other European city in these years
offered such support for new ideas about the past and future or
provided so many intellectual opportunities—historically unique
opportunities that all of these exiles seemed to recognize and exploit. Certainly, the French always kept themselves atop the cultural hierarchy, assuming for France the role of teacher rather than
student in the history of modern politics, theory, and literature.
Despite that self-assurance, however (or perhaps because of it), they
showed more than a little tolerance for the exile intellectuals
among them. The French may never have really understood or
cared about what the foreigners were doing, or they may simply
have accepted the presence of outsiders as flattering confirmation
of France's central, instructive role in European civilization.

In any case, the smug arrogance in that French view of their own
national glory was not altogether self-deceptive. Foreigners did
come to Paris in part because they too believed it to be the center
of European culture, politics, radicalism, and tolerance. Once settled in the capital, of course, they soon discovered that the reality
was more complicated than the legend, and so they embarked on
the creative, analytical process that this study has sought to explain. Heine, Marx, and Mickiewicz, and many other Europeans
in these years discovered themselves while they were discovering
France, and they drew upon Paris—a microcosm of modern Europe—in order to make major contributions to the literary culture,
social theory, and nationalism that have characterized European

society ever since. The history of exiles in July Monarchy France thus becomes also a history of the enduring connection between European thought and experience, and an example of personal and social processes that reappear constantly in modern world history.

Appendix 1

Prominent Foreign Intellectuals in France between 1830 and 1848

P. V. Annenkov	(Russian)	Moses Hess	(German)
Mikhail Bakunin	(Russian)	Zygmunt Krasiński	(Polish)
Cristina Belgioioso	(Italian)	Heinrich Laube	(German)
Vissarion Belinsky	(Russian)	Joachim Lelewel	(Polish)
Carl Bernays	(German)	Franz Liszt	(Hungarian)
Ludwig Börne	(German)	Karl Marx	(German)
Heinrich Börnstein	(German)	Giuseppe Mazzini	(Italian)
Albert Brisbane	(American)	Giacomo Meyerbeer	(German)
Frédéric Chopin	(Polish)	Adam Mickiewicz	(Polish)
August Cieszkowski	(Polish)	Arnold Ruge	(German)
James Fenimore Cooper	(American)	Julius Słowacki	(Polish)
Friedrich Engels	(German)	William Thackeray	(English)
Hermann Ewerbeck	(German)	Frances Trollope	(English)
Margaret Fuller	(American)	Ivan Turgenev	(Russian)
Karl Grün	(German)	Jakob Venedey	(German)
Heinrich Heine	(German)	Richard Wagner	(German)
Georg Herwegh	(German)	Wilhelm Weitling	(German)
Alexander Herzen	(Russian)		

Appendix 2

Prominent French Intellectuals
in July Monarchy France

Marie d'Agoult	(1805–1876)	Félicité Robert Lamennais	(1782–1854)
Honoré de Balzac	(1799–1850)	Pierre Leroux	(1797–1871)
Charles Baudelaire	(1821–1867)	Jules Michelet	(1798–1874)
Hector Berlioz	(1803–1869)	August-François Mignet	(1796–1884)
Pierre-Jean de Béranger	(1780–1857)	Charles de Montalembert	(1810–1870)
Louis Blanc	(1811–1882)	Alfred de Musset	(1810–1857)
Auguste Blanqui	(1805–1881)	Gérard de Nerval	(1808–1855)
François Buloz	(1804–1877)	Charles Nodier	(1780–1844)
Etienne Cabet	(1788–1856)	Constantin Pecqueur	(1801–1887)
François René Chateaubriand	(1768–1848)	Pierre-Joseph Proudhon	(1809–1865)
Victor Considérant	(1808–1893)	Edgar Quinet	(1803–1875)
Victor Cousin	(1792–1867)	Charles Sainte-Beuve	(1804–1869)
Eugène Delacroix	(1798–1863)	George Sand	(1804–1876)
Alexandre Dumas	(1802–1870)	Stendhal	(1783–1842)
Prosper Enfantin	(1796–1864)	Eugène Sue	(1804–1876)
Charles Fourier	(1772–1837)	Adolphe Thiers	(1797–1877)
Théophile Gautier	(1811–1872)	Augustin Thierry	(1795–1856)
François Guizot	(1787–1874)	Alexis de Tocqueville	(1805–1859)
Victor Hugo	(1802–1885)	Alfred de Vigny	(1797–1863)
Alphonse de Lamartine	(1790–1869)		

Notes

Introduction. Exiles in Paris and Intellectual History

1. For an informative, concise summary of exile themes in early Western culture, see Randolph Starn, *Contrary Commonwealth: The Theme of Exile in Medieval and Renaissance Italy* (Berkeley, 1982), pp. 1–9, 24–30; see also Paul Tabori, *The Anatomy of Exile: A Semantic and Historical Study* (London, 1972), pp. 40–65.

2. Starn (*Contrary Commonwealth*, pp. 31–147) analyzes the legal evolution of exile, the experience of Dante, and the Italian exile literary tradition; for the quotation from Isidore, see p. 1. Tabori *(Anatomy of Exile,* pp. 66–91) provides a less analytical survey for the early modern period.

3. The role of nationalism in modern culture and politics has been analyzed with much theoretical insight in Ernest Gellner, *Nations and Nationalism* (Ithaca, 1983). Gellner stresses the connections between nationalism and modern forms of government, education, and economic activity; he also describes the relationship between national culture and personal identity that I emphasize: "In stable self-contained communities culture is often quite invisible, but when mobility and context-free communication come to be of the essence of social life, the culture in which one has been *taught* to communicate becomes the core of one's identity" (p. 61). Other studies of the development and influence of nationalism include Hans Kohn, *The Idea of Nationalism* (New York, 1967); and Boyd C. Shafer, *Faces of Nationalism: New Realities and Old Myths* (New York, 1972). Citizens of the modern nation-state also developed new views of outsiders, as Hans Mayer explains in *Outsiders: A Study in Life and Letters*, trans. Denis M. Sweet (Cambridge, Mass., 1982).

4. Isaiah Berlin's description of Paris in the 1840s offers a partial justification and starting point for the study of this period: "The social, political, and artistic ferment of Paris in the middle of the nineteenth century is a phenomenon without parallel in European history.... It was a decade during which a richer international traffic in ideas, theories, [and] per-

sonal sentiments was carried on than during any previous period; there were alive at this time, congregated in the same place, attracting, repelling and transforming each other, men of gifts more varied, more striking and more articulate than at any time since the Renaissance"; see *Karl Marx: His Life and Environment*, 4th ed. (Oxford, 1978), p. 61. I have attempted to support Berlin's claim by listing prominent intellectuals who lived and worked in July Monarchy France; see Appendixes 1 and 2.

5. Debates about the relationship between social and intellectual history form a recurring theme in works that discuss the status of intellectual history. See, e.g., John Higham and Paul K. Conkin, eds., *New Directions in American Intellectual History* (Baltimore, Md., 1979); Dominick LaCapra and Steven L. Kaplan, eds., *Modern European Intellectual History: Reappraisals and New Perspectives* (Ithaca, 1982); Dominick LaCapra, *Rethinking Intellectual History: Texts, Contexts, Language* (Ithaca, 1983), and *History and Criticism* (Ithaca, 1985); Leonard Krieger, "The Autonomy of Intellectual History," *Journal of the History of Ideas*, 34 (1973): 499–516; Felix Gilbert, "Intellectual History: Its Aims and Methods," *Daedalus*, 100 (1971): 80–97; Robert Darnton, "Intellectual and Cultural History," in Michael Kammen, ed., *The Past before Us* (Ithaca, 1980), pp. 327–49; and Paul K. Conkin, "Intellectual History: Past, Present, and Future," in Charles F. Delzell, ed., *The Future of History* (Nashville, Tenn., 1977), pp. 111–33. These studies return frequently to questions about the interaction between contexts and texts and propose methodological alternatives that I would like to bring together in the history of exiles. My own view of the links between social and intellectual history appears in Lloyd S. Kramer, "Intellectual History and Reality: The Search for Connections," *Historical Reflections/Réflexions Historiques*, 13 (1986): 517–45.

6. I often join the term "exile" with "experience": I use "experience" to mean both a personal interaction with specific sensory impressions and the active, orienting response to sensory stimuli that results; it may therefore be understood as a process that is both sensuous and interpretive. The anthropologist H. G. Barnett has summarized this meaning of experience as follows: "Not only must a person orient himself; if he is to survive in a universe of unremitting sense impressions, he must order them; he must assign relationships and thereby structure them. . . . New experiences must be integrated with the old. They must be drawn into the matrix of the known before they can have any significance. Otherwise, they remain utterly alien, detached, and incomprehensible. In short, they must have meaning if the individual is to deal with them; and if they appear to be lacking in meaning, he consciously or unconsciously assigns some significance to them." This account provides a useful description of what happens to disoriented exiles who interpret their new experiences as something like a new text. See H. G. Barnett, "The Shaping of Experience," in George G. Haydu, ed., *Experience Forms: Their Cultural and Individual Place and Function* (The Hague, 1979), pp. 157–58.

7. The process of interpreting an alien place to make it fit certain expectations is part of every visitor's encounter with foreign countries. For discussion of how this semiotic process contributes to the experiences of soldiers, tourists, and imaginative writers (as well as of exiles), see Tzvetan Todorov, *The Conquest of America*, trans. Richard Howard (New York, 1984); Dean MacCannel, *The Tourist: A New Theory of the Leisure Class* (New York, 1976); and Peter Conrad, *Imagining America* (New York, 1980).

8. A good example of the psychobiographical study of this aspect of the exile experience appears in Frederick R. Karl, *Joseph Conrad: The Three Lives* (New York, 1979). Karl suggests how Conrad used his Polish heritage, psychological conflicts, and marginal, outsider status to develop the themes of his literature.

9. The relationship between self and other emerges as a much-debated issue in modern philosophy, psychology, literature, and social theory. As a point of origin for modern analysis of this problem, however, it is useful to go back to Hegel's discussion of self-consciousness. The creation of self, he writes, is a dynamic process of interaction with others, and self-consciousness "is essentially the return from *otherness*." For Hegel's extended discussion of how the self comes to consciousness, see *Phenomenology of Spirit*, trans. A. V. Miller (Oxford, 1977), pp. 104–19.

10. For a good account of the revolution that established the July Monarchy and created the social-political system upon which it depended, see David H. Pinkney, *The French Revolution of 1830* (Princeton, N.J., 1972); see also Pinkney's important study of French modernization, *Decisive Years in France, 1840–1847* (Princeton, N.J., 1986). Pinkney argues that the 1840s were decisive in the emergence of modern French society, and his description of the economic, social, and cultural changes that occurred in these years suggests why the experience of emigrating to France could be so influential for people from all parts of Europe. Biographies of Louis-Philippe and other leaders also provide good social-political surveys of the July Monarchy. See, e.g., T. E. B. Howrath, *Citizen-King: The Life of Louis-Philippe, King of the French* (London, 1961), and Douglas Johnson, *Guizot: Aspects of French History, 1787–1874* (Toronto, 1964). For discussion of the connection between social and political transitions and changes in the French language after 1830, see the classic study by Georges Matoré, *Le vocabulaire et la société sous Louis-Philippe* (Geneva, 1951), esp. pp. 17–109. William H. Sewell, Jr., also analyzes the issues of language and political consciousness, with special attention to the attitudes of workers, in *Work and Revolution in France: The Language of Labor from the Old Regime to 1848* (Cambridge, 1980). Finally, for an interesting summary of the new conditions and tensions in French cultural life during the era of bourgeois expansion, see Jerrold Seigel, *Bohemian Paris: Culture, Politics, and the Boundaries of Bourgeois Life, 1830–1930* (New York, 1986), pp. 3–30.

Chapter 1. The Capital of Europe

1. Catherine Gore, *Paris in 1841* (London, 1842), pp. 246–47. Gore (1799–1861), a novelist and popular writer, moved to Paris in 1832 and lived there for several years, writing both novels and plays; her book about Paris, however, is primarily devoted to descriptions of the city's famous monuments.

2. This is the title of an essay on Paris and Baudelaire in Walter Benjamin, *Charles Baudelaire: A Lyric Poet in the Era of High Capitalism*, trans. Harry Zohn (London, 1973), pp. 155–76. Other scholars have also discussed the special role of Paris in the 1840s; see, e.g., E. H. Carr, *Michael Bakunin* (London, 1937), p. 125; and André Liebich, *Between Ideology and Utopia: The Politics and Philosophy of August Cieszkowski* (Dordrecht, 1979), p. 113. See also Isaiah Berlin's description of Paris in *Karl Marx*, p. 61.

3. Charles Forster, *Quinze ans à Paris (1832–1848): Paris et les Parisiens*, 2 vols. (Paris, 1848), 1:9–10. (Where they are not otherwise attributed in the notes, translations in text and notes are mine.) Forster (1800–1879) went to Paris in 1832 and lived there for the next seventeen years. He worked as a journalist and traveled as a correspondent in Germany, where he lived after 1850.

4. Gaëtan Niépovié, *Etudes physiologiques sur les grandes métropoles de l'Europe occidentale, Paris* (Paris, 1840), pp. i–ii, 6–7. Niépovié, which means "will not tell" in Polish, was the pseudonym that Frankowski (1795–1846) used for this book. He left Poland in 1836 and traveled extensively in western Europe for several years. He differed from most Poles in the West because he had served in the Russian army and was not a political exile. He returned to Poland in 1841 and became the director of a school.

5. P. V. Annenkov, *The Extraordinary Decade*, trans. Irwin R. Titunik, ed. Arthur P. Mendel (1880–81; Ann Arbor, Mich., 1968), p. 165. Annenkov (1813–87) arrived in Paris in November 1841, returned to Russia in 1843, then spent several more months in Paris in the late 1840s.

6. Alexander Herzen, *My Past and Thoughts*, trans. Constance Garnett, rev. Humphrey Higgins, 4 vols. (London, 1968), 2:957.

7. Girault de Saint-Fargeau, *Les quarante-huit quartiers de Paris* (Paris, 1846), pp. 13–14.

8. Quoted in Liebich, *Between Ideology and Utopia*, p. 122. For more discussion of what the French experience meant to Gans, see John Edward Toews, *Hegelianism: The Path toward Dialectical Humanism, 1805–1841* (Cambridge, 1980), pp. 129–30.

9. Margaret Fuller Ossoli, *At Home and Abroad; or, Things and Thoughts in America and Europe*, ed. Arthur B. Fuller (New York, 1869), p. 214. Fuller (1810–50) went to Europe in the summer of 1846, visited England, and then spent the winter of 1846–47 in Paris. She wrote articles about Britain, France, and Italy for the New York *Tribune*. Her brother collected the pieces and published them in this book after her death.

10. James Fenimore Cooper, *Recollections of Europe*, 2 vols. (London, 1837), 2:311–12. Cooper (1789–1851) lived in Europe between 1826 and 1833, mostly in Paris. He became a close friend of Lafayette, entered a political dispute over the question of government expenditures in monarchies and republics, and found much to criticize in Paris as well as a culture to respect.

11. One exception was the American Fourierist Albert Brisbane (1809–90), who spent several years in Paris in the early 1830s and 1840s studying the works of Fourier, and the rest of his life preaching the French socialist's ideas to inattentive Americans. See his accounts of Parisian life in Redelia Brisbane, *Albert Brisbane: A Mental Biography* (1893; rpt., New York, 1969), pp. 65–68, 154, 187, 194, 211, 233–34, 239. For a comprehensive survey of American visitors' responses to France in the early nineteenth century, see G. Bertier de Sauvigny, *La France et les français vus par les voyageurs américains, 1814–1848*, 2 vols. (Paris, 1982, 1985).

12. Carr (*Bakunin*, p. 125) described the phenomenon most succinctly: "Everyone interested in the theory or practice of revolution was bound sooner or later to come to Paris."

13. Arnold Ruge, quoted in Pascal Duprat, "L'école de Hegel à Paris—Annales d'Allemagne et de France, publiées par Arnold Ruge et Karl Marx," *La Revue Indépendante* 12 (25 February 1844): 484.

14. Annenkov, *Extraordinary Decade*, pp. 69–70, 75–76.

15. Ibid., pp. 64, 165.

16. Ibid., p. 64.

17. Forster, *Quinze ans à Paris*, 1:76–77.

18. Ibid., pp. 77, 79.

19. See Louis Chevalier, *Laboring Classes and Dangerous Classes*, trans. Frank Jellinek (New York, 1973), pp. 2–3, 27. For one foreigner's horrified view, see Frances Trollope's discussion of a murder and a visit to the morgue in her book *Paris and the Parisians in 1835* (New York, 1836), pp. 193–98.

20. William M. Thackeray, *The Students' Quarter; or, Paris Five-and-Thirty Years Since* (London, 1875), pp. 55–56, 65. Thackeray (1811–63) lived in Paris in 1839–40; this book is a collection of letters that he wrote during that time. For more on Thackeray's experiences in France, see Roger Boutet de Monuel, *Eminent English Men and Women in Paris, 1800–1850*, trans. G. Herring (London, 1912), pp. 409–509.

21. James Grant, *Paris and Its People*, 2 vols. (London, 1844), 1:99. Grant (1802–79) was a journalist of Scottish origin who traveled extensively in Europe and Ireland and wrote travel books about many of the places he visited. His observations on Parisian life were based on a visit to Paris in 1843. He later served as editor of the London *Morning Advertiser* for more than twenty years.

22. Trollope, *Paris and the Parisians*, p. 381. Trollope (1780–1863) was one of the best-known English travel writers and novelists of her generation. She became famous (and controversial) with the publication of *The*

Domestic Manners of the Americans (1832), a generally unflattering portrait based on a four-year residence in the United States. Her Paris visit, in contrast, lasted only a few months during the spring of 1835; she went there to write a travel book and to find medical treatment for her ailing husband. A useful study is available in Helen Heineman, *Mrs. Trollope: The Triumphant Feminine in the Nineteenth Century* (Athens, Ohio, 1979).

23. The French scholar Jacques Grandjonc discusses this political emigration in "Etat sommaire des dépôts d'archives françaises sur le mouvement ouvrier et les émigrés allemands de 1830 à 1851/52," *Archiv für Sozialgeschichte*, 12 (1972): 492–93. Also see Jacques Grandjonc, "Les rapports des socialistes et néo-Hegeliens allemands de l'émigration avec les socialistes français 1840–1847," in *Aspects des relations franco-allemands 1830–1848*, ed. Raymond Poidevin and Heinz-Otto Sieburg (Metz, 1978), p. 86. Grandjonc is the leading authority on the vast and complicated subject of German immigration to France during the July Monarchy.

24. For an introduction to the revolt and the emigration that followed it, see B. Pawlowski, "The November Insurrection," and A. P. Coleman, "The Great Emigration," both in *The Cambridge History of Poland*, ed. W. F. Reddway, J. H. Penson, O. Halecki, and R. Dyloski, 2 vols. (Cambridge, 1951), 2:295–323. See also the study by R. F. Leslie, *Polish Politics and the Revolution of November 1830* (London, 1956); and the useful survey of revolutionary movements throughout Europe in Clive H. Church, *Europe in 1830: Revolution and Political Change* (London, 1983).

25. Annenkov, *Extraordinary Decade*, p. 196.

26. Jacques Grandjonc, "Eléments statistiques pour une étude de l'immigration étrangère en France de 1830 à 1851," *Archiv für Sozialgeschichte* 15 (1975): 287.

27. Grandjonc, "Etat sommaire," pp. 488–89; and Jacques Grandjonc, *Marx et les communistes allemands à Paris, 1844* (Paris, 1974), pp. 11–13. See also Mack Walker, *Germany and the Emigration, 1816–1885* (Cambridge, Mass., 1964), esp. pp. 1–102.

28. Grandjonc, "Eléments statistiques," p. 232. Some of the French view of Germans appears in Louis Huart's essay "L'Allemand," in *Les étrangers à Paris*, ed. Louis Desnoyers et al. (Paris, 1844), p. 166.

29. The second largest, Marseilles, grew in this period from 145,115 to 183,181; the whole of France from 32,569,223 to 35,400,486. All figures in this paragraph are from Charles H. Pouthas, *La population française pendant la première moitié du XIXᵉ siècle* (Paris, 1956), pp. 22, 98, 152; and from Louis Chevalier, *La formation de la population parisienne au XIXᵉ siècle* (Paris, 1950), p. 284. By way of comparison, population figures for other European cities during this period were as follows: Berlin (in 1840), 329,000; Vienna (in 1840), 356,870; St. Petersburg (in 1837), 468,000; London (in 1841), 1,825,714.

30. Pouthas, *La population française*, p. 148. Chevalier (*La formation*, pp. 37–50) also stresses the importance of immigration in the city's growth.

31. Pouthas, *La population française*, pp. 151–52, 157, 162.

32. Ibid., p. 162; Chevalier, *Laboring Classes*, pp. 194–95.

33. Pouthas (*La population française*, pp. 170–71) emphasizes the material conditions and crowding that the situation produced. For a detailed description of the crowded central city and of the massive construction projects during the Second Empire, see David H. Pinkney, *Napoleon III and the Rebuilding of Paris* (Princeton, N.J., 1958).

34. A. Cuchot, "Mouvement de la population de Paris," *Revue des Deux Mondes* 9 (15 February 1845): 721.

35. Chevalier, *La formation*, p. 285.

36. Cuchot, "Mouvement de la population," pp. 726, 730. His count placed all persons of a household in the category of the head of the household: e.g., a married lawyer with three children would count as five in the professional column. Most immigrants did not have children, and so the distribution of the working-age population would differ from the distribution that Cuchot provided.

37. Adeline Daumard, *Les bourgeois de Paris au XIXe siècle* (Paris, 1970), pp. 22, 27.

38. Chevalier discusses this pattern of "social deterioration" in *Laboring Classes*, pp. 275–80; his statistics on suicide appear on pp. 471–74.

39. Unmarried persons outnumbered married people by 57,000 in the 1846 census; see *Le parfait almanach de Paris et de ses environs* (Paris, 1847), p. 19. There were 119,567 out-of-wedlock births among the 365,432 children born in Paris between 1831 and 1846; see Chevalier, *Laboring Classes*, p. 476.

40. Chevalier, *Laboring Classes*, pp. 484–85.

41. Archives nationales (cited hereafter as AN), F[7] 3885, police bulletin of 16 November 1831.

42. Grandjonc, "Eléments statistiques," pp. 287, 290. Grandjonc notes that the number of foreigners had fallen to 390,000 by 1851, when they were counted for the first time in the census. The Revolution of 1848 and economic problems brought about a large-scale exodus from the country.

43. Grandjonc discusses these issues in ibid., pp. 231, 223.

44. Ibid., p. 228. The growth was slowest in 1836–41 (7,000 per year) and greatest in 1841–46 (11,081 per year).

45. See also the discussion of German immigrants in Grandjonc, *Marx et les communistes allemands*, p. 12.

46. Grandjonc, "Eléments statistiques," pp. 230, 235.

47. Desnoyers et al., *Les étrangers à Paris*, pp. xvii–xviii, 148–49. The book, with a chapter on every European nationality and many non-European as well, is an often ironic and exaggerated description of the foreign community in Paris. Its publication in 1844 suggests that the foreign presence was on more than a few French minds.

48. Grandjonc discusses the report in "Eléments statistiques," pp. 232–33.

49. *Galignani's New Paris Guide* (Paris, 1837), p. 108. James Grant (*Paris*

and Its People, 2:60–61) provided some other wage figures after a visit in 1843. Masons were making 2.5 to 3.5 francs a day, carpenters earned 4 francs, tailors averaged 3–5 francs, and shoemakers made 2–2.5 francs. Stonecutters (5–6 francs a day) and printers (4–5 francs) earned the best artisan wages. All these wages were lower than those in London. Henri Sée lists similar wages for artisans in this period in his *Histoire économique de la France*, 2 vols. (Paris, 1939, 1942), 2:179–81; he emphasizes, however, that many workers actually made less than 2 francs per day. Arthur Lewis Dunham makes the same point in *The Industrial Revolution in France, 1815–1848* (New York, 1955), pp. 194–95.

50. *Galignani's Guide*, p. 14. The price of bread remained fairly constant between 1830 and 1847. A kilogram of good white bread averaged 8 sous in 1830–32, dropped to less than 6 sous in 1833–35, and then averaged about 7 sous until the crisis in 1847, when the price reached 10 sous. For Paris bread prices throughout the July Monarchy (which were set and regulated by the police), see Jean Tulard, *La préfecture de police sous la monarchie de juillet* (Paris, 1964), pp. 98–99.

51. Trollope, *Paris and the Parisians*, p. 190.

52. *Le parfait almanach*, p. 19; Chevalier, *Laboring Classes*, p. 231.

53. *Galignani's Guide*, p. 12. The best hotels were the Hôtel des Princes and the Hôtel des Hautes Alpes on the rue de Richelieu, and the Hôtel Meurice on the rue de Rivoli; see *Le parfait almanach*, p. 12.

54. *Le parfait almanach*, pp. 129–31; AN F⁷ 3889, police bulletin of 22 December 1838.

55. Chevalier (*Laboring Classes*, p. 308) discusses the bad health that resulted from these conditions.

56. *Galignani's Guide*, pp. 34–35.

57. Ibid., pp. 112–13. Pinkney provides an excellent description of the congested Parisian streets in *Napoleon III*, pp. 3–24.

58. There are typical English comments (and complaints) about the Parisian water system in Trollope, *Paris and the Parisians*, p. 135, and in Grant, *Paris and Its People*, 1:31–32.

59. Trollope, *Paris and the Parisians*, p. 135.

60. Grant, *Paris and Its People*, 1:26. Similar complaints were recorded in *Galignani's Guide*, pp. 112–13.

61. Grant, *Paris and Its People*, 1:30, 51–52, 81; 2:120. Trollope (*Paris and the Parisians*, p. 80) also complained about dark side streets.

62. Thackeray, *Students' Quarter*, pp. 104–5; Gore, *Paris in 1841*, p. 1.

63. Cuchot, "Mouvement de la population," p. 718.

64. Ossoli, *At Home and Abroad*, p. 204.

65. Niépovié, *Etudes physiologiques*, p. 26.

66. Ibid., pp. 26, 216.

67. No one has explained the social and intellectual importance of this phenomenon better than the German critic Walter Benjamin, who believed that the modern crowd offered a new kind of historical experience. Ben-

jamin (*Baudelaire*, pp. 53–62) argued that there is "promiscuity" and freedom in a crowd because it brings individuals into contact with what is above and below them in the social hierarchy. The crowd is a leveling, non-hierarchical social experience. It resembles a "spectacle of nature" in that everyone shares the same space at the same time, despite the great diversity of personal and social characteristics. It also transforms each person into an object, an unknown commodity to be seen or bypassed in the way that customers look at merchandise: "The crowd is not only the newest asylum of outlaws; it is also the latest narcotic for those abandoned. The *flâneur* [stroller] is someone abandoned in the crowd. In this he shares the situation of the commodity. He is not aware of this special situation, but this does not diminish its effects on him and it permeates him blissfully like a narcotic that can compensate him for many humiliations. The intoxication to which the *flâneur* surrenders is the intoxication of the commodity around which surges the stream of customers" (p. 55). Benjamin's comparison of the crowd to natural and economic phenomena is precisely the conceptual framework that Frankowski applied to Parisian crowds in 1840.

68. Niépovié, *Etudes physiologiques*, pp. 7, 26, 106–7, 113, 216.

69. Ibid., pp. 108–9.

70. Ibid., pp. 221–22. Trollope *(Paris and the Parisians*, pp. 79–80) also commented on the noise: "The exceeding noise of Paris, proceeding either from the uneven structure of the pavement or from the defective construction of wheels and springs, is so violent and incessant as to appear like the effect of one continuous cause—a sort of demon torment, which it must require great length of use to enable one to endure without suffering."

71. Niépovié, *Etudes physiologiques*, pp. 109, 218.

72. Ibid., pp. 109–10.

73. Ibid., pp. 114–16, 217–18. The quotation appears on page 116.

74. Ibid., p. 175.

75. Grant, *Paris and Its People*, 1:81–82, 90, 95–96.

76. Ossoli, *At Home and Abroad*, pp. 204–5.

77. Niépovié, *Etudes physiologiques*, p. 59.

78. Ibid., p. 113. Frankowski provided a long account of the variety and richness of the merchandise in Parisian shops (pp. 38–60).

79. *Galignani's Guide*, p. 176.

80. Gore, *Paris in 1841*, p. 71.

81. Ibid., p. 70. Trollope *(Paris and the Parisians*, pp. 243–49) also recommended a visit and gave a lively description of the place.

82. Niépovié, *Etudes physiologiques*, pp. 62, 74, 95; Forster, *Quinze ans à Paris*, 1:140, 144; *Galignani's Guide*, p. 175; Gore, *Paris in 1841*, p. 67.

83. Gore, *Paris in 1841*, p. 71.

84. Forster, *Quinze ans à Paris*, 1:30.

85. Saint-Fargeau, *Les quarante-huit quartiers*, pp. 54–55; *Le parfait almanach*, pp. 86–87; *Galignani's Guide*, p. 175.

86. *Galignani's Guide*, p. 174.

87. Trollope, *Paris and the Parisians*, p. 138.

88. Annenkov, *Extraordinary Decade*, pp. 75, 165.

89. Trollope, *Paris and the Parisians*, p. 60.

90. Annenkov, *Extraordinary Decade*, p. 73.

91. Grant, *Paris and Its People*, 1:164–65. Grant was describing the "garrison" in 1843. The Galignani brothers also reported on the Paris military, listing about 30,000 regular troops and some 76,000 National Guard (*Galignani's Guide*, pp. 39–40).

92. Grant, *Paris and Its People*, 1:166–67.

93. Ibid., 1:177.

94. Ibid., 1:147; Trollope, *Paris and the Parisians*, p. 175; Annenkov, *Extraordinary Decade*, p. 165.

95. Ossoli, *At Home and Abroad*, p. 205.

96. Grant, *Paris and Its People*, 1:168–69. The newspaper circulation figures are from Charles Ledré, "La presse nationale sous la restauration et la monarchie de juillet," in *Histoire générale de la presse française*, 5 vols., ed. Claude Bellanger, Jacques Godechot, Pierre Guiral, and Fernand Tenou (Paris, 1969–76), 2:146.

97. Ledré summarizes the political positions of all the major newspapers in "La presse nationale," pp. 116–29; it should be noted, though, that the mass circulation newspapers tried to avoid the militant partisanship of the smaller political papers.

98. Radical journals naturally attracted the most attention. *Le National*, for example, received frequent criticism in police bulletins during a round of protests in the fall of 1840 (AN F⁷ 3890). *La Réforme* was also watched closely and blamed for many disruptions in the city. For several examples among many, see the bulletins of 5 July 1845, and of 7 and 12 March 1846 in AN F⁷ 3893.

99. Grant, *Paris and Its People*, 2:218, 232.

100. Ibid., 2:235–36.

101. Trollope, *Paris and the Parisians*, p. 366. Mrs. Trollope also had a very low opinion of contemporary French literature, holding it responsible for a large proportion of the suicides, murders, and antisocial behavior in Paris (pp. 52–53, 197–98, 340).

102. Forster, *Quinze ans à Paris*, 1:322–24, 327, 337–38. The quotation appears on page 337.

103. Grant, *Paris and Its People*, 1:224.

104. Grant (ibid., 1:250–51) counted at least twelve of the latter and reported that the admission price was only 4 or 8 sous.

105. Ossoli, *At Home and Abroad*, pp. 190–91. Other examples of the theatrical interest appear in Niépovié, *Etudes physiologiques*, pp. 320–460; and in Trollope, *Paris and the Parisians*, pp. 177–79, 199–203, 286–91.

106. Mme Emile de Girardin, *Le Vicomte de Launay: Lettres parisiennes*, 4 vols. (Paris, 1857), 4:82, 88–90. For brief sketches of some famous July

Monarchy salons and hostesses, see Cynthia Gladwyn, "Madame Reca-mier"; Joanna Richardson, "Madame de Girardin"; and Peter Quennell, "Madame de Lieven," all in Peter Quennell, ed., *Affairs of the Mind* (Washington, D.C., 1980), pp. 57–68, 71–83, 85–98.

107. Gore, *Paris in 1841*, p. 246.

108. Forster, *Quinze ans à Paris*, 1:57.

109. Niépovié, *Etudes physiologiques*, p. 522.

110. Ibid., pp. 527–37.

111. Trollope, *Paris and the Parisians*, pp. 156–57.

112. Ibid. Frankowski explained that he wrote in French because it was a universal language but never felt entirely comfortable when he spoke it; the words came slowly, and he could not use the enticing nuances of a native speaker. This linguistic problem apparently affected his social confidence in Paris; see Niépovié, *Etudes physiologiques*, pp. 274, 570. But many educated French people also expressed a strong interest in foreign words (especially English) during these years. For more discussion of the language of the salons and the vogue for certain foreign words in French society, see Matoré, *Le vocabulaire et la société*, pp. 60–61, 77–85.

113. Trollope, *Paris and the Parisians*, p. 254.

114. Ibid.

115. Forster, *Quinze ans à Paris*, 1:52–53.

116. Ibid., 1:54.

117. Trollope, *Paris and the Parisians*, pp. 179–187, 274–79.

118. Ibid., pp. 180–81.

119. Ibid., p. 264.

120. Ibid., pp. 263–64, 266.

121. Ibid., pp. 266–67. James Grant (*Paris and Its People*, 2:129–35) discusses the class of Parisian women called *grisettes*. They were young, single women who often worked in small shops and lived with a succession of male students as a kind of "temporary wife." It was an arrangement of convenience and economy for students and *grisettes* alike, and it carried a respectability that the Englishman described but could not understand.

122. Grant, *Paris and Its People*, 2:53–54, 120.

123. Trollope, *Paris and the Parisians*, pp. 38–39, 198.

124. Niépovié, *Etudes physiologiques*, pp. 177–78.

125. Ibid., pp. 178, 183.

126. Ibid., p. 183. Frankowski's account resembles the widespread French bourgeois view of Parisian workers. As Chevalier points out in his excellent study (*Laboring Classes*, p. 433), bourgeois observers emphasized both the violence and the biological traits of the lower classes. In fact, the class conflict was often perceived as a race struggle, "a conflict between two population groups differing wholly from each other, but above all in body; a difference not merely social but biological." For Chevalier's further discussion of these themes, see pp. 154, 361–62, 387, 392, 408, 423.

127. Niépovié, *Etudes physiologiques*, p. 184.

128. Ibid., pp. 178, 183–84.

129. Forster, *Quinze ans à Paris*, 1:43–47. Forster based his description on his experiences during the riots of June 1832.

130. Ibid., 2:91–92.

131. For example, Albert Montémont, *Guide universel de l'étranger dans Paris; ou, Nouveau tableau de cette capitale* (Paris, 1843), p. 3.

132. Grant, *Paris and Its People*, 1:119–20.

133. Ibid., pp. 114–15. Frankowski depicted the Paris welcome quite differently, reporting that Parisians answered inquiries rudely or not at all (Niépovié, *Etudes physiologiques*, p. 111), but the theme of French *politesse* seems more common in the contemporary literature.

134. Forster, *Quinze ans à Paris*, 1:55–56.

135. Ibid., 1:61.

136. Ibid., 2:62–63.

137. Gore, *Paris in 1841*, pp. 256–57.

138. The classical historical account of immigrant communities is Oscar Handlin, *The Uprooted* (Boston, 1951). Handlin's discussion of immigrant housing, social exchange, and institutions in American cities (chaps. 6–7) is relevant to the immigrant experience in all modern, urban societies. For sociological studies of the way newcomers join immigrant communities with the help of friends or relatives, see Joseph P. Fitzpatrick, "The Importance of 'Community' in the Process of Immigrant Assimilation," *International Migration Review* 1 (Fall 1966): 5–16; and Charles Price, "The Study of Assimilation," in J. A. Jackson, ed., *Migration* (Cambridge, 1969), pp. 210–12.

139. See Grandjonc's analysis of these patterns in "Etat sommaire," pp. 493–94, and in *Marx et les communistes allemands*, p. 13.

140. Grandjonc, "Etat sommaire," pp. 494–95. For a fuller discussion of German worker associations in France, see Jacques Grandjonc, "Mémoires d'un artisan allemand à Paris (1830–1834)," *Cahiers d'histoire, Lyon* 15 (1970): 243–49; and Hans-Joachim Ruckhaberle, *Frühproletarische Literatur: Die Flugschriften der deutschen Handwerksgesellenvereine in Paris, 1832–1839* (Kronberg, 1977). Babeuf (1760–97) was the leader of the "conspiracy of equals" who was executed for his attempts to bring about a more socialistic economic system during the period of the Directory in the French Revolution.

141. Grandjonc, "Etat sommaire," p. 495.

142. A good example of the suspicious French attitude toward the Polish Committee appears in H. Gisquet, *Mémoires de M. Gisquet, ancien préfet de police, écrits par lui-même*, 4 vols. (Paris, 1840), 2:473–75. Gisquet was prefect of police in Paris when the committee was expelled from France.

143. For concise discussions of the political factions and activities in the Polish Emigration, see Coleman, "The Great Emigration," 310–23; Wiktor Weintraub, "Adam Mickiewicz, the Mystic Politician," *Harvard Slavic Studies* 1 (1953): 150–55; and Joan S. Skurnowicz, *Romantic Na-*

tionalism and Liberalism: Joachim Lelewel and the Polish National Idea (Boulder, Colo., 1981), pp. 73–84.

144. The French police often reported on what happened at these meetings, who attended, and what was said. For one example, see the police bulletin of 29 November 1838 in AN F^7 3889.

145. Mme de Girardin discussed a Polish charity ball held by Princess Czartoryska in 1844 in *Le Vicomte de Launay*, 3:282–83. The worker-controlled *L'Atelier* published a report on the Polish community (December 1847, p. 42) that discussed bookstores and newspapers; it stated that the Polish library had collected over 16,000 volumes.

146. Beth Archer Brombert, *Cristina: Portraits of a Princess* (New York, 1977), pp. 74–75; Charles Neilson Gattey, *A Bird of Curious Plumage: Princess Cristina de Belgiojoso, 1808–1871* (London, 1971), pp. 33, 38–39. Belgioioso's salon was most important between 1835 and 1842 when she lived in the rue d'Anjou–Saint Honoré.

147. A useful account of Russian salons in Paris appears in Michel Cadot, *La Russie dans la vie intellectuelle française, 1839–1856* (Paris, 1967), pp. 73–79.

148. Grant, *Paris and Its People*, 2:171–73, 178–80; Desnoyers et al., *Les étrangers à Paris*, pp. 178–79; Henri d'Almeras, *La vie parisienne sous le règne de Louis-Philippe* (Paris, n.d.), pp. 52–53, 59–61.

149. Brisbane, *Albert Brisbane*, pp. 72–75; Liebich, *Between Ideology and Utopia*, pp. 124–26.

150. *Galignani's Guide*, p. 70. The university was "for men only," though women were admitted to lectures at the Collège de France; Margaret Fuller was denied entrance to a Sorbonne lecture hall, however (Ossoli, *At Home and Abroad*, p. 193).

151. AN 42 AP47. This report on universities, which was prepared for Guizot in the 1840s, argued that famous professors deserved more pay because they brought both honor and money to France.

152. Cieszkowski used his friendship with the Polish economist Louis Wolowski to meet Auguste Blanqui, Hippolyte de Passy, P. L. E. Rossi, P.-J. Proudhon, Victor Cousin, Jules Michelet, Edgar Quinet, Félicité Robert de Lamennais, Pierre Leroux, Louis Blanc, and Victor Considérant; see the introduction to *Selected Writings of August Cieszkowski*, ed. and trans. André Liebich (Cambridge, 1979), pp. 21–22.

153. *Galignani's Guide*, pp. 14–15; Galignani's Library, *A Famous Bookstore* (Paris, 1920), pp. 7–8, 15, 19. The shop later moved to the rue de Rivoli, where it is located today.

154. E. M. Butler, *Heinrich Heine: A Biography* (1956; rpt., Westport, Conn., 1970), p. 97.

155. Grant, *Paris and Its People*, 2:240.

156. Jacques Grandjonc, "La presse de l'émigration allemande en France (1795–1848) et en Europe (1830–1848)," *Archiv für Sozialgeschichte* 10 (1970): 96–98.

157. In ibid., pp. 109–26, Grandjonc provides a useful summary of titles, editors, publication dates, office addresses, and objectives of all the German press in Paris between 1830 and 1848.
158. Ibid., pp. 101–2; Grandjonc, *Marx et les communistes allemands,* pp. 33, 92.
159. Grandjonc, "La presse de l'émigration," pp. 109–10, 122–24; Grandjonc, *Marx et les communistes allemands,* pp. 25–27.
160. Grandjonc, "La presse de l'émigration," p. 111.
161. Ibid., pp. 103–5.
162. Ibid., pp. 110–11.
163. Ibid., pp. 99–101.

Chapter 2. Heine in Paris: Exile as Literary Identity and Career

1. Jeffrey L. Sammons, *Heinrich Heine: A Modern Biography* (Princeton, N.J., 1979), pp. 107–10, 115, 153–54. Sammons shows remarkable familiarity with the whole range of modern Heine scholarship and provides a scholarly starting point for the historical study of Heine's career. The complex question of Heine's ambivalent status as a Jew who converted to Protestantism to pursue a career in Germany receives detailed treatment in S. S. Prawer, *Heine's Jewish Comedy: A Study of His Portraits of Jews and Judaism* (Oxford, 1983), esp. pp. 1–43; see also Mayer, *Outsiders,* pp. 303–16.
2. These themes are all developed in Sammons, *Heine: Biography,* pp. 31–34, 40, 154, 210, 212.
3. Heine's explanations are scattered throughout his works. See the preface to *Der Salon* (1833), the preface to "A Winter's Tale" (1844), and the "Letters from Helgoland" (1830) that appeared in French editions of *De l'Allemagne,* all in *Heinrich Heine Säkularausgabe,* 27 vols., edited by Nationale Forschungs- und Gedenkstätten der klassischen deutschen Literatur (Weimar) and Centre National de la Recherche Scientifique in Paris (Berlin and Paris, 1970–80), 7:7–13; 13:147–48; 17:25–32 (cited hereafter as *HSA).*
4. From the preface to the German edition of *Der Salon, HSA,* 7:8. The translation here follows that in Gustav Karpeles, ed., *Heinrich Heine's Life Told in His Own Words,* trans. Arthur Dexter (New York, 1893), p. 213.
5. Heine, *Confessions,* in *De l'Allemagne, HSA,* 17:157. The translation here is from Havelock Ellis, ed., *The Prose Writings of Heinrich Heine* (London, 1887), p. 295.
6. Heine, *Confessions, HSA,* 17:158–59.
7. Ibid., p. 158. This translation is from Ellis, *Prose Writings of Heine,* pp. 296–97.
8. Heine to Ferdinand Hiller, 24 October 1832, *HSA,* 21:40. The trans-

lation here follows that of Louis Untermeyer in *Heinrich Heine: Paradox and Poet* (New York, 1937), p. 206.

9. Heinrich Heine, *Lutèce* (article of 17 September 1842), *HSA*, 19:161.

10. Ibid., pp. 161–63. Heine had complained about the machinelike English ten years earlier; see *De la France* (article of 1 March 1832), *HSA*, 18:43–45.

11. Karpeles, *Heine's Own Words*, p. 203. The quotations are from Karpeles's edition of Heine's "Memoirs," a collection of fragments whose authenticity is questioned by some scholars. However, similar ideas appear in the *Confessions*, *HSA*, 17:158–59.

12. The quotation, which is from Heine's work *De l'Angleterre*, appears in Joseph A. Kruse and Michaël Werner, eds., *Heine à Paris* (Paris, 1981), p. 93. Kruse and Werner published this catalogue in conjunction with a special exhibition at the Goethe Institute in Paris marking the sesquicentennial of Heine's arrival in France.

13. Heine, *De la France* (article of 10 February 1832), *HSA*, 18:41–42.

14. Heine's account of his early visits to Parisian museums, theaters, restaurants, and monuments appears in his *Confessions*, *HSA*, 17:158–65. A comprehensive discussion of the material conditions of Heine's life in Paris—his expenses, his income, his pensions, his literary market, etc.— is available in Michaël Werner, *Genius und Geldsack: Zum Problem des Schriftstellerberufs bei Heinrich Heine* (Hamburg, 1978), pp. 44–155.

15. Heine to Karl August Varnhagen von Ense, 27 June 1831, quoted in Kruse and Werner, *Heine à Paris*, p. 91; also *HSA*, 21:21. The image of an ocean here resembles Frankowski's description of Parisian streets as fast-flowing rivers.

16. Karpeles, *Heine's Own Words*, p. 204; Heine, *Confessions*, *HSA*, 17:163–65.

17. The addresses, almost all on the right bank, are listed in Kruse and Werner, *Heine à Paris*, p. 169. His longest residence in one place (1841–47) was in the rue du Faubourg Poissonnière.

18. Heine to Edouard de la Grange, 7 February 1834, *HSA*, 21:76.

19. Heine, *De la France* (fourth letter to Lewald), *HSA*, 18:156–57.

20. Ibid., pp. 154–55.

21. Ibid., p. 156.

22. Heine, *Lutèce* (articles of 7 February 1842 and 5 May 1843), *HSA*, 19:142–44, 188.

23. Heine discussed Rothschild and other bankers in *Lutèce*, ibid., (article of 5 May 1843), pp. 189–93. For the cousin's marriage and the Rothschild connection, see Sammons, *Heine: Biography*, pp. 223, 249–50. See also Mayer (*Outsiders*, pp. 311–12), who argues that Heine's interest in the Rothschilds reflected his attraction to power.

24. Kruse and Werner, *Heine à Paris*, p. 83. This estate placed Heine's wealth well above the average holdings of the Parisian bourgeoisie.

25. Heine, *De la France* (article of 19 April 1832), *HSA*, 18:70–71.

26. Ibid., p. 71.

27. Heine, *Lutèce* (articles of 11 December 1841 and 7 February 1842), *HSA*, 19:127, 142 (quotation, p. 127).

28. Ibid., p. 127.

29. Heine, *De la France* (article of 19 April 1832), *HSA*, 18:65.

30. Ibid. (article of 16 June 1832), pp. 99–100.

31. Ibid., p. 100.

32. Heinrich Heine, "The Romantic School," in Helen M. Mustard, ed. and trans., *Heinrich Heine: Selected Works* (New York, 1973), pp. 272–73.

33. Heine, *De la France* (articles of 19 April and 16 June 1832), *HSA*, 18:65, 101.

34. Ibid. (fourth letter to Lewald), p. 155.

35. Heine, "First Letter to Lewald," in Mustard, *Heine: Selected Works*, pp. 105–6.

36. Heine, *De la France* (third letter to Lewald), *HSA*, 18:150.

37. Ibid. (fourth letter to Lewald), pp. 153–54; Heine, *Lutèce* (article of 28 December 1841), *HSA*, 19:136. Heine also stressed the abstract qualities of German thought in an earlier article (27 May 1832) in *De la France*, *HSA*, 18:90–91.

38. Ibid. (fourth letter to Lewald), *HSA*, 18:153–54; Heine, "Salon of 1831," and "The Romantic School," in Mustard, *Heine: Selected Works*, pp. 101, 272–73.

39. Heine, *De la France* (third letter to Lewald), *HSA*, 18:151.

40. Ibid., pp. 150–51.

41. Ibid., p. 152.

42. Heine, "The Romantic School," in Mustard, *Heine: Selected Works*, pp. 238–39.

43. Heine, *De la France* (second letter to Lewald), *HSA*, 18:144–45.

44. Ibid., p. 145.

45. Heine, "First Letter to Lewald," in Mustard, *Heine: Selected Works*, pp. 107–8.

46. The quotation is from Heine's "Babylonian Anxieties," which formed part of the late poetry that was published in *Gedichte 1853 und 1854*. The poem is about Heine's anxiety at the thought of leaving Mathilde in Paris after his death. It appears in Hal Draper, trans. and ed., *The Complete Poems of Heinrich Heine* (Cambridge, Mass., 1982), p. 703. Heine's complaints resemble Frankowski's description of Paris as a "carnival of hell."

47. Heine, "First Letter to Lewald," in Mustard, *Heine: Selected Works*, pp. 106–7. See also Heine's comments about the freedom of married women in *De la France* (third letter to Lewald), *HSA*, 18:149–50.

48. Heine, *De la France* (seventh letter to Lewald), *HSA*, 18:170.

49. Heine's reliance upon the French press is discussed in Jeffrey L. Sammons, *Heinrich Heine: The Elusive Poet* (New Haven, Conn., 1969),

p. 220; and in Margaret A. Clarke, *Heine et la monarchie de juillet* (Paris, 1927), p. 8. For a detailed account of Heine's journalistic writing in the 1840s, see Lucienne Netter, *Heine et la peinture de la civilisation parisienne 1840–1848* (Frankfurt am Main, 1980); see also the discussion of Heine's journalism in Rutger Boos, *Ansichten der Revolution, Paris-Berichte deutscher Schriftsteller nach der Juli-Revolution 1830: Heine, Börne u.a.* (Cologne, 1977), pp. 119–67.

50. Heine, *Lutèce* (article of 7 October 1840), *HSA*, 19:84–85.

51. Heine, *De la France* (article of 19 April 1832), *HSA*, 18:66. Sammons defines Heine's concept of revolution as one of struggle against repression and for sensual emancipation (*Heine: Biography*, p. 167). He argues that Heine had "no concept of political institutions as such," but this passage seems to suggest otherwise. Although it clearly lacks an economic emphasis, the stress on contradictions between intellectual culture and political institutions is similar to the Marxist stress on the prerevolutionary contradiction between new productive forces and outdated political systems. One might say that in this passage Heine left Hegel standing on his head.

52. Heine, *Lutèce* (article of 4 November 1840), *HSA*, 19:87–88.

53. Heine, *Conditions in France* (article of 16 June 1832), in Mustard, *Heine: Selected Works*, pp. 97–98.

54. Sammons, *Heine: Biography*, pp. 153, 237. Sammons stresses that the actual weekdays of 1830 do not correspond to the dates Heine used and that there are allusions to events in the late 1830s; further, other 1830 sources suggest that Heine's response to the revolution was more muted than these letters imply.

55. The "1830 letters" were published in Heine's book on Ludwig Börne *(Heine über Börne,* 1840) and in the second edition of *De l'Allemagne* (letters of "6 August 1830" and "10 August 1830"), *HSA*, 17:26–27. For discussion of Lafayette's role in the 1830 revolution, see Lloyd S. Kramer, "Lafayette in 1830: A Center That Could Not Hold," *Canadian Journal of History*, 17 (1982): 469–92.

56. Among other places, the argument for Heine's disillusionment appears in Antonina Vallentin, *Heine: Poet in Exile,* trans. Harrison Brown (Garden City, N.Y., 1956), p. 172; and A. I. Sandor, *The Exile of Gods* (The Hague, 1967), p. 87.

57. Heine, *De la France* ("Salon of 1831"), *HSA*, 18:120.

58. Ibid. (article of 16 June 1832), p. 95.

59. Ibid. (article of 19 January 1832), pp. 30–31; Heine, *Lutèce* (article of 30 April 1840), *HSA*, 19:33.

60. Heine, *De la France* (article of 10 February 1832), *HSA*, 18:37; see also pp. 38–39 for a discussion of how these groups seemed to Heine utterly unrealistic.

61. Ibid. (article of 19 January 1832), pp. 29–31.

62. Ibid., p. 33.

63. Ibid., p. 32, and "Letter from Dieppe" (20 August 1832), pp. 109–10.

64. Ibid. (fifth letter to Lewald), pp. 159–60.

65. Heine, *Lutèce* (articles of 20 May and 30 May 1840), *HSA*, 19:49, 53–55.

66. Ibid. (article of 11 January 1841), pp. 99–101.

67. Heine, *De la France* (article of 19 January 1832), *HSA*, 18:34.

68. Ibid., pp. 32–35.

69. Ibid. (article of 12 May 1832), pp. 80–81.

70. Ibid. (article of 19 January 1832), p. 30.

71. Ibid. (preface to the German edition), pp. 18–19.

72. Heine, *Lutèce* (article of 13 February 1841), *HSA*, 19:105.

73. The compliments appear, among other places, in *Lutèce* (articles of 25 February and 12 November 1840), *HSA* 19:28, 95; and in *De la France* (article of 19 January 1832), *HSA*, 18:28. Sammons says that "Heine seems never to have doubted the widespread belief that Louis-Philippe was basically dishonest and insincere" (*Heine: Elusive Poet*, p. 238), but this does not seem accurate. Heine criticized the king's actions and his commitment to the July Revolution, but he did not really view the man as "basically dishonest."

74. Heine, *Lutèce* (article of 25 February 1840), *HSA*, 19:28.

75. Ibid. (Article of 6 November 1840), p. 92.

76. Heine also expressed great respect and sympathy for Louis-Philippe when his son, the duke of Orléans, was killed in an accident; see ibid. (article of 19 July 1842), pp. 155–57.

77. Heine, *Conditions in France* (article of 28 December 1831), in Mustard, *Heine: Selected Works*, pp. 87–88.

78. Sammons argues that Heine also sympathized with Louis-Philippe because he thought that the king and the poet were spiritual brothers. Both suffered from unfair attacks by opponents, both understood tragedy, and both favored peace in a world of warmakers. Part of Heine's frustration with Louis-Philippe therefore resulted from the king's inability to play the mythic, poetic role that Heine wanted him to play. See Sammons, *Heine: Biography*, p. 326; and Sammons, *Heine: Elusive Poet*, pp. 230, 247.

79. Guizot (1787–1874) played an important role as minister for public instruction between 1832 and 1836. Thiers (1797–1877) served in the same government, eventually becoming president of the Ministerial Council and prime minister before resigning in 1836. He served again as president of the council and foreign minister from March to October 1840; he was then replaced by Guizot, who became foreign minister and then prime minister until the Revolution of 1848.

80. Heine, *Lutèce* (articles of 6 January 1841 and 2 February 1843), *HSA*, 19:98, 173.

81. Heine published his defense of the pension in the *Allgemeine Zeitung*

after it became known to the public in the spring of 1848. See the explanation in Ludwig von Embden, *The Family Life of Heinrich Heine*, trans. Charles De Kay (New York, 1892), pp. 175–76.

82. Sammons, *Heine: Biography*, p. 224. See also Michaël Werner, "Heines französische Staatspension," *Heine-Jahrbuch* 16 (1977): 134–42.

83. Lucienne Netter, "Heine, Thiers, et la presse parisienne en 1840," *Revue d'Allemagne* 4 (1972): 115. Heine and Thiers had another point of contact in their common friendship with the editor of the *Allgemeine Zeitung*, the Baron von Cotta.

84. Heine to François Mignet, 1 September 1836, *HSA*, 21:61.

85. Heine, *Lutèce* (article of 13 February 1841), *HSA*, 19:108–9.

86. Gabriac's report is in AN 42 AP19, sec. 10; the specific recommendations appear on pp. 384, 402–3. Heine's pension is mentioned in an 1840 Foreign Ministry report on secret expenditures: "H. Heine, allocation established by M. Thiers and confirmed by M. Guizot (no written decision) 4,800 [francs per year]" (AN 42 AP1).

87. Embden, *Family Life of Heine*, pp. 174–75.

88. Heine to Edouard de la Grange, 25 June 1848, *HSA*, 22:284.

89. Alexandre Weill, *Souvenirs intimes de Henri Heine* (Paris, 1883), quoted in Heinrich Houben, *Heine par ses contemporains* (Paris, 1929), p. 161.

90. Ibid., pp. 163–64. Weill had the figures wrong, a good example of why his report should be taken loosely rather than literally.

91. Margaret Clarke (*Heine et la monarchie de juillet*, pp. 8–10, 126, 165, 212, 214, 218–19, 226, 231) argues that Heine was in fact a tool of the Austrian regime rather than of the July Monarchy and that the inconsistencies in his journalism reflected the needs of Austrian foreign policy. Behind the ambivalent discussion of monarchies and republicans in Heine's reports, suggests Clarke, one should see the hand of Metternich and his right-hand man Friedrich Gentz, who was close to the Baron von Cotta, publisher of the Augsburg *Allgemeine Zeitung*. Heine attacked Louis-Philippe like a radical when the Austrians wanted him to be criticized and defended him when they found him to be acceptable. All of this accorded with positions of the Augsburg newspaper, which followed the Austrian line. Clarke's argument rests on a supposition (textual inconsistencies require an external explanation) that overlooks Heine's own ambivalence in the changing French context, and it leads to an unconvincing theory.

92. Heine, *Lutèce* (article of 20 June 1842), *HSA*, 19:151–52.

93. Ibid. (article of 25 June 1843), pp. 207–8, 214.

94. Heine, *Confessions*, *HSA*, 17:169. Heine's images of the poor resemble those of Frankowski and other visitors who commented on the ugliness of these people.

95. Heine, *Lutèce* (preface), *HSA*, 19:15.

96. Ibid., pp. 15–16.

97. Ibid. (article of 25 June 1843), p. 208.

98. For a good introduction to Saint-Simonian theory, see Ghita Io-nescu, ed., *The Political Thought of Saint-Simon* (Oxford, 1976), pp. 2–57. Another useful account is available in Frank E. Manuel, *The New World of Henri Saint-Simon* (Cambridge, Mass., 1956), esp. p. 154: as part of his theory of human society, Saint-Simon believed that history evolved through stages and that the modern (fifth) stage had just begun; for him, each stage represented "the progressive expansion of the human intellect"—a notion of development that Heine also used.

99. For discussion of Heine's early interest in the Saint-Simonians, see E. M. Butler, *The Saint-Simonian Religion in Germany: A Study of the Young German Movement* (Cambridge, 1926), pp. 60, 63–65.

100. Ibid., p. 95; Sammons, *Heine: Biography*, pp. 155, 161.

101. The notice in *Le Globe* (which Sammons thinks Heine himself may have written) called Heine "one of these young and courageous men defending the cause of progress" (quoted in Sammons, *Heine: Biography*, p. 160).

102. Heine to Karl August Varnhagen von Ense, mid-May 1832, *Correspondance inédite de Henri Heine*, 2 vols. (Paris, 1866–67), 2:131–32; also *HSA*, 21:37.

103. Heine, *Lutèce* (article of 25 June 1843), *HSA*, 19:207–8. For an example of his continuing friendship with Saint-Simonians, see Heine to Michel Chevalier, March 1842, *HSA*, 22:20.

104. Heine's final judgment on the Saint-Simonians appeared in the preface to the 1855 edition of *De l'Allemagne*, the work he had earlier dedicated to Enfantin: "These former apostles who dreamed of a golden age for all humanity have made themselves content by propagating the age of money, the reign of this god money which is the father and mother of everyone and everything"; quoted in Georg G. Iggers, "Heine and the Saint-Simonians: A Re-examination," *Comparative Literature* 10 (1958): 307–8.

105. Prosper Enfantin to Heine, 11 October 1835, *HSA*, 24:340–43, 345–46.

106. Ibid., pp. 336, 342.

107. Ibid., p. 343.

108. Heine intended for *De l'Allemagne* to serve as an explicit refutation of Mme de Staël, a point that he emphasized in his *Confessions (HSA*, 17:167–68) and that Sammons also notes in *Heine: Biography*, pp. 188–89.

109. Sammons, *Heine: Biography*, pp. 161–62, 165; Iggers, "Heine and the Saint-Simonians," pp. 296–97, 308.

110. Butler, *Saint-Simonian Religion*, p. 169.

111. Ibid., pp. 141–43, 146, 154, 168. Butler seems to appreciate the forward-looking aspects of the doctrine (as opposed to the leaders) better than Sammons or Iggers; she can make a good case for the doctrine's influence on Heine while recognizing his ambivalence toward the leader-

ship. Other scholars argue that the religious aspect of Saint-Simonianism appealed to Heine more than its politics. They also suggest that Heine was happy to find a progressive social theory with a place for elites and an intellectual aristocracy: see Untermeyer, *Heine: Paradox*, p. 223; and Laura Hofrichter, *Heinrich Heine*, trans. Barker Fairley (Oxford, 1963), p. 63. There is also a useful evaluation of Heine's involvement with Saint-Simonianism in Nigel Reeves, *Heinrich Heine: Poetry and Politics* (Oxford, 1974), pp. 76–86.

112. The absence of reference to the Saint-Simonians in this respect becomes an even more significant silence. As Butler notes (*Saint-Simonian Religion*, p. 90), it is a "reticence that needs some special explanation." There was perhaps too much at stake for Heine to talk about Saint-Simonians in the style he used to talk about others.

113. Heine, *Lutèce* (article of 6 November 1840), *HSA*, 19:89–91. Coincidentally, perhaps, Blanc had said six weeks earlier that Heine misunderstood some of his (Blanc's) social philosophy; see Louis Blanc to Heine, 24 September 1840, *HSA*, 25:288.

114. Heine, *Lutèce* (article of 25 June 1843), *HSA*, 19:208, 211–13.

115. For a brief introduction to Cousin's thought and career, see D. G. Charlton, *Secular Religions in France, 1815–1870* (Oxford, 1963), pp. 96–103.

116. Heine's comment on Cousin in "The Romantic School" (Mustard, *Heine: Selected Works*, p. 211) suggested a rather low opinion of his philosophical abilities: "Mr. Cousin has expounded a lot of clever twaddle, but not German philosophy."

117. Heine, *Lutèce* (article of 25 June 1843), *HSA*, 19:209. Heine explicitly criticized Leroux's attack on Cousin in the same article, pp. 208–9, 211–12.

118. Ibid., pp. 210–11. See also ibid. (article of 19 May 1841), pp. 123–24.

119. Heine to François Mignet, 20 October 1843, *HSA*, 22:68.

120. Ibid.

121. Heine, *Lutèce* (articles of 19 May 1841 and 21 June 1843), *HSA*, 19:121–23, 204–6. The quotations appear on pp. 122, 206.

122. Sand's first dinner invitation to Heine stressed that she wanted to hear him talk and to ask for some literary advice; see George Sand to Heine, November 1834, *HSA*, 24:281. She later summarized her view of Heine in her journal (7 January 1841): "He is tender, affectionate, devoted, romantic in love—even weak and apt to submit to the unlimited domination of a woman. At the same time, he is cynical, scoffing, skeptical, matter-of-fact and materialistic in his talk (*parole*) to frighten and scandalize anyone who does not know his inner life and the secrets of his household. He is like his poetry, a combination of the highest sentimentality and the most facetious mockery" (quoted in Kruse and Werner, *Heine à Paris*, p. 100).

123. Heine to Sand, 17 August 1838, *HSA*, 21:288.

124. Sand to Heine, August 1838, *HSA*, 25:168–69.

125. Sand to Heine, 17 March (?) 1840, *HSA*, 25:249. Sainte-Beuve quoted Heine in a letter two days after Sand had urged him to come to dinner; see *Sainte-Beuve: Correspondance générale*, 18 vols., ed. Jean Bonnerot, (Paris, 1935–77), 3:252.

126. For an example of Heine's reassurance, see Heine to Sand, January 1838 (?), *HSA*, 21:250. When Sand wanted descriptions of Potsdam for her novel *Consuelo*, Heine sent translations from his travel book *Reisebilder* (which she did not cite). See Sand to Heine, [10 May 1843], in George Sand, *Correspondance*, 14 vols., ed. Georges Lubin (Paris, 1964–   ), 6:131–32.

127. Heine, *Lutèce* (article of 30 April 1840), *HSA*, 19:36–37, 41–43 (quotations, pp. 36, 42). Part of the discussion on Sand did not appear until Heine added some reflections to the article for publication in *Lutèce*.

128. Ibid., pp. 43–44.

129. Ibid., p. 44; Heine, "Tenth Letter to Lewald," in Mustard, *Heine: Selected Works*, p. 126.

130. Heine, *Lutèce* (article of 30 April 1840), *HSA*, 19:44–45.

131. Heine, "Sixth Letter to Lewald," in Mustard, *Heine: Selected Works*, pp. 109–11.

132. For an example of this early contact, see Heine's letter to Hugo introducing Professor Wolf, 2 April 1835, *HSA*, 21:100.

133. Heine, "Sixth Letter to Lewald," in Mustard, *Heine: Selected Works*, p. 110.

134. Ibid., p. 111; Heine, *Lutèce* (article of 30 April 1840), *HSA*, 19:44–45.

135. Ibid., p. 45.

136. Heinrich Laube, *Erinnerungen an Heinrich Heine* (1868), quoted in Houben, *Heine par ses contemporains*, p. 137.

137. See, e.g., the dinner invitation from Heine to Balzac, 27 February 1846, *HSA*, 22:207. Heine promised that his wife would provide good food and that others (including Théophile Gautier) would join the party.

138. Heine to Sand, 17 March 1840, *HSA*, 21:354.

139. Heine, *Lutèce* (article of 30 April 1840), *HSA*, 19:40.

140. The dedication appears at the front of the story and in *HSA*, 26:125. Mayer provides an interesting analysis of this dedication in *Outsiders*, pp. 313–15; he argues that Heine represented for Balzac the future world of bohemian poets (as opposed to wealthy bankers) rather than the actual reality of Germany or France.

141. Gautier's introduction to *Reisebilder*, in *HSA*, 14:14.

142. Gérard de Nerval to Heine, 6 November 1840, *HSA*, 25:296.

143. Extract from Heine's memoir on Nerval, in Karpeles, *Heine's Own Words*, p. 338.

144. For examples of compliment exchange, see Heine to Michelet, 20 January 1834, *HSA*, 21:74; and Michelet to Heine, June 1834, *HSA*, 24:267. Heine praised Michelet for writing history that combined art, philosophy, and belief in progress. Michelet reciprocated by calling Heine's prose "irresistible."

145. Heine, *Lutèce* (article of 1 June 1843), *HSA*, 19:202–4.

146. Edgar Quinet, "De l'art en Allemagne," *Revue des Deux Mondes* 6 (31 May 1832): 512–13.

147. Edgar Quinet, "Poètes allemands: Henri Heine," *Revue des Deux Mondes*, 3d ser., 1 (14 February 1834): 364–66, 368.

148. For an example of Quinet's practical help and critical assistance, see Quinet to Heine, 26 December 1837, *HSA*, 25:99. The letter describes his work on one of Heine's manuscripts and his communications with François Buloz, editor of *Revue des Deux Mondes*.

149. Heine, *Lutèce* (article of 1 June 1843), *HSA*, 19:203–4.

150. Extracts from Heine's *Reisebilder* appeared in the *Revue* in June and December 1832, and parts of *De l'Allemagne* in March, November, and December 1834.

151. The French editions of Heine's works did not sell well: less than 500 copies of *De la France* had been sold seven years after its first publication, and less than 700 copies of *De l'Allemagne* within the first six years (Werner, *Genius und Geldsack*, p. 79). They nevertheless served their reputation-enhancing purpose; see, e.g., Sainte-Beuve's sympathetic review of *De la France* (dated 8 August 1833) in C. A. Sainte-Beuve, *Premiers lundis*, rev. ed., 3 vols. (Paris, 1886–94), 2:248–59.

152. The articles appeared in *L'Europe Littéraire* between March and May 1833 and formed that part of *De l'Allemagne* called "The Romantic School."

153. Heine described his friendship with Bohain in his *Confessions*, *HSA*, 17:165–67. Butler (*Heine*, pp. 103–4) stresses that Heine met a long list of important French writers through the literary journals.

154. Heine to Karl Immerman, 19 December 1832, in *Correspondance inédite*, 2:135; also *HSA*, 21:42.

155. One scholar who has investigated these friendships reports that almost none of the French writers of the day mention Heine in their private journals or memoirs; see Joseph Dresch, *Heine à Paris, 1831–1856* (Paris, 1956), pp. 51–52. For another survey of Heine's French friendships, see Friedrich Hirth, *Heinrich Heine und seine französischen Freunde* (Mainz, 1949).

156. Heine, *De la France* (seventh letter to Lewald), *HSA*, 18:170.

157. Ibid.

158. Quoted in Dresch, *Heine à Paris*, p. 54.

159. Heine went often to the soirées of Princess Belgiojoso and of Mme d'Agoult (who also wrote about Germany in French reviews). According to Heinrich Laube, Heine defended German culture with wit and eloquence in Parisian salons, and he was not afraid to criticize his opponents in a discussion: ibid., pp. 60–62, 72; Butler, *Heine*, p. 105.

160. Astolphe de Custine to Heine, 1834, *HSA*, 24:282.

161. Heine, *Lutèce*, in *HSA*, 19:21.

162. Heine to the *Constitutional*, 7 June 1840, *HSA*, 21:356. Heine wrote this letter to deny rumors that he was an agent of Thiers, writing sympathetic pieces for the *Allgemeine Zeitung*. He was nobody's apologist, Heine explained, though he did admire Thiers and France. It must have been an awkward moment, since Heine began receiving his pension (recent research indicates) during the Thiers ministry in 1840.

163. Heine, "The Romantic School," in Mustard, *Heine: Selected Works*, pp. 129–31, 211.

164. Ibid., pp. 130–31.

165. Heine, *Confessions*, *HSA*, 17:168. The translation here follows Ellis, *Prose Writings of Heine*, p. 300. Pierre Leroux must have been one of the French thinkers Heine had in mind. Leroux once told Heine that his writings on Germany had convinced him that German philosophy was far less mystical than most French people imagined. See Heine, *Lutèce* (article of 2 June 1842), *HSA*, 19:148.

166. Heine, "The Romantic School," in Mustard, *Heine: Selected Works*, pp. 270–72.

167. Heine, "History of Religion and Philosophy," in ibid., pp. 295–96, 328–29.

168. Ibid., pp. 297–302, 324–28.

169. Ibid., pp. 303–4.

170. Ibid., pp. 324–28.

171. Ibid., pp. 324–25.

172. Ibid., pp. 285, 335, 395–96.

173. Ibid., p. 341.

174. Ibid., p. 340.

175. Ibid., pp. 367–69, 375–76, 379–80 (quotation, p. 380).

176. Ibid., p. 385.

177. Ibid.

178. Ibid., pp. 411–13.

179. Ibid., p. 410.

180. Ibid., p. 414.

181. He mentioned plans to write a book on the French Revolution in a letter to Varnhagen, mid-May 1832, *HSA*, 21:37. He also claimed to have written and then burned a manuscript on Hegel; see Sammons, *Heine: Biography*, pp. 77–78.

182. Heine, "History of Religion and Philosophy," in Mustard, *Heine: Selected Works*, pp. 418–19.

183. Ibid., pp. 403–4; Heine, *De la France* (article of 16 June 1832), *HSA*, 18:98–99.

184. Heine, *De la France* (article of 16 June 1832), *HSA*, 18:97.

185. Heine, "The Romantic School," in Mustard, *Heine: Selected Works*, p. 242. Heine also discussed the political awakening in German literature in ibid., pp. 198–99. Other prominent "Young Germany" writers were Heinrich Laube, Karl Gutzkow, Theodor Mundt, and Ludolf Weinbarg, all of whom were also included in the 1835 ban.

186. Ibid., p. 154.

187. Heine, *De la France* (article of 16 June 1832), *HSA*, 18:99.

188. Ibid., pp. 98–99, 101.

189. Heine, "History of Religion and Philosophy," in Mustard, *Heine: Selected Works*, p. 340.

190. Jakob Venedey to Heine, 10 April 1835, *HSA*, 24:306–7. See also Vallentin, *Heine: Poet in Exile*, pp. 177–78; and Max Brod, *Heinrich Heine: The Artist in Revolt*, trans. Joseph Witriol (London, 1956), pp. 279–80. Venedey later became a harsh critic of Heine.

191. Quoted in Vallentin, *Heine: Poet in Exile*, p. 178.

192. Heine to Laube, 27 September 1835, *Correspondance inédite*, 2:176; also, *HSA*, 21:121–22.

193. This is from a poem called "The Dragonfly," part of the collection of poems from 1853 and 1854; it appears in Draper, *Complete Poems of Heine*, p. 716. Note the reference to Dante as a suffering predecessor.

194. Sammons, *Heine: Biography*, pp. 133–34, 234.

195. Barthelemy Ott, *La querelle de Heine et de Börne* (Lyon, 1935), p. 35. Ott's study provides a detailed analysis of both the personal and political differences that led to the dispute.

196. Heine, preface to *Reisebilder*, in *HSA*, 14:17–18.

197. Ott, *Querelle*, pp. 68–69; Sammons, *Heine: Biography*, pp. 239–40. The complete text of *Heine über Börne* appears in *HSA*, 9:281–390.

198. Heine to Lewald, 1 March 1838, *HSA*, 21:257.

199. Heine to Varnhagen, 31 March 1838, ibid., pp. 272–73.

200. Heine to Julius Campe, 29 December 1843, *Correspondance inédite*, 2:445; also *HSA*, 22:91.

201. See Sammon's discussion of the friendship in *Heine: Biography*, p. 262. See also Ludwig Marcuse, "Heine and Marx: A History and a Legend," *Germanic Review* 30 (1955): 110–24; and Nigel Reeves, "Heine and the Young Marx," *Oxford German Studies* 7 (1973): 44–97. Only one letter from Heine to Marx survives. It is a friendly note from Hamburg that refers to their *Vorwärts* collaboration and sends along the *Wintermärchen* for inclusion in a future number of *Vorwärts;* see Heine to Marx, 21 September 1844, *HSA*, 22:130–31.

202. Grandjonc, *Marx et les communistes allemands*, p. 88.

203. By the 1850s Heine was recommending the story of King Nebu-

chadnezzar and other Biblical passages as useful lessons for arrogant "doctors" such as Ruge and Marx. He mentioned these former friends by name in the preface to an 1852 German edition of the "History of Religion and Philosophy" (*HSA*, 8:128). That preface also appeared in the second French edition of *De l'Allemagne* (*HSA*, 17:171–72, 177). For more of Heine's ambivalence about communism, see the preface to *Lutèce* (1855) in *HSA*, 19:15–16.

204. Heine to Varnhagen, 27 June 1831, quoted in Kruse and Werner, *Heine à Paris*, p. 91; also *HSA*, 21:21.

205. Heine, *Confessions*, *HSA*, 17:156–57.

206. Most scholars see Heine's alienation in Germany as primarily a consequence of his precarious Jewish status. See, e.g., Untermeyer, *Heine: Paradox*, p. 35; Sandor, *Exile of Gods*, pp. 76–77, Sammons, *Heine: Biography*, pp. 107–10, and Prawer, *Heine's Jewish Comedy*, pp. 10–43.

207. Heine, "Which Way Now?" in Mustard, *Heine: Selected Works*, p. 436.

208. Sammons, *Heine: Biography*, p. 171.

209. Heine, "Preface to the Salon" (17 October 1833), *HSA*, 7:12; the translation here follows Karpeles, *Heine's Own Words*, p. 215.

210. Heine, "Preface to the Salon," *HSA*, 7:9–10; also Karpeles, *Heine's Own Words*, pp. 214–15.

211. Quoted in Brod, *Heine: Artist in Revolt*, p. 278. The excerpt is from *Heine über Börne*.

212. Heinrich Heine, *Lyric Poems and Ballads*, trans. Ernst Feise (Pittsburgh, 1961), p. 161.

213. Draper, *Complete Poems of Heine*, p. 483.

214. Ibid., p. 482. Heine took care to avoid Prussian territory on his trips to Hamburg. For further discussion of this political poem, see Sammons, *Heine: Elusive Poet*, pp. 291–300.

215. Heine, *De la France* (second letter to Lewald), *HSA*, 18:147.

216. The quotation is an excerpt from *Heine über Börne* in Karpeles, *Heine's Own Words*, p. 277.

217. Heine to Princess Belgioioso, 30 October 1836, *HSA*, 21:166.

218. Sandor (*Exile of Gods*, pp. 60–61, 96–97, 109, 140) offers a number of pertinent observations about Heine's search for harmony in politics and art and about his conception of the poet as exile.

Chapter 3. Marx in Paris: Exile and the New Social Theory

1. Berlin, *Karl Marx*, p. 60.

2. For a good account of Ruge's and Marx's journalistic activities in Germany, see David McLellan, *Karl Marx: His Life and Thought* (New York, 1973), pp. 40–61.

3. Ibid., pp. 77–79. For more on the genesis and objectives of the project, see David McLellan, *The Young Hegelians and Karl Marx* (London, 1969), pp. 31–33; Beatrix Mesmer-Strupp, *Arnold Ruges Plan einer Alliance intellectuelle zwischen Deutschen und Franzosen* (Bern, 1963), pp. 69–100; and Emile Bottigelli, "Les 'Annales Franco-Allemandes' et l'opinion française," *La Pensée* 110 (1963): 50–51. Toews summarizes the economic and social problems that affected the work of marginal German intellectuals during these years; see *Hegelianism*, pp. 213–16.

4. Arnold Ruge, *Zwei Jahre in Paris*, quoted in David McLellan, *Marx before Marxism* (New York, 1970), p. 130.

5. Marx to Ruge, September 1843, in Karl Marx, *Early Writings*, intro. Lucio Colletti, trans. Rodney Livingstone and Gregor Benton (London, 1975), p. 206. The letter was first published in the *Deutsch-Französische Jahrbücher*.

6. McLellan, *Marx: Life and Thought*, pp. 79–80.

7. Bottigelli, "Les 'Annales Franco-Allemandes,' " pp. 62–63.

8. Marx to Ruge, September 1843, in *Early Writings*, p. 207.

9. Ibid., pp. 208–9.

10. Marx to Feuerbach, 3 October 1843, in Karl Marx and Frederick Engels, *Collected Works* (New York, 1975–), 3:349.

11. Ibid., p. 350.

12. On Ruge's unsuccessful contacts with French writers, see Mesmer-Strupp, *Arnold Ruges Plan*, pp. 101–21; and Bottigelli, "Les 'Annales Franco-Allemandes,' " pp. 54, 56.

13. Marx to Ruge, September 1843, in *Early Writings*, p. 209.

14. Louis Blanc, "D'un project d'alliance intellectuelle entre l'Allemagne et la France," *La Revue Indépendante* 11 (10 November 1843): 60–62.

15. Ibid., pp. 63–65. The importance of religious themes among left-wing radicals in France during the July Monarchy era receives detailed analysis in Edward Berenson, *Populist Religion and Left-Wing Politics in France, 1830–1852* (Princeton, N.J., 1984), especially pp. 36–73.

16. *La Réforme*, 13 November 1843.

17. Duprat, "L'école de Hegel à Paris," 481–86. Grandjonc, who also published this article in his study of German communists in Paris, thinks that Ruge actually wrote much of the text himself; see Grandjonc, *Marx et les communistes allemands*, p. 107. For further discussion of the non-response in the French press, see Bottigelli, "Les 'Annales Franco-Allemandes,' " p. 57.

18. Börnstein's review appears in its entirety in Grandjonc, *Marx et les communistes allemands*, pp. 115–21.

19. McLellan, *Marx: Life and Thought*, pp. 98–99.

20. For more on these Young Hegelian views of France, see McLellan, *Young Hegelians*, pp. 7–8, 24; and McLellan, *Marx before Marxism*, p. 154.

21. Marx, "On the Jewish Question," in *Early Writings*, p. 216.

22. McLellan, *Young Hegelians*, p. 10. See also Liebich, *Between Ideology and Utopia*, pp. 47–49; Liebich's introduction to Cieszkowski, *Writings*, pp. 11–13; and Andrzej Walicki, *Philosophy and Romantic Nationalism: The Case of Poland* (Oxford, 1982), pp. 130–51.

23. McLellan, *Young Hegelians*, p. 142; Isaiah Berlin, *The Life and Opinions of Moses Hess* (Cambridge, 1959), pp. 5–6.

24. Lorenz von Stein, *The History of the Social Movement in France, 1789–1850*, ed. and trans. Kaethe Mengelberg (Totowa, N.J., 1964), p. 96. This passage is from a revised and retitled edition (1850) of the original work. Stein himself was a conservative who described socialist ideas to inform German readers, not to convert them, but his work became an important source of information for the fledgling German radical movement. See also McLellan, *Young Hegelians*, pp. 36–37; and McLellan, *Marx before Marxism*, p. 94.

25. For further discussion of this German interest in socialism, see McLellan, *Young Hegelians*, pp. 11, 36–37, 142, 151; Berlin, *Life of Hess*, pp. 5–6; John Weiss, *Moses Hess: Utopian Socialist* (Detroit, Mich., 1960), pp. 3–4; Oscar J. Hammen, *The Red '48ers: Karl Marx and Frederick Engels* (New York, 1969), pp. 69–70; Liebich, introduction to Cieszkowski, *Writings*, p. 31.

26. August Cieszkowski, *Prolegomena to Historiosophy*, in *Writings*, p. 79.

27. Arnold Ruge, *Briefwechsel und Tagelblätter, 1825–1880*, quoted in Jerrold Seigel, *Marx's Fate: The Shape of a Life* (Princeton, N.J., 1978), pp. 138–39.

28. Grandjonc, *Marx et les communistes allemands*, pp. 60–62, 65; McLellan, *Marx: Life and Thought*, pp. 103–4.

29. McLellan, *Marx: Life and Thought*, p. 131.

30. Marx and Engels, *The Holy Family*, in *Collected Works*, 4:67–68. Szeliga was the pseudonym of a critic named Franz Zychlinski (1816–1900).

31. Ibid., p. 68.

32. Jenny Marx to Marx between 11 August and 18 August 1844, in Marx and Engels, *Collected Works*, 3:581.

33. Marx and Engels, *The Holy Family*, in *Collected Works*, 4:126.

34. Ibid., pp. 130–31. This connection between materialism and communism was rejected by French radicals such as Blanc and Leroux, who believed that materialism led to bourgeois ideologies and societies.

35. The essays appeared in the *Deutsch-Französische Jahrbücher* and in *Vorwärts*; the book was published in Frankfurt in early 1845.

36. Karl Marx, "Critical Notes on the Article 'The King of Prussia and Social Reform. By a Prussian,'" in *Early Writings*, pp. 410–11.

37. Ibid., pp. 412–13.

38. Marx, "On the Jewish Question," in *Early Writings*, p. 221.

39. Ibid., p. 230.

40. Ibid., p. 233.

41. Marx and Engels, *The Holy Family,* in *Collected Works,* 4:121–23.

42. Ibid., pp. 123–24.

43. Ibid., p. 119.

44. Marx, "On the Jewish Question," in *Early Writings,* p. 234.

45. Marx, "Notes on 'The King of Prussia,' " in *Early Writings,* p. 419.

46. Marx, "On the Jewish Question," in *Early Writings,* p. 234. For further discussion of Marx's response to the French Revolution, see Jean Montreau, "La Révolution française et la pensée de Marx," *La Pensée* 3 (1939): 24–38, Auguste Cornu, *Karl Marx et Friedrich Engels,* vol. 3, *Marx à Paris* (Paris, 1962), pp. 11–12; and François Furet, "Le jeune Marx et la Révolution française," *Le Débat* 28 (1984): 30–46.

47. The specific works included Eugene Buret, *De la misère des classes laborieuses en Angleterre et en France* (Paris, 1840); Constantin Pecqueur, *Théorie nouvelle d'économie sociale et politique, ou études sur l'organisation des sociétés* (Paris, 1842); Wilhelm Schulz, *Die Bewegung der Produktion, eine geschichtlichstatistische Abhandlung* (Zurich, 1843). Marx's careful reading of these texts and others is a major source of the "economic" sections of his *Economic and Philosophical Manuscripts;* see *Early Writings,* pp. 282–322. For a comprehensive analysis of how Marx drew upon these predecessors and upon the tradition of political economy, see Allen Oakley, *Marx's Critique of Political Economy: Intellectual Sources and Evolution,* 2 vols. (London, 1984–85), esp. 1:27–79, in which the focus is on Marx's period in Paris.

48. Marx, *Early Writings,* pp. 283, 287.

49. Ibid., p. 288.

50. E.g., Marx argued that the wage system described by the economists was the wage system of private property. In overcoming private property, communism would supersede the system of wage misery; see ibid., pp. 332–33, 345–52.

51. Ibid., p. 325.

52. Ibid., pp. 323–24.

53. Ibid., p. 326.

54. Ibid., p. 360.

55. Ibid., pp. 323, 342.

56. Ibid., pp. 360–61.

57. This historical emphasis in Marx's response to political economy has been noted by a number of scholars. See, e.g., Berlin, *Karl Marx,* pp. 65–66; and John Maguire, *Marx's Paris Writings: An Analysis* (New York, 1973), p. 60.

58. For more on Marx's contact with intellectuals in Paris, see Berlin, *Karl Marx,* p. 74; Cornu, *Marx à Paris,* p. 6; Grandjonc, "Les rapports," p. 80.

59. McLellan, *Marx: Life and Thought,* p. 104. For more on Marx and Proudhon, see also K. Steven Vincent, *Pierre-Joseph Proudhon and the Rise*

of French Republican Socialism (Oxford, 1984), pp. 91–95; and P. Haubtmann, *Marx et Proudhon* (Paris, 1947), p. 30.

60. See Haubtmann, *Marx et Proudhon*, p. 24; and Cornu, *Marx à Paris*, p. 56. The letter in which this discussion appears is from Proudhon to M. Bergmann, 24 October 1844, in *Correspondance de P.-J. Proudhon*, 14 vols. (Paris, 1875), 2:166.

61. Marx and Engels, *The Holy Family*, in *Collected Works*, 4:32.

62. Ibid., p. 31.

63. Marx, *Economic and Philosophical Manuscripts*, in *Early Writings*, pp. 332–33; for other critical references to Proudhon in the *Manuscripts*, see pp. 364–65, 368–69.

64. Cornu *(Marx à Paris*, pp. 51–54) provides an informative discussion of how and why Marx viewed Proudhon as a petty bourgeois reformer.

65. The influence of Hess on Marx's views of money and alienation is discussed in detail in McLellan, *Young Hegelians*, pp. 154–58.

66. Cornu discusses Ruge's view of Bakunin and the similarities between Bakunin and Proudhon (as compared to Marx) in *Marx à Paris*, pp. 45, 49.

67. Quoted in Carr, *Bakunin*, pp. 129–30. Carr offers one of the best accounts of the eventual break between Bakunin and Marx over policies of the First International; see pp. 424–40.

68. For discussion of this evolving language and class consciousness among French workers after the Revolution of 1830, see Sewell, *Work and Revolution in France*, pp. 194–218. Sewell stresses (pp. 154–61) that most workers of the period should be classified as artisans rather than industrial laborers and that most labor agitation involved this artisan class, partly because their real wages were falling in these years. See also Peter N. Stearns, "Patterns of Industrial Strike Activity in France during the July Monarchy," *American Historical Review* 70 (1965): 371–94.

69. Marx's letter to Ruge of September 1843 refers to the writings of French socialists such as Fourier, Proudhon, and Cabet *(Early Writings*, pp. 207–8). For a more detailed analysis of the ways in which French socialist writers may have influenced Marx's thought before and after he went to Paris, see David Gregory, "Karl Marx's and Friedrich Engels' Knowledge of French Socialism in 1842–1843," *Historical Reflections/Réflexions Historiques* 10 (1983): 143–93.

70. The argument appears, among other places, in Cornu, *Marx à Paris*, p. 39; and McLellan, *Marx: Life and Thought*, p. 97.

71. Cornu, *Marx à Paris*, pp. 7–8; McLellan, *Marx: Life and Thought*, p. 97.

72. Marx, *Economic and Philosophical Manuscripts*, in *Early Writings*, p. 365. The emphasis on *workmen* is in Marx's text; he clearly wished to make a distinction from, say, intellectuals.

73. Marx to Feuerbach, 11 August 1844, in Marx and Engels, *Collected Works*, 3:355.

74. Niépovié, *Etudes physiologiques*, pp. 178, 183–84.

75. See the discussion of these tendencies in Chevalier, *Laboring Classes*, pp. 154, 361–62, 387, 392, 408, 423, 433.

76. Quoted in ibid., pp. 403–4.

77. Ibid., pp. 383, 413–15.

78. Quoted in ibid., pp. 383–84, from Balzac, *La fille aux yeux d'or*.

79. Marx, *Economic and Philosophical Manuscripts*, in *Early Writings*, pp. 389–90. I follow Marx's use of "man" in this discussion to indicate all human beings.

80. Ibid., p. 350.

81. Ibid., p. 328.

82. Ibid., p. 329.

83. Ibid., p. 324.

84. Ibid., pp. 324, 336 (quotation, p. 336).

85. Ibid., pp. 329–30.

86. Ibid., p. 328.

87. Ibid., p. 327.

88. Ibid., pp. 325–26.

89. Ibid., p. 359.

90. Ibid., pp. 331–32.

91. Ibid., p. 324. For an insightful analysis of Feuerbach's critique of Christianity, see Toews, *Hegelianism*, pp. 327–55.

92. Marx, *Economic and Philosophical Manuscripts*, in *Early Writings*, p. 324. McLellan (*Young Hegelians*, pp. 106–7), who argues that Feuerbach was the greatest influence on the *Manuscripts*, suggests that Feuerbach's notion of man as a communal being may have influenced Marx even more than his critique of religious alienation. There has been a great deal written about Marx's notion of alienation, but few authors stress his German exile status in France as a major influence in the evolution of his views. This emphasis does appear, however, in the important work by István Mészáros, *Marx's Theory of Alienation* (London, 1970), pp. 70–73. Mészáros discusses a number of themes relevant to the present study in a chapter called "Genesis of Marx's Theory of Alienation" (pp. 66–92), though he does not explore the problem of Marx's response to the Parisian crowd or "bestial" workers.

93. Marx, *Economic and Philsophical Manuscripts*, in *Early Writings*, pp. 377–78.

94. Ibid., p. 348.

95. Ibid.

96. Ibid., p. 358.

97. The relationship between Marx and Hegel has of course been one of the most debated issues in Marxist scholarship. My own analysis of this problem differs both from those who believe that Marx broke decisively with Hegel in his later work (e.g., Louis Althusser) and from those who believe he scarcely broke with Hegel at all (e.g., Shlomo Avineri). Marx's

confrontation with Hegelianism seems to have been especially intense in Paris, and it led to a significant break from Hegel, but the lifelong interaction with the Hegelian tradition did not end there. See Louis Althusser, *For Marx*, trans. Ben Brewster (London, 1979), pp. 33–37, 43–86; and Shlomo Avineri, *The Social and Political Thought of Karl Marx* (Cambridge, 1968), esp. the introduction and chaps. 1, 2, and 4. The problem with both Althusser and Avineri, from the perspective of my themes, is that they do not give sufficient attention to the transformative effects of the French experience on Marx's relation with Hegelianism.

98. Marx, "A Contribution to the Critique of Hegel's Philosophy of Right," in *Early Writings*, pp. 244–45.

99. Ibid., pp. 251–52, 256–57.

100. Marx, *Economic and Philosophical Manuscripts*, in *Early Writings*, pp. 384, 396. Marx's discussion of Hegel focused on the *Phenomenology*.

101. Ibid., p. 384.

102. Ibid., p. 385.

103. Ibid., p. 396.

104. Ibid., p. 386.

105. Ibid., p. 385.

106. Marx to Feuerbach, 11 August 1844, in Marx and Engels, *Collected Works*, 3:356.

107. Marx and Engels, *The Holy Family*, in *Collected Works*, 4:20.

108. Ibid., p. 83.

109. Ibid., pp. 52–53.

110. Ibid., p. 153.

111. Ibid., p. 84.

112. Ibid., p. 135.

113. Ibid., p. 131.

114. Ibid., pp. 124–25, 128–29, 131–32.

115. Ibid., p. 63; also pp. 73–74.

116. Ibid., pp. 186–91.

117. Ibid., p. 191.

118. Ibid., pp. 23–54.

119. Ibid., pp. 33–37.

120. Ibid., pp. 33, 49.

121. Ibid., p. 41.

122. Ibid., p. 42.

123. Ibid., pp. 31, 43.

124. Ibid., p. 39. Few modern scholars know much about Bruno and Edgar Bauer except through Marx's criticisms. For an analysis of Bruno Bauer that returns to Bauer's own texts and critical projects, see Toews, *Hegelianism*, pp. 288–326.

125. For the Marx-Ruge dispute, see Cornu, *Marx à Paris*, pp. 24–25; McLellan, *Young Hegelians*, pp. 40–42; and H. P. Adams, *Karl Marx in His Earlier Writings* (London, 1940), pp. 118–119.

126. Marx, "Notes on 'The King of Prussia,' " in *Early Writings*, pp. 405, 409, 416.

127. Ibid., pp. 414–15.

128. Ibid., pp. 405–6, 413, 416–18.

129. Ibid., pp. 417–20.

130. Ibid., p. 420.

131. When Marx was expelled from Paris, he told Heine that he would miss him more than anyone else in France. "Of all the people I am leaving behind here," Marx wrote, "those I leave with most regret are the Heines. I would gladly include you in my luggage!" Marx to Heine, end of January–1 February 1845, in Marx and Engels, *Collected Works*, 38:21.

132. Marx, "Critique of Hegel's Philosophy of Right," in *Early Writings*, p. 245.

133. Ibid., pp. 245–48.

134. Ibid., p. 249.

135. Ibid., p. 250.

136. Ibid., pp. 250–51.

137. Ibid., pp. 253–54.

138. Ibid., pp. 253, 257.

139. Ibid., p. 257.

140. Ibid., p. 256.

141. Ibid., p. 255.

142. Ibid.

143. Ibid., p. 257.

144. Marx, "Notes on 'The King of Prussia,' " in *Early Writings*, pp. 415–16.

145. Ibid., p. 415.

146. McLellan *(Marx before Marxism*, pp. 156–57) stresses the importance of contact with French socialism as an influence in his discovery of the German proletariat. Cornu *(Marx à Paris*, pp. 7–8) emphasizes the contact with German worker groups.

147. Marx to Feuerbach, 11 August 1844, in Marx and Engels, *Collected Works*, 3:355.

148. Grandjonc discusses these complaints in *Marx et les communistes allemands*, pp. 87–88.

149. Guizot to Duchâtel, 9 August 1844, in ibid., p. 200.

150. E.g., the editors of *Le National* (17 September 1844) could not understand why Guizot should act at the behest of the Prussian government against a small, exile newspaper that was in fact friendly to France; similar criticisms appeared in the *Revue de Paris* and *Le Globe*. For a sample of this editorial comment, see ibid., pp. 202, 205, 208–9.

151. Ibid., pp. 91–92, 210.

152. The letter Bernays published in *La Réforme* appears in ibid., pp. 215–18.

153. Marx to Proudhon, 1 May 1846, in Marx and Engels, *Collected Works*, 38:38–39.

154. Proudhon's response, dated 17 May 1846, appears in Haubtmann, *Marx et Proudhon*, pp. 63–72.

155. Karl Marx, *The Poverty of Philosophy* (1847; New York, 1963), pp. 107–8, 111–14, 118–19.

156. Ibid., p. 119.

157. Ibid., p. 202.

158. Ibid., p. 126.

159. Marx stressed these points in a letter to P. V. Annenkov, 28 December 1846, in ibid., p. 192.

160. Ibid., pp. 144, 174–75, 190–91. Marx first made similar criticisms in his private notes in Paris; see, e.g., the *Economic and Philosophical Manuscripts*, in *Early Writings*, pp. 289, 332–33, 364–65.

161. Marx to Annenkov, 28 December 1846, in *Poverty of Philosophy*, p. 191.

162. Marx explained this purpose in his foreword, ibid., p. 29.

163. Marx paid for publication of the book himself. Only 800 copies were printed, and less than 100 of those were sold within the four months after they appeared in July 1847. Engels failed to find reviewers for the book in the French press that fall, and by the next winter the revolutionary events of 1848 were claiming the attention of the Parisian radical community. Proudhon himself may have planned a response, but he too eventually let the book pass without public comment. See Hammen, *The Red '48ers*, pp. 147–48; and McLellan, *Marx: Life and Thought*, p. 166.

Chapter 4. Mickiewicz in Paris: Exile and the New Nationalism

1. Another feature of Mickiewicz's youth is that he grew up in Lithuania and attended the university at Wilno. This heritage suggests that even within Poland, Mickiewicz's relationship to Polish culture was in some respects marginal. For more on his early life and exile in Russia and Italy, see Monica M. Gardner, *Adam Mickiewicz: The National Poet of Poland*, (1911; rpt., New York, 1971), pp. 31–78; Julian Krzyzanowski, *Polish Romantic Literature* (Freeport, N.Y., 1968), pp. 41–73; Wacław Lednicki, "Mickiewicz's Stay in Russia and His Friendship with Pushkin"; and Giovanni Maver, "Mickiewicz and Italy," both in Wacław Lednicki, ed., *Adam Mickiewicz in World Literature* (Berkeley, Calif., 1956), pp. 13–104, 197–201. See also Weintraub, "Mickiewicz, the Mystic-Politician," pp. 139–45.

2. Accounts of the insurrection (which was really a war, with more than 70,000 troops on each side) appear in Leslie, *Polish Politics*, pp. 134–255; and Pawlowski, "The November Insurrection," pp. 295–310. For discussions of the emigration that followed, see Coleman, "The Great Emigration," pp. 311–23, and the introduction in Harold B. Segal, ed., *Polish Romantic Drama* (Ithaca, 1977), pp. 22–46. Segal introduces *Forefathers'*

Eve, Part III, by situating Mickiewicz in the historical context of the Emigration and Polish Romanticism. Weintraub's analysis of this period in Mickiewicz's life stresses the possible implications of his guilt about missing the war; see Weintraub, "Mickiewicz, the Mystic-Politician," pp. 143–44.

3. Mickiewicz to Lelewel, 20 March 1832, in Jean Bourrilly, "Mickiewicz and France," in Lednicki, *Mickiewicz in World Literature*, p. 246.

4. Polish population figures appear in Grandjonc, "Eléments statistiques," pp. 213–14. For more information on the organizations within the Emigration, see M. Kukiel, *Czartoryski and European Unity, 1770–1861* (Princeton, N.J., 1955), pp. 209–28. See also Coleman, "The Great Emigration," pp. 311–20; and Walicki, *Philosophy and Romantic Nationalism*, pp. 31–41.

5. For accounts of the French response to the Polish situation, see Mark Brown, "The Comité Franco-Polonais and the French Reaction to the Polish Uprising of November 1830," *English Historical Review* 93 (1978): 774–93; Michel Fridieff, "L'opinion publique française devant l'insurrection polonaise de 1830–1831," *Revue Internationale d'Histoire Politique et Constitutionnelle* 2 (1951): 111–21, 205, 214, 280–304; and Lloyd S. Kramer, "The Rights of Man: Lafayette and the Polish National Revolution, 1830–1834," *French Historical Studies* 14 (1986): 521–46.

6. Gisquet, *Mémoires*, 2:469.

7. Ibid., p. 467.

8. Discussion of these French policies appears in ibid., p. 475; in Coleman, "The Great Emigration," pp. 316–17; and in Wiktor Weintraub, *The Poetry of Adam Mickiewicz* (The Hague, 1954), p. 200. The police kept especially close watch on Poles in the first year or two after the émigré regulations were enacted; e.g., reports on Polish gatherings and on Poles traveling without permission show up in the Parisian police bulletins of 25 March, 23 April, and 10 June 1833 (AN F[7] 3886). On Lelewel's émigré experiences in France, see Skurnowicz, *Romantic Nationalism and Liberalism*, pp. 73–84.

9. For more information on Emigration politics, see Walicki, *Philosophy and Romantic Nationalism*, pp. 31–63; Coleman, "The Great Emigration," pp. 319–20; Weintraub, "Mickiewicz, the Mystic-Politician," pp. 152–53; and Kukiel, *Czartoryski*, pp. 212–13, 217–19.

10. Mickiewicz's Parisian addresses are listed in Bourrilly, "Mickiewicz and France," p. 280. He lived at various times on both sides of the Seine, moving frequently from the more densely populated centers on the right bank to less crowded areas on the left bank and then back into the center of the city.

11. It is interesting that Mickiewicz repeatedly expressed the desire for wholeness that poststructuralist criticism, notably that of Jacques Derrida, has characterized as a major metaphysical tendency in the Western tradition. As the later sections of this chapter suggest, Mickiewicz was

constantly looking in history and in language for totalizing harmony or "full presence," which he often believed might be found in the spoken word. At the same time, his search was frustrated or denied by what Derrida might call contestations and escaping supplements—those forces, tendencies, and conflicts that always deny in history (as in language) the full reconciliation and totality that Mickiewicz wanted and anticipated. In these respects, Mickiewicz becomes an interesting exemplar of the metaphysical tradition. For an introduction to Derridean analysis of the "logocentric" Western tradition, see Jacques Derrida, *Of Grammatology*, trans. Gayatri Chakravorty Spivak (Baltimore, Md., 1976).

12. For discussions of Mickiewicz's place in the Polish Romantic tradition, see Segal, introduction to *Polish Romantic Drama*, pp. 28–36, and Julian Krzyzanowski, *A History of Polish Literature* (Warsaw, 1978), pp. 220–58.

13. Gardner, *Adam Mickiewicz*, pp. 129–30; Bourrilly, "Mickiewicz and France," p. 249. *The Books of the Polish Nation and of the Polish Pilgrims* may be found in English translation in George R. Noyes, ed., *Poems by Adam Mickiewicz* (New York, 1944), pp. 371–415.

14. A prose translation makes the work accessible to English readers; see Adam Mickiewicz, *Pan Tadeusz; or, The Last Foray in Lithuania*, trans. George R. Noyes (New York, 1917). One of the best critical discussions of the work appears in Weintraub, *Poetry of Mickiewicz*, pp. 221–64.

15. Quoted in "Mickiewicz as Journalist: Summary and Excerpts," in Manfred Kridl, ed., *Adam Mickiewicz: Poet of Poland* (New York, 1951), p. 98.

16. Léon Faucher to Mickiewicz, February 1839, quoted in Bourrilly, "Mickiewicz and France," p. 274.

17. The only dissenting deputy claimed that a chair in Slavic literature should not be given to someone who knew only one of the dialects. See Wacław Lednicki, "Mickiewicz at the Collège de France, 1840–1940," *Slavonic and East European Review* 20 (1941): 153; and Maxime Leroy, "Adam Mickiewicz in France: Professor and Social Philosopher," in UNESCO, *Adam Mickiewicz, 1798–1855* (Zurich, 1955), pp. 90–91.

18. Cousin's speech, which formed part of the debate on 18 June 1840, is quoted in Edmond Marek, *Destinées françaises de l'oeuvre messianique d'Adam Mickiewicz* (Fribourg, 1945), pp. 71–72.

19. Adam Mickiewicz, *Les slaves: Cours professé au Collège de France*, 5 vols. (Paris, 1849), 2:311, lecture of 14 December 1841. The published text of these lectures, gathered from notes and stenographers' transcriptions, surely varies in some respects from what Mickiewicz may actually have said.

20. Ibid., p. 312.

21. Mickiewicz to Cousin, 16 August 1840, in André Mazon, "Une correspondance: Mickiewicz, Cousin, Cyprien Robert," *Revue de Littérature Comparée* 14 (1934): 560.

22. Mickiewicz to Lelewel, 20 March 1832, in Bourrilly, "Mickiewicz

and France," p. 246. See also Manfred Kridl, "Two Champions of a New Christianity: Lamennais and Mickiewicz," *Comparative Literature* 4 (1952): 240–41.

23. Bourrilly, "Mickiewicz and France," p. 250.

24. Montalembert's preface appears in Kridl, *Mickiewicz: Poet of Poland,* p. 196.

25. Ibid., p. 197.

26. Sainte-Beuve's review, which was published in *Le National* on 8 July 1833, is in ibid., p. 198. Sainte-Beuve later became quite critical of Mickiewicz's mysticism.

27. This is the argument, e.g., in Kridl, "Two Champions," pp. 249–50, 262.

28. Lamennais to the Marquis de Corioli, 6 May 1833, in Kridl, *Mickiewicz: Poet of Poland,* p. 195.

29. Almost everyone who has studied the Lamennais-Mickiewicz relationship stresses these similarities. See, e.g., Kridl, "Two Champions," pp. 244–47, 250, 262; Marek, *Destinées françaises,* pp. 20–21, 31, 37; and Weintraub, *Poetry of Mickiewicz,* p. 198.

30. Kridl, "Two Champions," pp. 262–63, 266; Bourrilly, "Mickiewicz and France," pp. 254–55.

31. Bourrilly, "Mickiewicz and France," p. 256. Mickiewicz's financial problems became especially severe after he married Celina Szymanowska in 1834. They had five children by the mid-1840s.

32. Ibid., pp. 256–57. See, also, Wacław Lednicki, "Some Comments about Three Letters of Mickiewicz...(Mickiewicz and Alfred de Vigny)," *Polish Review* 1 (1956): 80–91. Much of the text of Mickiewicz's play has been lost.

33. Bourrilly, "Mickiewicz and France," p. 257. For details of Sand's assistance in the theatrical venture, see Wladimir Karenine, *George Sand: Sa vie et ses oeuvres,* 4 vols. (Paris, 1899–1926), 3:182–86.

34. Sand to Mickiewicz, May 1837, in Sand, *Correspondance,* 4:90. Sand continued to praise *Les confédérés* long after all attempts to produce it had failed, expressing hope that the project might be revived and even suggesting (in 1843) that it should be published without a performance; see Sand to Mickiewicz, 9 May (?) 1843, 6:130. On the friendship between d'Agoult and Mickiewicz, see Jean Fabre, "The Approach to an Understanding of 'Pan Tadeusz,' " in Lednicki, *Mickiewicz in World Literature,* pp. 286–88.

35. Mickiewicz to Sand, 3 June 1837, quoted in Karenine, *George Sand,* 3:185–86.

36. For examples of her support and interest, see Sand to Mickiewicz, March 1843 and 5 May 1843, in Sand, *Correspondance,* 6:88–89, 121–22.

37. George Sand, "Essai sur le drame fantastique: Goethe, Byron, Mickiewicz," *Revue des Deux Mondes* 20 (December 1839): 627 (the translation is from Kridl, *Mickiewicz: Poet of Poland,* p. 201).

38. Ibid.

39. Ibid., pp. 644–45 (Kridl, pp. 202–3).

40. Ibid.

41. George Sand, "De la littérature slave," *La Revue Indépendante*, 10 April 1843, p. 380.

42. Ibid., p. 378.

43. Ibid., pp. 382–83. Sand's sympathy for Mickiewicz's religion exemplifies part of the general interest in religious issues among French intellectuals in the 1840s.

44. Ibid., p. 380.

45. Ibid., p. 381.

46. Bourrilly, "Mickiewicz and France," p. 261; Leroy, "Mickiewicz in France," p. 92.

47. Edgar Quinet to Mme Quinet (his mother), 23 January 1838, in Z. L. Zaleski, "Une amitié franco-polonaise: Mickiewicz, Michelet, Quinet," *Séances et Travaux de l'Académie des Sciences Morales et Politiques*, July–August 1925, p. 104.

48. Quinet to Mickiewicz, 14 May 1838, quoted in Bourrilly, "Mickiewicz and France," p. 261.

49. Quinet's lecture of 20 March 1844, in Kridl, *Mickiewicz: Poet of Poland*, p. 204.

50. For examples of the Quinet-Mickiewicz correspondence and their mutual aid, see Zaleski, "Une amitié franco-polonaise," pp. 109–13. An interesting twist is that Quinet went into exile after Napoleon III's coup in 1851 and lived abroad for almost twenty years. The last letters from Quinet to Mickiewicz are therefore from a French exile in Brussels to a Polish exile in Paris.

51. Michelet to Mickiewicz, undated letter, quoted in Marek, *Destinées françaises*, p. 85.

52. These points are stressed by scholars who have studied the "Polish question" in Michelet's work. See, e.g., Maria Wodzynska-Walicka, "L'idée de la Pologne dans la pensée de Jules Michelet," *Europe* 51 (1973): 149, 161; Z. L. Zaleski, "Michelet, Mickiewicz, et la Pologne," *Séances et Travaux de l'Académie des Sciences Morales et Politiques*, July–August 1928, pp. 83–87, 144; and Marek, *Destinées françaises*, p. 86.

53. These themes in Michelet's thought are linked to Mickiewicz by the noted Michelet scholar Gabriel Monod, in *La vie et la pensée de Jules Michelet*, 2 vols. (Paris, 1923), 2:94–95.

54. Zaleski, "Michelet, Mickiewicz, et la Pologne," pp. 120–22; Wodzynska-Walicka, "L'idée de la Pologne," pp. 153–54; Bourrilly, "Mickiewicz and France," pp. 261–63.

55. Jules Michelet, "Le Collège de France," in Kridl, *Mickiewicz: Poet of Poland*, pp. 209–10.

56. Mickiewicz to Michelet, 19 May 1843, in Z. L. Zaleski, "A travers une amitié franco-polonaise: 12 lettres inédites d'A. Mickiewicz à Michelet," *Le Monde Slave*, August 1926, p. 247.

57. Jules Michelet, *Journal, 1828–1848*, ed. Paul Viallaneix (Paris, 1959), 22–23 February 1845, p. 592.

58. Ibid.; also 3 June 1845, pp. 604–5.

59. Michelet to Mickiewicz, 11 March 1845, quoted in Paul Viallaneix, *La vie royale: Essai sur l'idée de peuple dans l'oeuvre de Michelet* (Paris, 1959), p. 272.

60. Mickiewicz to Michelet [12 March 1845], in Zaleski, "A travers d'une amitié," pp. 250–51. A number of scholarly accounts draw attention to the differences between the two men. See, e.g., Zaleski, "Michelet, Mickiewicz, et la Pologne," pp. 108, 111–12, 114–15, 123–24; Monod, *La vie et la pensée*, 2:95, 98; Leroy, "Mickiewicz in France," pp. 92, 94–95; and Ladislas Mickiewicz, *Le trilogie du Collège de France* (Paris, 1924), pp. 11–12.

61. For a detailed analysis of Polish messianism, with special reference to Mickiewicz, see Walicki, *Philosophy and Romantic Nationalism*, pp. 239–67; see also the introduction in Segal, *Polish Romantic Drama*, pp. 32–35.

62. Mickiewicz, *Books of the Polish Nation and Pilgrims*, in Noyes, *Poems by Mickiewicz*, pp. 376, 378.

63. Ibid., p. 379.

64. Ibid., p. 380.

65. Ibid., p. 410.

66. Mickiewicz, *Les slaves*, 3:244–45, lecture of 17 May 1842.

67. Ibid., pp. 348–49, lecture of 28 June 1842.

68. Mickiewicz, *Books of the Polish Nation and Pilgrims*, p. 380.

69. Mickiewicz, *Forefathers' Eve*, Part III, in Noyes, *Poems by Mickiewicz*, p. 277.

70. Mickiewicz, *Books of the Polish Nation and Pilgrims*, p. 387.

71. Ibid.

72. Ibid., p. 394.

73. Ibid., p. 385.

74. Ibid.

75. Ibid., pp. 390–391; see also pp. 404, 405, 407–9. Mickiewicz suggested that Poles were "among strangers as shipwrecked men on a strange shore."

76. Ibid., p. 390. Mickiewicz went on to stress that if Poles did not recognize one another, it was because "some have put on the red caps of the French, and others the ermine of the English, and others the togas and birettas of the Germans. And the children thus disguised often their own mother will not recognize."

77. Ibid., pp. 382–84.

78. Weintraub argues that Mickiewicz developed his ideas on the religious, historical, prophetic function of poetry from his reading of the eighteenth-century French mystical philosopher Louis-Claude de Saint-Martin, whom he first studied in Russia. Saint-Martin (1743–1803) regarded both politics and poetry as essentially religious processes that demanded sacrifice and led to redemption. See Wiktor Weintraub, *Liter-*

ature as Prophecy: Scholarship and Martinist Poetics in Mickiewicz's Parisiàn Lectures (The Hague, 1959), pp. 15–17, 21, 61–63; also Weintraub, "Mickiewicz, the Mystic-Politician," pp. 145–46.

79. Mickiewicz, *Pan Tadeusz*, pp. 1–2. Weintraub discusses the "idealized past" of the epic in *Poetry of Mickiewicz*, pp. 222, 233, 236, 256.

80. Mickiewicz, *Pan Tadeusz*, pp. 14–15.

81. For a more detailed discussion of these themes in Mickiewicz's work, see Weintraub, "Mickiewicz, the Mystic-Politician," pp. 146–50, 177–78.

82. Mickiewicz, *Books of the Polish Nation and Pilgrims*, p. 379.

83. Ibid., p. 412.

84. Ibid., p. 376.

85. *Beilage zur Allgemeine Zeitung*, 9 March 1843 (published in Augsburg), in Kridl, *Mickiewicz: Poet of Poland*, pp. 183–84.

86. Sand, "De la littérature slave," p. 378.

87. Mickiewicz, *Les slaves*, 5:228, lecture of 23 April 1844.

88. Ibid., p. 185, lecture of 7 March 1844.

89. Ibid., pp. 183–84.

90. Ibid., 3:308–9, lecture of 14 June 1842. This emphasis on the relationship between religious experience and politics again suggests the influence of Saint-Martin: politics demanded religious commitment (or sacrifice), and one must be a saint to be a poet. The "sacrificial" aspect of the French Revolution especially appealed to Saint-Martin. See Weintraub, *Literature as Prophecy*, pp. 13–17; and Jean Fabre, "La France dans la pensée et le coeur de Mickiewicz," *Revue de Littérature Comparée* 31 (1957): 172–74.

91. Mickiewicz, *Les slaves*, 3:308, lecture of 14 June 1842.

92. Ibid., p. 309; a similar theme appears in 4:3, lecture of 6 December 1842.

93. Ibid., 4:3.

94. Mickiewicz, "Our Program," *La Tribune des Peuples*, 14 March 1849, in UNESCO, *Mickiewicz*, p. 235.

95. Mickiewicz, *Les slaves*, 5:134–35, lecture of 7 February 1844.

96. One example of Mickiewicz's hostility toward July Monarchy policies appeared in "Our Program," p. 234: "The political inertia of all French governments since the Restoration is due, not merely to their pusillanimity, but to their profound ignorance of European affairs and events—an ignorance that has more than once been pleaded by French statesmen themselves, both in official papers and public pronouncements."

97. Ibid., pp. 234–35.

98. For more on the Towiański-Mickiewicz relationship, see Weintraub, *Literature as Prophecy*, pp. 10–12, 72–75; Weintraub, "Mickiewicz, the Mystic-Politician," pp. 163–64, 171; Walicki, *Philosophy and Romantic Nationalism*, pp. 253–57; and Gardner, *Adam Mickiewicz*, pp. 206–7, 213–15.

99. Mickiewicz, *Les slaves*, 3:202–3, lecture of 29 April 1842.

100. Mickiewicz, "Our Program," p. 237.

101. Mickiewicz, *Les slaves*, 3:259, lecture of 24 May 1842.

102. Ibid.

103. Ibid., 5:109, lecture of 30 January 1844.

104. Ibid., 3:260, lecture of 24 May 1842.

105. The story of Mickiewicz's youthful encounter with French troops appears in a lecture Michelet gave at the Collège de France in December 1847. Michelet's account, based on conversations with Mickiewicz, has been translated in UNESCO, *Mickiewicz*, pp. 249–51. For more on the Polish cult of Napoleon, see Edouard Krakowski, *Adam Mickiewicz: Philosophe mystique* (Paris, 1935), pp. 33–34, 37–38.

106. Mickiewicz, *Les slaves*, 3:261, lecture of 24 May 1842.

107. Ibid., pp. 128–29, lecture of 5 April 1842.

108. Ibid., pp. 156–58, lecture of 12 April 1842.

109. Ibid., p. 366; 4:1–2, lectures of 1 July and 6 December 1842.

110. Ibid., 5:268–69, lecture of 21 May 1844.

111. Ibid., 4:12, lecture of 6 December 1842.

112. Ibid., 5:281, 286, 288, 300, lecture of 28 May 1844.

113. These comparisons appear in a number of lectures: e.g., 27 June, 22 December, and 26 December 1843, and 30 January 1844, in ibid., 4:503; 5:10, 19–20, 24, 90.

114. Ibid., 1:57, lecture of 12 January 1841.

115. Ibid., 4:211, lecture of 21 February 1843.

116. Ibid., pp. 211–18. Conflicting tendencies in Mickiewicz's lectures result from a generalized praise for Slavic culture and a specific hatred for the most powerful Slavic government—that of the Russian tsar; he wanted the French to lead the Slavic people to freedom from a Slavic government. There is also a question about the specific place of Poles within Slavic culture. In Mickiewicz's account they were of course Slavs, but they were a very special group: the chosen people within a chosen race. Weintraub refers to these problems briefly in "Mickiewicz, the Mystic-Politician," pp. 160–61, and Walicki assesses Mickiewicz's relationship with Russian Slavophiles in *Philosophy and Romantic Nationalism*, pp. 269–76.

117. Mickiewicz, *Les slaves*, 2:9–11, lecture of 4 May 1841.

118. Ibid., 1:373, 375, lecture of 24 March 1841.

119. Ibid., 5:91–92, lecture of 30 January 1844.

120. Ibid., 2:163, lecture of 1 June 1841.

121. Ibid., 1:87, lecture of 19 January 1841.

122. Ibid., 2:164, lecture of 1 June 1841.

123. Ibid., 1:2–3, lecture of 22 December 1840.

124. Ibid., 5:278–79, lecture of 28 May 1844.

125. Ibid., 1:72, 74–75, 83, lectures of 15 and 19 January 1841; 4:381–82, lecture of 16 May 1843.

126. Ibid., 4:277–78, lecture of 14 March 1843.

127. Ibid., pp. 274–75, 278, 279.

128. Ibid., pp. 275–77. To support his antiindustrial argument, Mickiewicz cited Ralph Waldo Emerson's complaints about the loss of *human* needs and duties amid the material values of industrial civilization. While Americans such as Emerson were longing for the simple pleasures of agrarian life, Mickiewicz saw no reason for Slavs to give up the virtuous agricultural communities that many Westerners so clearly missed in their industrializing urban societies. Emerson became an important reference in the development of Mickiewicz's Slavic theories, perhaps because he saw in Emerson a kindred antimaterialist voice or perhaps because the American was another writer on the margins of European society who was striving to define a new national culture and identity.

129. Ibid., pp. 394–95, 406, lecture of 23 May 1843. Here was a problem for Mickiewicz: "liberating" French armies brought with them their own set of "liberating" social practices.

130. Weintraub discusses these themes with a somewhat different emphasis in "Mickiewicz, the Mystic-Politician," pp. 159–60.

131. Mickiewicz, *Les slaves*, 4:455, lecture of 13 June 1843.

132. Ibid.; see also p. 445, lecture of 6 June 1843.

133. Ibid., pp. 319–20, 334, 358, 425–26, lectures of 2 and 9 May 1843 and 2 June 1843.

134. Ibid., p. 462, lecture of 13 June 1843.

135. Ibid., pp. 459–60.

136. Ibid., 5:14–15, lecture of 26 December 1843.

137. Ibid., pp. 15, 17.

138. Again, these arguments seemed to draw upon the views of the French philosopher Saint-Martin. For more discussion of Mickiewicz's antirationalist attitudes and the mystical tendencies in his view of literature, see Krakowski, *Mickiewicz: Philosophe*, pp. 217, 220, 225, 230, 241–42, 278–79; Weintraub, *Literature as Prophecy*, pp. 13–17; and Leon Kolodziej, *Adam Mickiewicz au carrefour des romantismes européens* (Aix-en-Provence, 1966), pp. 257, 261–62. One apparent consequence of Mickiewicz's interest in Emerson was his warm friendship with Margaret Fuller, which developed during her stay in Paris in 1846–47 and which indicated again how foreigners tended to meet one another in Paris. See Leopold Wellisz, *The Friendship of Margaret Fuller D'Ossoli and Adam Mickiewicz* (New York, 1947), pp. 9–39.

139. Mickiewicz, *Les slaves*, 2:368, lecture of 4 January 1842.

140. Ibid., p. 292, lecture of 29 June 1841.

141. Ibid., pp. 288–89.

142. Ibid., p. 294.

143. Ibid., 4:407–8, lecture of 23 May 1843.

144. Ibid., 2:292–93, lecture of 29 June 1841.

145. Delessert to Villemain 16 August 1842, in Krakowski, *Mickiewicz:*

Philosophe, p. 297. Krakowski published a series of French documents relating to Mickiewicz's case as an appendix to this book.

146. Delessert to Villemain, 4 May 1844, in ibid., p. 305.

147. Report for the Minister of Public Instruction, 4 February 1848, in ibid., pp. 322–23.

148. A. Passy, Under Secretary of State for the Interior, to the Minister of Public Instruction, 24 March 1844, in ibid., p. 302.

149. Passy to Villemain, 24 March and 30 May 1844, and police agent reports of 16 March, 21 March, and 29 May, in ibid., pp. 299, 301–2, 307.

150. Duchâtel to Villemain, 6 and 20 September 1844, and Villemain to Duchâtel, 7 September 1844, in ibid., pp. 309–10, 315–16; see also the Report for the Minister of Public Instruction, 4 February 1848, in ibid., pp. 322–23.

151. Discussion of Mickiewicz's move away from Towiański appears in Gardner, *Adam Mickiewicz*, pp. 253–63. For more on the Polish legion in Italy, see ibid., pp. 268–78; and Weintraub, "Mickiewicz, the Mystic-Politician," pp. 166–69.

152. For a good summary of these last years in Mickiewicz's life, see Weintraub, "Mickiewicz, the Mystic-Politician," pp. 169–77.

153. A group of Poles eventually transported his body back to Poland for burial in Cracow in 1890.

BIBLIOGRAPHY

*Unpublished Sources: Document Cartons,
Archives Nationales, Paris [cited as AN]*

F^7 3884–93
F^7 12.180–82
F^7 12.239–40
F^7 12.242–43
F^7 12.305–6
F^7 12.329
F^{18} 337

F^{18} 346
F^{18} 425
42 AP1
42 AP47
42 AP19
BB^{18} 1396–97

Works by Heinrich Heine

Correspondance inédite de Henri Heine. 2 vols. Paris, 1866–67.
Draper, Hal, ed. and trans. *The Complete Poems of Heinrich Heine.* Cambridge, Mass., 1982.
Ellis, Havelock, ed. and trans. *The Prose Writings of Heinrich Heine.* London, 1887.
Embden, Ludwig von, ed. *The Family Life of Heinrich Heine.* Translated by Charles De Kay. New York, 1892.
Feise, Ernst, trans. *Lyric Poems and Ballads.* Pittsburgh, 1961.
Heinrich Heine Säkularausgabe. 27 vols. Edited by Nationale Forschungs- und Gedenkstätten der klassischen deutschen Literatur (Weimar) and Centre National de la Recherche Scientifique (Paris). Berlin and Paris, 1970–80. [Includes *De l'Allemagne, De la France,* and *Lutèce.* Cited throughout as *HSA.*]
Karpeles, Gustav, ed. *Heinrich Heine's Life Told in His Own Words.* Translated by Arthur Dexter. New York, 1893.
Mustard, Helen M., ed. and trans. *Heinrich Heine: Selected Works.* New York, 1973.

Works by Karl Marx

Early Writings. Translated by Rodney Livingstone and Gregor Benton. London, 1975.
The Poverty of Philosophy. New York, 1963.
Marx, Karl, and Frederick Engels. *Collected Works.* New York, 1975– .

Works by Adam Mickiewicz

Noyes, George R., ed. and trans. *Poems by Adam Mickiewicz.* New York, 1944. [Includes *The Books of the Polish Nation and Pilgrims; Forefathers' Eve.*]
Pan Tadeusz; or, The Last Foray in Lithuania. Translated by George R. Noyes. New York, 1917.
Segal, Harold B., ed. *Polish Romantic Drama.* Ithaca, 1977. [Includes *Forefathers' Eve,* Part III.]
Les slaves: Cours professé au Collège de France. 5 vols. Paris, 1849.

Paris, Foreigners, and France, 1830–1848

Annenkov, P. V. *The Extraordinary Decade.* Translated by Irwin R. Titunik, edited by Arthur P. Mendel. Ann Arbor, Mich., 1968.
Blanc, Louis. "D'un projet d'alliance intellectuelle entre l'Allemagne et la France." *La Revue Indépendante* 11 (10 November 1843): 40–67.
Brisbane, Redelia. *Albert Brisbane: A Mental Biography.* 1893. Reprint, New York, 1969.
Cieszkowski, August. *Selected Writings of August Cieszkowski.* Edited and translated by André Liebich. Cambridge, 1979.
Cooper, James Fenimore. *Recollections of Europe.* 2 vols. London, 1837.
Cuchot, A. "Mouvement de la population de Paris." *Revue des Deux Mondes* 9 (15 February 1845): 719–36.
Desnoyers, Louis, et al., eds. *Les étrangers à Paris.* Paris, 1844.
Duprat, Pascal. "L'école de Hegel à Paris—Annales d'Allemagne et de France, publiées par Arnold Ruge et Karl Marx." *La Revue Indépendante* 12 (25 February 1844): 481–86.
Forster, Charles. *Quinze ans à Paris (1832–1848): Paris et les parisiens.* 2 vols. Paris, 1848.
Frankowski, Karol. See Niépovié, Gaëtan.
Galignani's New Paris Guide. Paris, 1837.
Girardin, Mme Emile de. *Le Vicomte de Launay: Lettres parisiennes.* 4 vols. Paris, 1857.

Gisquet, H. *Mémoires de M. Gisquet, ancien préfet de police, écrits par lui-même.* 4 vols. Paris, 1840.

Gore, Catherine. *Paris in 1841.* London, 1842.

Grant, James. *Paris and Its People.* 2 vols. London, 1844.

Herzen, Alexander. *My Past and Thoughts.* Translated by Constance Garnett, revised by Humphrey Higgins. 4 vols. London, 1968.

Houben, Heinrich. *Heine par ses contemporains.* Paris, 1929.

Michelet, Jules. *Journal, 1828–1848.* Edited by Paul Viallaneix. Paris, 1959.

Montémont, Albert. *Guide universel de l'étranger dans Paris; ou, Nouveau tableau de cette capitale.* Paris, 1843.

Niépovié, Gaëtan [Karol Frankowski]. *Etudes physiologiques sur les grandes métropoles de l'Europe occidentale, Paris.* Paris, 1840.

Ossoli, Margaret Fuller. *At Home and Abroad; or, Things and Thoughts in America and Europe.* Edited by Arthur B. Fuller. New York, 1869.

Le parfait almanach de Paris et de ses environs. Paris, 1847.

Proudhon, P.-J. *Correspondance de P.-J. Proudhon.* 14 vols. Paris, 1875.

Quinet, Edgar. "De l'art en Allemagne." *Revue des Deux Mondes* 6 (31 May 1832): 493–514.

——. "Poètes allemands: Henri Heine." *Revue des Deux Mondes* 3d ser., 1 (14 February 1834): 353–69.

Sainte-Beuve, Charles Augustin. *Sainte-Beuve: Correspondance générale.* Edited by Jean Bonnerot. 18 vols. Paris, 1935–77.

——. *Premiers lundis.* Rev. ed. 3 vols. Paris, 1886–94.

Saint-Fargeau, Girault de. *Les quarante-huit quartiers de Paris.* Paris, 1846.

Sand, George. *Correspondance.* Edited by George Lubin. 14 vols. Paris, 1964–   .

——. "De la littérature slave." *La Revue Indépendante,* 10 April 1843.

——. "Essai sur le drame fantastique: Goethe, Byron, Mickiewicz." *Revue des Deux Mondes* 20 (December 1839): 593–645.

Stein, Lorenz von. *The History of the Social Movement in France, 1789–1850.* Translated and edited by Kaethe Mengelberg. Totowa, N.J., 1964.

Thackeray, William M. *The Students' Quarter; or, Paris Five-and-Thirty Years Since.* London, 1875.

Trollope, Frances. *Paris and the Parisians in 1835.* New York, 1836.

Secondary Sources: Books

Adams, H. P. *Karl Marx in His Earlier Writings.* London, 1940.

Almeras, Henri d'. *La vie parisienne sous le règne de Louis-Philippe.* Paris, n.d.

Althusser, Louis. *For Marx.* Translated by Ben Brewster. London, 1979.

Avineri, Shlomo. *The Social and Political Thought of Karl Marx.* Cambridge, 1968.

Benjamin, Walter. *Charles Baudelaire: A Lyric Poet in the Era of High Capitalism.* Translated by Harry Zohn. London, 1973.

Berenson, Edward. *Populist Religion and Left-Wing Politics in France, 1830–1852.* Princeton, N.J., 1984.

Berlin, Isaiah. *Karl Marx: His Life and Environment.* 4th ed. Oxford, 1978.

——. *The Life and Opinions of Moses Hess.* Cambridge, 1959.

Bertier de Sauvigny, G. *La France et les français vus par les voyageurs américains, 1814–1848.* 2 vols. Paris, 1982, 1985.

Boos, Rutger. *Ansichten der Revolution, Paris-Berichte deutscher Schriftsteller nach der Juli-Revolution 1830: Heine, Börne u.a.* Cologne, 1977.

Boutet de Monvel, Roger. *Eminent English Men and Women in Paris, 1800–1850.* Translated by G. Herring. London, 1912.

Brod, Max. *Heinrich Heine: The Artist in Revolt.* Translated by Joseph Witriol. London, 1956.

Brombert, Beth Archer. *Christina: Portraits of a Princess.* New York, 1977.

Butler, E. M. *Heinrich Heine: A Biography.* 1956. Reprint, Westport, Conn., 1970.

——. *The Saint-Simonian Religion in Germany: A Study of the Young German Movement.* Cambridge, 1926.

Cadot, Michel. *La Russie dans la vie intellectuelle française, 1839–1856.* Paris, 1967.

Carr, E. H. *Michael Bakunin.* London, 1937.

——. *The Romantic Exiles.* 1933, Reprint, New York, 1975.

Charlton, D. G. *Secular Religions in France, 1815–1870.* Oxford, 1963.

Chevalier, Louis. *La formation de la population parisienne au XIXe siècle.* Paris, 1962.

——. *Laboring Classes and Dangerous Classes.* Translated by Frank Jellinek. New York, 1973.

Church, Clive H. *Europe in 1830: Revolution and Political Change.* London, 1983.

Clarke, Margaret A. *Heine et la monarchie de juillet.* Paris, 1927.

Conrad, Peter. *Imagining America.* New York, 1980.

Cornu, August. *Karl Marx et Friedrich Engels.* Vol. 3, *Marx à Paris.* Paris, 1962.

Daumard, Adeline. *Les bourgeois de Paris au XIXe siècle.* Paris, 1970.

Dresch, Joseph. *Heine à Paris, 1831–1856.* Paris, 1956.

Dunham, Arthur Lewis. *The Industrial Revolution in France, 1815–1848.* New York, 1955.

Furman, Nelly. *La Revue des Deux Mondes et le romantisme (1831–1848).* Geneva, 1975.

Galignani's Library. *A Famous Bookstore.* Paris, 1920.

Gardner, Monica M. *Adam Mickiewicz: The National Poet of Poland.* 1911. Reprint, New York, 1971.

Gattey, Charles Neilson. *A Bird of Curious Plumage: Princess Cristina di Belgiojoso, 1808–1871.* London, 1971.

Gellner, Ernest. *Nations and Nationalism*. Ithaca, 1983.
Goodwin, C. D. W., and I. B. Holley, Jr., eds. *The Transfer of Ideas: Historical Essays*. Durham, N.C., 1968.
Grandjonc, Jacques. *Marx et les communistes allemands à Paris, 1844*. Paris, 1974.
Hammen, Oscar J. *The Red '48ers: Karl Marx and Frederick Engels*. New York, 1969.
Handlin, Oscar. *The Uprooted*. Boston, 1951.
Haubtmann, P. *Marx et Proudhon*. Paris, 1947.
Haydu, George G., ed. *Experience Forms: Their Cultural and Individual Place and Function*. The Hague, 1979.
Heineman, Helen. *Mrs. Trollope: The Triumphant Feminine in the Nineteenth Century*. Athens, Ohio, 1979.
Hirth, Friedrich. *Heinrich Heine und seine französischen Freunde*. Mainz, 1949.
Hofrichter, Laura. *Heinrich Heine*. Translated by Barker Fairley. Oxford, 1963.
Howrath, T. E. B. *Citizen-King: The Life of Louis-Philippe, King of the French*. London, 1961.
Ionescu, Ghita, ed. *The Political Thought of Saint-Simon*. Oxford, 1976.
Johnson, Douglas. *Guizot: Aspects of French History, 1787–1874*. Toronto, 1964.
Kammen, Michael, ed. *The Past before Us*. Ithaca, 1980.
Karenine, Wladimir. *George Sand: Sa vie et ses oeuvres*. 4 vols. Paris, 1899–1926.
Kohn, Hans. *The Idea of Nationalism*. New York, 1967.
Kolodziej, Leon. *Adam Mickiewicz au carrefour des romantismes européens*. Aix-en-Provence, 1966.
Krakowski, Edouard. *Adam Mickiewicz: Philosophe mystique*. Paris, 1935.
Kridl, Manfred, ed. *Adam Mickiewicz: Poet of Poland*. New York, 1951.
Kruse, Joseph A., and Michaël Werner, eds. *Heine à Paris*. Paris, 1981.
Krzyzanowski, Julian. *A History of Polish Literature*. Warsaw, 1978.
——. *Polish Romantic Literature*. Freeport, N.Y., 1968.
Kukiel, M. *Czartoryski and European Unity, 1770–1861*. Princeton, N.J., 1955.
LaCapra, Dominick, and Steven L. Kaplan, eds. *Modern European Intellectual History: Reappraisals and New Perspectives*. Ithaca, 1982.
Langer, William L. *Political and Social Upheaval, 1832–1852*. New York, 1969.
Lednicki, Wacław, ed. *Adam Mickiewicz in World Literature*. Berkeley, 1956.
Leslie, R. F. *Polish Politics and the Revolution of November 1830*. London, 1956.
Liebich, André. *Between Ideology and Utopia: The Politics and Philosophy of August Cieszkowski*. Dordrecht, 1979.

MacCannel, Dean. *The Tourist: A New Theory of the Leisure Class.* New York, 1976.

McLellan, David. *Karl Marx: His Life and Thought.* New York, 1973.

———. *Marx before Marxism.* New York, 1979.

———. *The Young Hegelians and Karl Marx.* London, 1969.

Maguire, John. *Marx's Paris Writings: An Analysis.* New York, 1973.

Manuel, Frank E. *The New World of Henri Saint-Simon.* Cambridge, Mass., 1956.

Marcus, Steven. *Engels, Manchester, and the Working Class.* New York, 1974.

Marek, Edmond. *Destinées françaises de l'oeuvre messianique d'Adam Mickiewicz.* Fribourg, 1945.

Matoré, Georges. *Le vocabulaire et la société sous Louis-Philippe.* Geneva, 1951.

Mayer, Hans. *Outsiders: A Study in Life and Letters.* Translated by Denis M. Sweet. Cambridge, Mass., 1982.

Mesmer-Strupp, Beatrix. *Arnold Ruges Plan einer Alliance intellectuelle zwischen Deutschen und Franzosen.* Bern, 1963.

Mészáros, István, *Marx's Theory of Alienation.* London, 1970.

Mickiewicz, Ladislas. *Le trilogie du Collège de France.* Paris, 1924.

Monod, Gabriel. *La vie et la pensée de Jules Michelet.* 2 vols. Paris, 1923.

Netter, Lucienne. *Heine et la peinture de la civilisation parisienne, 1840–1848.* Frankfurt am Main, 1980.

Oakley, Allen. *Marx's Critique of Political Economy: Intellectual Sources and Evolution.* 2 vols. London, 1984–85.

Ott, Barthelemy. *La querelle de Heine et de Börne.* Lyon, 1935.

Pinkney, David H. *Decisive Years in France, 1840–1847.* Princeton, N.J., 1986.

———. *The French Revolution of 1830.* Princeton, N.J., 1972.

———. *Napoleon III and the Rebuilding of Paris.* Princeton, N.J., 1958.

Pouthas, Charles H. *La population française pendant la première moitié du XIXe siècle.* Paris, 1956.

Prawer, S. S. *Heine's Jewish Comedy: A Study of His Portraits of Jews and Judaism.* Oxford, 1983.

Quennell, Peter, ed. *Affairs of the Mind.* Washington, D.C., 1980.

Reeves, Nigel. *Heinrich Heine: Poetry and Politics.* Oxford, 1974.

Rose, William. *Heinrich Heine: Two Studies of His Thought and Feeling.* Oxford, 1956.

Ruckhaberle, Hans-Joachim. *Frühproletarische Literatur: Die Flugschriften der deutschen Handwerksgesellenvereine in Paris, 1832–1839.* Kronberg, 1977.

Sammons, Jeffrey L. *Heinrich Heine: A Modern Biography.* Princeton, N.J., 1979.

———. *Heinrich Heine: The Elusive Poet.* New Haven, Conn., 1969.

Sandor, A. I. *The Exile of Gods.* The Hague, 1967.

Sée, Henri. *Histoire économique de la France.* 2 vols. Paris, 1939, 1942.

Seigel, Jerrold. *Bohemian Paris: Culture, Politics, and the Boundaries of Bourgeois Life, 1830–1930.* New York, 1986.

———. *Marx's Fate: The Shape of a Life.* Princeton, N.J., 1978.

Sewell, William H., Jr. *Work and Revolution in France: The Language of Labor from the Old Regime to 1848.* Cambridge, 1980.

Shafer, Boyd C. *Faces of Nationalism: New Realities and Old Myths.* New York, 1972.

Simmel, George. *The Sociology of Georg Simmel.* Edited and translated by Kurt H. Wolff. Glencoe, Ill., 1950.

Skurnowicz, Joan S. *Romantic Nationalism and Liberalism: Joachim Lelewel and the Polish National Idea.* Boulder, Colo., 1981.

Starn, Randolph. *Contrary Commonwealth: The Theme of Exile in Medieval and Renaissance Italy.* Berkeley, Calif., 1982.

Tabori, Paul. *The Anatomy of Exile: A Semantic and Historical Study.* London, 1972.

Todorov, Tzvetan. *The Conquest of America.* Translated by Richard Howard. New York, 1984.

Toews, John Edward. *Hegelianism: The Path toward Dialectical Humanism, 1805–1841.* Cambridge, 1980.

Tulard, Jean. *La préfecture de police sous la monarchie de juillet.* Paris, 1964.

UNESCO. *Adam Mickiewicz, 1798–1855.* Zurich, 1955.

Untermeyer, Louis. *Heinrich Heine: Paradox and Poet.* New York, 1937.

Vallentin, Antonina. *Heine: Poet in Exile.* Translated by Harrison Brown. Garden City, N.Y., 1956.

Viallaneix, Paul. *La vie royale: Essai sur l'idée de peuple dans l'oeuvre de Michelet.* Paris, 1959.

Vincent, K. Steven. *Pierre-Joseph Proudhon and the Rise of French Republican Socialism.* Oxford, 1984.

Walicki, Andrzej. *Philosophy and Romantic Nationalism: The Case of Poland.* Oxford, 1982.

Walker, Mack. *Germany and the Emigration, 1816–1885.* Cambridge, Mass., 1964.

Weintraub, Wiktor. *Literature as Prophecy: Scholarship, and Martinist Poetics in Mickiewicz's Parisian Lectures.* The Hague, 1959.

———. *The Poetry of Adam Mickiewicz.* The Hague, 1954.

Weiss, John. *Moses Hess: Utopian Socialist.* Detroit, 1960.

Wellisz, Leopold. *The Friendship of Margaret Fuller D'Ossoli and Adam Mickiewicz.* New York, 1947.

Werner, Michaël. *Genius und Geldsack: Zum Problem des Schriftstellerberufs bei Heinrich Heine.* Hamburg, 1978.

Secondary Sources: Articles

Bottigelli, Emile. "Les 'Annales Franco-Allemandes' et l'opinion française." *La Pensée* 110 (1963): 47–66.

Bourrilly, Jean. "Mickiewicz and France." In *Adam Mickiewicz in World Literature*, ed. Wacław Lednicki, pp. 243–80. Berkeley, Calif, 1956.

Brown, Mark. "The Comité Franco-Polonais and the French Reaction to the Polish Uprising of November 1830." *English Historical Review* 93 (1978): 774–93.

Coleman, A. P. "The Great Emigration." In *The Cambridge History of Poland*, edited by W. F. Reddway, H. H. Penson, O. Halecki, and R. Dyloski, 2:311–23. Cambridge, 1951.

Fabre, Jean. "La France dans la pensée et le coeur de Mickiewicz." *Revue de Littérature Comparée* 31 (1957): 161–91.

Fitzpatrick, Joseph P. "The Importance of 'Community' in the Process of Immigrant Assimilation." *International Migration Review* 1 (Fall 1966): 5–16.

Fridieff, Michel. "L'opinion publique française devant l'insurrection polonaise de 1830–1831." *Revue Internationale d'Histoire Politique et Constitutionnelle* 2 (1951): 111–21, 205–14, 280–304.

Furet, François. "Le jeune Marx et la Révolution française," *Le Débat* 28 (1984): 30–46.

Grandjonc, Jacques. "Eléments statistiques pour une étude de l'immigration étrangère en France de 1830 à 1851." *Archiv für Sozialgeschichte* 15 (1975): 211–300.

———. "Etat sommaire des dépôts d'archives françaises sur le mouvement ouvrier et les émigrés allemands de 1830 à 1851/52." *Archiv für Sozialgeschichte* 12 (1972): 487–531.

———. "Les émigrés allemands sous la monarchie de juillet: Documents de surveillance policière, 1833–1848." *Publications Universitaires de Lettres et Sciences Humaines d'Aix-en-Provence, Etudes Germaniques* 1 (1972): 115–249.

———. "La presse de l'émigration allemande en France (1795–1848) et en Europe (1830–1848)." *Archiv für Sozialgeschichte* 10 (1970): 95–152.

———. "Mémoires d'un artisan allemand à Paris (1830–1834)." *Cahiers d'Histoire, Lyon* 15 (1970): 243–57.

———. "Les rapports des socialistes et néo-Hegeliens allemands de l'émigration avec les socialistes français, 1840–1847." In *Aspects des relations franco-allemands 1830–1848*, edited by Raymond Poidevin and Heinz-Otto Sieburg, pp. 73–86. Metz, 1978.

Gregory, David. "Karl Marx's and Friedrich Engels' Knowledge of French Socialism in 1842–1843." *Historical Reflections/Réflexions Historiques* 10 (1983): 143–93.

Iggers, Georg G. "Heine and the Saint-Simonians: A Re-examination." *Comparative Literature* 10 (1958): 289–308.

Kramer, Lloyd S. "Exile and European Thought: Heine, Marx, and Mickiewicz in July Monarchy Paris." *Historical Reflections/Réflexions Historiques* 11 (1984): 45–70.

———. "Intellectual History and Reality: The Search for Connections." *Historical Reflections/Réflexions Historiques* 13 (1986): 517–45.

———. "Lafayette in 1830: A Center That Could Not Hold." *Canadian Journal of History* 17 (1982): 469–92.

———. "The Rights of Man: Lafayette and the Polish National Revolution, 1830–1834." *French Historical Studies* 14 (1986): 521–46.

Kridl, Manfred. "Two Champions of a New Christianity: Lamennais and Mickiewicz." *Comparative Literature* 4 (1952): 239–67.

Lednicki, Wacław. "Mickiewicz at the Collège de France, 1840–1940." *Slavonic and East European Review* 20 (1941): 149–72.

———. "Some Comments about Three Letters of Mickiewicz . . . (Mickiewicz and Alfred de Vigny)." *Polish Review* 1 (1956): 80–91.

Ledré, Charles. "La presse nationale sous la restauration et la monarchie de juillet." In *Histoire générale de la presse française*, edited by Claude Bellanger, Jacques Godechot, Pierre Guiral, Fernand Tenou, 2:29–146. Paris, 1969.

Leroy, Maxime. "Adam Mickiewicz in France: Professor and Social Philosopher." In UNESCO, *Adam Mickiewicz, 1798–1855*. Zurich, 1955.

Marcuse, Ludwig. "Heine and Marx: A History and a Legend." *Germanic Review* 30 (1955): 110–24.

Markiewicz, Zygmunt. "George Sand et Mickiewicz." *Revue de Littérature Comparée* 34 (1960): 108–20.

———. "Mickiewicz dans l'oeuvre romanesque de George Sand." *Revue d'Histoire Littéraire de la France* 61 (1961): 429–33.

Mazon, André. "Une correspondance: Mickiewicz, Cousin, Cyprien Robert." *Revue de Littérature Comparée* 14 (1934): 555–64.

Montreau, Jean. "La Revolution française et la pensée de Marx." *La Pensée* 3 (1939): 24–38.

Netter, Lucienne. "Heine, Thiers, et la presse parisienne en 1840." *Revue d'Allemagne* 4 (1972): 113–53.

Pawlowski, B. "The November Insurrection." In *The Cambridge History of Poland*, edited by W. F. Reddway, H. H. Penson, O. Halecki, and R. Dyloski, 2:295–310. Cambridge, 1951.

Price, Charles. "The Study of Assimilation." In *Migration*, edited by J. A. Jackson, pp. 181–237. Cambridge, 1969.

Reeves, Nigel. "Heine and the Young Marx." *Oxford Germanic Studies* 7 (1973): 44–97.

Stearns, Peter N. "Patterns of Industrial Strike Activity in France during the July Monarchy." *American Historical Review* 70 (1965): 371–94.

Weintraub, Wiktor. "Adam Mickiewicz, the Mystic-Politician." *Harvard Slavic Studies* 1 (1953): 137–78.

Werner, Michaël. "Heines französische Staatspension." *Heine-Jahrbuch* 16 (1977): 134–42.

Wodzynska-Walicka, Maria. "L'idée de la Pologne dans la pensée de Jules Michelet." *Europe* 51 (1973): 145–62.

Zaleski, Z. L. "A travers une amitié franco-polonaise: 12 lettres inédites d'A. Mickiewicz à Michelet." *Le Monde Slave*, August 1926, pp. 240–53.

——. "Une amitié franco-polonaise: Mickiewicz, Michelet, Quinet." *Séances et Travaux de l'Académie des Sciences Morales et Politiques*, July–August 1925, pp. 97–114.

——. "Michelet, Mickiewicz, et la Pologne." *Séances et Travaux de l'Académie des Sciences Morales et Politiques*, July–August 1928, pp. 78–144.

INDEX

Library of Congress Cataloging-in-Publication Data

Kramer, Lloyd S.
  Threshold of a new world.

  Revision of thesis—Cornell University.
  Bibliography: p.
  Includes index.
    1. Paris (France)—Intellectual life—19th century. 2. France—Civilization—
Foreign Influences. 3. France—Exiles—History—19th century. 4. Intellectuals—
France—Paris—History—19th Century. I. Title.
  DC715.K73   1988   944'.3606   87-19899
  ISBN 0-08014-1939-5 (alk. paper)